What others are saying about this book:

"It's a nuts-and-bolt guide, written by a Southern California interior design firm, that provides loads of information on *lots* of decorating topics. Written for interior decorators and designers, the book takes readers through the entire process of selling, planning, measuring and buying for decorating and/or designing jobs.

There's no shortage of ideas, tips, advice and recommendations in this book. Even the most experienced decorators and designers, will have trouble not finding a particular decorating problem or subject *not* touched upon in this handy reference book." - Cathy A. Goetz, *Home Textiles Today*.

"Touch of Design, an interior design firm in Oceanside, Calif., has branched into the book publishing business with a career survival manual that offers tips and suggestions for succeeding in the design business.

Information on competing for jobs, keeping customers coming back and prospecting for new clients is included. So are some of the common mistakes and planning errors made by designers. Such topics as hidden enemies that deteriorate fabrics, steps to a sale and the effects of light on color are discussed." *A.S.I.D. Report*.

"A career skills manual for interior designers, this reference manual is a storehouse of information gleaned from years of experience from a Southern California design firm. It provides guidelines for securing interior design jobs, keeping customers satisfied and **making money**." *Vocational Educational Journal*.

"....interior designers and decorators will benefit most from the aggressive techniques outlined here, which were developed by a Southern California design firm. The unique information, geared to professionals, will help them polish their skills, expand their sales, and maximize their work potential." *Library Journal*.

"*Secrets of Success for Interior Designer's and Decorators*, is a book of salesmanship and customer psychology. It is an all-around job planning and measuring manual; a career skills reference for survival in today's market for design professionals." *Decorating Retailer*.

"Interior designers and decorators who want to develop good career skills receive not just the usual sales-oriented guide (though sales strategies are included), but an important set of tips on how to produce accurate measurements and estimates, how to make the right fabric and style selections, and how to work with customers. The practical focus on issues range from how sales are lost to handling reworks and choosing hardware makes for a virtual 'Bible' of tips for both beginners and those already working in the field." Diane C Donovan, *The Bookwatch*.

"....*Secrets of Success for Today's Interior Designers and Decorators*, by Linda M. Ramsay, really — no kidding, just about everything you need to know to begin a successful career as an interior decorator or designer." Broox Sledge, *The Book World*.

"Here is everything you need to know to be a successful interior designer. This book is for all interior designers and decorators who want to maximize sales, obtain more customers, plan their jobs correctly, and practice precise interior design skills. For seasoned designers and for those just now venturing into this lucrative field." *Best Books*.

SECRETS of SUCCESS

for **TODAY'S INTERIOR DESIGNERS and DECORATORS**

---

*Easily Sell the Job,
Plan it Correctly and
Keep the Customer Coming
Back for Repeat Sales*

SECRETS of SUCCESS

for TODAY'S INTERIOR DESIGNERS and DECORATORS

―――――――――❧―――――――――

By Linda M. Ramsay

Touch of Design™

Secrets of Success for
Today's Interior Designers and Decorators

*Easily Sell the Job,
Plan it Correctly and
Keep the Customer Coming
Back for Repeat Sales*

By **Linda M. Ramsay**

Published by: **Touch of Design®**

475 College Boulevard, Suite 6290, Oceanside, California 92057 U.S.A.

Ordering information in back of the book

Copyright © 1992 by Linda M. Ramsay
First Printing 1992, Second Printing 1993, revised; Third Printing 1996, revised
Printed and bound in the United States of America
10 9 8 7 6 5 4 3

Ramsay, Linda M. 1955—
Secrets of Success for Today's Interior Designers and Decorators: *Easily Sell the Job, Plan it Correctly and Keep the Customer Coming Back for Repeat Sales*/Linda M. Ramsay/1st edition
p. cm.
Includes: Index; Glossary
Preassigned LCCN: 91-91011
ISBN 0-9629918-3-X softcover

1. Career skills for interior designers and decorators. 2. Reference source — for accurate planning of all types of window treatments, measuring, information and planning for all types of hard and soft-window treatments, fabrics, slipcovers, upholstery, top treatments, specifications, accessories, fabrication, installation, hardware, color, and design. 3. Salesmanship guide — customer psychology, how to sell the job, service the customer, and keep receiving repeat sales. 4. Guidelines for prospecting and qualifying customers — ways to find qualified customers.

Table of Contents

Part 5   Measuring and Planning the Job for Window Treatments   117

Part 8   Bedspreads, Fabric Accessories, Slipcovers, and Reupholstery

Introduction

" Your Interior Design and Decorating Information Source"

Secrets of Success for Today's Interior Designers and Decorators, is published and presented to you by Touch of Design®, *your interior design and decorating information source.*

Touch of Design® is a Southern California interior design firm that is sharing *its secrets of success* with you, through *Secrets of Success for Today's Interior Designers and Decorators.*

Secrets of Success.... is a wealth of knowledge and professional advice for professionals in the interior design business. This book is designed to be an organized reference source for the interior designer and decorator who would like to maximize their career skills. **Whether you are *new* to this business, or have been a designer or decorator *for many years*, this book offers many ideas, tips, and suggestions for you.** You will be stimulated in your creativity on ways to find qualified customers, and shown how you can *maximize* each and every sale you make.

Secrets of Success.... is an easy-to-read and -follow, **all-around resource guide for everything an interior designer and decorator needs to know to get out there and successfully plan, measure and sell the job. This book extensively covers all the information needed, in the most important areas that the designer is going to encounter with this profession.** The hardest area of all, window treatments, has been thoroughly emphasized. **This book will teach you how to become a window treatment expert.**

Considerable time and effort has been put into this book. Touch of Design® has written and published what we consider to be a comprehensive training manual. This is *practical* knowledge *that works*. The information is based on years of practical application and experience, education, seminars, and research. Whether you work for a small or large firm, this information *will* apply and make your life *easier* and *more productive*. Touch of Design® has decided to share the information with every interior designer or decorator who truly wants to be a success.

Up until now, *little* of the information contained within this book was able to be acquired by interior designers or decorators. The knowledge was not readily available, even after many years of trial and errors on the job. Problems, pitfalls and expensive mistakes can be avoided before they happen, thanks to the information contained in this book. Costly errors and problems are what put interior design companies out of business. Errors and mistakes erode interior designers' and decorators' paychecks when they are forced to pay for them out of their commission or profits they have coming, at the completion of the job. Very few companies absorb mistakes made by their interior designers or decorators. Designers and decorators work extremely hard on jobs, only to have several "little" problems come up and dissolve away their commissions or profit that they have due them.

In the field of interior design, many, many, companies go out of business every day due to the erosion of profits, to mistakes that the designer or decorator could have easily caught, had they had the information and knowledge. *Don't just learn from your mistakes, eliminate them before they happen!*

This book will make a much more informed, trained, and educated interior designer or decorator out of you. This book picks up where most colleges leave off — *you are given the information on how to actually get out there and successfully **compete for and do** the job.*

Interior design sales is a very competitive business. **This book will put you ahead of the competition in the job market, and ahead of the competition you are up against out their selling the job. Eliminate your competition, easily and safely.**

This book has been carefully prepared and cultivated for many years. ***Secrets of Success* includes all relevant knowledge that an interior designer and decorator *must* have to be successful, today.** Touch of Design® is a successful company, and wishes to share the information in this book, which reflects our successful techniques and career skills.

Follow the guidelines outlined within this book to become a very *informed and aware* interior designer or decorator, with the ability to eliminate problems before they surface. **You will have the ability to accurately plan and measure for any situation that may arise and surface out there in the field — normal or unusual.** Become a sales professional, rather than an *"order taker."* Have the ability to increase each and every sale, and keep your customers coming back to buy from you again and again (even if a few problems should arise along the way).

If you should undersell a job, or run into problems, *Secrets of Success*, shows you how to get out of the jam! You are given guidelines on how to cut your costs on the job down safely, eliminating the need to go back to the customer and ask for more money, thus taking the chance on losing the sale. Guidelines for what can and cannot be reworked, are laid out for you. You will easily work well with your installer and workroom when the instructions within this book are followed.

Secrets of Success for Today's Interior Designers and Decorators is a manual of information for accurate planning and measuring for all types of window treatments, easy or difficult, soft, fabric and hard, material treatments. This book is your easy-to-follow reference for all types of interior fabrics, slipcovers, upholstery, top treatments, what specifications to use, fabric accessory planning, fabrication, installation, hardware, and how to *effectively* use color and design.

Broadly increase your sales and customer base. This book is your guide to customer psychology — **a complete salesmanship guide.** Much emphasis within this book is placed on how to sell the job, service the customer, and receive repeat sales again and again. Complete guidelines for prospecting and qualifying customers, and *ways to find* qualified customers, are set out within this book. Read the book, review it, and follow the directions. Any of the information may be easily found again and again through the use of the index.

Make the most of your career with the help of this book, and be a successful interior designer or decorator.

Disclaimer

This book is designed to provide information in regard to the subject matters covered. Great care has been taken to ensure the accuracy and utility of the information included within this book. Every effort has been made to make this book as complete as possible.

Neither Touch of Design®, nor the author, Linda Ramsay, assume any responsibility or liability for errors, inaccuracies, omissions, use, application of information, or any other inconsistency herein. The author and Touch of Design® shall have neither liability nor responsibility to any person or entity with respect to any loss or damage caused, or alleged to be caused, directly or indirectly by the information contained in this book.

Therefore, this text should be used only as a general guide and not as the ultimate source on interior design information. Furthermore, this book contains information on interior design products and application only up to the printing date. The purpose of this book is to educate on the application of interior design principles.

Any slights against any organizations or manufacturers are unintentional. Readers should consult an attorney or accountant for specific applications to their individual interior design ventures. If you do not wish to be bound by the above, you may return this book in resalable condition to the publisher within 30 days for a full refund.

Part 1

The Business of Interior Design and Decorating

Interior design and decorating is a *people* business. Customers who you will work with on decorating and designing their interiors will run the gamut in preferences for different types of styling, color favorites, fashion consciousness, and general wants and needs. Customers will vary culturally and economically in their attitudes, personalities, and lifestyles.

Interior design is also a business where accuracy is very important — if you would like the job to go in! Much of your time will be spent on paperwork and more paperwork.

Daily, you will make and return phone calls, take care of any messages and their problems, track orders, write service requests, work with customers who come into your studio, make house calls, figure up estimates, bids, write up orders, and try to troubleshoot problems that arise.

Murphy's Law

Custom decorating and design is the field that Murphy's Law really describes — *what can go wrong, will definitely go wrong!*

You, as a decorator or designer, cannot be too careful! Always write *everything* down. Always *keep* original worksheets. *Be specific* on all notes on all workorders for installers and for yourself. Always *record* all decisions, on your original worksheets and sales contracts so you can refer to them.

Always *verbally review* sales contracts with your customer. Carefully review *each* item decided. You will not only clarify to the customer what *you think* he or she has decided, but what you are *exactly* custom making, *and* you will catch many errors in the address, telephone, etc. Customers have the tendency to get mixed up *and think* they are agreeing to one idea (which you previously suggested), and now you are describing another idea. They end up thinking they have decided on one idea, and you think they have decided on another. **Surprise** at installation time! *The time to catch errors is when you are writing up the sales contract.* At this point it costs you your time only. *It is not pleasant to remake and rework the job with an angry customer.*

Slow delivery of goods *will help* your customer to forget what it is he or she has ordered. Having it down in black and white with their signature keeps everything clear and more problem free.

Always show fabrics once again before leaving. It is preferable to reshow the fabrics while reviewing the sales contract. You want to reconfirm that *this* is the fabric selection they are getting. Many times the customer has switched to a different shade of the same color. They may have confirmed it to you in a way that you did not see or hear, since you were concentrating on getting the job correctly planned and priced out.

Always try to work with the same installers, if possible. A consistent installer gets used to your style of planning jobs. On those occasions when you are not completely clear on the work orders, they are familiar with *you and your style* of the way you do your paperwork. A consistent installer tends to know *what it is* you are trying to do. They can second-guess a questionable situation if they cannot find you by telephone.

There will *still* be errors, regardless of how careful you are. Vendors will ship the wrong fabric. Workrooms will make up the wrong pattern or color, not spot the flaws before making up the item, etc. If the fabric gets cut and it is flawed, or the wrong fabric, although the manufacturer supposedly inspected it before it was shipped, you have a problem. Installers and workrooms make errors, also.

Your *accurate* planning and measuring of the job are only *a small part* of the whole job. Other people and materials are *also* part of the whole job. Realize that other people working on your job do not have nearly as big an interest in it as you do.

Customers Who Know What They Want

Some customers will have definite ideas on what they want you to help them with in decorating their space. Sometimes these ideas are strange, out-of-fashion, *seemingly* ugly, non-matching in style, wrong in color selection, faddish, non-functional, etc. Your job as a designer or decorator is to make appropriate suggestions, point out the negative aspects of their proposed selection, and show them better options and ideas. If the customer still wants their original ideas, *then let them have them.* Clearly spell out on the sales contract *"customer has selected _____,"* and describe their selection. Make notes on your worksheets about the suggestions you made that you felt were more appropriate, which your customer turned down. Keep these notes for future reference, in case the customer comes back and says, *"you told me to pick that."*

Many designers and decorators have big egos — they only want you to go with *their* ideas. Many are very dominant salespeople that are capable of getting the customer to agree to something the customer does not really want. The customer almost always ends up canceling before the three-day decision period is up. The customer will come back after the treatment is installed and say (rightly so), *"you talked me into this."* You will not only have to remedy the situation by remaking the job, but you will lose that customer for future sales. Normally, the customer will not complain later if they are definite on what they want at the time of the sale.

It is a pleasure to work with a customer who has *some* idea, or *definite ideas*, on what it is they want. Give it to them; if you do not, they will seek out someone else who will. If they are definite on what they want, they usually remain happy with you and the job. Just point out any negative aspects, make more appropriate suggestions, and then let them decide.

Architects and Contractors

Frequently, you will run into the situation where it appears the architect or general contractor has not considered placement of windows. They may also have used strange combinations of windows in proportion to each other, together, within the same room. Sometimes, it seems that they are not very aware of what products are available on the market, and certainly do not know how window treatments are planned for windows. You will get the job of trying *to make a silk purse out of a sow's ear.*

Windows will be mounted right up to a fireplace with uneven stone work, wavering in and out, right up to the glass of the window. Anything you put up on the window will gap and rub against the fireplace. Fireplaces will sometimes jut out into the glass of the window. You are limited to the products that can be fabricated with cut-outs and your customer will face an aesthetically ugly situation. Surcharges will be involved with the fabrication of the affected items. Sometimes there will only be 1" clearance on each side of the window.

If this situation should arise, drapery or vertical blinds *should* be made a one-way pull. One-way pulls are not as well-planned appearing as pairs, unless it is a butting corner situation, or two windows framing a fireplace, some other architectural feature, or it is a sliding-glass door.

If you go ahead and make the treatment a pair, the majority *of the side* of the drapery, with only 1" clearance, will cover the glass in the stack area, when the drapery is drawn open. Furniture arrangement will also be difficult with the mixed proportions of windows within the same room.

Your job as a designer or decorator is to create harmony within the same space. Make the window treatments consistent in height and length, and cover up the odd-proportioned windows. Take small windows mounted high into the walls, within the same room as floor-length patio doors, and plan the small windows in shutters or mini woods, the same color as the wall color. This is an effective solution. The odd-proportioned window will not stand out noticeably and will fade into the wall handsomely. Shutters are very effective on many odd-proportioned windows. They look exceptional on small windows, or wide and narrow-in-height windows. These windows look their finest when done in the same color as the walls. Shutters are the foremost-looking treatment for these type of odd-proportioned windows.

General Supplies for Interior Designers and Decorators

All supplies covered here are necessary for the interior design and decorating business. Some may be available from the company you work for and others you will need to provide for your success as an interior designer or decorator.

Automobile with a large trunk

A large trunk is needed so you may have readily available a large assortment of fabric and hard window samples. Carpet books, flooring books, and notebooks all take up maximum space. You will still need to constantly load and unload your car for personal trips when you choose to use your trunk for other non-decorating uses.

Try to find some sturdy boxes that fit comfortably in your trunk. Separate your fabrics into like-fabric categories and keep them sorted at all times. When you come out of a home after a sales call, quickly drop the samples back in the corresponding fabric box. This practice of placing the samples back in the like-fabric boxes will make life much easier for you. These boxes are also easily removed when you want to unload your car trunk for other uses.

Briefcase

Preferably one that opens from the top. Top-opening briefcases help deter small children from wanting to get in them and removing enticing items, when you have your back turned. Top-opening types of briefcases also *seem* to work the best with this type of business.

Calculator

Purchase one with large keys, for ease of use.

25'-30' tape measure

Retractable tape measure that is capable of staying rigid for 7'.

Clipboard

To slip into the briefcase; you will need to carry from room to room when measuring and writing up orders. The type of clipboard with the tray beneath is the best type and enables you to store estimate sheets, pens, price lists, and sales slips (sometimes you do not want to bring in a large briefcase for a small, easy-to-order blind or shade). This *is* a necessary item. Many customers see you with a pen in your hand and will not let you near their dining table or coffee table, even if the surface is padded. Carry the clipboard you will get hooked on it; it is more comfortable for you and the customer. You do not need this awkward situation to come up when you are out in the home, bidding on the job.

Appointment book

With a page for each day. One that is not so expensive that you feel uncomfortable stapling your daily appointment slips onto the pages.

Business cards and case

Having a case to slip them out of looks very polished when on an appointment. Make sure the cards are nicely done and actually list the services and items you specialize in. *If you do not tell the customer, they will not know.* Remind them any way that you can. Oversized cards may not be placed in a wallet because they are too big, and you may *lose* easy referrals if the customer does not have them handy.

Estimate sheets

Handy sheets that are easy to work off when giving bids. They also alleviate the possibility of you forgetting labor or fabrication charges when you are calculating complex bids.

Thank-you notes
Send one to every customer you make an in-home visit to, whether you were able to close the sale or not. This simple courtesy will make you stand out from the other bidders the customer has entertained. You show that you are willing to go the extra inch, and really *want* their business.

Graph paper
Especially necessary and important for planning floor-covering jobs and complex window treatments.

Large sheets of thin paper, masking tape
Used to make templates while at the customer's home.

Copies of current sales, flyers
Have available advertisements and current-sale flyers for your customers. They will be able to see your advertisement on the current sale in progress. Other items listed on the flyer or advertisement may also be needed by the customer. The flyer announcing the sale may be just what the customer needs, as an incentive, to get going on that additional item. You are also letting your customer know what else you do sell. They may not need the item now, but they may need the item in the future. They may share this information with friends, neighbors, and relatives.

Brochures
Carry a complete assortment of vendor brochures with information about the products you are presenting to your customer. They need this vital information to review the products they are considering. If you are unable to close the sale while you are in the home, since the customer must speak with their spouse, they now have a picture to show of the hard-to-describe item. You may have left important points and information out of your presentation; good brochures will help to fill in the gaps.

Envelopes
Assortment of envelopes in all sizes from letter size to large manilla types. Have envelopes stamped with your company name for more professionalism.

Specification sheets
Workorders to use for ordering of all items that you show and sell.

Purchase orders
You will need all-purpose, general purchase orders *and* your vendor's preferred and supplied purchase orders — when they just cannot figure it out unless its on their order form!

Prospect sheets
All appointments made should go on prospect sheets. These should have several layers of sheets that tear apart. Take the top sheet and staple it in your appointment book — no need to rewrite it.

Take the second sheet and leave in the studio as a control copy to see where the customers are coming from, what the lead count is, and which designer/ decorator received it and went on the appointment.

The third sheet is for you to follow up the sales call and write down what was the result of the sales call. Did you sell it? If not, *why not*? The control copy also tells management how you are doing with your closing rate; and shows you where you need to improve your skills to raise your closing ratio. Since this record is turned into your management, you are *forced* to improve your abilities. Review the sections in this book on how to get the sale.

**Magazines,
photo albums,
scrapbooks**

Decorating pictures and ideas to show your customer, to get them on the right track and wavelength with you when discussing interior design treatments and options.

Samples

A set of samples of everything you sell should be available to you for your use at all times. You should have your own individual sets of all hard-window treatments, unless the company you work for carries many different brands. If they do carry many brands, you should have available one set of the most popular and best-selling brand for your car. You should also have a general assortment of fabrics staples. Prints and highly individualized fabrics should be taken from the studio as the need is determined in the prequalification of the customer, before the sales call.

Profile of a Successful, Professional Designer or Decorator

The professional designer or decorator is knowledgeable about *all areas* of design and decorating. Additionally, a professional designer or decorator has a *well-rounded knowledge* of the current products available on the market. **A professional designer or decorator does not sell to the customer, *but helps the customer to buy*.** Additionally, a successful designer/decorator will have the following characteristics and abilities:

- A **well-kept appearance.**

- **Poise;** you need to like yourself and be comfortable with who you are. You need to appear and feel at ease in diverse situations.

- An **outgoing personality,** or the ability to act as if you have one.

- **No hesitancy in** coming right out and **asking for the sale.**

- Proficiency in **projecting warmth and enthusiasm** for people.

- **Enthusiasm** for the project you and the customer are working on.

- The capability of **approaching each customer with a positive attitude.**

- Ability to turn customers into friends.

- **Drive for making money.**

- Mastery for **selling to your potential.**

- Competitiveness; competition among peers to be the best you can be and the desire to make more sales than your competitors.

- **Ability to set goals and *focus* on the goals.**

- **Resourcefulness, industriousness.**

- Capability of putting forth immense effort.

- **Knowledge of the line of products carried.** To feel that you are doing a better job than 90% of the other designers or decorators, since you have taken the time to gain the knowledge and are prepared to do the job to your potential.

- **Good "*people*" skills**

- Excellent **time-management skills**.

- **The ability to do a few different tasks at once**.

- Capability to **warmly greet prospective customers**.

- **Expertise in pre-qualifying customers**.

- **Skill in presenting and showing merchandise to its fullest potential**.

- **Willingness to make suggestions** and offer design guidelines to fit your customer's situation.

- **Ability to overcome objections**.

- **Proficiency in selling up or adding on** other interior items.

- **The talent to adapt to many different people**, their varied personalities, and situations.

- **Good health and body condition; stamina and strength** to carry many pounds of samples *in and out* of homes.

- **Aptitude to be accurate and thorough**.

- Ability to work as a team player.

Self-control	**Patience**
Self-confidence	**Sincerity**
Courtesy	**Helpfulness**
Genuineness	**Friendliness**
Integrity	**Reliability**
Ambition	Common sense
Initiative	Punctuality
Intenseness	Alertness
Cooperation	**Honesty**
Good judgement	Loyalty
Optimistic attitude	Mathematical Aptitude

Designers and decorators have a variety of job descriptions. *A professional designer/decorator is a designer that pulls all elements of an interior together, while coordinating colors, textures, styles, line, form, space, light sources, etc. A designer/decorator is also a psychologist, financial analyst, mathematician, sales professional, and a manager of time, in addition to being a manager of people.*

A designer must be a self-starter type of person, not wanting or expecting management to hang over them, or to keep them going on schedule.

Paperwork must always be thorough, precise, and neatly written or typed. Sketches of ideas that are not readily clear, must be drawn in on the paperwork.

A professional designer must have very clear speech and good communication skills. Learn to communicate effectively by practicing communicating often with all types of personalities. Sell yourself first, then sell your abilities as a designer or decorator. Your outer appearance reflects your self image. When you look better, you feel better, and get more positive results.

Customers evaluate a person either consciously or unconsciously, whether in person or on the telephone. They try to *imagine* what type of person you are, your age, and your style. You give the same type of evaluation to the customers. Always endeavor to be warm, enthusiastic, and confident. Never talk down to what seems to be an unknowledgeable customer about custom decorating. They have chosen to come to you because you are a supposed expert in a field that is different from the field they are experts in.

Always keep a positive attitude. Strive to be friendly, honest, a good listener, helpful with suggestions on products, and remedies for their problems. Your customer will feel comfortable with you as a person if you project a positive attitude. Project confidence and knowledge when meeting with your customer. Be interested in your customer as a person, in addition to the decorating problem you are there to solve. Attempt to do *all* you can to help the customer, believe in yourself, your products, and your company. *If you do not honestly believe in yourself, your products, and your company, it will be projected to your customers.*

Try to be punctual to your appointments with your customers. If you are more than 30 minutes late or early, call the customer. Review the section on setting up the appointment and the *necessity* to say that you will be there *approximately* at such-and-such a time. If you are ill, call the night or day before so the customer does not stay home from work, cancel other plans, etc. If you do not give the customer notice that you are unable to make the appointment, they will be **furious** with you.

A professional designer or decorator trying to maximize their income tries to finalize each sale on the first visit. If you finalize most of your sales on the first visit you will have time to do the reams of paperwork that go with this type of business, put in your studio time, attend to more prospective customers, return telephone calls, and have time to prospect for more customers, as well as go on three to four appointments and callbacks daily. As it is, you will barely find the time to grab a quick lunch.

If you do not attempt to make the sale on the first visit, you will make repeated trips to the customer's home, many times never finalizing the sale. Much time necessary for you to make a living will be lost. *It is not cost effective* for you to go *repeatedly* to the home again and again. If you must go to the home twice, make the second call as short as possible. Preferably, try to get the customer to come into the studio when you will be there.

What Customers Expect from a Designer or Decorator:

- **Professionalism.**

- To **execute the job correctly.**

- **Pride of performance.**

- To feel confident that the **decorator or designer knows what he or she is doing.**

- **That you will fulfill and complete the job that you were paid to do.**

- **For you to be** *up on* **popular trends and current styles, in addition to being versed on working with traditional styles.**

- **If any problems should arise, to have them resolved quickly and painlessly.**

- **Honesty in correct pricing** of the job. If the customer is overcharged, the belief that you will refund the customer the overage.

- *To be candid and up front* about *why* the job is delayed; no untrue excuses or explanations.

- **Messages** from the customer **returned as quickly as possible.**

- *To follow through and get back* to customers with information, etc., **as promised.**

- **Friendliness and warmth in your personality.**

- **To feel comfortable in working with you.**

- **Sincerity.**

- **Concern.**

- **Confidence.**

- **Product and decorating education and knowledge.**

- **Well-kept appearance.**

Strangers decide within minutes whether they want to deal with you or continue dealing with you. You must be confident. You need to care about what the customer is conveying to you about their wants and needs, through their conversation and mannerisms. Realize you are dealing with another person who has feelings, dreams, and hopes. They are probably also insecure about their decorating project. Treat customers as you would want to be treated by a salesperson. You must display and convey confidence in your products to be able to sell them.

A professional develops and keeps a positive, optimistic, confident attitude about them. If you have product knowledge, know how your products perform, and their features, *you will be* confident and project this attitude.

The way to become professional and be proficient with your skills is to learn from the mistakes you will inevitably make. These mistakes will cost you money and will sometimes cost you future sales to customers, along with any potential referrals that customer might have given you. *Mistakes* are very expensive, in every way.

Always have the installer call to your attention any problem he or she *had* while installing the job. Many times these mistakes will be resolved by the installer or the workroom and you are never told what error you created. The same errors are repeated again and again — instead of having them called to your attention so you can find out the correct way to plan for that problem situation, and eliminate the errors from repeatedly showing up, again and again.

You need to be willing to repeatedly, all day long, every day, be interested in making suggestions, offering design ideas, and reminding the customer of correct design guidelines for them to follow with their decorating.

The customer wants to work with the decorating professional, not the hard-sell salesperson with no ideas, knowledge, and follow-through on the orders.

Part 2

From Customer Psychology, Steps to a Sale, to Servicing Your Customer

This section of the book covers the psychology of customers: why customers buy custom-made products; what they expect from you as a designer or decorator; the steps they have to go through before they will buy; the *levels* you must go through with the customer before you will make a sale; the customer's priorities; prospecting for customers; greeting your customers; how to handle "Is this a *"free estimate?"*; how to increase your sales; how to quickly qualify a customer; the in-home appointment; designer/decorator consultations; hard-to-work-with customers; how to help your customer find their style; presentation of samples; features, advantages, and benefits; your goal as a designer/decorator; the *"right and wrong words"* to use when making a presentation; handling objections; underselling or overselling the job; closing the sale; window treatment points to review before leaving the home; thank-you notes; why did you lose the sale; portrait of an unsuccessful salesperson; should you be present for the installation; the callback; customer service; angry customers. *This is the psychology of sales section of the book.*

Reasons Why People Spend Money on Decorating

Below is a listing of the real reasons why people spend money on interior decorating:

- **Comfort.**

- **Out of necessity;** there *may not be* a carpet on the floor or window coverings on the windows, as in a new home.

- To **get rid of ugly features** within the home or space.

- For **replacement** of existing furnishings that are worn out, tired looking, or were *there* when the home was purchased.

- To **create a focal point or conversation point.**

- Ownership of **easier-care items** that require less time and effort in their upkeep than existing furnishings.

- **To obtain useable window and floor coverings rather than nonfunctional window coverings or floor coverings.**

- The preference for **lighter-weight, airy window treatments that are insulating,** rather than heavy, overpowering treatments.

- To seek a *"new look."*

- The **enjoyment** of having and owning beautiful possessions to use and admire.

- **For recognition and prestige** of owning a properly put-together interior.

- **To be *"in style."***

- **A touch of luxury.**

- **To express their individuality and good taste.**

- **To realize a dream.**

- **Popularity.**

- **To emulate others.**

- **Pride of ownership.**

- **To attract the opposite sex.**

- **Reputation.**

- **To avoid criticism** from other people.

- The **desire to seek praise** from others.

- **To take advantage of sale prices** or reduced prices.

- **Protection for other possessions** that may be affected if a purchase is not generated, such as covering the window to protect the carpet and furniture.

- **Security and privacy** achieved by covering the windows with window treatments.

- To purchase **items with a longer life span.** The customer feels they are getting the most value for their dollars in their decorating purchases. This is preferable to purchasing limited-life or temporary items to fill an immediate need.

Decorating products need to appeal to these reasons and needs. **You must work with one or more of these buying motives to make a sale.** This is true when you are working with a customer face-to-face, or have appealed to customers through advertising by mail, newspapers, or other methods.

People are motivated to buy because they need or want the products. Customers may be anxious to have a certain styling or *"look."* They may have more money now and want their interior to reflect their opulence and grandeur. Some people are naturally interested in decorating and want their home to reflect their interest and talent.

Pride of ownership is a strong motive for the need to acquire and have nice possessions. The prestige and pleasure of owning a beautifully decorated home, of living in a beautiful environment, is a very strong motivator.

Most customers do not want just a pair of drapery, but want window fashion. You need to offer them the components to make entire *"dream"* window fashions or total window fashions.

A family wedding or party may be the final motivator for the consumer; they may be finally motivated to do something about their wants and needs in decorating.

Other people are *impulsive.* When they see what they want, or come across a good sale, they are moved to act *immediately* on realizing their dreams.

Some people like *change.* The item to be changed may be in perfect condition, but is now a couple of years old and they are bored with it.

Other people *dislike change.* When their item finally wears out, they will *choose* to replace the item with *a like item.* Change for them is psychologically difficult.

Reasons People Buy *Custom-Made* Interior Products

Here is the list of reasons people decide they want to buy *custom-made* decorating items for their home:

- **They have purchased custom interior products before**, and realize they are usually of better quality.

- **They have had them in other homes.**

- A home was purchased previously that came complete with custom drapery. **They were able to experience the difference** first-hand with custom-made interior products.

- **The difference in quality of custom-made products was visibly noticed** in someone else's home.

- **They want a luxury look** rather than a readymade look.

- The customer likes the way **custom products properly fit** the windows or furniture (slipcovers).

- **Higher quality fabrics and beautiful patterns and prints**, are desired.

- The **ability to be able to *line* the window coverings** if desired.

- Capability to **insulate the window, with proper planning, to its fullest potential.**

- **Broad array of styles and ideas** that are available.

- **Chance to get very creative.**

- **They have a certain *"look"* or idea in mind** that is not available in readymades.

- The customer **wants something *"different."***

- **Privacy that is obtained through the use of selected products and options.**

- The desire to have the window coverings **professionally installed.**

- Weary of the **inability of some readymades to function** correctly.

- **Disgusted with the quality available in readymade window coverings** and accessories.

The list is endless depending on the personality and the priorities of the person deciding to buy custom-made interior items.

Once a person has experienced custom-made interior items, he or she will find it very hard to accept readymades again. Even if the room is a secondary room and hardly used, the customer will never enjoy the readymade window coverings they select for those secondary windows as much as they will the custom window coverings.

A customer can plan their treatments just about anyway they like with custom window treatments. They may have whatever style, shape, size, or color they can imagine to fit their dreams and personality.

Designers and Customers

- *Customers bring you their wants and needs* for you to help them fulfill.

- Your job is to *help the customer* make the purchase.

- Try to give the customer *as much value* as possible for the money spent.

- The customer is the *reason* you are in this business. You, as a designer or decorator, are *dependent* on customers. Customers do not depend on you — they can always go elsewhere.

- The customer is not an *interruption* of your business or daily activities.

- When the customer calls you, he or she is doing *you* a favor.

Buying Decision Steps

Before a consumer buys a major purchase, they go through the following steps:

They become *aware* that they are dissatisfied with their present items. Or, they become aware that they are *dissatisfied with the lack of having the item.*

This awareness and dissatisfaction builds with time. More and more they think about it, until they finally get motivated to do something about it.

If a relative or friend is coming to visit — this can really be the motivator or the *crisis point* for moving the customer to finally do something about their interior. Unfortunately, this type of motivation will usually provide very short notice for the job to be completed for the decorating firm. The customer will demand short time limits in the sales contract. You run a *high risk* of cancellation from the customer if the job is not completed on time. An unresalable, partially completed job will cost you a lot if canceled! Decide if you are *easily* going to be able to complete the job before committing to it.

When the customer is in the panic stage of buying, it is very easy to make the sale. **At the panic stage, it is also very easy to lose the sale.**

If customer is not *particularly* in a big hurry to make a purchase, it is more *difficult* to get them to buy, unless you have a time-limited sale price. A customer who is not especially dissatisfied with their present interior is not in a big hurry to change it. They will have a few decorators over, *shop* their prices, and put the project on the shelf until they run into an enticing offer in the future that they cannot pass up. Usually, *none of the initial companies* that come out to the home will get the job. The customer is probably *surprised* at the price, and will let even *great* values go by. Later, they will realize what a good deal they passed up, and look for that *same* price. This will usually happen after prices have suffered an increase, or the companies are in their peak sales periods and are not as anxious or willing to take a smaller profit. This customer will also *finally* be motivated to buy when they have company coming. At this point, they will try to make their short time limit problem your problem.

You as a designer may have shown the customer everything you can think of, and they are just not excited about *anything*. The customer *needs to get excited and interested* in an item before they will buy. They may not care for the patterns and colors currently being shown.

A customer may just not have *any confidence* in their taste, and not even know what they really prefer. Do not spend too much time with a customer who is sending you these vibrations. They will shelve the project after wasting a few designers' time. They just do not know what they want and fear making a mistake.

If the customer has a *conflicting* personality with your personality, or does not feel you are being honest with him or her, you will not make the sale. They may actually love the products and ideas you are sharing with them. The customer may even feel that they cannot do without that particular item, but will not buy if from you, or your firm. They may go right behind your back and try to work with another decorator in your firm. A common problem is that they may go elsewhere, giving another designer the exact lot number and color off *your* sample. They may even end up paying a higher price for the same item. This customer may feel they cannot comfortably work with you, for one reason or another. The feeling is probably mutual.

In short, **people buy when their express interests and needs are answered with an appropriate benefit statement.** Sales professionals have to establish what *exactly those needs are. Do not make the mistake of telling a customer what their needs are; let them tell you what their needs are.* Draw their needs out of them, through appropriate questions and suggestions. **To motivate people to buy, use the feature, advantage, and benefit approach.** Try to express to the customer that you can give them something that they cannot get elsewhere. **It is much easier to *help* the customer to buy, rather than *"sell"* them.**

Levels to a Sale

To make a sale, sales pass through three levels. These are: **getting the customer's attention; presenting and relating to the individual the benefits of the product that** *pertain to them,* **specifically; the closing of the sale.**

You must fulfill your customer's wants and needs for these stages to happen.

Below is an outline of the steps that need to occur for the above stages to take place:

- **Greeting** of the potential customer.

- **Proper qualifying** of the customer.

- **Presentation of appropriate selections.**

- **Discussion of the benefits** (what's in it for him or her) of the product.

- **Overcoming objections.**

- **Selling up or adding on sales.**

- **Closing the sale.**

Priorities of Customers

Customers are individuals. You need to establish their wants, needs, and preferences. Treat customers the way you would like to be treated. You will get more sales initially and get many referrals from your customers.

Generally, *the first priority for a customer, pertaining to a particular item, is the color.* They will pass up beautifully textured selections if the color they are seeking is not there. When showing fabrics or other items to the customer, pull out their color preference *immediately,* before they look at the top color and *reject* the whole group of colors.

Style is the next consideration. Style can be the prime motivator or driving force in the beginning to motivate the customer to make a change.

The next important consideration to a customer is the texture. The customer is looking for a texture that is both attractive and appropriate.

Long-lasting, good looks or performance is the next feature of importance to a customer. Will it stay looking good? Will the upkeep be hard or easy? How long will it last?

Price is a strong last consideration. Although a customer may have this as a *prime* consideration, and may inquire *immediately* about the price, hold them off on the subject until you have shown them color, style, and then texture. Make them fall in love with the item and *have to have it,* before telling them the price. The *"love"* of the item is going to help cushion the price blow. They will find a way to have it.

Always have financial tables handy for different interest rates, to be able to tell the customer how much it will run them per month, if the item is financed. This is true whether you finance at your firm or they will be using their major credit card. Be able to give a customer a price per month as an option for purchasing the item.

Be prepared to show the customer several grades of similar fabrics and textures if the price is too expensive. Have a less-expensive, alternate plan available. *Let the customer decide what they can afford and must have.*

Designers and Decorators are Salespeople

The resolution to have a career in designing and decorating homes is the decision to be a sales professional. If you are unable to close the sales, you will not have a career. *Sales is everything to the career of designing and decorating.* If you cannot sell and work easily with customers after reading and applying yourself with this book, forget this line of work. A large quantity of sales is crucial for your survival.

Today, large companies (especially decorating companies) are purely considering not a person's design skills and knowledge, but how well the prospective decorator can sell. They do not care as *much* about your knowledge of the field as they now do about your sales ability. This is sad for the customer who thinks he or she has a design professional in their home, when in essence they have an arm-twisting salesperson who prides himself or herself on his or her ability to oversell and add on needless items, and who couldn't *care* what their customers buy. Designers and decorators who have worked hard educating themselves and trying to do an all-around, total job as exceptional designer/decorators, with the best interests of the customer always in mind, feel very disgusted with this *new criterion* for a designer or decorator's preferred qualifications.

The customers would be shocked to find out that the person holding themselves out to be a designer/decorator in their home has no background or education in the field. Chances are the so-called decorator is also faking their so-called design ability to do the job.

Review this whole section covering salesmanship on a regular basis until the techniques become a natural to you. *You* will be able to *vastly improve* your sales closing ratio, and be the designer or decorator with the design skills and knowledge that *should get* the sale. If you spend the time with the customer, you certainly deserve the sale.

Designer and Decorator Studios

Designer and decorator studios are a very *intimidating* place for an average customer to just casually walk into. *They must be enticed in*, through the projection of a warm and friendly environment. The atmosphere should project to the customer that they are welcome to come in and browse. This ambience is created in the way you advertise, display your windows, the way the samples are displayed, and in the amount of warmth you as a sales professional extend to the customer.

Consider putting prices on the displays and samples, to give the potential customer some idea of what they are looking at in price. Having items priced out is much more comfortable for the customer than having to ask you every few minutes what the price is on certain items. You will make many more add-on sales if you use this technique.

Greeting the Customer

Do not consider a customer to be an *interruption* of your work. They are the reason you are in business. The customer is the reason you are in this particular business of interior design and decorating.

Everyone has a different personality. Everyone will differ in the way they approach and greet a customer. You should never do or say anything that you feel uncomfortable about. If you do not seem sincere, you will appear overbearing and artificial.

Your initial greeting should not last more than seven seconds. Build trust through your greeting with your prospective customer.

When a customer walks into the studio and pauses to look at something, do not *pounce* on them. Give them a warm smile and a hello, letting them know you realize and care that they are there. This will make them feel welcome. Give them a few minutes to look around, unless it is obvious by their body language that they want instant attention.

Smile and approach the customer. *Do not stand too close to them, or too far away.*

Since the old standby, *"May I help you,"* has been so overused, customers are conditioned to automatically respond, negatively, when asked in this manner. **Start your greeting with comments such as the ones below:**

- Introduce yourself; tell the customer you are happy to help them.

- *"What may I show you?"*

- *"We have a beautiful line of fabrics that has just arrived, would you like to see them?"*

- Ask a question such as, *"What do you think of the new display we just put up?"*

- *"What do you think of the top treatment chosen to finish off the treatment?"*

- Make a comment on the item the customer has paused to examine. *"That is a beautiful treatment, don't you agree?"*

- *"That is a fine quality _____."* This type of comment reaffirms to the customer that you think they have excellent taste and make good choices.

- Compliment the customer about something they are wearing.

- Anything warm and friendly you feel comfortable saying will do. **Make the customer feel comfortable in your studio *any way* that you can.**

To develop that friendly, warm feel, *you need to look and sound as if you like your work.* Show sincerity, enthusiasm, and patience. Always handle your samples as if *they are something very special.* Also, *allow and encourage the customer to handle the samples.*

If you are cool, aloof, or non-caring, that customer is going to most likely flee, never to darken your door again.

Every time you approach a new customer, think to yourself, *"Here, if I handle it right, is a good sale!"* There is a type of sales professional who expects to sell *every customer.* When you **expect** to make the sale, most of the time you will close the sale.

Every potential sale should be approached with a positive attitude. Sell to your potential, adding on extra products and windows if they are needed, to give a more complete, finished look.

The salesperson who goes out to give an estimate, does just that — ends up *giving a free estimate.* Their time is wasted, and they do not end up getting the order.

The sales professional thinks of each estimate as a battle to be won. Have a plan of attack to win the battle. Approach it with proper planning and logic. You plan to make the sale and expect to make the sale. If you look for reasons to fail, or lose the battle, you probably will. The sales professional **plans a strategy** for the individual customer, and what *expected sales resistance* that customer will raise.

Prospecting

Why Prospect?

Why should you bother to prospect? Mainly because *you will increase your business and make considerably more money.* By prospecting, you build your confidence, self-esteem, and pride in yourself when your sales are increased due to the small extra efforts you did.

It is proven that if a salesperson contacts five new people a day for his services, he or she will build a base that will make him or her a success and keep him or her constantly busy. You have to keep your appointment calendar full and the sales constantly coming in.

You should never stop prospecting, even if you are very busy. Get your studio assistant to help you with the prospecting program. If you stop one month from now, you will have fewer customers two months from now, since your efforts to bring them in have stopped.

Try to increase your sales every month by setting goals. Any goals should be obtainable. They should also be challenging. Write them down and reexamine them daily. Review them, until you subconsciously know how much you have to sell, to make your goals, daily. Start each day with a list of articles to accomplish, and actually accomplish them. Do not carry over to the next day more than a couple of uncompleted items from the day before. Force yourself through good organization to get more and more items done daily.

Set goals for the amount of new leads you are going to generate on your own. If you do not set goals, you will quickly relax from working toward the goals and get sidetracked.

Determine *where* can you get more customers that have the needs and income to purchase your goods and services, similar to your present customers.

- **Why did your present customers come to you?** Find out the reason; really focus in on this reason as a prospecting tool to increase contacts within the same area.

- **Do your customers appear to be of the same financial level?** Or do they vary? Are their occupations the same? If patterns show up here, target those groups.

- **What groups could you target that have similar needs, along with the financial income needed** to purchase your goods and services?

- **Who uses your products?**

- **Where are your products used?**

- **How can you best reach your potential market?**

- **Which advertising methods** are the better ones to use?

- **What prospecting methods** are the superior ones to use?

- **Which present and past customers should you repeatedly ask to refer you** to additional customers?

- **How can you create a need** for your decorating/design services? Consider decorating a retirement home, model room, to show prospective new move-ins. Retired people in a retirement home have the time to look at your exhibit of services. They usually also have the means to pay for them.

- Get involved in doing model homes, or with other groups of designers decorating showcase houses in your area.

- **Where can you have a public display** that will be seen by many people? Banks, utility companies, and mall displays are very high traffic areas that are usually willing to allow you to do set up a display for a fee.

- **How can you improve your prospecting?**

- **Which methods shall you add? Which methods shall you continue to use?**

- **Adapt your presentations to fit the personalities of the individual customers** you are working with on their interiors. *Present the right style of samples to go with the style the customer perceives as the "look" that they want.*

- You must have the expertise to **appear instantly credible in your ability to decorate.** *People make snap decisions about people.*

By prospecting, **you help your customers know what you sell.** You are also letting them know that you are willing to help them with their decorating needs. Always treat customers in a positive manner that conveys to them that you care about their decorating wants and needs. Treating you customers in this manner also lets them know that you care about them as human beings.

By prospecting, *you help yourself* by making larger commission checks and more income. Your company is helped by being supplied with constant business. You become an invaluable employee that has the ability to generate leads on your own.

Work floor time in your studio if advertising draws customers into your place of business. Even if you do not have the item the prospective customer wants, but you presume you can get it, take their name, telephone number, address, and get back to them whether you can or cannot get the item. This practice helps *keep your name current*; if they ever do business with your company, they will probably ask for you. If they are treated well by you, they will also refer potential customers to you.

Always try to get any visitors to your studio to sign a guest list so they may receive mailings of future sales and promotions. Explain to the visitors *why* you want them to sign in. Have a box to check on the list, they are filling in, asking the customer if they would like to be contacted by *mail or telephone* about future sale events and new products. Periodic coupons, sent regularly as incentives to buy, work extremely well.

If the customer's name and address are directly supplied by an individual decorator's efforts, *all* mailings to that potential customer should include that decorator's business card.

Try to let anyone and everyone whom you encounter daily know the business that you are in. Freely distribute your business card to all these prospects. Let them know they are welcome to call you for a consultation on decorating.

Let your friends and neighbors know exactly what your career is and specifically *what* you do. Ask them to refer you to people whom they hear talking about your field. Let them know when you are having exceptional sales, so they can help get the word out.

If your company is a good company with a good reputation, remember to mention this to all customers, and also *refer to it* in your advertising efforts.

The referral from a satisfied customer is the finest quality lead you can possibly get. Ask your customers to mention you to their friends and neighbors who admire the completed decorating project. Be sure to give the referring customer extra cards to pass around. *Ask all of your customers at least once to refer you, and ask some of them repeatedly.*

Put on a referral program any customer that you think may be in a position to refer you *often* to many customers. Pay them a small amount, a small percentage of the sale, or give them a reduction on the price for their decorating projects, as discussed below under *Referral By Business People.*

Let each customer that you are working with know that you do other areas of decorating and design besides the area you are helping them with. If you do not *specifically* indicate to them the scope of the services you do, later when they need those services they will go elsewhere, not realizing that you also took care of that design area. You may think everyone knows what you do as a designer/decorator, but really *few* people know the true realm of the position. Have business cards printed up, listing all areas that you are capable of handling in the decorating/design field.

Find businesses that are in related fields around your area, where you may leave cards and flyers for potential customers to pick up. Allow these same businesses to leave their sale literature at your place of business, to be picked up by your customers.

As new products come out, immediately try to have a display in your studio made, exhibiting or incorporating the new product in a total treatment. In advertisements, telephone calls to customers, flyers mailed to your mailing list, or when speaking to present customers in their home, let the customers know the product is displayed for their examination in the studio.

Keep literature on products current and well stocked. If *new*, exciting products arrive, make a point of keeping your mailing list informed about the new arrivals; get them interested and enthusiastic about your current products and services.

Give any new customers an additional $50 savings on their decorating selections if they buy the day you come out for the in-home appointment. You will have to come up with a minimum sales amount to make this feasible. *This works as an easy incentive to get them to buy.*

Set up displays at fairs and in malls, where lots of foot traffic passes by. Hand out sales flyers and cards to all who pause when they pass your exhibit. Have potential customers sign a guest list to get them on your mailing list. Try to get the potential customer's name and telephone number so you may call them back to ask about setting up an in-home appointment. Stage a free drawing for a custom bedspread or other custom article, to get them to provide you the necessary telephone and address information on the guest list.

Try to turn any complaint call you return to the home on into an add-on sale, by suggesting additional items to finish the room. This is actually very easy to do. Simply look around the room and honestly tell the customer what they should now purchase to give the room a more custom-finished look.

Prospecting with Direct Mail

Try the following technique to increase your prospects and subsequent sales. Send a letter out to your past customers. Enclose your sales promotion flyer with a Post-it note attached, in a contrasting color, on the flyer. Write a small note on the Post-it, saying something similar to one of the ideas following: *"This is the sale I told you was coming up." "This is the sale I told you I would let you know about." "Do not pass up this exceptional savings." "The price on this product is going to go up June 3rd." "This is a particularly great value for this product."*

Follow up by calling the customer a day or so after the customer will have received the mailing and your note, and try to make an appointment. See below for the guidelines to the prospecting phone call.

Every three months or so, *work* your mailing list. Mail out a letter and flyer to your past customers and *any other* leads you have obtained. Include all past customers on your Christmas card list.

Add all customers to your mailing list that belonged to decorators that have *left* your company. These customers were probably satisfied, well taken care of, and would like to continue working with your company in the future. They will appreciate being retained by you, on your mailing list, so they may receive notification of sales. Send each customer a letter inviting them to do business with you, letting them know your credentials and experience. Let them know you are happy to be their designer or decorator.

Include on your mailing list those leads who you came close to closing, but lost to a less-expensive bidder. These leads are still potential targets. These people probably were not treated that well by the lower-quality company, with the probable lower-quality products. The customer probably now regrets buying from the competitor. If you continue pursuing them as customers, you will probably get the next project. This is especially true if everything did not go *perfectly* from start to finish with the other company. They probably regret not giving you the sale in the first place. They can see that you, indeed, really do want their business, due to the effort you expend in pursuing them with mail-outs. *They may be embarrassed for not giving you the sale.*

Sending them flyers and letters, show them you are inviting them to work with you on future projects, with no bad feelings from you.

Your past customers will appreciate knowing what is on sale, so they can take advantage of the sale prices. They are also able to mention these sales to their friends and relatives, when these people express any desire for decorating. The people referred by your past, satisfied customers, are the best potential customer you can get.

Every two years review your prospect mailing list and purge prospects names from the list you have never sold. Remove any customers' names from the list who have moved out of the area. Do not remove customers' names you have sold, unless you do not want to do further business with them.

Make up a complete package of information to mail out to prospects. Not only about your sales and promotions, but about the services you and your company offer. Hand these out to any prospects who come in to your studio looking around. Customers welcome you to mail them out information. Follow up with a telephone call to see if they are interested. Information about new products, store promotions, and upcoming sales are welcome, because you are helping them to save money and stay current about what is new by doing so.

After discussing this with your customer, develop a letter that you may mail or place on the doors of neighbors. Place this letter on the two houses on either side of the customer's residence, and the three homes directly across the street. You want to inform these potential future customers that you are working on the decorating project for their neighbor, Mrs. Neighbor (name the neighbor and the address). Invite them to come see the job when finished. You are, in essence, letting them know that you are also happy to work with them.

Mrs. Neighbor is going to be happy to show off her new decorating project, if the job went in well. To keep her happy you will have to stay on top of the job, keeping her well informed every step of the way. If you *do* stay on top of the job, she will give you many glowing referrals to her friends and the neighbors.

The neighbors will have your card already, and the satisfied customer will help to keep your name current and first in the minds of these acquaintances.

Let the customer know that a satisfied customer referring you to friends and neighbors is the finest source of leads you can possibly have.

If mailing to the neighbors of your customer, make sure to note addresses when you are out there on the appointment, or check the crisscross directory for the addresses. Crisscross directories may be subscribed to, or are available at your local libraries.

Watch the business section of the newspaper for newly promoted citizens at various companies. Send them your packet of information. These people now have a higher status with their new promotion, may now be entertaining more, and may need a more impressive interior. With their new promotion, they may now have the money to achieve some of their longed-for dreams for their home. They may also want to redecorate their new office. Find their address in the phone book white pages or send the packet of information to them at their company's address.

In the business section of your local paper are the announcements of any new companies that are moving into your area. These new companies may require a whole building full of window coverings, furniture, furnishings, and floor coverings. You may not make as much profit per item, but overall you can make considerable money obtaining jobs like these. You may be selected to do only one portion of the job, such as the windows, but *you are looking at potentially many windows.*

Send the packet of information to the address where they are vacating, in addition to their new address. Send a note or letter telling them to order now and have the interior *done* before they move in. The packet of information under their nose, twice, will reaffirm that you are anxious for their business. It will also keep your name very current in their minds.

Sign up with mailing lists that give you the new homeowner's address and name. This is a source of prospects that has *immense potential*, depending on how abused it is already in your area.

It is not uncommon in Southern California for new owners to receive a stack of advertisements from various design and decorating companies, 1" thick. When this happens, you will give many estimates. Each company will compete against each other, over a few dollars difference from estimate to estimate.

Customers, if given a stack of advertisements that say *"free estimate,"* will take advantage of getting as many designers or decorators to their home as possible. They also get different ideas and free advice from all designers and decorators that come out. They will usually end up very confused and worn out.

Customers generally buy from the lowest bidder or end up waiting, because of the cost factor, to do most of it in the future, piece-by-piece.

If you go this route, have a well-put-together ad, and a coupon for extra savings, to be used only for the *first* in-home appointment. Find less-expensive sources to sell down to in addition to higher-quality sources you may sell up to. Make a request on the ad for the customer to *"Call me and my company last when you are ready to buy, due to the extra savings available at the time of the initial in-home appointment."*

Estimates on houses needing many interior items are going to take a lot of your time. Try to eyeball and give the customer an idea of the price up front by making a *guess* of the price. Eliminate the unqualified customers from the qualified customers this way. Three hours later, you do not want to hear the customer say, *"Your price is much more than so-and-so company's price,"* or *"I cannot afford to pay that much."* If they are going to say you are too expensive, get them to tell you before you have wasted your time with them.

Spend your time with the qualified, likely-to-buy customers. Whole houses are potentially outstanding sales, but generally with lower profit per item, and are harder to secure, due to lots of competition. Be sure to give the customer an exact quote, or an idea of how much it will run them monthly, if they finance through your company or other financial sources.

Your local courthouse also has a listing of the new homeowners who have closed escrow. This is where the mailing list houses get them. This will be a free source of the names and addresses of potential customers, if you are willing to work to get them. You will have to go there twice weekly, research and spend time, and then hand address the labels.

The advantage is that you will get the information on the new names and addresses before the other competing companies get them. You can beat their mailings by at least a week.

Be ready to *jump right on the appointment immediately* and offer that extra $50 savings if they will buy that first visit without any delay. If your company tends to be a more expensive company, *this is the only way to go.* Customers will spend more money and buy higher-quality than they need, if they do not know they can get it less expensively with less quality elsewhere.

Many customers want to get right to taking care of their window covering and floor covering needs. You are probably the only company mailing to them *immediately*, with a dated, extra-savings offer. They will not know about all the other companies *yet* — especially if this is a new area for them.

Once potential customers find out about all the other companies available in their area, they become instantly educated, and much harder for you to obtain the sale from.

- Find out from **loan companies, newspapers, and county records who the people are who have taken new home loans out to fix up their homes.** Get to these prospects before others do. Go to the county recorder's office twice a week *at least*, for a listing of these records.

- Check the **newspapers for building loans applied for and granted.** These will be both commercial and residential. You will have both names and addresses of potential customers with the money in hand. Do some cold calling and mail out packets of information to these people.

- Obtain the **new marriages and births recorded at the county recorder's office.** You may obtain some names of more affluent couples that want to redecorate and fix up their homes.

- Always try to **schedule prospecting mail to arrive on Wednesday or Thursday.** Most businesses seem to get large quantities of mail on Monday and Tuesday. You do not need yours lost in the shuffle.

- On mail-outs of all types, **make clear to all prospects that you do the whole job.** From the proper planning of the job, helping the customer make appropriate selections, and the fabricating of all selected items, to the installation of all products. Let them know that financing is available or may be obtained through various sources.

- If you are **well-educated in interior design and decorating, very experienced, or affiliated with any interior design organizations,** always mention these facts in your mailings and on your business cards. You want to appear very credible in this diverse market. If indeed you are the best, look and act like you are.

- Mailing houses are available to take care of mail-outs for you. You supply them the labels, pay a modest fee per insert and label, and they take care of the rest. They will even deliver the ready-to-mail letters to the post office. Some of them will let you use their company bulk-mail permit *free*, so your company avoids a currently $60 yearly charge for the permit. Check with the mailing houses in your area on the services they have available for you.

- Computers are great time-savers for word-processing letters, planning your advertisements, and keeping track of your mailing lists. But if you just cannot get it done, contract it out rather than avoid doing it. Hire a computer-literate student to come by as needed, to help you out at a modest cost.

Prospecting by Telephone

Calling past and present customers for prospecting purposes:

These are the circumstances where your customer will welcome your prospecting call:

- When the call is about **new products, store promotions, and upcoming sales.**

- The customer **had previously expressed interest in other future items** and sales.

- **They are not busy** when you call — such as serving dinner, getting the children to bed, etc.

- **You are not overly pushy** about trying to sell them something they have not seen yet.

Call past customers two or three months before the holidays and remind them that **now is the time to order if they want a holiday delivery.** Having a sale to tell them about makes an excellent combination when prospect calling.

These are the reasons your follow-up call may not be welcome:

- **You are overly pushy.**

- **The call is made when the customer is busy.**

- **The customer feels you are trying to push them into buying something they have not even seen.**

Cold Call Prospecting via Telephoning

Cold calling prospective customers is an *exceptional* way to get leads you probably would never have. This may be done by you or by a telephone solicitor you have trained to set up appointments for you. Follow the guidelines outlined below for the approach to take in making this type of telephone call.

An overview of the preferred strategy to take in cold calling prospects is: *Send out a packet of information and flyer about your company and your upcoming sales and promotions.*

Wait about a day after they would have received the information, and follow up with a telephone call to see if the prospect is interested.

Invite them to take advantage of your sales and services. Try to set up an appointment with them now. Keep control of the situation. Give the prospect a couple of choices of times when you are available to meet with them.

Inquire if the spouse *needs to be there* to help pick out the wanted decorating items and to review everything selected.

Mention to the customer there is a $50 extra savings available to them if they purchase the day you come to the home.

Remind them that they are also covered with a three-day cancellation policy if they should change their mind about the purchase.

The telephone call should follow these guidelines:

- **Identify yourself by name, then state the name of the company** that you are representing.

- **State the reason you are calling.** *"I sent out some sales information to you and wondered if you had the chance to review it yet? Are you interested in my services for decorating?"*

- **Say something to benefit the customer.** *"We are having an excellent sale and I wanted to be sure to let you know. Participating in the sale will save you a substantial amount of money."*

- **Let the customer know that if they make a purchase the day that you come out to their home you will give them an additional $50 off the sales price.** Almost everyone *loves* what they perceive to be an outstanding deal, and find it hard to pass up.

- **Answer any objections the customer may raise.**

- **See what the prospect's reaction is.**

- **Give them the course of action to take,** if interested. *"Would you like to set up an appointment to have me come out to your home?"*

Successful Telephone Selling

After all your hard work trying to get your name out to customers so they will call you when they need your services, be prepared when the telephone rings to take care of that customer. Have pens and referral sheets to take down customer information, price books, and your appointment calendar ready by the telephone.

Answer the telephone as promptly as possible when it rings. If you are on the other telephone line and are the only one in the studio, place the person you are talking with momentarily on hold. Answer the other line, ask to take the customer's name and number, and explain that you will call them right back. Try to find out the reason the customer is calling before hanging up. When you call the party back, you want to be ready with the information at hand. Let the customer feel you are eager and enthusiastic to discuss their area of concern.

Have accurate product knowledge about the lines of products you carry. If you are informed and know what you are talking about, this is projected in your actions. The customer will gain confidence in you. Customers want to work with knowledgeable, experienced decorators and designers.

Review all the features and benefits of the products you carry. Study the products until they are familiar to you and easily expressed by you to your customers. Tell the customer the truth about the product in question. Never assume this customer has any product knowledge at all, about the product being considered. Go right down the product's list of features and consequent benefits for the customer.

Anticipate the objections the customer may present to you. *Think out* possible answers to these objections. Give complete, but honest, answers to all the objections.

When discussing products, group items such as pleated shades, blinds, and honeycomb shades together in one group. You want to make the in-home or studio visit as short as possible and these are similar products. When interest is projected by the customer to one of the groups you are discussing, *then* delve into the individual products.

Always, **practice basic salesmanship rules.** *Listen* to what your customer is expressing to you. Take notes on points covered and possible choices the customer will want to see, and review. This will make your in-home visit shorter and more to the point.

Ask leading questions or open-ended questions to get to the necessary facts. If you use open-ended questions, the customer will come up with needs he or she never thought about. By careful questioning on your part, you will help the customer to create his or her own needs.

Elaborate on special, limited-time sales and promotions you are having. This will create urgency for the customer to act now. He or she will want to make the decision to buy before the sale is up.

Empathize with the caller. Put yourself in the customer's shoes. Put yourself at the customer's level when speaking and using vocabulary.

Space out the selling points. Give a customer a question that he could answer with a *"no"* when you are ready to ask the customer to buy. You want to be able to answer and satisfy the last objection and then close the sale.

When you are ready to ask the customer to buy, use the *"which or what"* one would you like choice. It is very hard to say no when given this choice. Do not give the *"if you buy"* choice. Get the customer to commit him or herself. Keep trying this method until it becomes natural and you become good at it. With practice, if you work with the customer in the studio, you will be able to wrap the sale up before getting to the customer's home. You will only need to go out to the home to measure and confirm the color selection.

Close the sale — if the customer gives you positive buying signals. *Do not oversell or undersell the customer.* Give them what they actually need. **Come right out and ask for the order.**

Always show you customer appreciation for allowing you to discuss or work with them on their decorating needs, whether they buy from you or not. If they buy elsewhere, you will probably see them later, after that great deal they could not pass up turns out to be a poor-quality loser with them as the victim.

Referrals by Business People

Pay a referral fee to anyone who refers you customers. Give them a set amount for any customer they refer — *that you sell.* Set an amount of $5 to $10 for each referral that turns into a sale, or a set percentage of 1% of the gross sale's price. When you pay money for referrals, most people will go out of their way to supplement their income. They will repeatedly refer you to potential customers. It is the easiest money that can be made by people in the right position to do it. Below are ideas on who these people are.

If you work in a large department store with a custom-decorating department, have the other departments that are related, such as the furniture department, readymade drapery department, domestics, or catalogue department (customers return those skimpy readymades they order), refer the customer over to your department.

Have window companies, drapery-cleaning companies, installers and estimators, moving companies, carpet cleaners, drapery dry cleaners (they see the damaged drapery and are able to immediately refer you), insurance company agents (they get damage reports on interior furnishings all the time), refer you any potential customer.

Nearby furniture stores, shops, house cleaning businesses, florists, should all have your cards and flyers to place on the counter or hand out to customers. You should also reciprocate and do the same for them. Ask the customer where they heard about you. If a customer tells you this was the source of the lead, you should pay the store's employee a referral fee to keep the referring person inspired.

Work out a plan with the local drapery dry cleaning companies to have them to refer you business. Reciprocate by also referring them business. You are both in a preferred position to do this for each other. They see the potential customers who need replacement drapery first, before anyone else does. You get calls from past customers, asking you who you recommend for dry cleaning.

Moving companies, building inspectors, real estate appraisers, financial lending agents, insurance agents, real estate agents, escrow personnel, are all potential businesses that should be on your referral program. Real estate people and support personnel such as lenders, appraisers, escrow personnel, and insurance agents know of homes closing escrow weeks before the deed gets recorded at the county recorder's office.

Insurance agents also work with customers on damaged interiors, due to flooding, fires, etc. They are able to actually *request* that the customer call a specific company, or they may call the company themselves, requesting for you to do an estimate of the interior replacements. This area has so much potential and can work so well that I would put these people on a percentage of 1½% to 2% for their consistent referrals. The potential is there to get extremely easy sales working with them. It is not the customer's money, but the insurance company's, and if they are willing to pay off the claim, the customer is usually willing to go along with the insurance agent's request and recommendation to call you.

Get to the potential customer before everyone else's pile of advertisements get to them. If they get your ad first, and do not see any other ad for the next day or so, they will call you because they are not aware of anyone else to call. They are not aware of the many companies out there *at this point.* They need their windows and floors covered fast. Customers need privacy. After the pile of competing advertisements arrive, the customer becomes instantly educated. They know they can get free estimates, free ideas, will shop you against the next company over a few dollars, etc.

Visit the above people frequently and keep them paid up and interested. Once they earn a couple of checks by simply having you call the customer, or referring the customer to you, they will be interested in pursuing *the easy money.*

Supply any potential referring people with a good supply of your cards and always ask new customers if anyone referred you to them. Always make sure the referrer gets taken care of monetarily. You must keep them inspired. Not paying them just one time is the quickest way to uninspire them. Always ask the customer how they found out about you and your company. It may have been months ago and they finally called you for an appointment. Surprise the referrer with an unexpected check.

Work out cooperative advertising with reputable drapery dry cleaners, furniture stores, floor covering stores, carpet cleaners, etc., to share advertising expenses.

Place Sales Information and Business Cards Everywhere

See a moving van? Stop and give the people moving your packet of information. Also, leave a packet in the home being vacated for the new move-ins.

Stop at homes where you see a sold sign. Hand out your information packet to the people moving, ask for the name and number of the new owner. If they do not have the information or will not supply it, again, ask them to leave the packet of information behind in the home when they move.

Slip your information packet through doors of *"for lease"* buildings that you think will need your services. Be careful that the sales promotions and flyers do not have expiration dates on them. Use the first-time visit, undated $50 savings coupon. Some of these buildings sit unoccupied for months before a new tenant takes over.

Make notes en route to your appointments of any homes that look like they need your services from the outside. You will see the torn draperies and dangling window coverings that degrade the home's value. Send out sales information or place your sales information at the home. Be sure to include information on financing the purchase — this may be the reason the customer is putting off doing something about the situation. Follow up your information with a call to the customer. Find their telephone numbers in the criss-cross directory. They need your services. They may be putting off the purchase until they have the money saved, so have ready financing information on paying for the products monthly, rather than all at once.

Local building materials stores usually have bulletin boards where you may place your business cards or a small ad. If they have a store newspaper, place an ad in it. Also let the employees know you pay for referrals of customers that place an order with you.

Post notices and your cards in common area laundry rooms of condominiums and townhome communities. Also place notices and cards on laundromat bulletin boards. Not everyone has a washer and dryer, and those that do occasionally have theirs break down or wash larger items in public large-capacity machines.

Other potential targets are grocery store bulletin boards or other bulletin boards anywhere else around your area. Replenish these notices and cards, regularly. Both competitors and interested potential customers remove them. Try tacking or stapling up a small pile of cards, so a few people may take them. There are businesses around that regularly service these bulletin boards for you.

The whole idea here is to keep your name current in a prospect's mind. If they ever need your services, they automatically feel you are the company and person to call.

Flyers Everywhere

Contribute money to local youth organizations to hand out your flyers with your card attached. They must not place the flyers in mailboxes; you will receive an angry call from the postal service.

Try direct canvassing to specific neighborhoods. Knock, smile, introduce yourself and your company. Then hand the potential customer your packet of information with the incentive coupon for them to look over. Invite them to call and make an appointment with you for your services. This has much more impact than just placing a flyer at the front door. Potential customers do not feel very intimidated by you if you have already introduced yourself and invited them to call you.

Potentially, you might be able to work certain neighborhood areas and get some of your customers in the same general area. This will save you time in travel when going for in-home estimating and installation calls. Pick the homes that obviously need some help on their window coverings, in addition to the homes that look complete. The ones that look complete may not have done the bedrooms yet, or may have only opted for the undertreatment to start with, and are now ready to do the fancier overtreatments.

Place flyers on cars in shopping centers. This cannot be done usually at the largest shopping centers that house your largest department stores. If the mall security observes you doing this, they will probably warn you, rather than ticket you. Try the grocery store or the other smaller malls that do not have obvious security. This is a good method for getting the word out about your company. Include the incentive coupon, with the expiration date, to get the customer propelled toward immediate action. This is obviously quicker, easier, and more prospects can be reached, than with a person walking around a neighborhood handing out flyers. Unfortunately, you will not be able to tell the homeowners from the renters.

If you work in a large department store with many departments, hand out flyers, with your business cards attached, to all customers who pass by your strategically positioned spot in the store. If you are not located strategically, place your body in an advantageous spot in the store, where most of the foot traffic goes by. Give all potential customers a smile and say *I would like to introduce you to our custom decorating department and give you our current sale sheet to let you know what we do in our department, and what excellent buys we have. My card is attached and I invite you to call me on any decorating questions you may have.*

Have Seminars

Put on seminars for various women's clubs, organizations, retirement communities, and retirement homes in your area. The people attending generally have the needs, means, and desire for custom decorating. Older people do not have much energy to shop competing companies to compare prices. There is a local company that is very successful giving periodic seminars at a large retirement home with older people. They also did the models for the prospective move-ins to inspect.

Every one of these potential customers is faced with doing the window treatments for their new apartment. These customers have had to get rid of a lifetime's supply of household goods, and many of them are simply opting to start over with completely new interiors for a change. This particular company stays on top of the situation by keeping its name current in the minds of these older people by appearing regularly before its affluent audience.

Join any clubs, organizations, or networking groups that seem interested in your field. You will get the opportunity to speak before the club and use its mailing lists to mail out advertisements to all club members.

Talk to the club about the decorating trends and new colors forecast for the future. Show before and after photographs during your speeches. Show samples of new fabrics, treatments, styles, and window coverings. Give all who attend one of your sales packets and invite them to call you for an appointment.

Advertise decorating seminars to be held in your studio. Teach potential customers how to put together different looks and how to combine different elements. Show any new products and ideas you have displayed. Seminars will get people excited about what you have to offer and the lines you carry. Give the extra incentive coupon in addition to a sale price for first-time buyers.

Previous Decorator's Problems that Arise

Agreeably take care of problems that arise from designers or decorators that are no longer employed with your company. *There is the definite potential of turning problem calls into additional sales by suggesting add-on purchases to finish the room.*

While you are there taking care of the problem, the customer will perceive you to be more of an expert than the original designer or decorator. The customer will happily welcome your suggestions. This customer may also find they prefer working with you. They may desire any decorating items that they need for the future to be fulfilled by you, the expert designer/decorator. Always add any new contacts to your mailing lists.

Customers Not Sold by Other Decorators

Customers not closed and sold by other decorators may be closed by another, stronger decorator under certain circumstances.

Some customers just do not blend well with your personality. They may mesh with another designer or decorator's personality very well. Relinquishing a customer may be done if the original designer or decorator willingly turns the customer over to another designer or decorator, or if the designer/decorator leaves the company.

Do not work with a customer of another designer or decorator unless the decorator turns that customer over to you. This is the easiest way to cause problems in any studio amongst fellow designers/decorators. You should never fall to this level, ever.

If one designer or decorator works with a customer, all subsequent purchases should be made with the same decorator. This is especially true *if* the designer or decorator has kept that customer on his or her mailing list and continued to keep the customer current on sales and on follow-through, with any problems that have arisen.

All customers should always be asked, *"How did you hear about us?"* If they are a past customer, they will come right out and say they are when asked this question. The customer should then be asked if they remember their designer's/decorator's name. Have the studio assistant look up the file if the customer does not remember the designer's/decorator's name. At this point only is it the option of the customer to change their designer or decorator. And this option to change designers or decorators only belongs to the customer.

The customer simply may not have been happy or comfortable with their previous designer or decorator. Make sure the customer understands, if the previous designer or decorator asks the person who set up the appointment, why the customer is set up with another designer or decorator, that the reason/reasons the customer changed their designer or decorator will be revealed to the previous decorator.

Peace and fairness in the studio must be maintained, even at the cost of a customer. Another decorator should have enough integrity not to grab another's customer. Not all customers realize that you are on commission and many will just not think to ask for you, even if you did an exceptional job in the past for them. Make it a rule that whoever is making the appointment ask, *"How did you hear of us."*

You may want to try this technique with a friend that works with a competitor. Tell the customer who is being price or time-resistant with you, that you have a friend who is also in the decorating business and works for a competitor.

Possibly, he or she may be able to get this job installed for the customer faster. Tell your customer, if they are going to shop your price, that you will have a friend from a competitor call them to give them a comparison price.

Discuss with your friend you are referring the price quoted to the customer, the sizes and styles that were decided, and the fabric selection. Let the competing designer or decorator underbid you on the job. Work out an arrangement with the other designer or decorator to reciprocate and do the same for you. Split the commission on the job to keep it fair.

If you do not want the customer to know your arrangement, let the other decorator mail out sales information to the customer or put a flyer on her door. Have the decorator follow through with a phone call and set up an appointment. The decorator will know what it is the customer wants in style, sizes needed, type of fabric, what pricing not to exceed, etc. This will be a fast sales call and an easy sale to obtain.

Yes, this is fair — as long as a fair price is given to the customer, and the customer is not taken advantage of in any way. You worked hard on the sales call that you did not get paid for, didn't you? If the customer had any feelings for you and your time, they would have come into the studio and asked for approximate prices, and found out what the price was approximately going to be — before you came out and spent hours of your time with them — free. They ended up with your time, your ideas, and did not make the purchase from you. Is that fair to you?

Contact Past Customers That You Did Not Close the Sale With

Contact past customers that you did not close the sale with, and try to sell them again on the decorating items that they did not buy. You may be having a better sale now, or want to let them know that this is the last chance for them to order at the quoted price, before the price goes up. People have a tendency to put affairs on hold, look around some more, or need to come up with more money. They will appreciate being notified of a better price. They will also appreciate notification of price increases and having one last chance at purchasing the item at the lower price.

Keep trying for the sale through follow-up telephone calls and repeated mailings periodically to keep your name fresh. You want to let the customer know that you definitely want their business. *They are obligated to you for your time spent with them and you should indirectly remind them of this fact. Make them feel that they owe you a sale.*

Before calling a customer back for a follow-up call, *ask yourself,* **what would make me buy this? What can I say to get the sale?** Would you like to be waited on by a salesperson like yourself? Have you thought through your sales pitch recently?

Also, call customers you did not close in the past to see if they now need any decorating items. Let them know that you are still happy to work with them. Time is available to work with them now, and there are several exceptional buys, that you thought they might be interested in.

For customers that needed financing, that you did not take care of with the financing, arrange a financing plan, call the customers, and let them know that you now have financing available.

Make every customer feel that you are a friend that is going to help them get the most value for the money. They should feel you are going to give them the right styling and products for their needs. Make them feel that you are going to follow through on exceptional service and delivery. Let them know you are there for them to call back in the future for questions and concerns about the current purchase, in addition to other decorating needs. You will build confidence with your customers if you have friendly business relationships.

Successful Sales Professionals

People successful in sales are not born that way but *desire to be that way*. Successful sales professionals act on taking care of tasks faster. They balance elements out mentally before making decisions. Successful sales professionals perceive and believe they can do the job.

Invest in sales seminars to improve your sales ability and write them off on your taxes as a business expense. Improve your sales ability by reviewing this section of the book, again and again.

"Is This a *Free Estimate?*"

Many customers will call you up and inquire if the services of having a decorator/designer come out are free. Unfortunately, you may be advertising in this fashion, to compete against your competitors, since they are advertising in this manner. Possibly in the future, more and more companies will opt to charge a small amount for estimates, to discourage people from having numerous designers and decorators out to their homes.

Presently, the trend is to have numerous designers and decorators out to the home, to get their ideas *free*. Some of these customers end up doing the decorating themselves, using your ideas.

Since most companies have *"free estimates,"* if you charge for the estimate, you may not get as many customers. A small charge would encourage the customer to do a bit of the leg work and come into the studio with their measurements, to get an idea of the price before wasting your time.

The charge could be applied toward their purchase. Decorators and designers are like other professionals — it takes education and hard work to become a professional. Other professionals never work for free, why should we?

If the customer calls and says, *"Is this a free estimate?"* *"Is there any obligation to buy?"* — that customer is probably getting other bids, or just *wants ideas*.

Instruct you studio personnel to say, *"No there isn't any obligation to buy. But, realize that the decorator/designer is coming to your home, spending his or her valuable time to help you with your decorating needs, and does anticipate that you are going to purchase the items discussed. If there is a question on pricing, may I give you an idea of the pricing before the decorator/designer comes out? Would you like me to set up a time to meet the decorator/designer in the studio, to go over pricing and selections before he or she comes out? You will need to bring in approximate measurements when you come in."*

If you instruct your coordinator to say the above, this is really going to make all questionable calls much more productive. This will get the questionable customers into the studio, where they may turn into customers, or may go on their way to the readymade store. Other non-serious customers will make the appointment, think about what the assistant said to them, call and cancel the appointment — not wanting to face you, after they used your time — *free*.

It will take much less of your valuable time to work with them in the studio, then run out to their home, hauling piles of decorating items in and out of the home. Always try to narrow down the desired selections to see in the home, for a quicker trip out there.

How to Increase Your Sales

There are key techniques for you to use below, to make the most out of each sales call.

- Always be **warm** and **friendly** to all customers.

- Be **complimentary** to your customer and their home.

- **Take an interest** in your customer and their decorating problems.

- **Listen** to the customer. Note the clues to wants and needs they are giving you.

- Carry and **show current ideas and pictures.** These may be pictures of the jobs you have done in the past, magazines, or window-covering books.

- **Make suggestions** — but do not get angry or offended if the customer *wants what they want*, or does not care for your suggestions.

- Have **accurate product knowledge** of the products you carry and show. Know the correct products to use for the particular situation.

- Try to **upgrade the customer to higher quality** if the need is there. Do not sell the highest-quality if the need is not there. To preserve a good reputation, do not sell or show poorer quality products *at all*.

- **Add on other windows or layers of window treatments,** to give the room or home a more finished look.

- **Suggest slipcovers** for spring or summer months to give a lighter, fresher look.

- **Be observant** while in the home. **What else do they need to finish off the room. Make suggestions** and tell them to call you when they want to replace that carpet — as you do carry a beautiful line of carpeting, competitively priced. **Let them know when they are ready, you are happy to help them on that project, also.** If you do not speak up and tell them, when they are ready to do the project they will seek a local carpet store or other source instead.

  When you make suggestions to the customer about adding undertreatments, top treatments, accessories, etc., they may be able to make the purchase that minute. What you are doing is *planting seeds for future purchases.*

- **Ask the customer if they are going to continue that same treatment, fabric, or theme into the next room.**

- When measuring and planning any immediate window treatments, **always leave room to add future top treatments, sheers, or undertreatments.** Sell the future needed rod initially, to take care of easily adding future sheers. Think ahead; **suggest finishing treatments and get future sales.**

- Take and **keep the customer's name and number for future sales.** If the customer is expressing interest in items that are not on sale now or have not arrived yet, due to being new, always try to take the customer's name and number so you may contact them in the future. Call them back, when you get the information and let them know that you are wanting to work with them on this project. Keep your name current to the customer, so they will ask for you when they call or come in.

- Always **bring up the subject of floorcoverings, upholstery, wallcoverings, etc., and specifically indicate to the customer what other services you provide and what other products you sell.** If you do not tell them, they probably will not realize you also cover that area, and will go to another source when they need these items.

- **Send out sale information sheets and promotions** that you are having regularly to all past customers. Keep your name current in their minds for future sales. This also keeps your name current for future referrals they will make for you to their friends and relatives.

- Take and **keep notes on what your customers want to purchase now, and what they need to purchase in the future.** Call the customer back and send them information when the items they need go on sale.

- **Measure for future items. Keep note files on any needed future items for present and past customers.** This can turn into a quick sale when the customer comes to the studio and orders the item which you have already measured.

- Try to **turn any complaint call that you go on into an additional sale.** Be observant and let the customer know what they need to finish off the treatment or the room.

Qualifying the Customer

Qualifying

As you start to work with various customers, you will be able to absorb a lot about them by observing them in action. This will be projected in the way they are acting, the way they are dressed (conservative, flamboyant, stylish), how they combine elements together, etc. Their projection may be deceiving. *Do not ever underestimate a person's ability to buy, if they appear overly casual* — this is probably their day to rush around and get tasks done.

When qualifying the customer give them an idea of pricing:
Give them an *idea* of the price of the items the customer is considering purchasing. Take the time to give the customer a price, whether you look up the price, or using your past sales experience, you give a realistic, approximate price by guessing.

If you do not know what the price would be approximately, look it up. This practice of giving the customer a price gives them something to go on, and qualifies the customer — it realistically lets them know if they should continue to pursue the idea, use even more of your time, or consider another course of action or selection.

If you do not make it a practice of pre-qualifying your customers, this is typically what happens: three and one-half hours later, at the *"free-estimate,"* in-home appointment, when you finally get around to a price, the customer goes into shock. This is true with very affluent customers as well as ones with more moderate means.

Work with the customer in the studio qualifying and showing samples:
When customers go out of their way to come into your studio, spend a few minutes working with the customer showing samples and products. Discuss their situation and needs.

Your role as a designer consultant is to *advise and educate* the customer **on what is available** for their particular situation, and guide them to an appropriate selection. Give only the amount of information that is needed. Do not *confuse* the customer into not being able to decide, by plying them with too much information. Use simple terms and explanations when explaining about the products you carry and the planning of the job.

Help the customer become clearer on what it is they want. Your customer may need to take care of any final confusion and overcome the fear of buying. You should again state the benefits and the good value they are getting if this is the case. Take care of the customer, and they will become long-term clients and refer you many friends and relatives.

Spend time working with customers in the studio. Show them different fabrics, give suggestions, demonstrate selected displays, and show pictures.

This practice will give you a much better idea of what you will be working on when you arrive at the customer's home. Many times you are able to narrow down the customer's selections to the right type for the customer. Your visit will be much shorter, and you will have less to carry in and out of the house and studio. This approach also allows the customer to see a total selection of what you have available.

Working with the customer in the studio, additionally, gives you *more of a possibility* of making a sale during the initial in-home visit. Otherwise, you may make subsequent visits back to the home with other more appropriate merchandise to show.

Even if you go to their home several times, bringing more and more samples, customers still may not feel obligated to buy from you. This will occur especially if you advertise *"free estimates."* Your time is valuable. Get customers to come in and see what is available. When they come in, they can also get an idea of the price. Suggest this when they call your studio for a designer or decorator to come out on a *"free estimate."*

Many decorators like to go ahead and make an appointment for an in-home visit, and possibly work *free* for three or more hours in an estimate situation. Why not spend your time, gasoline, and wear-and-tear on your car by visiting pre-qualified customers who are most likely going to buy?

Immediately upon your first encounter with the customer, put that customer at ease. You may be meeting the customer for the first time at their home or in the studio. Either place, get that customer comfortable with you. Be warm and friendly to all customers. Project that you are excited to be here and working with that customer. Extend to the customer that you are happy to help, knowledgeable about all the customer's options, and *you* are the right person for the job.

Let the customer know your qualifications, education, and experience. If you are *not* educated and experienced, act confident that you do know what you are talking about. You should spend all your extra time learning the business by studying and following other experienced designers or decorators around, if they will let you. Work extra hard, until you gain product knowledge and know what you are talking about. Do not lie to the customer if they ask how long you have been doing this! Be honest — *if they like you, they will probably want to work with you anyway.*

Seek Information from the customer by asking questions such as:

- **Which room** are you doing?
- What **color scheme**?
- Which **type of texture** do you prefer?
- Do you prefer **printed or plain fabrics**?
- What **style is the furniture** in that room?
- What **color is the carpet**?
- Do you want **a casual feeling** or a **formal feeling**?
- **How big is the family and what are the ages** of the children?
- How well **do the children take care of their possessions**?
- Will you be **changing the wall color**?
- **How soon** do you need this installed?

Customers are Either *"Decision Makers"* or *"Not Decision Makers"*

Customers fall into the categories of either being "decision makers" or "not decision makers."

When a *"not a decision maker"* meets a salesperson who *does not* show and tell them what it is exactly that they need — taking control of the situation — the response from the customer is usually, *"I want to look around some more before making up my mind."* They look around until someone takes charge of the situation and convinces them that **this** is the right choice. The salesperson who takes control of the situation will end up making the sale. If you are not a decision maker type of person, you will not see the customer again.

When a *"decision maker"* meets a take-charge type of sales professional, the result is the same as the *"not a decision maker"* working with the salesperson who does not take charge of the situation. *"Do not even assume you know what I need. No, I do not like that, that is not what I had in mind, etc."* You can show them everything in your studio and in your car and the results are the same.

Determine what type of customer you are dealing with before coming on too strong or too weak. **Adapt and tailor yourself accordingly** in your personality and presentation. *Combine* yourself with the customer and come up with a complementary combination.

Regardless of whether the customer is *"a decision maker"* or *"not a decision maker,"* always *assume* they are going to buy, and act like they are going to buy.

If the customer is a *"not a decision maker,"* start asking questions to formulate in your mind the correct course of action to take to help them to decide to buy in their mind. However, do not come on too strong and scare the customer away.

If the customer projects to be a *"decision maker,"* start reviewing the features and benefits, just giving enough information to instill confidence in your knowledge. *How thorough*ly you cover the information will decide if this customer gives you the sale.

Be sure to discover the customer's wants and needs before starting to show samples.

After establishing the customer's wants and needs and narrowing down the possible selections, try to make an in-home appointment with the customer.

Qualifying a customer allows you to spend your time with the customers *who are most likely to buy* from you. Qualifying a customer, before spending too much time with them, is necessary for the following reasons:

- Qualify the customer to see **if they are a custom decorating customer**. Make sure that they are willing to spend the extra money to have a higher-quality, custom product.

- Qualify a customer to make sure that they have **the means to buy your products and services**.

- Qualify you customer to be sure that they can and will **wait the amount of time needed** for you to supply your products and services.

You should start to qualify the customer the minute the customer telephones you, or on the first visit by the customer to your studio. Your time is valuable and you want to spend it with buying customers.

Start qualifying a customer by sharing ideas; books, with pictures of different styles and products; magazines; photo albums that you have, or have put together.

Find out by listening and discussing with the customer what their wants and needs are. **Wants are the emotional reasons for buying, needs are the rational reasons for buying.**

Qualify a customer by listening, observing, and asking these types of questions:

- **How will** this product **be used?**
- Are there **any problems** that you foresee?
- How much **use** will the item receive?
- Are there **any unusual conditions?**
- **What have you had in the past?**
- **What did you like about it?**
- **What are you looking for** in the new one?

Be willing to *immediately show and discuss* various products and fabrics that you feel would be appropriate selections for them. If the customer does not respond favorably to your perceived solutions, be willing to show other selections. Keep showing other selections until you are able to narrow it down to the appropriate group of products and fabrics that gives the customer the right style and selection.

Some decorators or designers are taught the contrary by their companies and management that employ them. They want you to go on every call, cold. You end up spending vast amounts of time in customers' homes not even knowing beforehand if they are a custom customer.

You do not want to waste your time (probably about three hours) and energy. Calls take time — selection of fabrics and samples, bringing in tons of samples from your car, selection of styles, and estimating various treatments, in different ways. You are probably on commission. If you take the call cold, the company you work for probably will lose only the mileage to the home.

Determine ahead of time if the prospective customer is willing to spend the kind of money and time that it is going to take to realize their dreams.

Pre-qualify every customer down to what they think they are interested in, then give them an approximate price on what you think it will run them before proceeding to set an in-home visit. If the price does not seem to disturb them, then proceed to make the appointment for you to come out to the home.

If the pricing shocks the customer, then you have saved hours of your time by finding out right away. After the initial shock sets in, they may absorb and digest the price.

After they have comparison shopped, the customer will probably be back to set the appointment with you, if the price you gave them was competitive. It is better to get the shock over with in the studio, rather than after spending hours in the home. At that point, the customer has to think it over, absorb and digest the price, before buying.

Give the prospect your business card with the approximate price on the back of the card. **Be sure to spell out the words,** *"approximate price based on these measurements, in this selection of fabric or product."* You do not want to be held later to the estimated price if the customer comes back with an actually needed, much larger size, or a different selection. Some customers will claim that is what they told you, and that is what you gave them the price on initially.

The practice of working with the customer in the studio also helps narrow down what the customer wants you to bring to the home, and what they are interested in discussing when you get there.

Setting the In-Home Appointment

If the customer is *still* with you after you have given them an idea of the price, than go ahead and make an appointment for you to come out to the home.

Check your appointment book, even if you know that you have plenty of time open. Appear very busy to the customer, even if you are not. You are in demand for your expertise. Your time is valuable, and you are going to share some of it with the prospect by coming out to their home and helping them with their decorating needs.

Always try to book your appointments during the week, filling the day slots if possible. Depending on what schedule you personally prefer, have certain time slots set aside for appointments. First slot would be 9:00 to 10:00 in the morning. Next slot would be 1:00 in the afternoon and then 3:00, for a three-appointment a day schedule. Add in another appointment for 5:00 or 5:30 for a four-appointment day.

To go on callbacks and complaint calls, you will need to work the four-appointment day. You will also need to run back to previously held appointments, to pick up samples or bring new samples for the customers you did not satisfy with your initial selection. Squeeze these repeat calls in *after or before* the individual appointments, when you can.

You will also need to run into the studio when you can, to do paperwork, return telephone calls, put in your floor time, meet customers in the studio, etc.

Remember, **dusk and evening hours are poor times to pick colors.** If you have no alternative but to do the appointment at that time, leave the samples *behind* with the customer, so the customer may view them during the day. Either pick up the samples later or get the customer to return the samples to your studio.

Save Saturday appointments for people who work during the week and get off late in the day. Saturday appointments usually turn out to be your best appointments. The prospects who book Saturday appointments have limited time to shop around, have the means to buy, and are serious about buying, or would not waste their limited time having you come out to their home.

Try to book appointments with married couples when both can be there to participate. This is especially true if one spouse cannot come to a decision without the other. You will end up hearing at the end of your presentation, *"I have to discuss this with my husband or wife and get back to you."* **They almost never get back to you,** so again, you have wasted your time.

Come right out and **ask if both husband and wife need to be there to make a decision.** They will indicate at this point whether you are about to waste your time. *"I want to get a price first, and then discuss it with my husband." "My husband wants me to narrow down what I want before we decide."*

Insist on **giving the customer a price before coming out to the home**, and have the customer discuss it with their spouse. After they have discussed the price, still try to make the appointment when they both will be there. You may alienate some customers here, but *they were not going to buy in the first place.* They wanted a *"free estimate and free ideas."* You will have saved your time and let them know you are happy to work with them when they are serious about buying, but not before.

Try not to make next-day appointments. Next-day appointments make you appear as if you are not very busy. The exceptions to this are: the next day may be the best time to go because you have had a cancellation, or the customer is here from out of town. Then go ahead and make the appointment, letting them know they were lucky, you have a slot open the next day due to a cancellation from an ill customer.

Write up an appointment slip as the customer relays address and telephone information to you. Record any information about what they are interested in, samples they want to see, selections they have made, product possibilities, color preferences, textures, styling, directions to their home, etc.

By finding out before the appointment what the customer is interested in, you save yourself needless extra trips to the home. You are also able to think about your presentation of the items before you arrive at the home. When you think your presentation through, you are able to make a better presentation. Otherwise, it will be a spur of the moment presentation, when you go out to your car and pull the item out of the bottom of your trunk and bring it in.

Ask and record on the appointment slip how the customer heard about your company. Make sure to give credit to any designer or decorator whose efforts led the customer to you.

Give the customer your card with the date and approximate time recorded on the back of the card. Be sure to tell the customer that the time is approximate, although you do try to be on time. Reaffirm the date and time with the customer as the customer is leaving, or before you hang up the telephone with the customer.

Record the customer's name, address, and telephone number in the master studio appointment book at the date and time of appointment. The master appointment book is the schedule with every decorator's schedule listed in it, so everyone can accurately set up appointments for each other at available time slots.

Use an appointment slip that is double or triple with carbon or N.C.R. paper. Tear off the top copy, or two top copies (if recorded in triplicate), of the appointment slip and staple into your appointment book under the date of the appointment. Place the other copy in the pile of appointment slips left, in order, in the studio. These slips later can be reviewed to see how prospects are hearing of your company and where to keep spending advertising dollars.

The initial appointment slip or the second copy should be returned and verified on the slip if the lead was sold. If the sale was not sold the reason, should be given. Most interior design and decorating firms require this procedure to show them how you are doing. It also helps you to see the areas that you need to improve upon, to close more sales in the future.

Preparing for the In-Home Appointment

Carry the following items for in-home appointments:

- Appointment book

- Bring price books of everything you sell. Double check that the price lists for the items requested are current.

- Samples of all hard-window coverings you carry.

- Samples of most frequently sold fabrics, variety of assortment.

- Samples that the customer has specifically requested.

- Bring a clipboard to write on.

- Photo albums, idea books, magazines of current and traditional styles.

- Calculator, pens, tape measure

- Estimate sheets, business cards, sales contracts

- Briefcase to carry the majority of the above in. The type that opens from the top works very well, so items can easily be slipped in and out. Small children seem to stay out of this type of briefcase better when your back is turned.

In-Home Appointment

After establishing a customer's wants, needs, and preferences by either working with them in the studio or over the telephone, try to make an in-home appointment with the customer. You are now an invited guest to help the customer make informed decisions.

Show the products in the setting and environment they will be used under. The other members of the family may also participate and give their opinions. Since you have lugged samples, spent time with the customer in the home and probably in the studio, made trips to and from the home, the customer may (should) feel obligated to buy from you. At the in-home appointment, you are now able to sell up and add on other needed merchandise.

The prices given in the home become bids or exact prices, rather than an estimate of the cost given over the phone or in the studio.

Take other selections with you to the in-home appointment. Have a range from expensive to less-expensive. Make sure you also have variations of the desired color in a range of pricing. What may have looked like a perfect match in the studio, under fluorescent lighting, may not look too great in natural or incandescent lighting of the home. You are there to close the sale, not to come back again with a broader selection due to the first selections not being a perfect match.

- Be on time. Do not be earlier or later than 15 minutes.

- Walk up to the door with a business card in your hand if you have never met the customer before.

- Carry only your appointment book, briefcase, and clipboard to the door of the home. Carrying any more will make you appear overloaded and will overwhelm the customer at their first glance of you. Some decorators/designers do not bring anything in with them when they arrive initially. Since you are destined to make many trips to and from your car daily, bringing in your support supplies initially helps cut down the extra trips.

- Knock or ring bell.

- Smile, introduce yourself, and present the customer with your business card if you have not already presented a business card to the customer in the studio.

- Be friendly and break the ice. Set the customer at ease. The customer may feel uncomfortable and apprehensive having you come out to their home. The customer has probably gone to a lot of effort to get the home ready for you to see. The customer probably stayed up late and got up early to get the home clean and in order for your visit.

- Bond with the customer by *sincerely* complimenting him or her about something in the home. Regardless of how sparse or meager the home may be, find anything to compliment the customer about. *This is a very important step, since you will be enhancing the customer's self esteem by complimenting them. Do not skip this step.*

- If you are nervous at first on your in-home visits, the nervousness will soon disappear. The customer is far more nervous than you will ever be. Meeting all types of people from all cultures and backgrounds will become the most interesting part of this profession for you, *if you like people.*

Successful sales come from idea-selling, confident, and knowledgeable decorators/designers. After learning the basic principles of color and design; the rules of measuring; proper planning of window coverings and other interior treatments; the correct way to do the paperwork; service the customer after the sale, you will gain the confidence needed to be a success in this business.

One of the foremost favorable elements of being a decorator/designer are the wide diverse group of people you will encounter from various countries, cultures, lifestyles, economic groups, personalities (from very easy-going to very closed and stiff), from casual in manner to ultra formal, etc. *You need to be able to bond with each type of person to make a sale.* You do not want to turn anyone off by your manner or the negative way you treat someone.

Be sincere to your customers; treat them with *genuine* warmth. You have to really like all types of people, not just tolerate them. You need to be able to take an automatic liking to people and be able to get to know them quickly, while setting them at ease.

Enhance the customer's self esteem. Make them feel important by treating them warmly, smiling, using their name, complimenting them on their home. Show them that you care enough to come to their home to help them with their decorating.

Share empathy with the customer. Put yourself in their shoes, understand where they are coming from. Customers, while communicating, show a variety of emotions. Understand how the customer sees the situation and where they are coming from.

Even though the home may not be overly pretentious, the customer may be financially well-off. They may need your help pulling a striking interior together. Do not judge a customer's ability to buy by his clothing, grooming, automobile selection, or their home that may have tastelessly put together furniture. Do not prejudge their means to buy (if you have already given them an initial idea of the price, and they are still interested), until you ask for the sale, they sign the contract, and give you a deposit.

Appear to admire and show interest in the proposed selections that your customer is making. Point out the features of the various proposed selections that will give your customer the most value for their particular situation and really emphasize these features.

Always act excited about the aspect of being able to help the customer decorate their space. *If you are excited, they will get excited*, you are sure to make the sale and get them going on the project.

Talk to you customer about the pride of having such a treatment/selection — *make the customer just have to have it!*

Designer/Decorator Consultation

Start your interview of the customer by asking a few very revealing questions. *Ask friendly, nonprying questions.* Do not get overly personal, unless the customer voluntarily reveals personal information.
"To help you make the best possible selections, *do you mind if I ask you a few questions?*"

- *"How large is the family and what are the ages of children? Who are the other members of the family?"* This tells you how durable the products need to be, how much abuse the items will get, what fabrics to stay away from.

- *"Have you ever had custom-made decorating items before?"* The answer to this question tells you a lot. If a *"no"* answer, give the customer an idea of the price *immediately,* before spending any more of your time.

   If the answer is *"yes,"* then proceed with your presentation. Try to find out if the customer made the purchase themselves or if the custom items came with the house. Does the customer have a grasp on the pricing? If not, give them an idea before spending any more time. If the customer made the purchase themselves, then start at the beginning and take him or her through the process of buying.

- *"How much were you planning on spending for the decorating project?"* The designer/decorator must work within the realm of the customer's budget. Since the customer probably does not have a realistic idea of what things cost, they may not be able to finish the total job at once and must do it in stages. Spend the money where it will show up and count the most. By finding this out early in the consultation, you can focus your time on the projects to be done now, rather than later.

- *"How soon do you need the decorating items/interior completed?"*

- *"Do you own the home?"* Are they going to go to the expense of decorating someone else's property?

- *"What is this room used for?"*

- *"Is the room used for other activities? What activities?"*

- *"Are **other changes** going to be made to this room?"*

- *"What **type of atmosphere** do you want to create?"*

- ***"How are the new treatments/floor coverings to differ** from the ones you had previously? **What did you like or dislike about the old ones?"***

- *"What type of entertainment do you do? How many people are usually present?"*

- Try to find out what the customer and spouse do for a living. This will tell you a lot about what quality, possible tastes, etc. This may not be easy to find out unless you come right out and ask the customer. Customers tend to want to work on the subject at hand and not talk about themselves too much.

- ***"How long do you plan to live here?"*** *This information indicates quality of the item and the price the customer will probably spend for the item,* such as lined versus unlined drapery, elaborate top treatments versus simple top treatments, simple top treatments versus no top treatments at all.

- ***"What type of style and 'look' were you thinking about?*** *What styles do you prefer?* **Do you have pictures to show me of the styles you like?** *What do you think you would like to do here?"* You, as a decorator/designer, want to express the customers personality. ***"Shall I start giving you some ideas?"***

- ***"What type of fabric and texture** do you prefer?"*

- ***"What color scheme** are you considering?"*

- *"What is the main idea you are trying to achieve with the new treatment? What are your expectations for the new selections?"*

- *"Have you purchased or **do you already have the focal point or major accessory to be used in the room? Is the palette of colors found within the accessory, or found in the focal point? Are these the colors to be used in decorating the room?"*** Mauve means many different shades of pink to peach. If the customer has an idea of the shade, fine. When you bring your samples in, you will have 25 different shades of mauve. If the color needs to be matched up to a certain item, be sure the customer has the item out or *available* for the appointment.

- *"What style or styles is existing furniture to be incorporated into the interior?"*

- ***"How much maintenance** are you willing to do? Is there a housekeeper?"*

- *"Do you like plants?"*

- *"Will pets be coming into the room?"*

- *"Do you need extra storage? Should you incorporate storage needs into your design ideas?"*

- *"How much do you want to spend monthly?"* Ask this if they want to pay for the decorating items by the month.

- *"Is there any other item we did not cover concerning the selections for this room?"*

Additional questions to consider for window treatments:

- *"Are the window treatments **to be the focal point** of the room?"*

- *"Do you want to make the window treatments **as beautiful as possible?"***

- *"Do you want the window treatments to **stand out and be noticeable, or fade unobtrusively into the wall color,** not calling attention or being obvious?"*

- *"**What fabric/window treatment did you have in mind for the windows? Have you found a style or a fabric that has really caught your eye?"***

- *"**How often will you open and close these windows?** Will the treatment be drawn open and closed frequently to expose the glass of the window?"* This answer tells you *how functional* the treatment for the window needs to be.

- *"Do you want to consider the most **functional products or treatments?"***

- *"Do you want **a center-open, or a one-way pull?"***

- *"Is **insulation** an important factor?"*

- *"Will the treatment be **lined?"***

- *"Is **privacy** a main factor?"*

- *"Shall I consider **light control?"***

- *"Will the planned treatment **need to stack-off completely for the view?"***

Additional questions for floor coverings and carpeting:
- *"Do you want a floor covering/carpeting that is **as functional as possible?"***

- *"**How durable** does the floor covering/carpeting need to be?"*

- *"**How much maintenance are you willing to do?** How often do you vacuum/mop?"*

- *"Is noise control a consideration?"*

- *"Does the surface need to be nonslippery?"*

- *"What is your **color preference?"***

- *"**What type of floor covering/carpeting do you like?"***

- *"What is your **style preference?"***

- *"What **type of life do you need** out of the floor covering/carpeting?"*

Additional questions concerning commercial projects:
- Be careful to find out **exactly how the spaces are to be used.**

- **All functional aspects of the space must be considered. Maximum use must be obtained in commercial situations.** Additionally, efficient flow and operation within the space are of prime importance. Lastly, an attractive environment to work in and receive clients is very important.

- Find out the style that the business *projects.* Traditional, contemporary, innovative?

- Incorporate the business's logo and any specialized graphics, if possible.

When you find out the **priorities** that are important to the customer, then you are able to focus your presentation on these main ideas. By asking these questions, you will be able **to take the customer's input and ideas and apply them appropriately, with the end result a satisfied customer.** Otherwise, you will end up with a customer that hates what you did, because you did not express their wants and needs. Instead, *you expressed your own wants and needs.*

Unless, the customer is decorating to put the house on the market to sell, **sell long-term style, color, and quality.** Do not make the decision for the customer to look at lesser quality, rather then better quality. If possible, they deserve to have nicer selections.

Try not to be too faddish. If the customer keeps going in that direction, point out to the customer what they are selecting is faddish. **Let the customer** *decide* **if they still want to work in that direction.** The customer may be in a position to redecorate every three years or they may need styling, color, and quality to last them 10 to 15 years.

A professional designer/decorator reviews the range of ideas that the customer and the designer/decorator arrive at and **decides if the ideas will work** in the room, with the customer's lifestyle.

Customers have practical wants and emotional wants. A customer may want a particular product, but may not need it. People may want to update their interiors, but may not need to, since the interior they have is still in good shape. Show concern, have respect for a customer's wants and needs, and for what they can afford.

Listen to What the Customer is Saying

Pay attention and listen closely to what the customer is saying. What do they really mean? The object of listening is to get your customers comfortable enough to freely discuss and tell you what they want. Both parties want to get the subject of the visit covered. Cover the matters at hand, and any perceived problems that are important to the customer. Try to draw out of the customer as much information about the situation as possible, so you may make appropriate recommendations. You want to solve, correct, or minimize the problems, and create great-looking interiors.

While listening to the customer, always act interested and be understanding of the problems and situations. Express empathy (put yourself in their shoes).

While listening, do not make the mistake of arguing, interrupting, making decisions, or passing judgement too quickly, before hearing all the facts. Do not cut the customer short, assuming you know all the facts and have all the answers. Let them tell you what *they think they want.* Use these methods if you want to effectively come up with the right solutions to take care of the problem, and if you want to make a sale.

After listening to the customer, drawing out as much information as possible, clarify back to the customer what the customer has projected to you. Clarify to get additional facts, and to review all sides of a problem. To clarify back to the customer what you perceive the customer has projected to you, use the following type of leading explanations and clarification of the facts.

- Specifically, you feel that....................
- Can you explain the problem to me?
- You feel the problem is......................

Single out the problem, listen to what the cause of the problem is, and help figure out the solution or right course of action to take to correct the problem.

Restate the facts, to see if the customer means what you think they mean. Restating the facts also shows you are interested, understand, and are listening to the customer. This will also encourage the customer to further elaborate on the specific problems, as they perceive them. Review and restate the relevant facts, any problems, reflect on the situation, and the different solutions.

Summarize the probable, correct way to go to bring about the best overall results for that customer's individual situation. Pull out the correct selections to do a properly planned job for the situation.

Keep Notes on Possible Future Purchases

During your in-home visit, always keep notes on what rooms and items the customer mentions to you that they may want to work on in the future. After the job you are there to do is completed to the customer's satisfaction, some of the other items needed may go on sale. Contact the customer by telephone and let them know about sales of the needed items. Invite the customer in to see new fabrics when they come in. Even though the customer may not like the fabrics you call them to come in and see, you are establishing rapport with that customer. They feel you are looking out for them and care about their needs. The customer will become more of a friend. If they see something else that they really like elsewhere, you probably will be asked to get it for them.

Hard-to-Work-With Customers

Some customers have literally *no taste*. They may be insecure about what they want, and show no preference, when you make suggestions. After you make suggestion after suggestion, they sometimes will venture forth and *finally* give you an idea that they have, but were not comfortable in expressing it to you immediately.

More often, the customer does not know anything about fabrics, types of textures, styling, ideas, etc. The customer probably has not even looked in any magazines, decorator studios, fair displays, or model homes, for ideas on styling, fabric types, products, or colors. When you get the *"I don't know"* answer, you envision yourself there, three to five hours later, for just a few items, *finally* arriving at a price. Then, the customer says to you, *"Well, I never thought about doing it that way, or doing it in that style, or color, and I have to think about it."*

The customer *now* has to take time to absorb the ideas, because they never took the time to investigate what they really might want to do before calling a designer/decorator to come out to their home.

In this business, *this type of customer is an irritation.* They use up your and everyone else's time, and get everyone's ideas. They think long and hard about doing the project, shop everyone's price against each other for a few dollars differential, while letting the sale prices they received the bids on end. When, and *if,* they do come back later, you will have to re-estimate the job in a different price or fabric.

The original designer/decorator who gave the customer the idea they want to use and spent the time narrowing down the selections and styles will probably not get the job. The bid will be beaten, using your ideas, from a competitor who is willing to do the job for a few dollars less. The competitor will spend a minimal amount of time to get the customer to make decisions on the elements that you and the customer spent hours making.

The best way to handle the above situation is to **tell the customer ahead of time** when the appointment is made, *"The day the designer/decorator comes to the home, there is an additional discount of $50, if the customer signs the order and buys on the initial visit to their home."* Warn the customer ahead that they will forfeit the additional savings if they do not make a decision that day.

If the customer protests that they are getting other bids, then tell the customer to get the other bids first, than have the designer/decorator come out after they have gotten the other bids. Explain to the customer that it costs money to send the designer/decorator repeatedly out to their home, *in time, wear and tear on their car, and gasoline.* If they can finalize the sale in the first visit, then the customer is offered the additional savings. The job becomes an easier one for the subsequent designer or decorator, because the customer is now more in focus as to what they really want.

Take the name and number of the customer and call them back in a week to see if they are *now* ready to make the appointment. Call them back if they do not initially make the appointment for a later date, when they call or come in the first time.

The danger is that the customer may run across a designer or decorator that they were able to bond well with, and they go ahead and give the designer or decorator the order. Usually, customers will still call you in to see what your price is, if you let them know that you are happy to work with them. You may lose a few customers (which probably would have only gotten a price from you, anyway), but you will save much more time and make many more sales over a long period of time this way. This works.

Customers Who Speak Negatively About Competitors

Sometimes you will arrive at a customer's home and they will say very negative comments about another company that has tried to work with them. The customer canceled the order because something went wrong and the customer got mad. *Beware!*

The customer may be saying negative things about the other company's overall quality of product, quality of the job, or the other company's way of handling problems. You may be called in to *redo* the job that the customer canceled with the other company.

If you are fortunate, the original job may still be in the home, not yet picked up by the company that put it in. Look and listen *carefully* to the customer's complaints. *The customer is now at a very low tolerance level.* If anything goes wrong with your job, the customer is really going to give you a hard time, while spreading negative thoughts about you and your company around to many people.

Examine the existing problems of the job, if the items are still in the home. Are the complaints justified? *Can and will* your company do a better job? Do you foresee any problems working with this negative customer? Do you want to go ahead and take the chance on doing the job — knowing that your job may also have problems come up?

If you do choose to take the job, realize there is a strong possibility that the customer may cancel on you, over a small problem. Any errors may eat up all your profit. Additionally, the customer will probably be hard to work with.

Hard-to-Please Customers

Some customers cannot ever be pleased. They seem to sit around and study each valance, measure each pleat's spacing, study the way every pleat falls, measure the distance off the floor at regular intervals, etc. We all are *somewhat* particular, and *some* of these complaints are legitimate. The redoing of the problems, and the service calls, will quickly erode *any and all* profits. Jobs may end up *costing* your company money, to finally satisfy the ultra-particular customer.

As you look around the home, does it seem especially meticulous? Is the customer giving you clues about the problems that he or she has encountered in the past when decorating?

Be very careful when quoting the job. Pump up the profit margin so potential reworks, possible remakes, and adjustments can be taken care of. You will have to pad the price to make any money on the job. It seems some people will find any minute question or problem to get you or your installer back out to their home to reassure them, or to fix *a nothing problem.* All of these trips cost you and your company money.

Always try to do a great job. Some customers just cannot be satisfied. Some customers will find any fault or use a small delay to get an adjustment out of you. This type of customer will haunt you regularly, if not daily. You will come out at the end with hardly any profit. These types of customers are the ones for you to pass up.

How to Help Your Customer Find Their Style

The most successfully decorated interiors are the ones which express the occupants' personality, interests, and feelings about life. A customer must find a style to call their own. Customers need styles that they are comfortable with, which reflect their lifestyle.

Some people are born with an inherent sense of knowing what they like, excellent taste, the ability to choose and blend elements, to create design that reflects their style. Other people cannot easily do this.

You need to narrow down the style to decorate the home in, because there are so many styles and choices *available to decorate with.* A customer that does not have direction will become overwhelmed and not be able to put together successful combinations.

To help a customer find his or her style, or the direction to go in, observe these following points:

- **Where do they live?** City or country? Suburbs? Is the house architecturally very modern, traditional, Spanish, English, French, Mediterranean, Oriental, very old, brand new? You really cannot fail if you flow with the style and look of the home, keeping the initial theme consistent.

- **Is the home dark, overly sunny, light and airy?** If the home is dark, then lighten it up in color, furniture, possible skylights, mirrors, etc. If the home is overly sunny, take care of the sun problems when planning decorating ideas.

- If a customer has chosen a **distinctively styled home** over another, this probably is a conscious or subconscious **preference for that particular style.** They may want to continue the same style in their interior to make the home really flow.

- Look at the **existing furniture** to see what the customer has chosen in the past and tends to prefer. Ask the customer what they intend to keep. Work with these items in color and style.

- Have the customer decide **what are their favorite colors**, and *which of their favorites* could they live with for a long period of time.

- Eclectic styles are always a very comfortable way to decorate. We all like many different effects. We sometimes simply must have something that does not necessarily go with our intended decorating style. Eclectic arrangements and combinations add interest and relief from too much of the same look.

- Customers may want to study and invest in artwork. Use the artwork as the focal point. Use the colors of the artwork to decorate the room around.

- Have customers save all **pictures of color schemes and rooms** which are decorated in styles that they favor.

- **Have customers look through books, magazines, books of jobs** you have done in the past, etc. **See what they consistently seem to prefer.** Have them point out why they like certain elements and ideas over others.

- Have customers **save fabric and wallpaper samples** that they come across and especially like.

- Customers will gain insight in going through **model homes** and seeing the actual rooms decorated. Have them **snap pictures of ideas** they come across that they particularly admire.

- Visiting friends' and neighbors' homes will give customers a range of ideas.

- Your **studio decorated in a range of colors and styles**, in different layered treatments, will pay for itself time and time again, when customers can come in and see the actual treatments up.

- A customer's **occupation** will also reflect in their decorating selections and preferences. Does the customer need to unwind in a calm setting, or is their work rather unstimulating and mundane? They may want and need to have a stimulating interior.

- Does the customer **entertain a lot**, and wants to have elaborate treatments to show his or her status in life? Is the home primarily a backdrop for entertainment?

- Be sure to consider **animals and children** when helping the customer determine appropriate selections. Does the customer really need a more durable, cleanable fabric, or will the fabric be used minimally?

- What is the **customer's interpretation of their home?** Are they home often? Do they put the home to full use or do they just come home to sleep, bathe, and change clothes? Are they seeking a comfortable, cozy feeling, or is an extremely clean atmosphere desired?

- Consider the **ideal use for the room.** Not the use the architect planned when the home was built.

Try to draw out of the customer how *they really want their interior to look*. They are the ones who must live there with the interior selections. The customer should have what they want. If what they want is not affordable, do the decorating in stages, so you can give them what they truly want in the finished treatments.

Describe other jobs you have done. *"I just did a beautiful job on drapery over in the next block. We put up beautiful lined, printed drapery over pleated shades and cornices, that matched the drapery on all the living and dining room windows. We chose stylish tiebacks to complete the window treatment look. Let me show you pictures to give you a better idea. A similar idea would be exceptional in these rooms also, as the layout of the floor plan is similar."*

Some customers know *exactly* what they want, so your role is to guide them along keeping them on the right track, helping them avoid expensive mistakes.

When you and the customer decide which design direction you are going to go in, assemble all the fabric samples (purchase a yard each, if samples are very small), flooring samples, and wallpaper samples. Look at all the samples together in the home. Let the customer live with the combination for a few days to see if they are happy with the combined group.

Try to fit you customer into a general style and then adapt the style to their own individual personalities and needs.

The House and Adjacent Rooms

During the in-home visit, look around the home to see what the customer already has and what their taste is like. Note the following key items important for successful decorating:

- Does the **home have attractive features**, or are there features that you will have to disguise?

- Note mentally **where the room is located** in correlation to the rest of the home. How does the space flow? The whole house flow?

- What is the **room arrangement**?

- What are the **focal points**?

- **How much sunshine** comes into the room? Is the **room generally comfortable** in temperature? Were you comfortable with the coldness or the heat of the space?

- Is there **a view** to play up and accent? Or is the outside unattractive, and you **need to disguise it**?

As you look around the home during your visit, look to see if the customer is a perfectionist. *Signs of perfectionism tell you that some of your selections will not satisfy this customer.* These selections should be avoided.

Items such as verticals that have horizontal patterns that will not match up, nor are never attempted to be matched up; drapery fabrics such as moire may not hang in perfect folds; antique satins with slubs will never be smooth and perfect hanging, etc.

If you pick up on these clues about the customer being a perfectionist, pad the price for the reworks, select all samples carefully, and beware if the customer is making negative comments about other companies that have attempted to work with them in the past. See the section on *Customers Who Speak Negatively About Competitors.*

Presentation of Samples

After building a rapport with the customer, and getting an idea of the colors and style that the home is to be decorated in, you have an idea of the family that the fabrics or hard window covering falls in.

You can then go to your car trunk and bring in piles of samples from the fabric family you envision they should pick from. After hauling in many pounds of samples, your customer may want a texture out of a completely opposite family.

Customers generally do not know much about fabrics and will only know the type of fabric when they see it.

Note: too many selections of fabric or hard window covering samples overwhelm the customer. Get the customer excited by showing a limited, beautiful selection of fabrics and hard window coverings.

Always show the customer the samples that first caught their eye, and then samples similar which are slightly higher in quality.

If the customer seems completely unsure about which type of fabric or other sample would be their preference, invite them out to your car trunk and let them grasp the range of fabrics and samples available to them. While at your trunk, if the customer expresses an interest in a certain type of fabric or family of other products, pull other *similar* fabrics or samples from the same family. Bring these selected samples into the home for consideration.

There are two thoughts on the right way to present samples to a customer. **The first thought** is to allow the customer to thumb through the samples, unattended by you, while you go off and measure.

The second thought about presenting samples is to sit down with your customer, present the exact color selection to the customer out of each sample book, and then have the customer accompany you while you measure each window.

Many designers/decorators will go out to the car, choose the selections for the customer to see, bring them into the house, lay them on the table in a stack, and then ask the customer to look through the samples to see what they like. While the customer looks through the samples, the decorator goes off and measures the windows. *It is possible to save some time doing it this way.*

There are two dangers here. The customer, if not versed in fabrics or other samples, will look at the top color of the sample, placed first in the sample book, and decide that they do not like the fabric because they do not like the top color. They *never* thumb through the sample colors, to the right color to suit their needs. They decide, based on the top color, that it is not the sample or fabric for them.

When you return to the room, all the samples are neatly stacked and the customer says they did not see anything that they liked.

Now, you attempt to re-show them the samples, pulling out the appropriate color selection for their situation. They have already prematurely decided they do not like the sample. *Customers will not get very far looking at samples alone.* The customer does not *usually* know what is right for their situation, what they really want, or actually like.

The second danger is that you are off measuring the windows by yourself. You are really taking a chance on measuring without the customer standing right there in the room, discussing and planning exactly how the treatments are going to be. If you do not have the customer right there watching you measure and plan the job, then you are going to have to be willing to redo the windows when they arrive in a different length, width, or do not stack-off the window, as the customer silently perceived that they would.

The second thought on sample presentation is, after bringing in the samples, place them on the table, and go through every sample. Pull out the right color and texture selections for the interior from each sample.

Comment on each selection's benefits, features, and pricing (if the customer is price conscious). Discuss the fiber content and finished looks of the various samples, eliminating them and stacking the discards as you go along.

Fold the colors back or pull the sample out, so the right selections may be viewed. Handle the samples with care and treat them like they are very valuable. Eliminate them as you discuss each sample. If the customer has a hard time making selections, spread the samples out on the table or the floor.

When you are down to a couple of selections, review the pricing and fiber content of the remaining selections with your customer, if one happens to be a better value in price or quality.

Many customers say, *"I don't care what it costs."* **And they think they mean it,** until you tell them what it is going to cost to do the job. Try not to press the point about which is the better price, because the customer's pride is involved. *In the end they will care what it costs,* and will probably balk as badly as the customer who warned you going in that the price was a main concern. When it comes to money, people are extremely prideful, even when they cannot afford to be.

Leave them laying on the table and ask the customer to accompany you to the windows that are to be measured. Ask questions about every measurement and decision as you go along, for every window. Make the decisions together, while the customer receives your guidance. The job goes in without any surprises to the customer, and you have a happy, satisfied customer without any remakes or reworks.

Ask questions such as, *"What do you think of this sample? How do you like this?"* By asking these questions, you will see if you are on the right track, or on your customer's wavelength with the sample selections.

You must be the one controlling the presentation, through to the close. You are in charge of the situation and are the salesperson and authority on interior decorating.

The second thought on sample presentation is more time consuming and may be slightly irritating to the customer. If you take the time to explain to the customer that the reason you want them to accompany you to measure the windows is that you want to make sure both of you are on the same wavelength. You want to make the items fit, just the way the customer wants them to fit. If you explain why, the customer is really going to like your style.

This way of proceeding is the best way to do your measuring, planning, and sample presentation. You will eliminate the majority of mistakes right then and there. Always head off any potential problems that can arise by covering them, so they will not happen.

View the samples at the window and against the wall:

Pleat the selected samples in the sample books with your fingers (as best as you can) and hold up to the window. Holding the sample to the window allows the light to filter through the fabric or other material. Observe the color — *sunshine filtering through fabrics or other materials will change the color.* Next, lay the sample against the solid wall. Observe the color again. Is the color still right?

If the drapery or other treatment is to be lined, place the lining to be used with the fabric, or double up the selected sample with a fabric the color of the lining. Pleat the two fabrics or samples of self-fabric up together. Place fabrics over the window and against the wall to observe and verify the correct color.

Customers have trouble visualizing with a small swatch of fabric, or swatch of a hard-window treatment, what their finished treatment will look like. This is why many pictures of the same treatment or similar treatments, executed in various colors, help the customer get a truer picture.

Select the style of treatments for the windows:

Show pictures, describe, or draw styles to get the customer narrowed down to the desired style for the windows. Narrow down the styles to one or two selections.

Measure up the windows. Keep the customer on their feet, accompanying you, so you have their complete attention. Ask them questions as you go along, about every decision to be made, while measuring. Record every decision on your worksheet.

You are helping the customer to decide what they want. You are not making the decisions, but are guiding the customer along the whole planning process. Do not take a different attitude here, unless you do not mind (and can afford) to have a large quantity of reworks and remakes. Designers and decorators have always been perceived to pick out the selections with little help or input from the customer. Not today. Any problems that arise are very expensive in materials and in labor to correct. The wrong attitude here will put a small firm and a large firm (if it repeatedly happens) right out of business.

If you did your preliminary work by working with the customer in the studio, then you have already narrowed down the fabrics to a few. You will have suggested styles to the customer that the customer is now mentally pondering.

The customer will now contemplate for several days the solutions you have already offered to the decorating problems. When you arrive for the house call, the customer probably now has a feel for what direction in style, and what direction in fabric and samples they want to go.

Many customers, probably not realizing how much time and effort it takes, or possibly just not concerned for your time, will request for you to figure the windows treatments out many different ways. For example, you may be requested to give prices on lined versus unlined treatments(an acceptable request), this style versus that style, with stationary panels versus full drapes, with pleated shades versus honeycomb shades, etc. *This is an extreme amount of computing and estimating on your part.* This amount of estimating in itself will cause you to make errors due to all the figures on your worksheet. Also, this amount of estimating will take up a lot of your time.

The solution to this problem, is to try to give the customer an idea of the different prices by making a guesstimate. *"That will run you about $300 more that the other style. Stationary panels instead of full drapery will cut the price down about $700, etc."* To alleviate this situation, and to avoid a major headache (literally) on your part, ask the customer, *"How do you really want these treatments? That is the way we should make them up."*

If you do not take this approach, after all your intense refiguring, your customer will be thoroughly confused and have to think about it. You probably will not be able to close the sale with the customer, because they have now decided to shop around.

You will also get confused. Two hours later, you *may* make a sale to the customer, incorrectly concluding that the customer wants you to do it a certain way that was discussed one hour before.

The customer, not knowing the terminology, will be thinking that they are agreeing to do the treatment a different way, that was also previously discussed. When the treatments come in, the customer is very unhappy because, *"That is not what I ordered."* You, of course, have it down in black and white, in terminology that is foreign to the customer. Right or not, the unhappy customer needs to be taken care of until they are satisfied.

If this problem should arise, you need to try to talk your customer into keeping the treatments. **Use your best salesmanship principles under these circumstances. While making your presentation, sell these points:**

- **Sell the beauty, quality, effect** of the fabric or other treatment. Sell the fabric or sample's texture and pattern.

- **Sell the benefits** of the particular fabric or treatment.

- **Sell the esteem and pride of owning** a custom treatment.

- **Sell the workmanship and quality** of having a custom-made product.

- **Sell the quality of service** that you and your company will be providing the customer, when allowed to do the job for the customer.

Possession of product knowledge makes you the expert. During the presentation, involve the customer by letting them handle the samples, making decisions while measuring, deciding what it is that they want. Demonstrate features, **discuss the benefits.** Ask the customer for their reaction, *"How do you feel about this particular feature? What do you think?"*

Features, Advantages, and Benefits

Features describe the characteristics that the product possesses. You can actually **see and touch** features. **Features describe benefits.**

Advantages describe how to use the features. You are unable to touch advantages.

Benefits turn the advantages into buying motives. They are the reason the customer should buy. **Benefits will make the sale for you.** You can turn advantages into benefits by phrasing sentences with beginning words such as, *"What_____;" "You_____;" "The reason_____;" "The advantage to owning this particular_____."*

What Feature	*It Will Do* Advantage	*For The Customer* Benefit

Studies on what makes people buy reveal that *sales are made when the customer's express need is answered with a benefit statement.* Before you can answer with an appropriate benefit statement, you need to discover what the customer's needs are.

Do not tell the customer what they want; let them tell you what they want. Achieve this by asking questions. By asking questions, you get a clearer picture of what they really need, not just what they think they need.

Tell the customer that they can save money. Telling them that they can save money will get their attention. Customers want items that will be easier for them to take care of, and items that will save them time. Customers also want items that will wear for awhile before looking worn.

Motivate customers to buy by using features, and then the feature's advantages. Follow up with a benefit about your product that will benefit *that particular customer.*

Gain and hold your customer's attention. While in this stage, get the customer to express a need so you can follow through with a benefit statement. *Once you have sufficiently followed through with giving the benefits of the product, you need to follow through with closing the sale.*

Do not bore your customer with too much technical knowledge. Convert the technical knowledge to simple, understandable features, advantages, and benefits.

Other key points:

- **Enhance the customer's self esteem.** Make them feel good by smiling, calling them by name, and finding ways to sincerely compliment the customer.

- Put yourself in their shoes and **empathize with them.** Understand where they are coming from. You do not have to agree with their point of view, just understand where they are coming from.

- As you show merchandise, **watch the customer's body language** to see if they are interested.

- **Romance and use showmanship** of your products when working with your customer. Match their perceived needs with your line of products. Once the customer has expressed a need to you, answer with an appropriate benefit. If you have sufficient product knowledge, you will be able to do this.

- **Keep the customer interested by being enthusiastic.** Your enthusiasm will cause them to be enthusiastic and excited. You must be able to sell yourself to the customer. Until you can do this, you will not be able to sell the customer anything.

- **Tell the customer** that **you are glad they made these particular selections.** Always **use eye contact** and keep your rapport up when working with the customer.

- **Let the customer see, feel, examine, and handle the samples** and proposed products. Place the samples right in their hands and give them the feeling of owning it. Give them the feeling of having to have the product. Show pictures of similar treatments to visually show the customer, what the treatment will look similar to.

- **Show** the potential customer **how this merchandise** or treatment **will help solve** his or her **wants and needs.**

- **Express** to the customer **the ease of adding or blending additional items** later to go with the proposed purchase.

- Let the prospect see that **they will be getting their money's worth.** *Pack the treatment or merchandise full of value for the dollars spent.* If the customer feels the money outweighs the merchandise, they will not buy the merchandise.

- **A customer who has not gone through all the steps of salesmanship** and the steps of the presentation **will feel overwhelmed and unable to decide to buy.**

- **Make the product easy to buy.** *"It will only be 'x' amount per month with 'x' amount as the down payment."*

- Consider this plan: **The more the customer buys, the bigger the discount they get.** This could potentially turn a couple of windows into a whole house full of treatments by giving the customer a real motivator or incentive to do the whole project. You will not make as much per item but the overall sale will be larger.

- Find a **financial institution or loan broker** to work with you on **providing financial arrangements, to offer your customer for financing.** You may be able to earn extra commission from recommending customers to them, for the delivery of filled-out loan applications. You also end up with sales you would not have. Why should you pass up these customers if your company does not carry their own paper or have a plan available to you? Some Visa and Mastercards will not carry the whole amount, have higher interest rates, and/or may be already at their limits.

- Give a **better guarantee** than your key competition does. Top them and win the customers.

- Supply the **finest service** of any decoration business around. Keep your customers referring you and coming back for repeat sales.

- **Build a reputation** for being the foremost place to get decorating services. Why would the customer want to go anywhere else? Only if they want problems and headaches!

Third Parties Present for the Presentation

It is hard enough to come to a decision with the husband and the wife agreeing, let alone a neighbor, a friend, a relative, etc., *getting involved*. If the customer wants these people present for the presentation, try to discourage having anyone present other than immediate family members. If you do not, you will probably not make a sale. Tell the customer, in your experience as a designer or decorator, the third party will not *like* what the customer likes. It is not uncommon for customers to go along with what the third party likes, and end up very unhappy with the selections. These were selections that the customer did not choose or even prefer.

The third party always *seems* to know of a less-expensive source to refer the customer, to get another bid before deciding. They are put in the authority position by the customer, and tend to take charge of the situation. Everyone has a *"decorator"* in their circle of family or friends.

Assure the customer that they are the ones whose opinions count, because *they* have to look at the selected treatments every day. Why would a person's opinion, who only occasionally comes to visit, carry that much weight? Tell the customer if they want to be discouraged, then by all means, invite the third party over and come to *"no decisions."* Discourage the third-party visit during your presentation at all costs. Be honest about the reasons for your discouragement of the third party attending.

If at no warning to you the third party is present, do not take sides when the difference of opinions start flying. If you express your opinion, do it very diplomatically, honestly, pleasantly, and professionally. Do not alienate or anger anyone.

Your Goal as a Designer/Decorator

Your goals as a designer or decorator should be to decorate and be creative, while helping customers to select the right product for their needs. If the customer does not follow through and make the purchases, you have not been paid for your time, efforts, and education.

In the decorating and design field, you will have a full range of tastes, opinions, likes, and dislikes expressed by your customers. As a sales professional, you must be able to work with a wide range of lifestyles, cultures, and economic levels.

You will not succeed with the attitude that you are the decorator and your customer has to go with your selections. If you make a customer feel that what they want is ugly, out of style, in bad taste, etc., you will not be successful in working out a sale with that customer. They will go elsewhere. If you succeed in changing their minds to what you want them to have, they will call and cancel the order before it makes it through the three-day cancellation period. If the customer does not cancel at that point, they will cancel after the order gets installed or delivered. Let the customer have what they want in the first place.

Customers who know what they want almost never call and say they dislike the item, because they generally love it! It is their house, and you can only gently make more appropriate suggestions. If the customer wants to stick to their original plan, then let them. You are there to make a sale, and to acquire satisfied customers for later additional sales. Yes, you have been trained to decorate properly and that is also one of your goals. Save these goals for the homes where they have no idea what they want.

If you live in a large metropolitan area, many of your customers will be from a variety of ethnic groups. As a sales professional, there is no room for discrimination and prejudice in this line of work.

You are there to help the customer to buy, to help fill the customer's wants and needs. You are there to make appropriate product suggestions, and give decorating ideas.

After determining your customer's buying motives, means to pay, and maturity level, make your selections to be shown to that customer reflect that customer's personality, financial level, and status.

Use Positive Comments When Selling Custom Decorating Products

Romance the customer with the words and descriptions you use to describe their selections. Tailor your explanation and vocabulary to fit the products you have estimated and planned for him or her. When reviewing the job with the customer, **focus in on the specific wants, needs, and buying motives that this individual has** for making the purchase. Choose your words to describe the job carefully. Be very thorough on your description, so the customer will feel and know that they are getting quality and a lot of features for their money.

When presenting and reviewing custom products with your customer, use positive comments similar to the ones shown below, to get the message across to the customer. Even if the customer does not go through with the order that day, upon leaving review the job in a descriptive manner.

- This window treatment will be **professionally installed and remeasured.**

- The window treatment you have selected will include 118" seamless, imported sheers under a moire satin, lined drapery.

- The valance is a balloon, tailored style; mounted on a covered board, fully lined, with pleated tiebacks to match.

- Included in your order is **all the hardware necessary** to do the job properly.

Review pricing and all elements that were planned to make up the job. On sales slips, estimates sheets, bids, or business cards, write out a description of what your bid includes, in addition to the fabric or sample name, lot number, color name, and number. Figure out how much of a down payment is needed, what the payments will be, and also record this information on the bid.

Any competitor is going to simply jot down the price, the name of the fabric, and the treatment style — such as, *"balloon shades."* Your competitors will not romance the customer with a complete description and a review of all the components that will make up the total job.

Below is the **type of conversations** to have with your customer **when verbally summarizing the job, before attempting to close the sale.** Again, you are **expounding on the merits of the job** *you* will provide for the customer.

"In addition to this treatment looking superb on the window, the treatment is also going to be very functional. You will easily be able to pull it up and down to get the treatment off the window."

"This particular treatment will protect your interior furnishings, while allowing light to filter through and still allow you privacy during the day. At night when you have your interior lights turned on, simply close the overdrapery for privacy."

"The design and colors of the treatment you have selected are going to work well in making the colors flow throughout the home."

"Using an elegant treatment as the focal point of the room is very stylish and sophisticated. The colors and fabrics you have selected will really make a beautiful backdrop for the room."

"You have chosen one of the nicest quality and most beautiful fabrics that we have."

"I agree, lining a fine treatment like this is the only way to go. You will double, if not triple, the life of the treatment. The treatment will hang nicer, look better, be more private, and add insulation to the room. It will now feel warmer in here in winter, and cooler in the summer."

"These draperies will hang and look exceptional for their life, with regular vacuuming and dry cleaning as needed."

"Since custom drapery are made up with proper fullness, they take on a quality, rich look — a luxury look."

"I am so glad you have decided to go with a beautiful top treatment. That particular style is going to be luxurious and elegant in the fabric you have selected, on that window!"

"The addition of the tiebacks will finish off this treatment. In future years, if you want a different look, leave the tiebacks off after you have the drapery cleaned. The drapery will also look handsome, free hanging."

"You will be happy to know that we only use top-quality, heavy-duty hardware. This hardware is made to take heavy use and will stand up to the wear-and-tear of long-term use. Wall-to-wall, wide treatments and also floor-to-ceiling drapery with heavy lining will not cause these rods to fail."

"Everything we have discussed today is guaranteed to preform and fit properly. We are making up the treatments in the fabric, style, and measurements to fit your windows. To be perfectly sure of the measurements and of the installation, we like to do a remeasure. This way we have two expert opinions about the planning of the job and the paperwork. This ensures that the job will go in problem free."

Study and use the enclosed list of *"right words"* to use versus *"wrong words"* to use when selling. Use the right words as much as you can to form a mental picture of what you are describing to your potential customer. Tailor the words to the individual customer you are dealing with at the time. *Some customers want to be conservative, while others want to be the other extreme,* so choose your words accordingly.

List of right words to use:

- use the customer's name
- investment
- elegant
- understand
- graceful
- proven
- enhancing
- health
- conservative (depends on the customer)
- easy
- strong
- guarantee
- powerful
- money
- bold
- safety
- flamboyant (depends on the customer)
- save
- dramatic
- value
- style
- nice
- home
- authorize
- color
- vital
- deluxe
- simple
- you
- airy
- light
- advantage
- dignified
- playful
- new
- amusing
- love
- plain
- right
- magnificent
- results
- youthful
- truth
- current trend
- current style
- comfort
- luxurious
- proud
- elaborate
- enjoy
- leisure
- transformation
- lavish

Below is a listing of words *that are the wrong words to use*. If used, these words are a *"turnoff"* to your customers. Try to limit the use of these words while trying to make the sale. Substitute appropriate *"good words"* from the list above, in their place.

List of wrong words to use:

- offbeat
- ordinary
- deal
- pay
- sign
- worry
- hurt
- death
- sell
- price
- hard
- obligation
- fail
- ugly
- house
- cheap

- common
- dull
- cost
- contract
- try
- loss
- buy
- failure
- sold
- decision
- difficult
- liable
- liability
- angry
- bad

Handling Objections

Your customer will come up with objections to going ahead and making the purchase for three reasons: They have received *misinformation* about the product or item; they have *incomplete information* about the product or item; or *they are covering up their real reason for their buying resistance.*

As a customer looks around at various sources before buying an item, they gather inaccurate or incomplete information. This misinformation may show up in objections to the item you are presenting to the customer. *Prove your points about the misinformation.* Back up your answers by showing the customer printed proof in your sales materials or brochures.

As a sales professional, you should welcome objections. This is your chance to reassure the customer about the selections he is making. You have to convince the customer that the selections he or she have made are going to be beautiful and enhance their home. If it is what the customer wants, and you do not necessarily agree with the selection, sell it to them anyway. If you do not, some other company will. If the customer really wants the item, they will turn out to be a happy customer.

When the customer gives you objections, you know that the customer is seriously considering purchasing the item. Even if you did a fabulous job of making the presentation to the customer, the customer is going to raise some objections. Answer any and all objections completely. Do not skim over, skip, or leave any objections unanswered or incompletely answered. If you do not have the information, call the manufacturer and find out.

Listen to what the customer has to say. Do not interrupt prematurely. Do not presume you know what the customer is going to say, therefore cutting the customer short. Do not argue with the customer. Always be agreeable and friendly when disagreeing with the customer and answering their objections.

One of the best techniques for handling objections is to start your answers with, *"Yes, but,"* give them *a choice next, or ask a question, or start over, re-presenting your presentation.*

Some of the typical objections you will encounter, and some better ways for you to answer, are listed below:

Objection: *"I have to think about it."*

Answers: *"Is there something I have not been clear on?"*

"Why think about it?"

"If you go ahead today, you get the additional coupon savings."

"Remember, everyone has three days to cancel their order, provided to you by our truth in lending laws. You will lose nothing if you exercise your right to cancel within the three-day period."

"When will it be convenient for me to stop back?"

"When will it be convenient for me to call you?" Make sure to always call back customers who put you on hold. They *really are* obligated to you. They have used your time, experience, ideas, gasoline, and car, to get you over to their home for a large portion of the day. Some will act indignant when you call, too bad!

"If you are happy with what you have picked out, as I think you are, let's just go for it!" Why put it off?

"If you get this ordered, this gives you one less detail to worry about. Let's get this off your mind."

Create urgency, but be sure to be truthful. *"If you wait you lose the sale price." "This is the lowest I've seen this price this past year." "We are having a price increase on this fabric the 1st of the month." "This fabric is going to be discontinued, that is why the price is fabulously low. If you wait at all, I cannot guarantee delivery." "We have been given a special promotion on this particular product. This is a brand new product, and the manufacturer wants to launch it with a great promotional sale price." "This is a great one-time price, so don't pass it up."*

Objection: *"I have to discuss this with my spouse."*

Answers: *"What do you need to discuss with your husband/wife?"*

"What do you anticipate that your husband/wife will have questions about?" "Will the main concerns be the styling, fabric selections, the down payment, the price?" Review thoroughly with the customer any proposed questions that the spouse may have. **Help the customer sell it to their spouse** by making an itemized list of what your package consists of. You want that spouse to have a clear picture of what they are getting for the money. Additionally, list the monthly payment and the minimum down payment required. If your delivery is fast, state that fact. If you have similar window treatments displayed somewhere, let the customer know where, so they may come to see the quality you will be giving them. Make sure your customer understands what amount of insulation will be provided from the selected products.

   Go ahead and try to write up the sale, pending the spouse's confirmation. You can go out to the home and pick up the sales slip, or have the customer bring it to the studio. This will make the customer **feel more obligated and confident** when discussing it with their spouse. Go ahead and set another appointment for you to meet with the spouses together, in the studio. This will also give you the chance to show off the quality of the job they will be getting, by showing them your studio displays.

"Will your husband/wife like the selections you have chosen?" Give that customer as much **confidence and knowledge to defend their selections** if the husband/wife seems unreceptive to them when the customer discusses the selections with the spouse. Again, thoroughly review the benefits and features until the customer fully understands what they are getting. Now write out a complete description of all the items.

"Would you like me to wait, while you call him/her?"

This will work in your favor most of the time. The husband/wife called is usually busy at work and usually seems to make a **favorable decision if the wife/husband really wants the items.**

If the husband/wife at work is too busy even to talk a minute about the decision, they will tell your customer to tell you they have to think about it. They may be surprised at the price. **The answer in the end is usually unfavorable.**

If the spouse is present, suggest that they take a few minutes to talk privately. Let them go into the other room and discuss the purchase. They can ask you more questions, and you may immediately clarify any questions that come up.

Objection: *"This is more than I want to spend for this item."*

Answers: *"The particular _____ that you have selected will last a long time due to the high quality construction and materials used. For the quality you have selected, this is a great price."* If the item is an insulative window treatment, *"The insulation values of this window treatment will cut your utility bills way down, and actually end up saving you money. The treatment will literally pay for itself over a period of time. The lining/protective backing will protect the drapery/carpet/furniture exposed to the strong sunlight."* Mention the benefits of custom-made products over readymade products. Review the section on **Customers Considering Readymades.**

Objection: *"I can't afford it right now."*

Answers: *"The price is going up April 1st due to a price increase (say this only if it is true)."*

"If you pay for the items on a monthly basis you will be able to have the window coverings now, and be able to protect your furnishings and carpeting."

"Would you prefer to start with one layer of the treatment at a time? Or would you prefer to do a few windows at a time, as you are able to pay for them? Let's do these windows in this room first and then you can see how nice they come out. As you are able to do the rest, we'll do the rest."

Objection: *"The price seems too high for that."*

Answers: *"How much did you plan to spend."*

"You realize this is custom made in the style and fabric of your personal selection?"

Determine if the price, seeming too high, is really the **motive** for the objection. When a customer complains that the price seems too high, they actually are asking you to *justify* the **price to them.** You need to clarify that the price is, indeed, a fair price for the product. Review the points below again to the customer:

Review the product's value points. Discuss with the customer how many widths you are using, what quality and features those particular fabrics or products have, your guarantee, your service, information about the installers you use, etc. **Anything positive you can say, say!** If you still don't have the sale, upon leaving list those items out for the customer.

Justify the price by reviewing the features and benefits of the products. You need to be familiar with the lines your competitors carry, their sales, and promotions. Know what better features your product offers at a similar price range. Remind the customer of your company's fine reputation and superior service.

"You deserve it! This will become the focal point of the room! These treatments will make the house look beautiful! Let's start on this room, at least, and see!"

"You only need a down payment of $___. If you need a little more time to come up with the balance, when the treatments are ready, don't take immediate delivery for a couple more weeks." If the customer agrees to this, write on the workorder for the workroom, to hold off fabricating the order so it will not get wrinkled. Sheers need to be hung over a hanger for several weeks to achieve a proper hang. See the section on *Sheers*.

Get your customer to realize that the *"cost"* of the treatments is more important than the *"price"* of the treatments. The cost is low when you get your customer to stop and realize that they last many years and give much value for the price. Higher-priced items cost less because they last longer. Price is the only way lower-quality companies can attract the customer. They give high cost and low value for the money spent.

Estimate how many years the item will probably last. Divide the estimated years into the price of the item. Now, divide the months into the subtotal to arrive at a price or cost per month. This is an effective tool to use when comparing a competitor's inferior, short-life product against your higher-quality, longer-life product. The more expensive product will be a less-expensive cost, with a longer life. Your customer will be getting more value for their dollars by buying your higher-quality product.

The finest quality a customer can afford will be their best value. It will be uneconomical years later to have settled for lesser quality. The exception here is when they are redecorating the house to put it on the market.

Objection: *"I can buy that readymade for much less money."*

Answers: *"You want the quality of custom made. You realize that readymades are much lower quality, skimpy, poor-functioning, and that standardized sizes will not work well in your situation."* Review the section on *Customers Considering Readymades*.

"It will run you only $___ per month!"

"You have picked a very high-quality fabric — should I show you a less-expensive fabric to help get the price down?" Determine if they can afford that particular fabric or any fabric. The price may be way beyond their means.

Objection: *"I like a fabric I saw at another studio better."*

Answers: *"Will they give you the great price and service that I guarantee? We take pride in doing a quality job, thus turning our sales today into future continuous sales."* If the customer really prefers the other fabric, then tell the customer that you can probably get it for him or her, if they can give you the vendor and the fabric information. Realize you are taking a chance letting the customer venture back into the other studio to get the information. The other firm may win the customer over.

Objection: *"I want to look around more before I buy."*

Answers: *"If you want to look around more, I have more in my car or studio to see." "Let's make another appointment to meet in the studio. Will you be free this afternoon?"* Do not make much of a time lapse between your visit and the next meeting. You want to wrap up the sale, not lose it to your hungry competition.

"You want to get this in for the holidays, don't you? If we wait, the workrooms and the installers are going to get very busy. We don't want either to be in a rush when they do your order."

Objection: *"$7,000 to do these windows!"*

Answers: *"You have 19 windows, many with multiple layers and top treatments. That is $368 per window."* Estimate out the whole package price, count the windows involved, and divide the windows into the package price. Give the customer the average price per window. They may not realize they have as many windows as they have.

Objection: *"I received a less expensive price from...... for the same thing."*

Answers: *"In the decorating field, you tend to get what you pay for in quality of products. What you have selected is a high-quality _____. Although the competitor's product may look similar, I am sure it is not the high-quality brand that this one is. In fact, I have given you a discount price of 40 percent off on this product. By doing this, I have cut our profit margin way down. If we go any lower than that, we lose money on the sale. If the competitor has given you a lower price than I am giving you, then they are showing you a lower-quality product. If you want the product to hold up and look outstanding for a period of time, you need to buy quality."*

"When I planned the job, I used ____ widths of fabric for the treatment. The treatment is lined, on heavy-duty, top-quality hardware, etc. The other company has cut corners, somewhere. They may have used less fabric, a lower-quality fabric, less-expensive hardware. Would you like me to show you similar fabrics that are less money? Would you like me to cut the fullness down? Would you like to forego the lining?" Review the section on *Cutting The Price Down* for more techniques.

"Although our price is slightly more expensive than _____, we provide excellent service and if anything should go wrong, you are going to be taken care of in the right way. We have an excellent reputation, and I can give you the names of customers to call, if you are in doubt. We have beautiful displays of our products' quality displayed in my studio. Please come in and look." Ask the customer to give calls to the lower-priced competitor's customers. *"Compare who is really going to give you the higher-quality product and service. Then make a decision. If you are still in doubt, please try us out on several windows and see if I know what I am promising you here."* Bend over backwards to provide the finest-possible service for this customer. Prove to them you are really what you say you are.

Try making a list of all the positive aspects of making the purchase from you, versus the customer making the purchase from your competitor. List everything positive you can think of, especially the points that would be important to the customer.

Now list the negative things about buying the item from your competitor. *Do not say or write negative things about your competition.* Simply say your company has higher-quality, better service, and will follow through on any problems that arise. Your company takes care of its customers.

Objection: *"I'm getting three bids."*

Answers: *"Shall I give you a bid on something else? I have other less-expensive treatments and fabrics."*

Review again exactly what you are providing. If you still do not have the customer's order when you leave, write everything out in romancing language.

"Make sure when you get the other bids that they compare exactly with what I am providing you. There are so many variables that it is extremely hard to compare window treatment bids against each other. The planned size may differ, they may price you out in unlined, instead of lined treatments, the quality of the fabrics vary, the fullness may be cut down, the quality of the construction may be inferior, the quality of the hardware may not be what our standard is, the delivery may be slow, the service may be poor, and there may be no real guarantees."

"How can you be sure they are going to give you everything I'm going to give you?"

"Why would you want to go to all that work? This is work for me, this must be work for you, having other decorators over. Do you want to keep going through this?" Explain that you are competitive in your pricing and promise to do a high-quality job. Their satisfaction is

guaranteed. Try to find out who is coming over and why they are coming over (is the customer trying to get a less-expensive price, see more selection, etc.).

"Do you need more questions answered? Are the selections you have made not what you want?"

"Is the price going to be the deciding factor? Doesn't quality, service, and a promise of great service matter?"

"Who are the other bidders?" Many customers will not tell you. Expect resistance on this question. If the customer will tell you, you have that much more ammunition.

It is never good salesmanship to say anything directly bad about another company. You may also be sued. Just indirectly say, *"Mrs. Jones, be careful. You get what you pay for in quality and service. We have a good reputation. Some of the companies do not. That is all I am going to say, without naming any names. I promise you if you let me do this job, I will do my very best to make sure that everything is done to your specifications. I will see to it that you are, in the end, a happy customer that will want to continue working with me and my company."* Who is going to turn you down!

The customer may still get the other bids, but will see you later for the sale. They will be so wary of anyone else, and will want the safety and personal guarantee that you have given them.

You may also try relaying true stories that you know about, of some of the bad things that have happened to some customers whom you have ended up with on the rebound. These things do happen, and after awhile you will have heard some horror stories. *Again, do not name names under any circumstances.* Your potential customer will become very apprehensive about working with another company.

If it appears that the customer has been shopping around, inquire, *"Have you already gotten other bids?"* Ask the customer how you compare. Some of the customers will not tell you. Do not press the customer if this appears to be the case. Again, **review specifically what you will give the customer for their money if you are given the job.** List a lot of value for the money. Chances are, the other bidder hurriedly jotted down a price for the customer when they found out the customer was going to seek other bids. Now the customer does not even know if the price includes tax, let alone what else it includes. Do the most professional presentation. Pack your bid full of value, and get the sale.

Objections are an opportunity for the professional decorator/designer to tell the customer more about the selected items and your quality service. **A customer must be comfortable with the decision to buy before that sale may be closed and kept closed.**

Sometimes the customer may need more explanation. You may not have convinced him or her due to your having inadequate product knowledge. Bring up any points you may have skipped or skimmed over. Go back and review these areas with the customer.

Do not skim over or brush off any objection that the customer brings up. Though you may not feel that is an important consideration, your customer may find the objection that they raised a real concern. The customer feels that it is important and would not have brought it up if he or she did not. Treat all objections as if they are valid objections.

Customers want to be assured that they are getting their money's worth. **Try to give a package price, rather than breaking down the price to price per yard of fabric or carpet.** If you do break it down, the next question the customer asks is, *"How many yards do I need."* They then multiply the price out and come up with a figure that falls far short of your package price you are quoting them. They of course have not added in fabrication, installation, lining, hardware, etc. This will turn the customer right off. Customers do not like to see visible profits.

If the customer insists on knowing the price per yard, tell them that the fabric is $29 per yard and you would like to figure up the whole package price for them.

If they persist in wanting to know how many yards, *they may be pumping you for the amount of yardage to buy, because they want to make the treatments themselves. Tell them you haven't a clue as to the amount of yardage needed.* You figure the widths and the lengths and work off a chart that is based on the fabric's base price, with all costs built in. You then take the sale discount off the whole package price — less the hardware. You will not have the yardage figured out until you do the workorder and place the fabric order. This explanation usually suppresses the question of yardage, unless they have something up their sleeve.

Next try telling the customer, *"When you buy a new dress or suit, do you ask how many yards are in it? You also have to pay the designer, the person who sewed it up, you have to pay for the thread and notions, the cutter, the presser, the store, the sales clerk, etc. It is not a package that just consists of the fabric."*

Determine between false excuses and real objections. Sometimes people will say they do not like the texture of the item rather than admit that they think the price is out of line. Carefully inquire through questions, determining what the customer really means. If the real reason seems to be that the price is too high, suggest paying for the items by the month.

Leave any literature on the desired items with the customer if they insist on getting back to you about making the purchase. Customers and their spouses tend to have a hard time visualizing anything decorative.

Keep informed of advertising and specials your competitors are running, in addition to the lines of products and guarantees that your competitors offer. If you are well informed when told by your customer, *"I am having _____ come over tomorrow to also give me a price,"* you can say to the customer, *"I also saw their ad. That carpet they are going to show you, I am familiar with. That carpet does not have the finishes that the one I have showed you has."* If you are working with window coverings, say, *"The blinds they have on sale are not the quality of the ones I have shown you today. Make sure you see a sample of them hung up; test them like you have tested mine. You will see the difference immediately when you pull them up and down. The brand I carry is much longer lasting. Be sure to compare like products to like products, if you must compare prices. That is the only way to assure which is the better value."*

If the customer opts to do only a partial job now, try to get them to select something very decorative *to do first.* This may be hard, as the customer may want to do the undertreatments first. If the customer chooses something highly decorative first, they will be inspired to find the money to continue the project. If they start on the undertreatment first, they are not going to get as excited about the overall decorating project.

Make sure that the customer is aware that quality varies. Products must *very carefully* be compared to each other. Explain to the customer that the quality is not always readily apparent by looking, for a non-expert. In this field, *you tend to get what you pay for.*

After answering the objections, remind the customer how much per month the item will run, if the payments are spread out over a period of time.

Review the section on *Cutting Down the Price,* if the customer insists that they must have a lower price. Price may be more important to the customer than the finished looks of the treatments/furnishings.

If the customer is obviously discriminating, then be careful which techniques you use to cut the price down.

Customer Considering Readymades?

If faced with the situation where the customer feels that custom window products are out of their budget, and are considering going the readymade drapery, route, **use the comments below to sway the customer back to your custom products**. Nicely, make these comments and suggestions to your customer. Do not come on too strong and alienate him or her. Do not hard sell these following points. Simply point out the pitfalls of readymade products. They may still purchase them, but after examining them, they are sure to return them and come back to you.

"Custom-made window coverings are made to fit your exact window measurements, in the fabric of your selection, and in the style you would prefer to have."
"You realize that readymade products are generally very skimpy — using much less fabric, slats, materials than custom products do, don't you?"

"Readymade products are generally of very poor construction and quality. I would not buy readymades for windows where I expected the treatment to be functional. After pulling the treatment open or up and down a few times, they tend to fall apart and cease functioning."

"Readymades come only in standardized sizes — I do not think you can get them to work on your windows."

"Readymades are generally unlined, not lined. Therefore, they are not going to provide you with a very long life, nice hanging ability, insulation, or the privacy you need to have."

"You realize that you will have to put the rods and the drapery up yourself, don't you? This is not an easy job, even for someone who is very handy. You have to use the right hardware so the rod will not pull out of the walls."

"Since some of the panels and valances only come in small widths, you will have to take them apart and seam them together, to get anywhere near enough fullness."

"If you use readymades on these windows, you are going to have to cut them off and hem them; otherwise they will be too long."

"If you have ever had custom window treatments before, you will not be happy with readymade quality."

"The pleats on the drapery are about 5" apart and not very deep on readymades — consequently, you end up with a very cheap look."

"Half the beauty of a custom drapery is in the proper hanging and installation of the treatment. Do you know how to properly install window treatments and break the crinoline?"

"Installation is an art, and well worth the extra money spent to have it done right — with the quality, hardware products available through custom. You end up spending the same amount of money for inferior, readymade hardware as you do for the heavy-duty, custom hardware."

If the customer *is still not convinced* with the above comments, then ask them to go ahead, order the readymade products, and install them. If the customer does not like the readymade drapery's shoddy quality and poor hanging ability, tell the customer to save all the wrappers, boxes for the hardware, receipts, and *return them. Invite* them to call you back so you can get their order under way, if they should change their mind. *It is almost a guarantee that after you have pointed out all the above faults, the customer will not keep the product, even after they go to the time, expense, and frustration of installing them.*

Be sure to show the customer pictures of the quality, fullness, fit, and hanging ability that **you will supply** with custom products if they should change their mind.

You, as a professional, know that if the customer spends the small amount of money that cheap readymades cost, they are going to come flat folded, horribly wrinkled, and hang very poorly. The only way to get some of the wrinkles out is to take them to a dry cleaners and have them professionally pressed. A customer trying to spend the minimum will never spend the money to take them to the cleaners for pressing.

The customer is going to take one look and agree with you. You warned him or her ahead of time; since they listened to you, they saved the receipts and can return them. **Make sure this customer gets a follow-up call several weeks later, inviting them back to place their order.**

There are made-to-measure lines available, also. These lines of drapery are generally 200 percent fullness for the overdrapery, and 250 percent fullness for the underdrapery. Generally available for an optional cost is 250 percent fullness for the overdrapery, and the underdrapery to have 300 percent fullness. These are made to the customer's specifications and are comparable in price, or may be more expensive, than having a custom drapery made. This hold true, unless the made-to-measure drapery are offered at an exceptionally reduced sale price.

Draperies are shipped uniformly, pleated up, hung over hangers and covered in plastic. They are ready to be installed by the customer. The customer may hire an installer to professionally measure them and hang them.

If the installer does not measure them, the customer does. How many customers know how to measure? If the customer orders them wrong, they are stuck with them, without recourse. An installer making two trips out to the home will cost the customer some money.

If that same customer would have the drapery custom made, they would get a much fuller drapery, have them professionally measured, receive help on the proper selection, obtain a professional installation and quality hardware, complete with a guarantee that the draperies will properly fit and are properly installed.

Made-to-measure lines are not serious competition for you. They are expensive, inconvenient, and come with no insurance, as custom window coverings usually do. Unless the customer knows how to measure, knows exactly what they need, and knows how to install them, they are not going to come out ahead going the made-to-measure route.

Using Existing Hardware

One of the most common mistakes in planning the job is the reuse of the customer's existing hardware. If the hardware has already lived through one drapery life, will it actually live through another? Probably not, if the existing hardware was not top-quality, heavy-duty hardware to begin with. Definitely not, if the existing hardware is decorator rods.

- Old, existing regular traverse rods have usually been painted, and the existing glides will not function properly.

- The new drapery will hang differently, heavier or lighter, and the old rod is going to pull differently.

- The new drapery may have more pleats, so more glides will have to be added to the old rod.

- The cords may be old, stretched, dirty, and possibly frayed. The weight of the new drapery may cause the cords to break shortly after installation. If you have the cord restrung because it is frayed, the new cord will also fray. This happens due to sharp interior parts in the headrail of the rod.

- The new drapery may be heavier and additional supports may be necessary, but unobtainable, due to age of the rod, or the rod may be an unfamiliar brand.

- On decorator rods, there may not be enough rings. You may not recognize the brand, and do not know where they may obtain more rings.

- Your installer is going to be a much happier installer if he can go in, take down the old hardware and put up new hardware, if the existing hardware is in any way questionable.

If the old rods and hardware are in great shape, appear to be high quality, are going to hold a similar-weight drapery, and the customer is resistent to changing them, then go ahead and use the existing rods. **Always write on the sales slip,** *"customer is responsible for use of existing hardware."*
Some customers want you to move existing hardware to the new planned position of the new treatment. This will incur extra charges for remounting of the hardware. Be sure to tell the customer that for a few more dollars they can have a new rod. Your installer will not be happy about remounting the existing hardware, and they may not be able to remount the existing hardware in the new position. The installer will have to come back with the appropriate hardware, delaying the installation. This creates the necessity for you to get back together with that customer to collect the additional money needed for the additional cost of new rods.

Underselling the Job

Always show a range of fabrics and samples from inexpensive to moderately more expensive, if the fabrics and samples are correct selections for the planned situation. Let the customer decide to spend *more or less* money on the fabric or sample selection. Do not put yourself in a position to be faulted later because you did not show or tell the customer that also available were nicer or less-expensive fabrics that would have achieved the same type of a look for the situation.
If the customer can and will pay for extra fullness in the drapery, give them the option. You do not want the customer to come back and say the treatments or drapery are not full enough or that they look inadequate. Do not cut the fullness of the drapery or other treatment down, unless the customer knows you are.
Always suggest lining. Let the customer have the option. Five years from now when the unlined draperies you sold that customer fall apart, and that customer comes in angry, be able to pull out the old job

jacket and look on the sales slip and old workorder and say, *"I suggested lining the drapery. You said no, you did not want to pay the extra money."*

Most customers have the money, but need you to convince them with reasons to part with it. They will purchase the minimum, unless you point out to them they are doing a disservice to themselves by not opting to go with the added optional features that are available to them. Be very clear what the added features and options do for the product in longer life, styling, performance, and looks. Most customers want to spend the least amount of money as possible. Your job is to guide them into the right products for the particular situation, not underestimating their needs and ability to pay. Always try to sell complete window dressing, complete with a top treatment or decorative rod to finish the treatment off.

You will earn more commissions from a job with add ons and receive many more customer referrals when friends, relatives, and neighbors see a more complete job. The same customer will probably want to add on more rooms, later. The customer will feel they cannot do it without your input and give you the future jobs.

Selling Up

When you are working with a customer, try to show your better quality items within the group from which you are working. Show and offer the better blinds, better shades, or better fabrics.

Your customer may not want to spend the extra money for the better items and may have to go with the minimum quality. Make sure you sell the benefits of the better quality product, and make sure the customer knows the better product is longer lasting, more durable, and probably better looking with fewer problems likely to arise in the future. The better product will give you fewer headaches because it will hold up much better. There will be far fewer complaints from your customers. If the customer will not sell up or cannot spend the extra money, just make them aware of what quality and the limitations of the quality they are receiving.

Overselling the Job

There is a danger in overselling a customer too many products for a window. The window may appear too heavy. Too many layers may obstruct the woodwork, the look may be too heavy, the window may not easily be opened, light may not be able to filter through the window, and the view is obstructed. If this happens, the customer will probably cancel the job after the treatments are installed.

If a simple top treatment is wanted with an under shade or blind, do not sell opaque sheers with overdrapery and a heavy top treatment to finish it off. Give the customer what they want. They will go on their merry way, happy and non-complaining. Your customer will show off the treatments whenever anyone comments on them, mentioning where they made their purchase, and from whom — probably giving out your card. If the treatments are not what they wanted, and you refuse to change them, they will also go out of their way to tell everyone they get the opportunity to tell.

Service

Sell the quality of service you will be providing. And be sure to follow through with great service. Get right back to the customer when he or she calls you. Stay on top of the order and keep the customer *honestly* informed about any new developments, delays, and changes in the order.

By staying on top of the situation with your customers, any problem or delay that does arise will be more readily accepted by the customer with whom you have stayed in close contact. The customer you have not spoken with since you took the order and whom you are now calling to report a delay, when the order is already two weeks late, is not going to be a very accepting customer. The customer whom you have ignored is probably going to lose their patience, cancel, or demand an adjustment and threaten to cancel.

If you know any news or information about the order, keep the customer informed. Touch bases with the customer, just to tell them that the order is progressing as it should be.

Progress calls show your customer that you are interested in working with them. **If something goes wrong, explain that *this* is that type of business. Interior decorating jobs hardly ever go in completely smooth.**

There are too many variables that can come up along the way. The customer, who you have kept informed, will want to continue working with you in the future, even if the job was not problem free.

Always call the customer after installation to make sure the customer was treated with great service by everyone. Then make an appointment to go out and see any problems that came up with the finished job.

Closing the Sale

Keep your confidence throughout the presentation and the close, that this customer is going to buy. Closing is narrowing your selection down, justifying the price to your customer, writing up the sale, obtaining a deposit and an approval to go ahead (signature) from the customer.

Always assume the sale when working with a customer. How can they pass this deal up? Ask the customer leading questions such as; *"Which one would you like — this fabric, or this other fabric?" "Are these treatments to be lined?"* This type of questioning will cause the customer to make decisions whether or not to buy in his or her mind, and bring out any further objections they may have.

Work on closing the sale at every opportunity. You will see the customer make mental decisions after you have satisfied all objections and questions. If you see the customer making a mental decision to buy, close the sale right then and there.

Buying signals vary with each customer from strong to weak. You will need to adapt your closing style with each customer according to their buying signal strength. By choosing the proper maneuver to close the sale you will increase your closing rate.

Be aware of the positive buying signals that the customer gives, when the customer acts positive toward the merchandise. As soon as you observe these buying signals, try to close the sale. Some of the possible ways to close are:

Buying Signals:

Extremely strong signals

Assume the sale. Act like they are buying the item. Start writing up the order. If the customer does not stop you, they are ready to buy. If they do stop you, answer the objection and again proceed to write up the sale.

Strong signals

Use a direct question close. Come right out and ask for the sale. Ask questions that must be answered with a positive answer. *"Can we go ahead today and place the order, so you can take advantage of the extra $50 savings?" "If we place this order today, we can probably get this installed for you by the holidays. Shall we go ahead?"* This type of closing technique gives the customer the opportunity to say *"Yes, lets go ahead,"* or *"No ,not yet, tell me again about the _____."* After satisfying the new objections, attempt to close again. *"May I write the order up now, or did you want to add another room?"*

Medium signals

Use the choice close. *"Which color, package, or_____ would you like?"* Offer a choice of color, fabric, style, or amount paid by the month, if financed.

Weak signals

Use the suggestion close. Give that customer a specific reason. Suggest that the customer buy the item today for the sale price, or additional discount to receive the item as soon as possible, to avoid any further delay, etc. *"Let's get this order in now so we can get these windows insulated before the hot weather hits." "Let's get this order in now so we can have these treatments installed before you move in, so you avoid having to put sheets on the windows." "If you match everything up now, all the colors are coordinated; you will not have a problem in the future if this color becomes hard to find."*

Weaker signals

Review the presentation. Go back over everything that the customer decided. Remind the customer of the benefits and features. Review what is included in the full price and package. Next, try the choice close, above. *"Which one would you like?"* If that does not close the sale, use the suggestion close, above.

Review with the customer the **needs and wants they expressed to you** at the beginning of the presentation, and **reaffirm** how this particular selection **satisfies these needs and wants.**

If the company you work for has financing available, be able to quote what the job will run them monthly. If you do not have financing available, but do carry Visa and Mastercard, obtain a finance table and ask them what their credit card interest rates are for their Mastercard or Visa. Quote a monthly price. Remind the customer that the deposit goes on the card immediately; the balance goes on after the job is complete, when the customer is satisfied.

Give a **full package price without the sales tax included.** Add the installation and the labor to the base price and **quote the price plus the tax.** Example: $2,567.34 plus tax, $134.78 = $2,702.12, total price. The reason you break up the tax and show the tax separately from the base price, is that your competition has surely done this when they bid on the job. The competition never seems to get around to figuring the tax, and certainly will not want to include it in the price, making their price that much higher. *If you add the tax in, your price appears more than the competitor's price, without the sales tax!*

Always **review what is covered** in the package price. **Review the features, the benefits, the service** of your company, **the quality of the job** you promise to do, and your **guarantee of satisfaction.**

Always **reassure the customer of the wise, good value they are getting.** Emphasize that the customer is getting a lot for the money, while letting them know exactly *what* they are getting.

Reassure the customer **that they have made beautiful selections in style and color.** The customer likes what they have chosen, but need you to affirm that they are wise choices. The spouse or friends of the customer may throw some doubt into the selections later when it is discussed. If you have agreed with the customer that what they have selected is beautiful, they feel more confident and assured. It depends on how secure your customer is with their ability to make the right selections.

Another technique to improve your closing ratio is to **give out names and telephone numbers of other satisfied customers.** Potential customers may want to call and possibly go view the finished window coverings or other treatments. If you readily supply names and numbers for references, at least your potential customer feels more secure with you, whether they exercise the option to actually call the references or not.

Give the customers who help you out as references **special discounts** on their decorating needs. Or, you may want to do some work without making a profit, to keep the positive comments and visits from potential customers welcome.

Always **write up bids on sales slips** — they appear obligating to the customer, and will also save you time when the customer says to go ahead with the order.

Practice getting over the fear of coming right out and asking for the sale. The customer's rejection is not really going to hurt. As a sales professional, you need to let rejections roll right off of you. Do not let rejections get to you and bother you. You need to **ask many times for the customer to buy** during the presentation. **When you get those positive buying signals — whenever they happen — ask for the sale.**

Ask them to make a decision, now. Use this technique after you receive a positive buying signal.

A customer will generally not ask you to take their order. As a sales professional, you have to draw it out of them, unless the customer is particularly decisive. They need your help reaching and making this big decision. If the customer did not have an interest in what you are there to show him or her, they would not have come in to see you, or invited you to come to their home. Having you over is also work for them.

Asking for the order is not high-pressure salesmanship. **If you have gone through the steps to a sale, taken all the customer's wants and needs into consideration, and answered all objections raised, they should now be *ready* and *want* to buy.**

Write up the customer's order. Review thoroughly everything that the customer is going to get. Get the deposit, and signature from the customer, to go ahead with the order. Thank the customer for the order and reaffirm to them that what they have selected will give them much value and beauty for their money. Reassure the customer that they will love the results. After covering all of these areas, leave immediately.

If they do not buy, act very surprised. Reaffirm that this is an exceptional value, especially with the extra $50 savings available to you by buying today.

Window Treatment Points to Review Before Leaving the Home

After the customer has given you their approval to go ahead with the order, be sure to **review** the following window treatment points with the customer **before** leaving the home. Reviewing these points also clarifies in your mind exactly what the customer thinks they are getting. You are catching costly errors by thoroughly reviewing what you are planning for the job.

- The **window treatment placement in width and height.**

- **Placement of cords and wands.**

- **Placement of traverse rods.**

- Decide **whether or not the customer is doing their own removal of old hardware.** If removing their own hardware, the customer should always be reminded about the removal by the person setting up the installation, before the installer comes out.

    Always record this information on the workorder, so the installation set-up person can readily see it when they call to make the installation appointment.

    If you do not remind the customer, some customers who say they will do their own removal, do not do it. When the installer arrives, they end up spending extra time removing hardware free to get the new installation completed.

- **Review all fabric selections, color choices, and lining selections;** hold fabrics up to the windows, with lining behind the fabric if the fabric is to be lined.

- **Bunch up any sheer fabric** to note true color.

- **Again, show styles to be fabricated.** Customers do get confused. You may think that the customer has selected a different style than the customer is thinking that they have selected. **Many mistakes are caught here, if you take the time to review.**

- Note **how the item/items are to be fabricated;** such as center-open, one-way pull, no returns, etc.

- **Review the fullness decided** for the drapery or treatment.

- Discuss the **type and style of the hardware and rods** that will be used. Sometimes the customers think they will be decorative, even under a top treatment, if you do not remind them that they are going to be plain traverse rods.

- Discuss with the customer and note on sales slip **any variance in the measurements from floor to ceiling.** Discuss and note any other variance you come across, such as a fireplace placed into or right against the window you are covering.

- **Remeasure all measurements** before you leave the home. Remeasuring again helps you to double check all measurements and catch errors. Remeasuring also allows you to make better decisions on which course of action to take with the planning when you review the situation again.

- **Review pricing of yardage, lining, labor, fabrication, and extra fabrication charges.**

- Reassess again **how the customer is going to pay for the items.**

- **Reread sales slip to the customer, completely.** Note any discrepancies in phone number, address, etc. Be very thorough.

The above list is especially important when planning and dealing with window treatments. Anything ordered custom made needs to be thoroughly reviewed with the customer. Adapt the above points to whatever item you are selling the customer. **Always thoroughly review the sales slip and catch any errors or points you overlooked then and there, not after the fabrication of the item.**

Accurate Planning and Measuring for Window Treatments

All measurements taken for window treatments *must* be accurate. *If the measurements are not accurate, the installation of the window treatments will not occur on the first trip.* Additionally, sufficient fabric must be ordered to complete the fabrication of the treatment. The only way the treatment you have planned and sold to your customer will fit correctly is from accurate planning and precise measurements.

Always try to have a remeasure done by the *same* installer who will be installing the treatment. While remeasuring, the installer may review any unusual conditions about the installation, the precise measurements to use, and information for the fabrication and installation. Doing a remeasure for each job is the same as buying insurance for each job. For a price of $30 to $40, the installer goes to the installation site, reviews the job and paperwork, and catches errors before they happen. Remeasures save time and money in reworks and remakes.

If you are unsure about the way an item *should* be fabricated, the way an item should be ordered on the workorder, or what measurements to ask for, always call your workroom to discuss the situation. They dislike reworks as much as you do.

Your customer expects the new window coverings to fit well and have the appearance of what they imagined; what custom window products are and should look like.

Always try to be right on the money with the price. *Never be short on the money charged to the customer.* Review the *Accuracy in Pricing* section.

If you should overcharge the customer, be sure to send the excess money back to them. This practice makes you appear to be very honest. You appear to be a person with whom the customer will want to continue doing business.

Thank-You Notes

Send all customers a thank-you note the day you go on the call to their home. Send a thank-you note for finalized sales and for all estimates and bids you have not yet closed the sale on. Personalize each thank-you note with a personal, individual note. You are really inviting them to reconsider giving you the job, if they have not already done so. Hardly any designers or decorators will do this, so you will probably be the only one with enough courtesy to send a thank-you note.

The thank-you notes should arrive just before you follow up with a telephone call. Think about it; the customer just received a thank-you note from you and now you are following up with a telephone call. Appears as if you really want their business and would really deliver great service as promised, doesn't it?

Why Did You Lose the Sale?

After an appointment that you were unable to close and finalize the sale with, always review in your mind and list on your copy of the referral slip the reason you *feel* you did not get the sale. Be honest and realistic when you list the reasons. You are the only one to see these notes. Analyze the reasons. If the reasons are in your control, try to learn from them and improve your sales ability. Attempt to overcome the situation if it should arise again. If a sale is lost, you do not get paid. You work to get paid. Strive to improve each month to achieve a higher closing rate.

You, of course, are in this business to make a profit, or as much commission as you can. Never lower your prices to the point that you will not make a profit. Let the other company down the street have the sale, and the potential problems after the sale, that will absorb the profit. Let them provide their probable, poor service that will be provided due to their lower profit margin. You may see that customer on their next purchase, due to the poor-quality job they received. This will happen if the customer makes the price their deciding factor in going with another company.

Place one copy of the referral slip of any customer whom you did not close the sale with, three days later in your appointment book. Do not wait any longer than three days, so you will still have a very clear picture of the in-home call in your mind. See the section on *Telephone Prospecting* to see the general tone and procedure to use when calling the customer back.

If you did not get the sale, ask yourself, why didn't you? *Didn't you ask for the order, again and again?* If you did not make every effort, you are the one to blame. Next time, do not repeat the same mistakes.

Portrait of an Unprofessional Sales Professional

A profile of an unprofessional sales professional would be a salesperson who is basically unwilling and uninterested in their customer. They will not take the time to listen, do not care what the customer is saying, will not make appointments to suit the customer's time frame, rather their own preferred time frame, and tends to have very low patience.

This type of salesperson is inclined to be pushy, talks excessively, and decides for the customer what they need, without considering the customer's wants and needs. He or she will shove the customer's objections aside, discounting and skimming over the objections, without answering them.

An unprofessional salesperson will talk very technically about a product, not bothering to speak in terms their customer can relate to. Benefits to fit their customer will not be pointed out or discussed.

Try to be Present for the Installation

All designers/decorators should **strive to be present for their major installations.** The person scheduling the installation should inform the designer or decorator when the installation is, and time to attend the installation should be blocked out on your calendar.

Customers will appreciate your presence, and will feel you really care what their final job's outcome will be. If present, **you will be able to help the installer on various decisions** that will come up at the installation. You are the designer. On the other hand, the installer usually has very little design education.

One argument for your presence during installation is if you have not been unusually clear about everything on the workorders, the installer may not know where everything goes, how it is supposed to look, and exactly what it is that you are trying to do.

The callback may be made at the time of the installation. Both the callbacks with the customer will be taken care of, and this practice will keep your installer happy, allowing a smoother job for everyone involved. If anything goes wrong, you will be there to discuss with the installer what he or she is going to do about it, concerning their portion of the paperwork, and what you are going to do about it, with your portion of the paperwork for reworks, remakes, and service requests.

If you are present for the installation, you are able to reassure the customer that everything will be taken care of. You may also apologize in person for any delays.

Being present for the installation saves you time in the end, if the job does not go in perfectly (they hardly *ever* do). Your presence goes a long way for smoothing the situation out with the customer, if the job does not go in perfectly. Otherwise, you still will have a telephone call to the customer, when all does not go well, to set up an appointment to go out to the home to see the problems. If everything went in well, you should still make a visit to the home to admire and take pictures of the job.

If you are present for the installation, the customer sees and hears from you the day the order goes in. Though the customer may have already paid your company and you have been paid, your presence assures the customer that you are still interested in the job coming out the way you promised that it would.

Being present for the installation puts you in the position to **suggest appropriate additions to finish off the job.** Additionally, you will also **gain future business from the customer and their relatives and friends by making them feel you followed through with fine service** to the completion of the job. This is the way to promote customer happiness and future business. You and the installer together can demonstrate correct operation of the new treatments, and give tips on how to clean and maintain the items.

The Callback

If you were not present for the installation, telephone customers when their installation is complete to see how the customer regards the new treatments. Follow up and make callbacks whenever possible. This is also your opportunity to thank the customer again. Follow up the telephone call with a visit out to the home to admire the new decorating items. You and the customer, after speaking and working with each other a few times, now know each other fairly well and it is hoped are on very friendly terms.

Callbacks by telephone (at least) and in another visit to the home show a customer how interested you are in following through and providing the service, that you promised them you would. It shows that you indeed care to find out if everything went in according to your specifications, in addition to the customer's perceived specifications.

Be sure to bring the job jacket, so you can see what is installed and what is possibly missing. You will be able to note any inconsistencies that the customer is bringing to your attention — that they thought the job was going to include or look like. Any inconsistencies or disputes that may arise will be very clear if you wrote all information down in your notes and on the sales slip, as you should have.

This is the opportunity to complete and finalize any extra touches needed to finish off the treatments or items with workorders.

While making callbacks, you are able to make add-on sales to finish off the room. Look around, make suggestions, mention items that the customer mentioned previously that they wanted to do in the future. All this information should have been noted on your worksheets.

Now is the time to also suggest taking measurements of any anticipated future purchases. Explain that you will keep these measurements on file for the customer. When you get the items needed on sale, or if appropriate new samples of items arrive, call the customer back and let them know. The measurements will be in the customer's file; if the customer comes in and likes what you show them, they may buy right on the spot. This has the potential to become a very easy sale for you. If you add an easy, extra sale every day because you took the time to measure while on a callback, you will indeed increase your income.

In six months or so, your customer may be able to add the wanted purchases onto their credit account, and not increase their monthly payment they are now used to making. They have paid down the account for six months, and instead of decreasing or shortening the payment period, would prefer to add other needed items on, maintaining the same type of payment amount. Do not underestimate this idea. People live on credit today.

While making a callback, you are in a great position to *remind* your satisfied customers to refer you to any friends, relatives, or other potential customers who compliment and admire the new treatments. Give them a supply of your cards to refer you with. Since you should have already asked them to do this before, you are reminding the customer to do this for you. Now they are sure to remember to do this for you, after being reminded again.

Ask them at this time if they have names, addresses, and telephone numbers of any prospects you may contact that might be in need *now* of decorating products.

While at the home for the callback, compliment the customer on their selection of style, fabric, and colors chosen for the decorating items. This practice will help enhance your customer's self-esteem, while reassuring them they made some very complimentary selections. They will not question their selections later if they receive a derogatory remark on the new treatments or items by a spouse, relative, or friend.

Callbacks are the time to snap pictures of your finished treatments to record and put in your picture book of finished jobs, to show to other potential customers. Even if the treatment is simple in your eyes, take a picture or two. Picture-taking confirms to the customer that their treatment is something special and worthy of showing to others. This picture-taking also confirms to the customer that the treatment is hanging correctly and looks finished off. You are the perceived expert in this field, not the customer.

While on the call back, again discuss the way to have items cleaned for best results. Do not assume your customer knows the proper techniques or where to have the cleaning done. Take the time to test each window treatment item for smooth operation. The installer **should** have done this, but may not have done so.

Callbacks provide higher customer satisfaction, repeat business, additional leads, will take care of potential complaints (which are best taken care of before escalating into a very angry complaint), and allow you to **teach the customer proper techniques for cleaning and maintaining the items for long-lasting, good looks.**

Follow up the callback visit to the home with *another* personalized thank-you note.

Customer Service

When a customer telephones or walks into your studio, remember that a decorator studio is an intimidating place to the majority of customers, who do not consider themselves to be decorating experts. Always try to immediately set the prospective customer at ease. They need some help in the decorating area or they would not have come in or telephoned. Drop what you are involved with and *greet that customer warmly. Offer to help the customer, be willing to discuss pricing, show products, and samples.* See the section on *Qualifying Customers* for more information on why to work with customers on their first visit into your studio.

Always answer the telephone in the name of your business, and then follow with the name of whomever is answering the telephone.

Be willing to give approximate prices to a customer's inquiry about pricing, over the telephone or in person. If you suspect that it is your competition calling, then ask for their telephone number so you can call them back with the information. If it is your competition, they will not leave you their number.

You do not want to waste your time going on a house call to a customer who has no idea what decorating items cost. You will probably put that person into shock when you finally do quote the price two to three hours later, and will never see or hear from that customer again. *It is better to give the customer an approximate idea of what their proposed decorating treatments cost* — let them be shocked, reassure them that is what the going rate is for that type of treatment. Remind the customer that you are a competitively priced studio that does a good quality job. Also reassure them that you work with good-quality products, fabrics, and vendors. Lastly, inform the customer that you and your studio follow up all jobs with good service, delivery, and quality installations.

Be willing to provide the customer with the needed information about pricing and your decorating establishment — in a friendly, warm manner. If the truth is known, most companies in the decorating business will not give any prices until the in-home visit. *Most designers or decorators, and other employees of decorating companies, are very hard to work with. They are known for their rudeness, abruptness, and unwillingness to provide information (it has to be pulled out of them), giving poor service, bad installations, and using poor-quality products, with guarantees that mean absolutely nothing.*

This type of company is running rampant through the decorating field and is very difficult for the customer to work with. If they do get a customer and make a sale, the chance of that customer returning or referring a friend to them is remote.

If a problem arises, as they always do, and you are a company that tries to provide good service and take care of the problems that do come up, your customer is going to be reassured and not get very upset. This is especially true if you have been working with the customer throughout the whole job, instead of dropping him or her right after you took the deposit.

Do not let certain addresses or casual appearances by prospective customers deceive you into thinking that this is not a custom customer. Some of the most immaculately groomed, well-dressed people who seem very affluent, spend more than they make, have poor credit, and their homes are in terrible condition.

Conversely, the person who rushes in casually dressed, not perfectly groomed from head to toe, will turn out to be a person who works hard and has a beautifully well-kept home. They devote more of their time to keeping their home up and rush around on days off to get errands done. Both situations will happen countless times to you in this business.

The person or the studio assistant who is taking down the information to set up the appointment for the decorator to go out on an in-home visit should carefully record the customer's name, address, work and home telephone numbers, appointment date, and approximate time of the appointment. Nearest cross streets should always be requested and recorded on the appointment slip, along with any directions for hard-to-find homes that the customer volunteers. All this information should then be repeated to the customer to verify that it was correctly recorded. If the customer is in the studio making the appointment, then the appointment time and date should be written on the designer or decorator's card who will be making the in-home visit.

Clearly spell out to the customer that *this is an approximate time*, not a right-to-the-minute, exact time. Whatever the designer/decorator has run into on the previous appointments that day will dictate if the decorator is running a bit early or slightly late. If you are running more than 25 minutes late, pick up the phone and call your customer and let them know you will be there, but are running a bit late.   Most customers will be accommodating. If they seem unreasonable, they may not be a customer you want to be working with on a decorating project anyway. Sometimes you realize you have forgotten vital samples that the customer has requested you to bring, and you must go back to the studio to pick them up. Sometimes, you get lost on the way to the customer's home, have difficulty finding the home, or finding a telephone to call the customer.

The person taking the call or the studio assistant should attempt to discover what it is that the customer wants to discuss and look at during the in-home visit. The designer or decorator needs to know what samples and information to bring with them. Finding out this information also ensures you that you indeed sell and carry the products or items needed.

If the appointment is for the very next day, or so soon that the decorator may not be coming into the studio before then, then the person making the appointment should pick up the telephone and call the decorator and let them know they have made an appointment for them at that time. If it is not a satisfactory time, then it should *promptly* be rescheduled.

Any inquiry calls for more information from prospective or ongoing customers, or problem calls, need to be taken care of as soon as possible. If the designer or decorator is off or out on appointments, the studio coordinator should attempt to estimate when the designer or decorator will return to the studio, and when the decorator will be returning the call to the customer. The studio assistant should take accurate information about the question and/or complaint the customer has, and record this information on the message left for the decorator. This allows the designer or decorator to check on the order, call the installer, research the problem or look up the information, before calling the customer back.

Anytime a studio assistant can follow through on a problem or question, they should do so, even if it means keeping the customer on the line while trying to get the situation resolved. Get the problems and questions resolved as quickly as possible, while relieving the designer/decorator of a few tasks to do. Why keep the customer waiting for a designer or decorator to call them if the studio assistant can quickly come up with the answer? The idea is to keep the customers happy and provide as good as service as you can.

A good studio assistant is essential for survival. I recommend paying a good person an additional 1% to 2% of gross commission, in addition to their hourly rate of pay. Make them interested in every sale going through smoothly, and interested in resolving problems as painlessly as possible for everyone. If they are getting a percentage of all sales, they will want to keep the decorator out on as many sales calls as the decorator can handle, giving them full support back at the studio.

The studio assistant can track the orders periodically and keep the customers informed of how their order is going, so they do not end up with any surprises at the deadline. Giving the studio assistant a percentage also ensures that any potential customer is going to be treated the way you want your customers treated. They will receive 100% attention over the phone and in person. You will complete the job with happy customers that feel they were taken well care of, and will give you many referrals for years to come.

Call the customer before heading out to the home for a house call. Call one or two days ahead to discuss what type of fabrics, prints, colors, styles, etc., the customer wants to see. Also, inquire if the spouse will be available at the time of the appointment. You may want to reset the appointment to accommodate both of them being there, if one of the spouses will be unable to attend. If the wife cannot make a decision without him, why go there when he will not be there? Usually, the reason is it is a more convenient time during the day for the designer or decorator. Think about it — go on a Saturday or at night, after the spouse is off work.

As a professional, always show up on your sales calls. Never, not show up without calling the customer. You will have lost the customer forever. Matters come up in a designer or decorator's life, just like everyone else's. If you are sick, or an emergency arises, if at all possible, call the day or night ahead. Your customer may have taken off work or put off doing something else in order to meet with you. Do not be unreliable or undependable. You may end up giving a bid, but you will not get the job.

If you should arrive and the customer is not there, sit in your car and wait at least 30 minutes. If you are early, wait until 30 minutes past the time of the appointment. If the customer still does not come home, leave a card with a message on it that you will call and reschedule them. Do not forget to make the call to reschedule them. If they honestly forgot, or an emergency came up, they will immediately call you back, very apologetic. They may have already called to reschedule with you due to something coming up, but you could not be reached by the studio assistant.

Studies on Customer Satisfaction

Studies on customer satisfaction show that *unhappy customers who have problems come up, and are not properly taken care of with these problems, will tell 10-15 other people about the problems that occurred.* They will also tell them how you *did not* resolve their problems.

On the other hand, *a happy customer will tell only 5-7 people about a good job you have done for them.* This is the best customer you can obtain, one who is referred to you by another happy customer. To increase the number of customers referred to you by a happy customer, ask and ask again, repeatedly, for customers to refer you to people who compliment the completed decorating assignment. Explain to the customer that this is the best customer you can get — the one referred by another happy customer.

A person in business cannot afford the above odds of the quantity of people an unhappy customer will go out of their way to tell about the poor-quality job you did and what a bad company you are. This type of advertising will put you right out of business. It is better to attempt to satisfy a customer and take care of perceived problems than to let them spread around bad news about you.

Customer Service — Handling Problems

When a customer calls in upset or reporting a problem with the products you have sold him or her, you and the studio assistant should handle the call in a manner that shows concern. Share empathy with the customer, make them feel that you care.

Have the studio assistant take accurate notes about the problem, the customer's name, and telephone number where they can be reached.

Have the studio assistant thank the customer for bringing the problem to your attention and apologize for any inconvenience for the problem arising in the first place. They should then sympathize and put themselves into the customer's shoes regarding the problem. They should then finish the call by reassuring the customer that the problem will be solved, but will take a bit of time to do so. The amount of time depends on the problem — whether or not it is just a service request, or if something has to be reordered or re-fabricated to correct the problem. Inform the customer that your company will start correcting the problem right away.

The studio assistant should then set an appointment for the decorator of the job to go out and view the perceived problem, while he or she still has the customer on the telephone. The customer should be told that the decorator will be able to offer possible solutions to the problem when he or she sees the situation. Problems are usually not described very well over the telephone by a customer that does not know much about decorating products. If the problem may be solved by the installer's input, get the installer involved, immediately. Have the decorator immediately return the call to the customer, reconfirming the appointment date and time to come out to see the situation.

After the decorator goes out to the home, the decorator, owner of the company, and installer should discuss the right course of action to take to correct the problem and get back to the customer for the customer's agreement.

If possible, on reworks try to put back up the old window coverings or put up loaner window coverings for the customer so the windows will be covered in the interim while the treatment is reworked.

If the window treatments must be remade to satisfy the problem, then leave the defective treatment up until the new, corrected one arrives. Try to correct and solve the problem as quickly and as painlessly as possible for the customer. To keep a very irate customer from canceling, offer an adjustment of 10% to 20%. Follow the job closely to completion. You will have given an adjustment and spent more money to correct problems. At this point, you cannot afford for the customer to cancel the order.

Customer Complaints

Be sure to get right on customer complaints, immediately. Take care of the situation, correct it, keep the customer happy and ready to refer you. Strive to keep the customer coming back again and again to buy more.

The longer you wait to react to a complaint, the angrier your customer will get. Do not turn the dissatisfaction with the product or the job to dissatisfaction with you as a designer or decorator. At this point, they are not angry at you, only dissatisfied. It is not personal, unless your suggested ideas fell flat and are not what the customer expected or wanted. It is always better to go out and take a look for yourself. It may not be the way you were expecting it to come out either. Take care of the customer and keep them happy.

Angry Customers

Many customers, after putting the purchase of window coverings or other decorating items off, finally get around to ordering — and they want it *"tomorrow."* This is after they put you off for a couple of weeks, while they absorbed the price, shopped the price, etc. Any delay due to backorders, defective goods, or delivery problems turn them into angry people who will take it out on the studio assistant and you, the designer or decorator. They were as amicable as could be on the first couple of encounters and now are unrecognizable, due to their over-reactive behavior. They may use threats of canceling, of bringing suit against you, swear at you, make mean comments, etc. Any hold-up or adjustment to the fit of the treatment may bring this attitude out. How people can put such importance on such a minor part of their life is surprising. It is only *"a decorating item,"* not anything more important than that.

After many discussions with fellow peers in this business, we have concluded that most of the very uptight, excessively angry people are probably so stressed out, financially. They are running on stress due to being overextended. They lose their temper over something very trivial. I work in a rapidly growing, northern area of a large county. Everyone moving there was generally from a very large city to the north. The southern, central, western, and eastern areas of the same county were highly populated areas consisting of people who had lived in the area for years, or were originally from there. They are so much more relaxed. Interestingly enough, the northern area also wants very fancy treatments and fabrics. All the other areas also like nice treatments, but are more conservative and basic in their overall taste.

Never fail: the customers who you bend over backwards to give the great price to, the best service, or you go out of your way to get the sale, will turn out to be the customer who will demand an adjustment, require excessive service, will telephone you all the time, and will never seem satisfied. This will probably happen to you time and time again.

Part 3

Elements of Color, Lighting, Design, Texture, and Pattern

Color

Color Terminology and Overview

- **Hue**   Means the same as the term, *color*.

- **Value**   Value is the lightness to darkness of a color. Every hue ranges from light to dark. Light values are termed high values and dark values are termed low values.

- **Tints**   Tints are light shades that are created by adding white to colors or hues. Tints can vary from very light, almost white, to a shade slightly lighter than the original color that white was added to.

- **Tones**   Tones are dark shades created by adding black to a color or to a hue. These tones can vary from almost black, to a shade slightly darker than the original color that black was added to.

- **Intensity** Intensity is the brightness, dullness, or lack of grayness of a color. Intensity is the degree the original color has been grayed or neutralized.

Color Psychology

Color can give people a feeling of well being. *Color affects people differently due to inherited and learned responses.* Women differ from men in their responses to color. Depending on your income level, culture, and the geographical area that you are from, you are going to vary in your response to certain colors. These responses reflect your total makeup; you feel differently about colors than someone with a completely different background does.

Color can be used to expand space, to create certain moods, give or take away the illusion of light, or influence the way people will react when exposed to certain colors.

Variances in color selections **from light to dark** will make a **room appear larger or smaller.** You may elect to select color for treatments or wall colors that fade into the walls or surrounding elements. By selection of color in this fashion, unfavorable architectural features may be camouflaged and hidden. On the other extreme, **color can call attention to centers of interest.**

Calm, quiet, lower-energy people tend to like cool, calm, color schemes with not too much contrast. Select harmonious, neutral versions of colors for this type customer.

Energetic, active, outgoing-type personalities tend to like contrast in their color schemes. Select stronger tones with more contrast within the space for this customer.

Colors and Their Effects

All colors have a blue-based or a yellow-based undertone. Do not mix blue-based colors with yellow-based colors. They will not look comfortable or harmonious together. If in doubt as to what base a color has, hold a true yellow and a true-blue fabric next to the color you are indecisive about. You will readily be able to see if the color fights and conflicts with the opposite based color.

All color families listed below will vary in their preference and responses, depending on the intensity, shade, tint or tone of the colors. Additionally, color preferences will vary with the base of the color itself — whether it is a color with a blue undertone or a color with a yellow undertone. The texture the items are made up in must also be considered.

Color families:

- **Pink** Includes mauve shades. Suggests cleanliness, happiness, youth, perkiness, and warmth, while enhancing most skin tones. Implies good health. The pink family is preferred by women over men. Combines well with black, white, gray, burgundy, violets, blues, and greens.

- **Red** High energy, passion, warmth, comfort, wealth, grandness. Red causes adrenalin to flow, psychologically. This color will encourage you to spend more, eat more, and encourage you to stay longer. Reds are preferred colors for commercial establishments. Reds come in blue-based and yellow-based tones. Men prefer the yellow-based reds; women prefer the blue-based reds.

- **Purple** The purple family is preferred by women over men. Violets and purple reflect dignity, but may remind people of death and funerals. Symbolizes elegance, sophistication, is regal and rich looking. Purples are usually at their best when used as an accent color. Purples mix well with blues, pinks, yellows, whites, grays, and greens.

- **Black** This color denotes sophistication, elegance. Better for women than for men. Can be successfully used as a neutral or accent color with most colors successfully.

- **Gray** Neutral color that goes well with many colors and *gives* other colors life. Indicates sophistication, coolness, calmness, dullness, unliveliness, and creativity. Mood varies with the intensity of the gray. Cool gray is easygoing, while deep gray is dignified and somber. Grays are either blue grays or brown grays and the two groups *do not mix well* together.

- **Brown** Browns are considered to be neutral colors. The brown family combines well with other colors and tends to neutralize brighter colors. Most people are comfortable with browns. Browns may be boring, dull, and too subdued.

- **White** A neutral color. Sophisticated, classy, elegant, denotes luxury, cool, clean, spacious, open, airy. White comes in off-whites, which are tints of another color plus pure white. Some whites are in the cool families and others are in the warm families.

- **Yellow** Sunny, bright, optimistic, happiness, warmth, cheerfulness, youthfulness, energetic, makes people feel good. Yellow is a very noticeable color. Can be irritating to some people, psychologically. People on medication may need to use a higher dose of medication to calm down. Some people may lose their tempers easily when exposed to yellow. Yellow is usually better used as accents than in large amounts in larger areas of rooms, to avoid possible negative responses from visitors.

- **Green** Refreshing, cool, lively, soothing, reminds you of nature. Greens are easy colors to live with. Greens combine well with most colors. If customer has many plants, make sure the selected green for use goes well and enhances plant greens.

- **Orange** Designates warmth, heat, comfort, is stimulating, cheerful, energetic. Depending on the intensity, orange may cause irritation, nervousness, tension, hyperactivity. The orange family includes peach shades. Peach shades are preferred by most people. People from all backgrounds prefer this color. Again, peaches come in blue-based peaches and yellow-based peaches.

- **Blue** Relaxing, calm color, widely preferred by many people. Time seems to pass slowly in a blue atmosphere. To avoid a depressing environment, combine blue with other lively colors. Blue combines well with other colors.

- **Teal** Teal blue, teal green, turquoise, seafoam blue, seafoam green; in general, colors preferred by women, liked by few men. More easily accepted in regions where the color has gained popularity, such as areas where Southwestern looks are popular.

Color preferences and fashions come become popular due to regional, economical, fashion, and political influences, in addition to styles and palette of colors available and popular at any given time.

Color Schemes

Successful decorating evolves around a comfortable color scheme. Outlined below is an overview of color schemes and how to use them.

Monochromatic This color scheme is **based on one color and variations of that same color.** Different values and intensities are combined, all based on the same color. **Vary the values and intensities of the color.** Accent with black, white, one-metal tone.

One color and white This color scheme is **based on the use of white and another color.** The particular white selected may be a contrasting white or a complementary tint of the primary color you have chosen. Some tints of white are in the cold family and others are in the warm family, depending on what color the tint is a tone of. When selecting this scheme, you may **use white as the dominant or the secondary color.** If used as a dominant color, use on the largest areas, picking up the secondary color in the accessories and smaller pieces. The opposite would hold true if white was the secondary color and the other color was the primary or dominant color. Add neutrals to finish off this scheme.

Related or analogous This color scheme is composed by **using colors which are immediately next to each** other on the color wheel. This scheme gives a wide variety of choices while still being related, harmonious, and unified.

Complementary This type of color scheme is a contrasting color schemes. Complementary schemes are created by **selecting one color on the color wheel, and then another color *directly across* from the selected color,** on the other side of the color wheel. This can be a very exciting color scheme to work with.

Note: When selecting color schemes, use all colors from the yellow-based families, or all colors from blue-based families. They do not interchange successfully.

Factors to Consider When Making Color Selections

- **Where the home is located** — country, city, garden-like area, concrete environment.

- **Climate** of the locality. Where is home or building located?

- The **surrounding landscape.**

- **Natural lighting** — which sides are exposed to the south and west?

- **How the room is to be used.**

- **What is the atmosphere to be created.**

- **Existing furnishings and any existing color** you need to incorporate into the scheme. Any existing colors in the room will affect and limit the addition of other colors to the home.

- **Personality** of the customer and family for whom the decorating is being done.

Use cleaner colors rather than muddy, drab, dull, tiresome colors for the color scheme. Do not pick colors that are extremely intense, too bright, or too clean. This will give the interior a cheap, youthful effect.

The lightest, most neutral in color areas should be the largest areas within the space to be decorated — the walls, floors, ceilings, drapery or window treatments. These larger areas need to be decorated in neutral or muted tones so as not to overpower and close in the room, making it appear smaller.

Use medium tones of color on the larger pieces of furniture, counters of the kitchen, bedspreads, drapery or window coverings, floors, etc.

Stronger, more intense colors should be utilized in the accent pieces and accessories.

There is some overlap in the way color may be used, depending on the effect you are trying to achieve. By making distinctive choices with color, you may create exciting, dramatic effects. You may want the window treatments to stand out with a medium tone or to be as light and airy as possible by using a lighter tone. Either selection is correct, depending on the atmosphere desired for the room.

Contrast Color Values

Contrast color value for all colors used within the treatments or decorating planned. **Use variations of color value when combining colors.**

Varying of values is especially important when placing different colors of very close value on top of each other, as in placing trim or banding on a drapery or top treatment. **Variance of values is very important when placing colors too close in value right next to each other.** Examples: the placement of sheers, shades, etc., against overdrapery or other treatments. *The difference in the colors will not show up and stand out against the other colors used, unless the values of the colors are contrasted.* If you select colors too close in value, you will lose the effect you are probably striving to achieve, due to low color contrast.

Light-to-Dark Ratio in Color

For successful decorating with color, **have a light-to-dark ratio, or medium-to-light ratio, or medium-to-dark value contrast.** Include darker elements, probably the smaller pieces and accessories; some lighter elements, usually the larger pieces; and some bright and dull elements, for successful decorating. **If you use the same value, or intensity of color, throughout the space, you will finish with a very dull scheme.**

To achieve light-to-dark value contrast, select a light neutral for the floor covering, and a contrast of light-to-dark in a pattern for the wallcoverings. Use medium tones for the window coverings and furniture. Choose darker, brighter tones for smaller items and accessories.

Color in General

The following list is a collection of general guidelines to follow when using color:

- **Most colors will go together** if the right shades of the colors are used together.

- **Texture and light will change the color.**

- The most successful way to combine colors together: **select the preferred dominant color and a group of related colors.** Next, try out **contrasting colors with the preferred colors** to see what contrasting color is the best selection.

- Color choices will change constantly. What the trend is today will be different next year. You may see a similar hue, but the shade of the hue will be different. And the way you will combine it with other colors will be different.

- Rooms that are successfully decorated usually have the color scheme based on tones of one dominant color. **Only one color should dominate.** Use contrasting colors as accents in small amounts.

- Use this basic rule: **One color is the predominant color; introduce some texture** in this **predominant color** and **use value contrast of the predominant color** within the room.

- Several colors fighting to dominate make the room appear busier and smaller.

- Fewer colors make a room appear larger and quieter.

- **Bolder colors** jump out at you and **make a room smaller.**

- **Quieter colors** are more subdued and **make a room appear larger.**

- **A well-put-together color scheme can unify and blend disunified furnishings of different styles and periods.**

- **Balance color throughout the room;** do not give one corner too much color, while another corner appears to have little or no color.

- On larger areas, keep the tone of the color less intense.

- **Light colors reflect the sun** much more effectively than darker colors, which absorb heat.

- Lighter colors used on walls and ceilings take away your awareness that the ceilings are low.

- **Light colors reflect light,** making rooms that are light in color appear lighter, more spacious, larger, and airier. Light colors let our eyes flow through a space and keep going, unobstructed. Therefore, light expands space.

- In smaller rooms, use less intense, lighter, fewer patterns to help the room appear larger, rather than smaller.

- **Use the brightest-intensity colors in the smallest amounts.** This may be a contrasting color or another related color. Use intense colors in the accessory items, such as, lamps, vases, dishes, pillows, and trim, on treatments, pictures, etc.

- **Darker, deeper colors will make a room appear smaller** and more closed in.

- Cool colors, or low-intensity colors, with **lighter values make a room appear larger.**

- **Use cool colors in rooms with southern or western exposures,** to cool the rooms down.

- **Pastel and paler colors reflect light and expand space.** You may use pale colors to make artificial lighting more effective. Pastel colors are ideally used in small, cramped, low-ceiling rooms. Ceilings in pale colors will recede or appear higher.

- **Warm colors have the tendency to close a room in.** Warm colors stimulate, make it appear and feel warmer than it is, may make you uncomfortable, uptight and nervous. This will vary in the degree of uncomfortableness, depending on the depth of the colors used.

- Large rooms can be made much more intimate with warm colors. **Warm colors absorb light, requiring more natural or artificial lighting.** The use of warm colors on high ceilings that need to be lowered are an effective use of warm colors.

- **Rooms with northern exposure will be warmed up with the use of warm color.**

- **Do not use warm colors in a hot, southern or western exposure.** The room will get unbearably hot.

- Combinations of pale pastel colors and stronger colors for wall colors can be used together to help change the proportions of a room. An optical illusion will be created. The stronger-colored wall will advance, while the pale walls will recede. Change the plainness of a rectangular or square-shaped room this way.

- Color can rearrange and change the shape of a room. Paint or paper one or two walls of the room in a contrasting color from the other three walls, to make a narrow room appear shorter or wider.

- **In rooms where a lot of time is spent, select colors that are quieter rather than lively and bold,** as you might select for an area such as an entry, that you are only in for limited periods of time.

- **Do not select colors too intense in their shade for large backdrop areas.** The milder, more subdued shades are more successfully used here.

- **In smaller rooms, do not use bright colors, or too many colors.** It will make the room appear busy and confining.

- When working **with smaller areas, try to make the small space appear larger. Achieve this by using fewer patterns, lighter colors, and lightweight furniture.**

- On a studio apartment, or a small space to be decorated, use natural tones rather than a fashionable color scheme. Natural tones are more livable in a confined space, over a period of time, than definite colors.

- **Select one or two neutrals to go with the selected color scheme.**

- **Select one metal color to be used** within the room: chrome, brass, gold, etc. Do not use more than one metal color, unless the metal colors come from the manufacturer mixed on the accessory to be used. For example, a gold lamp with chrome trim.

Selection of a Color Scheme From a Pattern

The easiest way to help a customer choose an exciting color scheme they will like is to **have your customer select a patterned fabric, decorative rug, painting, or wallcovering that he or she wishes to use as the palette of color for their decorating scheme.**

Match the colors in the pattern, using the same intensity, a tint, or a tone of the featured colors. If **a color is particularly dominant in the amount used, then ideally use the same proportional amounts of the color within the room. Use the secondary and other colors in proportionately the same amounts shown in** the pattern you are working with. Try to keep all the colors in the same proportions as shown within the pattern, for successful decorating. If the pattern has a background of blue, then blue would be an ideal color to use in the larger areas — such as the carpet, or on several walls. If the secondary color shown in size and amount in the pattern is salmon, this would be an excellent color selection for the sofa or other medium-sized color areas within the room. Then coordinate other items to the colors and prints.

Working With Existing Furnishings

Most people own some furniture they want to incorporate into their new decorating scheme. This may be due to monetary or sentimental reasons. *You must find a way* to bring these pieces into the plan, harmonious with the rest of the decorating scheme. You have to do this to keep your customer happy, and prevent the customer from going to another studio. The other studio will probably do this for the customer. whether the existing furniture matches or not.

Furniture your customer is planning to keep and use (rather than replacing, changing the upholstery on distinctively styled furniture, artwork, etc.) must be considered when deciding the color scheme. **When you are using existing furnishings that need to be used within the room you are decorating that have distinctive colors,** *the distinctive color may be used as the primary or the secondary colors.*

Existing, hard-to-match in color furnishings:
Do not use colors with these existing hard-to-match in color furnishings that are extremely bright. Extremely bright colors will make the pieces look even more worn, faded, old, dull, and drab, than the existing furnishings probably already look.

Introduce the Neutrals

Neutrals are tints and shades of whites, blacks, grays, and browns. Additionally, pure black, pure white, deep gray, off-whites, gold metals, chrome metals, etc., are also neutrals.

After selection of the primary and secondary colors for the scheme, bring in the neutral colors to accent the color scheme. Select one or two neutrals, but **do not mix metal colors.**

Wood Tones

Before deciding the wood tones to use for the interior, consider the tone of the wood in the existing cabinets, banisters, and other architectural features in addition to any existing wood furniture that is going to be incorporated into the scheme you are planning. **Similar to color, woods have either a pink undertone or an orange undertone. Stay within the same undertone family, when selecting wood tones.** Try to contrast the values of the wood tones within a space, to create interest. Too much of the same tone is boring and heavy.

Link Spaces With Color and Unify the Home

Color needs to flow from one space to another. **Select one color to flow in varying degrees of shade or tone throughout the home, to create unity and flow.** You may change your dominant color used in the primary rooms to a secondary color in connecting spaces of the home, as long as the original dominant color is being used in *some* amount within each room. The color scheme will appear subconsciously to be harmonious. The home will appear more spacious; the furniture and accessories will be interchangeable from one room to the next.

The key is to **pick an interesting scheme with a bit of life and excitement to it rather than a dull, non-personality combination.** There is a fine line drawn here, as selection of a color scheme that is over exciting is not the way to go, either.

Limit color scheme to only a few colors:

Limit the color scheme to only a few colors. In some rooms, play up other colors that you used in smaller amounts in other rooms. *Use only two or three different values and intensities of a color.*

Accenting or downplaying architectural features:

For architectural features you would like to accent or stand out, paint in a contrasting color or in two shades of color, darker or lighter than the surrounding wall areas or nearby window treatments. Outlining the architectural features with a contrasting color, or a color two shades darker or lighter, will also make the features stand out and call attention to them. Depending on the intensity of the accent color against the background color, the effect will vary from dramatic to subtle. A strong contrast in color will create a focal point for the room.

Architectural features you wish to downplay or hide, paint the same neutral shade as the wall color.

Color palettes have limited availability:

Anytime a particular color palette is selected for use, always instruct the customer to purchase all needed decorating items in a distinctive color within a relatively short period — two years or less. This is due to the frequent change of color palettes that come in and out of fashion, which stay in style only for short durations. If your customers wait too long to buy furnishings in distinctive colors, they will not be able to easily find their needed colors, or will not find the needed colors at all.

Show swatches of fabric in proportion to the size of the amount to be used:

When presenting color boards to a client, or demonstrating visually the fabric selected, show fabric selections in the proportional size to the other size swatches of the amount you are actually going to use. Keep these swatches in proportion to each other, whether the swatches are of wallcoverings, paint, ceramic tile, fabrics, etc. You do not want to show a large swatch of vibrant, overpowering color for use only in a small accessory, against a small muted-toned carpet swatch. The customer will not get a true perspective of the perceived, overall finished look. If you use too large of an accessory sample color, the larger sample color will make it appear that your accessory color selection is overpowering.

Always check swatch samples in the lighting conditions to be used in. Colors *do* change in natural day lighting, natural evening lighting, or artificial lighting.

Selection of color from a small swatch:

When making color selections from small swatches, recognize that colors have the tendency to get more intense and brighter when used in a large area. Therefore, swatches of paint and fabric appear about a shade lighter than they will appear in reality on the walls, or hung up at the windows. Try to use a slightly less-intense tone of your preferred color, to lessen the possibility of being overwhelmed by the color, when the item is actually fabricated or applied.

Lighting

Light and Glare

Natural light is comfortable light that brightens up the room. If the contrast from light to dark within the room is broad, glare will be created. Glare, is actually created from having *too much* light, rather than *not having enough* light placed in the wrong areas of the room. **If light comes from more than one direction within the room, the light will lighten up the dark areas and brighten up the room.**

If placement of the window is near the ceiling, and if the window is left unobstructed, the top portion of the room and ceiling will be lighted up from the natural light. A window with this placement will probably light up the *whole* ceiling of the room, rather than a window placed much lower on the wall that will only light up a portion of the room.

The use of fabric or metal awnings, patio covers, or other overhangs on the exterior of the home will cut down on glare and make any light coming in, more comfortable to the eye. If you use a fabric awning, the color of the awning is reflected into the room. The reflected awning color creates a beautiful effect — if the awning color enhances the interior colors. If awnings or other overhangs are used, remember, while you are cutting down on the summer's harsh sunlight coming in the window, you are also cutting down on the winter's warming sun rays coming through the same windows.

- Windows with southern exposures will let in welcome sun during the winter. If you eliminate the problems that you have with summer's southern exposure in a permanent manner, you have eliminated any sun coming in during the winter, when it is welcome.

- West-facing windows will allow the heating rays that filter in to warm a cold house in winter.

- Windows with eastern or northern exposure, if not properly covered, will let the cold in during the winter.

Non-glare glass is available if the glare situation is out of control and the customer does not want to correct the problem with window treatments or awnings. Tinted shades will also drastically help this problem.

Effects of Natural Light on Interior Colors

Interior colors are affected by natural light from outside filtering into the room. Fabrics will vary in their color due to the amount of light shining on them and which direction the light is coming from. This color variation will also vary throughout the day as the natural light changes. Natural light changes as the day gets later and later. Early morning light has a pink and orange glow to it. As the day goes on, the light changes to yellow as the sun rises. About noon, light is reflected from the sky and takes on a white and light blue hue. Later in the day, when the sun sets, the color reflected is orange and pink.

Windows with southern and western exposure get more yellow sunlight reflected than those windows with northern or eastern exposure. It is preferable to use cool colors when decorating these warmer rooms. Use warm colors to warm-up cooler rooms and balance out the situation.

Small windows or windows with multiple layers not allowing much light through will make interior colors darker and less intense.

As night falls, and the use of artificial lighting is employed, the colors will be affected again. The practice of allowing a customer to borrow the samples and see them at night in addition to viewing them during the day is a wise decision — unless you do not mind remaking items that took on an unmatching hue when the artificial light was turned on.

Effects of light on color:

Colors differ in their way of absorbing, reflecting, and transmitting light within a space when combined with lighting. Natural light, artificial light, the color that is affected, surroundings, and the color used, will determine how the color will reflect or absorb light.

Color	Type of Lighting	Effect of Color
Pink	Natural Light	Brightens, and makes colors of the pink family appear clear, warm, and rich in appearance.
	Fluorescent	Pink colors appear richer and brighter.
	Incandescent	Gives pink colors an orange tint and makes the pink family brighter, richer, and warmer.
Red	Natural Light	Red colors appear richer, warmer, full of life, and clear.

Red   **Fluorescent**   Lighter colors of the red family are clearer and brighter appearing. Bright reds are slightly yellowed in appearance. Deeper reds and rust tones appear browner in color.

               Incandescent   Red colors appear more orange. Affects most reds by making them warmer, richer, and more vibrant.

Blue   **Natural Light**   Blue colors appear clearer, richer, and brighter.

               Fluorescent   Blue colors appear lighter, more clear in color, and richer.

               Incandescent   Blue colors appear more yellow or greenish in general. Deeper colors appear dulled and darker.

Green   **Natural Lighting**   Green colors become darker and also take on a gray tone.

               Fluorescent   Lighter-green shades become brighter and clearer. Deeper shades become deeper and warmer in appearance.

               Incandescent   Greens are darkened and take on a tone of yellow or brown.

Yellow   **Natural Lighting**   This lighting tones down yellow colors.

               Fluorescent   Yellow colors become brighter, warmer, and have a warm, soft-yellow glow to them.

               Incandescent   Yellows become warmer and richer in appearance.

Design

To have a beautifully decorated room, design elements such as proportion, scale, emphasis, balance, form, line, unity, harmony, and repetition must be considered in addition to color, texture, and pattern selections. Below, the elements of design are outlined with their important considerations when decorating a space or a room:

Form:

Form must follow function. Why create a room and select items to furnish that room that are not functional? Consider this element first, then apply the other design guidelines around form. Form is a three-dimensional formation, and is often used interchangeably with the term, space.

Proportion and Scale:

Proportion is the relation of one part of an object to the whole. Compare the length of a valance to the overall length of a drapery. When you choose, select, and plan correct proportions you create a comfortable feeling of continuity.

When you pick the wrong proportions, you create a top-heavy feeling or a deficient feeling. If the top of the treatment or object is too heavy and deep in length, you feel as if the top is going to fall down on you. If too inadequate in length, your treatment looks as if you have missed the point.

- When deciding what size or length to make a treatment or other object, remember that proportions in increments of three-eighths and one-thirds are more pleasing to the eye than one-halfs.

- **Arrive at the correct proportional length for a top treatment by determining one-fifth to one-sixth of the overall length of the drapery.** Hold your tape measure at the wall at the top of the top treatment placement and down. Look at both the one-fifth and the one-sixth length, compare and determine which length your customer and you both prefer — the longer or the shorter of the two.

- **Keep in proportion — line, color, form and textures within a room.** Over-emphasis or under-emphasis of any design element will be overkill or underkill within the room.

- **The scale of the size of an object to another object must be considered. Additionally, the scale of an object to the size of the room or area must be considered.** If the room is small, you should not choose to use a heavy, dark colored, overbearing treatment. You would want to strive for a light, airy feel and look.

- **Keep the scale and size of the window treatments in scale with the overall look and size of the room.** Scale must be considered with every object selected and placed within the space. All furniture should be in proportion or scale to the room, in addition to being in scale to other furnishings in the room.

Emphasis and Focal Points:

Emphasis is the focal point within a room, used and needed to relieve monotony. You may want the focal point to be a beautiful drapery treatment, a beautiful painting, an interesting architectural area, or a beautiful view. **Decorate the room to flow to the focal point, to flow to the point which holds the most emphasis.**

Every room should have a main center of interest, in addition to secondary centers of interest in other areas of the room.

To create a focal point, use exciting patterns, pieces, accessories, contrasts in line, shapes, textures, or colors. Fireplaces are an ideal focal point to arrange furniture around. Lighting may be used to direct the eye over to the focal points.

Balance:

Balance is in two forms: symmetrical or even balance, and *asymmetrical balance,* the more interesting uneven balance. **Even balance can be achieved by placement of the same amount of relative mass, color, or weight on each side.** *You do not necessarily need to use identical items.*

Incorporate balance by distributing large, heavy, dark, or dominant colors around the room. Do not place them all together in the same areas of a room.

Objects or color equal in mass will balance each other. Placing mass on one side without placing it on the other, or in a lesser amount, will create asymmetrical balance. Placing the same amount of mass or weight on both sides will create symmetrical or even balance. Always **balance opposite walls** within a space or room.

Harmony and Unity:

Keep all furnishings and decorating elements harmonious to each other in style, color, texture, size relationships, line, and form. All furnishings should flow with the effect you are creating and be in the proper scale. The various furnishings and their corresponding elements should appear as if they were planned to be together. The furnishings should not appear as if they are competing against each other, or are just thrown together. Harmony is achieved when variety and unity are combined in a favorable manner.

Unity is pulling everything together in a harmonious manner. Apply the principles of balance, proportion, and contrast to create unity. *Each part, together, makes a whole.*

Line:

Line is an important design element to remember when decorating. When deciding what type of line you will use as the theme of the room, remember to **use one type of line predominately.**

Try to use consistency in the lines within the space. If the furniture is curved, choose curved lines for the lamps and all other accessories. If the lines used in the sofa and wood furniture are very angular, keep accessories and other furnishings within the same theme.

- **Vertical lines** are **masculine, calm,** and give **height.** Vertical lines combined **with horizontal lines** appear **classical and strong.**

- **Curved lines** have **personality, rhythm,** are **active, romantic,** and have the tendency to be more **feminine.**

- **Avoid** the use of **diagonal lines.**

- Use **straight lines** to accentuate **height and width.**

Rhythm and Repetition:

The flow of the space or room is the feeling of rhythm. **Rhythm is created by using lines, spaces, forms, colors, patterns, by movement of lines, and by progression** — the use of forms from small to large or large to small. Rhythm is movement, flow, repetition. Repeating colors, patterns, and forms around the room creates repetition and rhythm.

Use repetition throughout the space. When a print has a certain type of motif or style, or a rectangle form is predominant, or a similar pattern is found in an accessory that is similar to the dominant print being used, repeat this pattern to create repetition and rhythm.

Contrast:

Use contrast to **create interest** in decorating a room. You would not want to keep *everything* the same tone, size, color, pattern size, etc. Use contrast among the selected elements to make each element stand out on its own. Some elements are preferred and selected to be more dominant, while others are secondary, but *all are important.* Keep within the same families and style, but **use contrast to add personality** to your decorating.

Flow of Traffic Patterns:

When arranging furnishings for conversational groupings and traffic patterns throughout the room, make it comfortable to get in and out of the conversation areas and be able to walk through the room easily. The traffic pattern should move around the conversation areas, not through them.

Basic Design Points

- *Odd numbers* of decorative accessories or furnishings are **more interesting than** *even numbers*.

- **Keep large furniture and area rugs parallel to** the larger **walls** of the room.

- Use **one dominating pattern** within the room.

- **All patterns** used together **should coordinate.**

- Do not place **decorative accessories above eye level.**

- **Minimize** decorating accessories that do not have a function.

- Keep the family pictures, trophies, or hobbies in the bedrooms, recreation areas, or hallways.

- **Patterned rugs and flooring** selections **take away from** the **furniture** sitting on them.

- The use of **mirrors adds depth** to a small room and makes it appear larger.

- **If the room is really cut up** by numerous doors and windows, **paint the moldings the same color as the walls.**

- If there are many windows and doors, and if you would like them to stand out, paint the moldings of the windows and doors a contrasting color.

Texture and Pattern

Textured Fabrics and Window Treatments

The way we use texture, and the way we combine texture in our interiors, adds interest and excitement to our decorating schemes. **To properly combine textures, they need to have texture and style compatibility.** You want to use formal textures with other formal textures. A heavily textured fabric and window treatment make a good combination when contrasted with a smooth, textured, or patterned leather sofa. If you are using casual looking fabrics or textured treatments, then also use other casual elements and accessories within the same room or space. **Stay within the same families of styles and types of texture** when coordinating textures together — whether the texture is smooth or heavy. **Use one texture predominantly** throughout the space. **Do not mix one *extreme* style of texture with another *extreme* style of texture.**

The use of textures in our interior fabrics and window treatments stimulates our sense of touch. Psychologically, we feel comfortable and secure. *Texture adds depth to a room.* Light and color are reflected in varying shades, because of the textural surface, rather than showing up as a flat solid color.

If a fabric is made up of a moderately-intense color, the color is going to appear less intense if made up into a soft or rough-textured fabric or window treatment. Rooms will appear smaller when mostly heavy-textured elements, or many soft textures have been used.

The use of identical textures throughout a room or space is very boring and dull. Even if the combined colors are a good combination, you need to provide surface contrast.

To keep a neutral color scheme from becoming too monotonous and dull, use texture to give it style and life. Contrast smoother textures with nubby, heavily textured accessories; use smoother textures to balance heavier-textured fabrics and other interior elements. Some of the accessories to use to add texture are: dried flower arrangements, baskets, plants, etc.

Below is a listing of many interior elements and the textural categories textures are classified in. As you review the following list, note there is a degree of overlap in the various categories. If the items that overlap are used with other like items in the same class, then the tendency is that the texture falls into the category of being more of a *smooth* rather than more of a *hard* texture.

Textural Categories

- **Soft Textures**　　Includes interior use of several fabrics together. Cottons, chintz and polished cottons, linens, satins, silks, velvets, corduroys, quilted fabrics, tweeds, wool, cashmere, plush carpeting, Oriental rugs, Dhurrie rugs, Kelims, woven throws, afghans, patterned wallpaper in non-geometrical designs, silk flower arrangements, fresh flowers.

- **Smooth Textures**　　Glass, mirrors, plexiglass, satins, silver, chrome, brass, finer, closed-grained wood furniture, leather, vinyl, formica, Ikebana.

- **Hard Textures**　　Vertical blinds and mini blinds made of aluminum or vinyl. Marble, ceramic tile, stone, slate, granite, glass, chrome, wood flooring, parquet flooring, travertine, brick, cork, plaster, vinyls with shiny surfaces, formica, cane, rattan, wicker, brass, chrome, ceramic tile, terracotta tile, mahogany, oak, pine, teak, walnut, lacquer, porcelain.

● **Rough Textures** Basketry, wicker, rattan, dried flower arrangements, rustic pottery, hand-woven fabrics, wall hangings, heavily slubbed fabrics; nubby, coarse textures, rough-hewn furniture, unrefined items.

The Use of Pattern in Decorating

The use of pattern in decorating adds rhythm and life to an interior. Before selecting a pattern or texture to incorporate into an interior, you must **consider the style of the design and the scale of the pattern. The style of the motifs**, within the patterns, **should relate to the other patterns**; unless the patterns are geometrics, stripes, or plaids. These fabrics cannot relate in style, but should be in the same color family and be of a related fabric. **The types of fabrics combined together should relate to each other in style or family.** *The style or family should complement what style or "look" is already occurring,* rather than starting a new theme of its own.

Your objective is to achieve a comfortable flow between the patterns and their various sizes. You do not want shocking extremes with the size of the patterns used together. *Never use the same size patterns together in the same room.*

● **The colors used in patterns must relate** with other elements in the interior. Additionally, colors need to relate to the other patterns and colors used within the patterns.

● Use some solid plain areas mixed in with patterned areas. Otherwise, you will create a room that is too busy. It is better not to place patterns right on top of each other. Patterned drapery is at its best when placed on top of plain walls, rather than on top of patterned wallpaper.

● Patterns placed on top of each other have the tendency to fight each other and create a busier look. Placing two patterns right next to each other will work, if the patterns used are a medium-large pattern used with a smaller or tiny pattern.

● The combination of patterned fabrics and solid woven-in-patterned fabrics will work well together.

● Use patterns with other colorful patterned fabrics of a different scale, or with stripes or geometrics. Using a **large pattern in a small area will make the area appear smaller and may overpower the area.** The use of a **small pattern in a large area will lose the pattern in the larger space, and make the pattern seem insignificant.**

● **Larger-scaled patterns work well with medium and medium-small scaled patterns; and medium-sized patterns go well with smaller and tiny patterns. Do not put large patterns together with very small or tiny patterns.**

● **Patterns give height and depth** to a space or a room.

● Placement of **a pattern on the ceiling** will tend to make the ceiling **appear lower.**

● Use of vertical lines in patterns on walls tend to make the ceiling appear higher.

● Use of **an abundance of pattern will lessen the need** for the customer **to have a lot of furniture.** The patterns will give the illusion that the room has a lot of life and rhythm — lack of furniture will not be noticed.

Selection of Patterns

When making pattern selections for a room, keep in focus the size of the room in proportion to the amount of pattern you want to use.

The scale of the pattern you are considering — does the pattern or print accent the style of the treatment you are using it on? Does the style of the pattern go with the style of the sofa? How will the pattern look placed on that piece of furniture? How will the pattern look gathered up if used on a gathered window treatment? Pleated up? **Always try to use the largest patterns on the largest areas or furniture you are decorating.**

Consider the intensity of the colors that are used within the pattern being considered. If the pattern is very intense, the pattern is going to appear to occupy more space and make the room appear smaller.

Always pick the dominant pattern, then the secondary pattern, and then the other fabrics to coordinate to the dominant pattern. The dominant pattern should stand out the most and be the most important pattern. *Do not choose a secondary pattern with more intense colors.* If you do, when you stand back, the secondary, more intense pattern will stand out more than the dominant pattern. Choose the secondary and other fabrics to be less intense, or *if necessary*, the same intensity. Always select all the prints from the same color family. If the dominant fabric is formal, all patterns selected for the space must be formal.

Stripes, plaids, checks, geometrics, small-patterned goods, dots, and tweeds are ideal secondary patterns.

Combining Print Fabrics

To combine print fabrics, always start by picking one pattern to dominate. You may use this dominant pattern in other areas of the room also. Then, **select the secondary patterns to relate in color, style, and general fabric type.** The scale of the patterns should be different. **The fabric patterns should be similar in style, but different in pattern.** Leave large areas of plain, unpatterned relief within the room or space.

Patterns are found in decorative elements such as sofas, drapery fabrics, wood grains, wallcoverings, flooring, carpeting, rugs, and accessories. **All patterns within the room will need to relate and blend with one another.**

When combining fabrics, do not strive for a *perfect* match among the fabrics. Some fabrics that are available with companion prints to mix and match are an easy alternative if you are unsure of combining fabrics. **You can create more interesting effects by combining fabrics from other groups if you follow the rules outlined below.**

- **First, look for fabrics that have similar colors used in them.** The colors do not need to be an exact match, as long as they are tints and tones of the same color (light or darker versions of the same colors). Use reverse-background colors if the fabrics look good together.

- **Look at the scale of the prints you are considering. Contrast the size of the prints.** A good combination is to use one large print with a much smaller (not tiny) print. You do not want to pick a tiny print to go with a very large print. Select a print that is about one quarter to one-third the size of the other print. Strive to show there is a difference in the size of the prints.

- **Use consistency when selecting the types of fabrics you are working with, to combine with each other.** The fabric types in style, fiber content, and motif style need to relate well to each other.

Prints come in very formal fabrics and very casual fabrics. *A formal fabric is not going to relate to a casual fabric.* The fabrics will not relate, even if the fabrics have the same type of motif. Example: a very formal jacquard used with an informal cotton dull-finished printed fabric, with the same motifs. Stripes and geometrics need to follow the color-matching rules. *Stripes and geometrics do have more flexibility in the size of the stripe that may be used together, or with printed fabrics.* Your eye sees that a stripe is different from a print, so a large stripe may be used with a large print very successfully. The exception to this is the use of a tiny all-over print with a large, boldly striped fabric. *This use would reflect a too-extreme contrast.* Stripes and geometrics used with other stripes and geometrics need to contrast in the size of the stripes and geometric patterns that are used together.

Part 4

Fabric Selection, Wearing Ability, Lining, and Maintenance

Fabric

Every fabric has its own personality. A fabric's personality is composed of all the elements that make up its texture, pattern, colors, fiber content, and finished hand. All of these factors must be considered when making fabric selections. The textile's ability to be cleaned and the durability of the fabric are also major considerations.

Window treatment elegance is achieved by properly balancing the fabric's color/colors, texture, draping ability, and style with the overall effect and look of the room, furniture selected, and the lifestyle of the inhabitants.

The use of textiles gives a room warmth and personality. Fabric is a warm medium for window treatments. In addition to being a very attractive medium, textiles insulate against heat, cold and noise. Fabric filters and controls light, provides privacy, and keeps drafts of cold air from coming in.

Cloth may be draped, swaged, tailored, trimmed, gathered, and pleated.

The proper selection of different patterns and colors can camouflage a window's poor proportions, increase the apparent size of the window, or call attention to the window, making it the room's focal point.

Before deciding that a particular fabric is the one to be used for a particular window treatment, determine how the particular fabric is to be used.

- Will the selected **fabric perform** the tasks needed?

- If the preferred window treatment style is to be particularly drapey, will the selected **fabric drape well**?

- Will the **fabric take the abuse** it will be subjected to?

- Consider **the fabric's cleaning ability and durability** for the particular situation the fabric is to be used in. Will it **withstand the sun**? How will it **react to humidity**? Is the fabric going to be **subjected to hard use and abrasion**?

Fabric Durability

The durability of the fabric is determined by the following components and elements:

- **Fiber content** of the fabric.

- The **weave** of the fabric.

- Whether or not the fabric is **lined**.

- The **exposure of elements** to the fabric.

- How much **sunlight** the fabric is subjected to.

Fabric Considerations for Selection

Fabric points to consider when selecting fabric for use in an interior:

- **Fabrics should be protected from the sun.** Use lining, and possibly interlining, when working with fragile fabrics. Blinds or shades should be drawn closed during the day if the sun is strong, and outside awnings should be employed.

- Winter's sun and the reflection of the sun off of snow are more harmful than summer's sunshine. **Window glass magnifies the destructive elements from the rays of the sun.**

- Keep in mind that tightly woven fabrics are easier to work with than loosely woven fabrics.

- **Loosely woven fabrics stretch and shrink with the humidity levels.** Lock-stitch, woven patterns are available with some fabrics to eliminate this problem.

- **Small rooms will appear larger with the drapery fabric the same color as the walls.**

- **Floor-to-ceiling treatments give height to a room.**

- **With the careful selection of fabric, a room may be brightened or lightened up.**

- **Poorly proportioned windows may be softened, camouflaged, or concealed.**

- All over, printed fabrics are easy to work with. **Printed fabrics will hide any imperfection that would be visible if the item were made up in a solid color. If the design of the fabric is very small, do not attempt to match it up.**

- **Small patterns can hide the ugly proportions of a window.**

- **Large patterns can make a window appear larger.**

- **The use of a fabric the same color as the walls will make the window unnoticeable.**

- **Contrasting colors in the wall color or other fabrics adjacent to the window treatment will call attention to the window.**

- **Vertical stripes will give height to a window.** The amount of height will be related to the style, color, and selection of the stripe. Bold, brighter, deeper stripes give more height than subtle pastel, off-white stripes.

- **Horizontal stripes will make a window appear wider.** The amount of width will be determined by the boldness of the stripe. Bright, deep colors will give more width to a window than subtle off-white ones.

- **The wider the fabric, the fewer seams it will have.**

- **If the selvage appears tight and the fabric to the side of the selvage looks puckered, have the workroom trim off the selvage completely.** Trimming off the selvage will prevent the drapery or window treatment from having conspicuously puckered seams. The only way to remedy puckered seams is to rework the drapery or window treatment and remove the selvages.

- **Fabrics absorb noise.** Their absorption is **based on these factors: the amount of fabric used, the heaviness of the fabric, and whether or not the window treatment or drapery is lined.** Textured, heavy, lined drapery are best for noise control, inside and outside.

- Darker fabrics, lined window treatments, tightly woven fabrics, and heavier fabrics will allow very little light to filter through. Depending on the color of the undertreatment and the window treatment, the light and glare coming in will be affected in different degrees. **Lighter fabrics filter sunlight, while sheer and loosely woven fabrics will filter both light and glare.**

- Trees and shrubbery outside window areas protect the windows from sunlight, glare, and fading of interior fabrics and carpeting.

- The more layers of window coverings, the more insulation and light control you will have.

- Some fabrics have more finishes than other fabrics. Special finishes are available on some fabrics that help prevent mold and mildew and allow higher soil resistance.

- A home that is being completed in stages of furnishing and decorating is going to appear more comfortable, more furnished, and warmer if fabric is the selected material to be used for the window treatments, rather than another material.

- With the use of fabric, you may change a room's proportions and hide ugly architectural features.

- Fabrics do wear out — they are not indestructible. The amount of wear that a fabric will give will vary with the amount of use and abuse they receive. Additionally, a fabric's life is affected by the amount of protection that it has from the sun and other elements. Lastly, some fibers and weaves are stronger than others.

- Drapery fabric that is tightly woven, opaque, and also light in color will reflect the sun's rays.

- Woven fabrics add warmth and interest to a room that is otherwise decorated in smooth textures.

- Abrasive upholstery fabrics will be uncomfortable to bare arms and legs.

Interior Fabrics

Fabrics selected for interiors should be carefully considered for their fiber content and for their weave.
Fibers are spun into yarns and woven into various weaves, depending on the methods used and the effect desired by the manufacturer. The same fiber may be made up as a see-through voile, a rough, slubby, homespun fabric, or a very elegant satin.
Fabrics made for interiors do not always exhibit the same qualities for their use as clothing fabrics do. For example, interior wool fabrics are less prone to wrinkle than wool fabric for use in clothing.

Care of Fabrics

Every fabric sample and book with the fabric's specifications in your studio or possession, has the care instructions and fiber content for the fabric noted on it. As a professional designer or decorator, you want to educate your customer on what to expect from a particular fabric, and how to care for the fabric.
Strive to avoid complaints from your customer. Do this by giving them fabric that will satisfy their needs. Make it a habit to point out to your customers positive and negative points about the fabric. They will know what to expect and will be more tolerant of the fabric's shortcomings. Do not wait and let them find out the negative points after the fabric arrives. Point the negative points out ahead of time, and keep your customer a repeat customer, rather than a surprised, unhappy customer that will buy elsewhere in the future.
When presenting possible fabric selections to your customer, remind them of the following points. Review the corresponding sections on these specific areas for more information.

- **Fabrics are an investment** and need to be protected from the sun to have a long life. **They need to be lined.** Undertreatments should be drawn closed during the sunny times of the day. Exterior awnings, trees, and shrubbery are wonderful interior fabric preservers.

- **Dry-clean all fabrics to preserve the fabric finishes and the treatment's crisp, well-fitting appearance.** Use a reputable dry cleaner that specializes in home furnishings and drapery cleaning. Vacuum fabrics regularly to remove the dust sitting on them. Very few fabrics benefit from being washed. Sheer fabrics are the exception.

- **The length of the draperies will fluctuate slightly, due to the humidity or dryness of the air.** No fabrics are completely stable. Fabrics breathe and absorb moisture from the air. This causes the fabric to stretch or shrink.

- **Fabrics do wear out.** They wear according to the amount of use they are given, atmosphere they are subjected to, and the fiber content and weave of the fabric.

- **Soil-resistant finishes help resist spotting, staining and soiling.** The fabric has to be maintained and cared for, regardless of the finishes that have been applied. Spots and stains need immediate attention, or the soil-resistant finish on the fabric or carpet will fail.

- **Sun fading can occur regardless of the quality of the dyes used for the fabric.** No dye is completely resistant to sun fading. Lining is necessary for any medium to darker-toned colors. The hems on the back of the leading edges of drapery will still fade. Undertreatments, window tinting, transparent shades, awnings, exterior trees, and shrubbery all work to prevent this problem.

Fiber Information

Fibers for the home must be durable and hold up for use for many years. **Fibers need to be resistant to abrasion and sunlight, and in most cases, insulative.**

The **three major categories for fibers are: natural (plant and animal); cellulosic; and synthetic (manufactured).**

- The **natural fibers** and their sources are: wool, animal source; cotton, plant source; silk, animal source; linen, plant source.

- The **cellulosic fiber group** is made from plant fibers that are reduced to a chemical broth and then respun.

- **Synthetic fibers** are generally made of petroleum. They are made by being twisted into yarns.

Common fibers used in home furnishings are outlined below. In the first paragraph the positive and the negative aspects of the fiber are listed; in the second paragraph the negative aspects of the fiber are noted; in the third paragraph the suggested uses for the fiber are recommended; the fourth paragraph outlines the way to care and maintain the fiber.

Acetate	A cellulose fiber. Originally classified as a rayon fiber. May be spun or crimped, many different ways for different appearances. Has a lustrous appearance, drapes well, and has a soft hand. Acetate is poor on sagging and stretching if loosely woven, but is better if tightly woven. Fair to good sun resistance, fair to good abrasion resistance, resists mildew and moths, good resilience and fair wrinkle resistance. Acetate is an inexpensive fiber; will take dyes easily, is colorfast if solution dyed, blends well with other fibers, and is not affected by static electricity. Moderately low cost.
Negative features	Weakened by abrasion, weakened by sunlight, will melt and dissolve when exposed to heat or various chemicals. Colors fade from atmospheric fumes.

Positive features	Silky appearance, drapes well, and is mildew resistant.
Preferred use	Favored use is for lined drapery, especially when combined with other fibers resistant to abrasion and sunlight.
Care and cleaning	Dry-clean and press with low-temperature iron.

Acrylic

A synthetic fiber. Made up of a combination of carbon, hydrogen, and nitrogen. Acrylic is lightweight, warm, soft, fuzzy, bulky, and is a staple fiber. May be spun in a variety of ways. Usually blended with fur, cotton, wool, acetate, or nylon. Acrylic resists abrasion, is moth and mildew resistant, resists wrinkling and fading, is strong, has a soft hand, and excellent draping ability. Acrylic fabrics will sag and stretch, are extremely resilient, wrinkle resistant, and creases may be heat-set in. Not affected by sunlight, smoke, fading, and is shrink resistant. Has excellent color fastness if solution dyed, easy to maintain, not easily soiled, and is flameproof. Moderately expensive.

Negative features	Pills up from abrasion. Static electricity problems. Pile fabrics will require special maintenance.
Positive features	Wool-looking appearance, moth, mildew and sunlight resistant. Excellent color fastness, strong, and durable.
Preferred use	Favored uses are for drapery and curtains. If using for upholstery fabric, use a fiber blend of nylon or polyester to help fabric retain its shape.
Care and cleaning	Dry-clean acrylic fabrics. Some fabrics may be handwashed or washed on the gentle cycle of the washer if labeled washable. Iron at a low temperature. Fabric softener will cut down the static electricity problems.

Cotton

A natural fiber. Grows from the seed of the cotton plant. Cotton is a seed-hair fiber. Twisting of the fibers together creates the yarn. Low-cost fiber, most versatile of all the fibers, absorbent, dull-luster, strong, durable, excellent draping ability, and has a soft hand. Comfortable fabrics, abrasion resistent, good sun resistance, will not stretch, unless wet. Cotton when stretched has low resiliency, is not affected by static electricity, takes dyes easily, and has good color fastness. Cotton fabrics feel cool to the touch and are easy to maintain. Low cost.

Negative features	Shrinks and wrinkles easily if not treated for resistance. Sunlight will weaken over a long period of time, will mildew, poor resilience, will burn and yellow.
Positive features	Very versatile for all interior fabric applications. Drapery or any other furnishing item in the sun's path should be lined or protected by tinted windows, transparent shades, or other undertreatments. Usually a long-wearing fabric for drapery. Blending with other fibers enhances the good qualities of cotton. Strong, insulative, dyes easily.
Care and cleaning	To retain crisp finishes and good fit, dry-clean cotton fabrics. May be washed if the fabric is labeled washable. Press with iron on medium to high heat.

Glass

A silicate fiber. Nonabsorbent, resists sun damage, moth and mildew resistant. Glass fibers will not shrink or wrinkle, will not stretch, has poor resilience, elasticity, not affected by static electricity, and is naturally flameproof. Moderately, expensive.

Negative features

Fibers will break and shred from the very least amount of abrasion. May wrinkle and shrink if not finished to resist. Excessive sunlight will weaken the fiber. Cannot be used where the fabric will be handled or the furniture will rub up against. The glass fibers may scratch or may become airborne.

Positive features

Glass fibers are strong fibers. Sunlight resistent, resists staining, good insulative abilities, flameproof.

Preferred use

Use for drapery only. Drapery should be lined.

Care and cleaning

May be handwashed, gently (wear gloves). Do not twist, wring, or fold up. Hang back up while still wet. Do not press with an iron or have dry-cleaned.

Linen or Flax

Natural fiber. Derived from a cotton-like plant. Twice as strong as cotton. Absorbent, slightly lustrous surface, strong and durable, good draping ability with a medium hand, poor sagging resistance, can lose shape easily, lacks elasticity, takes dyes easily, good to poor color fastness (prints will not hold their color as well as solids). Excellent sun resistance, poor resilience, feels cool to the touch, easy to maintain. Spots are easier to remove than from cotton fabrics. Expensive.

Negative features

Easily wrinkled, creased or shrunk if not treated to resist. Quality may vary. May mildew and has poor abrasion resistance. May grow or shrink in length in humid climates. Linen is stiff, fibers may crack in creases or folds. Colors may fade from prolonged exposure to sunlight. Bright or deep colors may run if washed; expensive.

Positive features

Strong and durable fiber with attractive surface sheen and texture. Will hold up to sunlight. Strength varies with the weave of the fabric. Linens are considered excellent for drapery if in a plain color, and good for drapery if a printed fabric.

Care and cleaning

Dry-cleaning is preferred. May be handwashed gently or on the gentle cycle of the washer, if labeled. Press on both sides with a high-temperature iron, while still damp, to regain luster. Over starching of the fabric will cause the fibers to break.

Modacrylic

Synthetic fiber. Nonabsorbent, resilient, and wrinkle resistant. Not affected by sunlight, moth and mildew resistant, will take dyes easily, easy to maintain, and is flameproof. Moderately expensive.

Negative features

Not very abrasion resistant or very durable. Will melt at a low temperature. Static electricity problems. Fur-looking fabrics require special maintenance and care.

Positive features

Wrinkle resistance and resilience, not affected by sunlight, moth and mildew resistant, dyes easily, and is flameproof.

Preferred use

Favored use is for drapery and curtains.

Care and cleaning

Dry-clean. May be handwashed gently or on the gentle cycle of the washer if labeled washable. Let drip dry, press with a cool iron. Fur fabrics should be dry cleaned only.

Nylon

A synthetic fiber. Nonabsorbent, strong and durable, excellent abrasion resistant, moth and mildew resistant. Nylon has good draping ability, soft to stiff hand, and will not sag. Resists wrinkling, has good recovery and resilience, easy to maintain, takes dyes easily, good colorfastness. Moderate cost.

Negative features

Static electricity problems. Will pill from abrasion, poor sunlight resistance, will fade and weaken, melts under high heat.

Positive features

Fairly versatile interior furnishing fabric. Drapery should be lined if the drapery has a color to it, other than off-white. Preferably used in combination with other fibers that are absorbent to help eliminate static electricity. Good resilience and elasticity, a strong and durable fiber.

Care and cleaning

Dry-clean. May be handwashed gently or on the gentle cycle of the washer, separately (nylon will easily pick up another color) if labeled. Dry on low heat. Remove from dryer immediately, to avoid wrinkles. May be pressed with an iron at a low temperature. Fabric softener will help eliminate static electricity problems.

Olefin

A synthetic fiber. Nonabsorbent, strong and durable, abrasion resistant, moth and mildew resistant, resists stains and spills, wrinkle resistant. Moderate cost.

Negative features

Olefin has a low melting point. Static electricity problems. Poor appearance, preferred use is combined with other fibers.

Positive features

Best use is combined with other synthetic fibers for upholstery or outdoor furniture uses. Lightweight fiber, good insulator, strong and durable, resists stains and spills, wrinkle resistant, abrasion resistant, inflammable.

Care and cleaning

Dry-clean. May be handwashed gently or on the gentle cycle of the washer if labeled washable. Remove from dryer immediately to avoid wrinkles. May be pressed with a warm iron. Fabric softener will help eliminate static electricity problems.

Polyester

A synthetic fiber. A chemical process where long chains of hydrogen, oxygen, and carbon are combined to create polyester. Versatile, nonabsorbent, durable and strong, sun resistant, abrasion resistant, wrinkle resistant, moth and mildew resistant, excellent draping ability and soft hand, good resilience, will hold its shape, will not sag, stretch or shrink, can be pleated or creased permanently, sunlight and heat resistant. Not affected by moisture, acid, or alkalis. Polyester is non-allergenic, easy to care for, takes dyes moderately well, with good color fastness. When combined with natural fibers, adds positive properties to the natural fiber. Moderate cost.

Negative features

Static electricity problems. Does not dye easily. Will deteriorate over time from repeated sun exposure.

Positive features

Very versatile, excellent fiber for fabric interior furnishings. For slipcovers or upholstery uses, select a fabric with a blend of other synthetic fibers for absorbency. Polyester sheer fabric may bruise easily. Strong and durable, resists wrinkling, and is moth and mildew resistant. Polyester fiber makes stable fabrics and is also a fiber that blends well with other fibers.

Care and cleaning

Dry-clean. May be handwashed gently or separately on the gentle cycle of the washer (polyester will easily pick up another color) if labeled washable. Dry on low heat. Remove from dryer immediately to avoid wrinkles. May be pressed with a low-temperature iron. Fabric softener will help eliminate static electricity problems.

Rayon

A cellulose fiber. The first manufactured fiber. Rayon fiber is partially synthetic and partially a manufactured fiber. May be spun or extruded many different ways to create many appearances, plain or novelty. Absorbent. Fairly good sunlight resistance, lustrous surface effect, excellent draping ability, and has a soft hand. Rayon is poor on sagging and stretching, if loosely woven, but better in tighter weaves. Good resilience and elasticity, will not knife edge or crease, resistant to shrinkage, moth resistant, sheds dirt, good abrasion resistance, resistant to pilling and picks, fairly durable, static resistant, and is non-allergenic. Rayon fabrics feel cool to the touch, take dyes well, and have good color fastness if solution dyed. Finishes may be applied to stabilize, resist spots, stains, and shrinkage. Low cost.

Negative features

Easily sun damaged and weakened, will mildew, and will wrinkle. Once rayon is wrinkled, the wrinkles are hard to remove. Unless finished, rayon will shrink and stretch.

Positive features

Low cost, drapes and hangs well, versatile, dyes easily, easily blends with other fibers, inflammable.

Preferred use

Favored use is for drapery. Drapery should be lined if placed in direct sunlight. If used for slipcovers or upholstery applications, select a fabric that has a blend of other synthetic fibers (cotton, acetate, or linen) with stronger durability.

Care and cleaning

Dry-clean only. May be pressed with a medium-hot iron.

Silk

A natural fiber. Absorbent, good draping ability, will not sag, medium to soft hand, good resilience, durable and strong, wrinkle resistant, mildew resistant, poor sun resistance, cool to the touch, takes dyes well, good color fastness, wrinkle resistant. Expensive cost.

Negative features

Fades easily from the sun or interior lighting. Will rot and fall apart if exposed to excessive sunlight, easily damaged by abrasion, will water spot. An expensive fiber.

Positive features

Has lustrous appearance, dyes in beautiful colors, good draping ability, strong and durable, absorbent, good resilience and elasticity, mildew resistant, will not burn easily.

Preferred use

Favored use is for drapery. Drapery should be lined. Not recommended for any application where durability or heavy use is anticipated. Because of the expense of this fabric, coupled with poor sun resistance, silk is not readily available in a large range of fabrics.

Care and cleaning

Dry-clean only. Press with a medium-temperature iron.

Wool

A natural fiber. Absorbent, good recovery, durable, wrinkle resistant, sunlight resistant, abrasion resistant if tightly woven, takes dyes well, crease resistant. Expensive.

Negative features

Shrinks easily, poor abrasion resistance and strength unless tightly woven, not moth or mildew resistant. Wool has a scratchy hand, static electricity problems, is weakened by sunlight, and is expensive.

Positive features

Strong and durable, insulates well, dyes easily, good draping ability, mildew resistant.

Preferred use   Only real use is for upholstery.

Care and   Dry-clean only. Press with a warm iron and steam.
cleaning

Man-made or Synthetic Fibers

Manufactured or synthetic fibers *were and are* formulated to improve natural fibers' limitations. Natural fibers are very expensive and sometimes hard to get. When natural fibers are hard to get, manufactured fibers fill the requirements.

- **Performance of the manufactured fibers will vary with the weave.**

- **Synthetic fibers, except nylon, will resist damage from the sun.** This is an important point to consider for homes in very sunny climates.

- **If the home is located in an area of high humidity, select fibers that are less absorbent and more stable,** such as synthetic fibers — fiberglass, acrylic, or polyester.

- **The easiest care interior fabrics are composed of polyester, polyester-cotton blends, and glass.**

Combining Man-made Fibers with Natural Fibers

By combining the better properties of one fiber with the better properties of another fiber, we end up with far superior fabrics than we would if we used 100% of one fiber or 100% of the other fiber. Fabric resulting from combining various fibers usually results in fabrics that have a better hand.

Economically, natural fibers are more expensive than manufactured fibers. Combining natural fibers with manufactured or synthetic fibers gives the fabric the desirable properties of the manufactured fibers, while reducing the overall cost.

Below are the characteristics that are achieved when natural fibers are combined with manufactured or synthetic fibers:

- **Less cost.**

- **A considerably better-performing fabric.**

- **The resulting fabric will have a better hand.**

- **Improved spinning or weaving process, resulting in yarn uniformity in finished fabrics.**

- **Has the ability to have a natural-woven effect.**

- **Cross-dyeing effects may be achieved by combining fibers which will take dyes differently.**

- **When combining** natural fibers with man-made or synthetic fibers, **the disadvantages of a fiber are minimized or eliminated.**

Weaves

Warp and weft yarns:
- Warp yarns are the yarns or threads which run vertically or lengthwise in woven fabric.

- The horizontal yarns or threads running across the width or across the grain are called weft threads or yarns.

Weave points:

- The sturdiest, longest-lasting weave is the closely woven plain weave.

- The least durable weaves are the satin and twill weaves.

Dye Processes

There are **two color substances: dyes and pigments.**

Dyes are substances which are **soluble** — they penetrate the fiber and are fixed (colorfast) with chemicals, heat, etc.

Pigments are color particles which are **insoluble** and held mechanically on the fabric surface by binding agents such as resins.

- Dyes will vary in their life expectancy, depending on the dye method used.

- Dyes improve a fabric's looks.

- Piece-dyeing is the process of dying woven fabrics (grey goods) by putting the fabric through a dye bath.

- Solution-dyeing is the method used to dye manufactured or synthetic fibers, while still in the spinning process. This dye process happens before the fibers are formed. This is the most permanent dye process available.

- Cross-dyeing color effects are achieved by combining different fibers together and the way they individually take the dye. These are extremely resistant to washing and to sun fading.

- The yarn-dyed process is when the yarn (group of fibers twisted together) is dyed, rather than dyeing each individual fiber, before being woven in to the finished fabric.

- Ombre is a shaded, graduated in color effect, usually used in striped patterns. The color will range from light to dark within the color area.

Dyelots

Dyelots will vary from dye batch to the next dye batch. Manufacturers do try to keep consistency in their dyelots. And they do a very close job of it, generally. If an exact dyelot is necessary, always call the fabric vendor and send for a cutting of the particular fabric in question. Another solution is to note in writing on the purchase order, that you are having several items fabricated with several purchase orders of the same fabric, and need the same dyelot. Request this by writing, *"cross match with P.O. 13456 and P.O. 45679."*

Sending a swatch of the fabric to be matched-up to is another alternative when you must have a matching dyelot.

Fading of Fabrics

All dyes available today are capable of fading from sunlight. Colors may fade by oxidation, or *"gas fading."* Impurities in the air may also cause as much fading as the direct rays of the sun. If the fabric is stored unaired for a long period of time, the fabric will also fade. Some colors will fade more than other colors.

Make sure that interior fabrics are protected from the sun. Tint windows, use transparent shades, line drapery, or use exterior awnings, trees, or shrubs to protect interior fabrics.

Maintain fabrics by vacuuming them regularly; professionally clean; or tumble them in the dryer on the air cycle. Drapery and window treatments made of fabric regularly need to have dust and impurities that have settled on them removed to reduce the fading from oxidation.

Fabric Printing

Fabric printing is the process of applying designs to fabrics. These designs may be one color or many colors. There are several processes used to achieve this. These are roller printing, block printing, and screen printing.

Additionally, there are also different color processes. These are direct printing, discharge printing, and resist printing.

Today the bulk of fabrics fall into the screen printing process. The fabric background is first vat-dyed and preshrunk, before going through the various screens to impart the design to the fabric. Each color used requires the engraving of an additional roller. This is the most efficient and economical method we have in use today.

Stain-Resistant Finishes

There are many competing applications available on the market that are applied to various fabrics to help aid in soil, stain, and spotting resistance. All of them appear to help, and *any* of these applications on a fabric are going to be better than the fabric without any stain-resistant finish applied at all.

Stain-resistant finishes work by causing fabrics to shed fluids and resist oily, greasy stains. Most of the offending stains can be wiped away. Any fabric with a stain-resistant finish needs to have the spot or stain immediately attended to or the finish will fail.

Fabric Finishes

The finishes that are applied to a fabric are as important as the fiber content and the fabric construction of the fabric. Fabric finishes improve fabric performance and looks. Some of the highest-quality greige goods may have the quality cheapened by having short-cut finishes applied. Nothing will enhance or improve a fabric more than the correct application and selection of finishes.

Some of the finishes produced by mechanical means are brushing, embossing, napping, calendaring, and shearing. These are used to give texture to the fabrics. We also apply chemical finishes to fabrics. The following are the reasons fabrics have finishes applied to them:

- **Fabric durability** is improved.

- A fabric's **draping ability is improved.**

- **Fabric shrinkage is controlled.**

- **Body** is added to fabric.

- **Fabrics may be softened.**

- **Fabrics may be stiffened.**

- **Creasing of fabric will be broadly cut down.**

- **Permanent creases may be added** to fabrics.

- **Permanent press, wash and wear features may be added** to a fabric.

- The fabric's **luster may be increased.**

- The fabric's **luster may be decreased.**

- **Pilling** for some fibers **may be reduced.**

- **Colorfastness may be increased.**

- **Water repellency may be added.**

- **Oil repellency may be added.**

- **Aids in stain and spotting resistance may be added** (all spots and stains still need immediate attention).

- **Added flame resistance.**

- **Added anti-static abilities.**

- **Added germicidal properties.**

Glazing

Glazing is an applied finish for fabric to add sheen and shine usually to cottons and cotton-blend fabrics. The results are polished cotton or chintz-type fabrics. Unfortunately, this type of fabric is limited in its life span if washed. The finishes will wash off. Dry-clean glaze finished, polished cottons or chintz types of fabric.

Glazing gives a fabric elegance and also makes the fabric's pattern and design, more distinct, making the colors sharper and clearer.

Flameproofing

When decorating a home, flameproofed fabrics are necessary when placed on windows near a range, stove, heater, or fireplace. Glass fibers, polyesters, acrylics, and modacrylics are naturally flame resistant. Other fibers such as cottons, linens, rayons, and acetate will easily burn.

On commercial installations, flameproofed fabrics are a necessity. Some fabrics need state and local certification for installation, verifying that they are flameproofed. Arrange to have the fabric flameproofed from your fabric vendor or arrange to have the fabric flameproofed locally. Check your yellow pages under cloth finishing. If not available in your area, check the larger nearby metropolitan areas.

Be sure the selected method of flameproofing will meet the requirements of the state certificate of flameproofing, before proceeding.

Some commercial fabrics are available already flameproofed. The fibers of the fabric are flameproofed during the manufacturing process, before being woven into fabric. This is known as inherent flame-frees. This method makes the fabric flame-free for life of the fabric.

The applied or processed methods of flameproofing are available in three types: inherent, applied, and renewable.

The inherent method of flameproofing: the fiber is flameproofed during the manufacturing process and then woven into yardage.

The applied method is implemented after the fabric is woven. This is achieved by dipping the fabric in the flameproofing solution. This applied method will usually last through 18 to 20 **dry cleanings.** This process may be applied to about 90% of all fabrics. The fabric exceptions would be the fabrics which have had stain or water-repellant finishes applied.

The renewable, applied flameproofing will not be retained when the fabric is dry-cleaned or washed. This type of flameproofing must be reapplied after each cleaning.

Velvet and napped fabrics are not recommended for flame proofing.

Fabric Testing

Fabrics are tested **to determine their efficiency of performance, show weaknesses and flaws, and to determine the finished quality.** Most mills will **determine the thread count per square inch in warp and fill (weft). They will also determine the fiber content or composition. Fabric mills test the fabrics physically, chemically, and optically.**

Physical testing tests the twist, strength, size and quality of the yarns. The fabric's woven strength, weight, and shrinkage will determine the overall grade and quality of the fabric.

Chemical testing determines fiber content, colorfastness and any special finishes needed to be applied. Defective fabric and the cause of the defect will be partially determined here.

Optical testing confirms fiber content and cause of the defect of defective fabric.

All three methods of fabric testing determine the following:

Breaking strength	How much pressure will be needed before the fibers will break.
Elasticity	Tension is applied, the fabric is stretched, and the amount of recovery is determined when the tension is released.
Flexibility	How pliable is the fabric without reaching the breaking point? Is the fabric able to maintain a certain position? This test becomes necessary for fabrics that may be permanently creased or pleated.
Resilience	Amount of recovery the fabric has when crushed or wrinkled up.
Abrasive resistance	How much wear and abuse will the fibers take before obviously breaking down.
Fabric stability	The fabric will be resistant with sufficient elasticity to bounce back, after hanging or cleaning. Is the fabric consistent in design and able to maintain proper width during weaving and other processes. This is measured with the use of chemical and mechanical resistance.
Resistance to light	How much light does it take to fade the fabric?
Seam slippage	Will the seams slip during sewing and how easy is the fabric to cut?
Absorption	How much water will the fabric absorb.

Buyers of greige goods will consider all these areas before purchasing fabrics.

Carefully scrutinize fabrics before selecting them to be carried in your line. What you choose to carry in your line says that you in essence are saying, *"This is a great fabric and we will be liable for any problems that come up."*

If a fabric starts to have problems show up, immediately remove that fabric from your line and substitute with another fabric.

Fabrication Materials

The following are materials used in the workroom to add body and shape to drapery, top treatments, and other accessories made of fabric. Some are used to add sunproofing, lightproofing, and warmth.

Buckram	Coarse, almost rigid woven fabric stiffened with heavy sizing. Made of white cotton or brown jute, available in various weights. Used in drapery or curtain headings, as well as in tiebacks.

Crinoline Lighter-weight, finer-textured version of buckram. Usually made of cotton or cotton blends. Comes in white only. Used in drapery, curtain headers, or tiebacks.

Flannelette Soft, napped, medium-weight fabric used for interlining in light to medium drapery for added warmth, body, and shape. Usually made of cotton or a cotton blend.

Non-woven stiffeners Matted, synthetic fabrics similar to felt, neutral colors, in many weights. Used to shape and add body to top treatments and accessories.

Seamless Fabrics or Railroaded Goods

Railroaded goods are wide-width, imported European seamless goods from 115" to 118" wide. *Railroaded goods are turned on their side, or in the opposite direction from 48" goods.* The width becomes the length. A sheer or drapery out of this 118" fabric can be made continuously as wide as needed, without a seam. Unless you make the sheer or drapery into a pair, there will not be any seams or overlaps in the middle of the drapery. Seamless fabrics are usually sheer fabrics and loosely woven fabrics.

Points to remember:

- **The use of seamless goods will generally result in lower costs than the use of 48" wide goods.**

- **You cannot exceed a finished length for a drapery of 100". The extra 18" is used for the hem and headers.**

- **There are no seams across the width of the draperies.**

- **118" goods are easier to fabricate in the workroom**, as the workroom only sews the edges, hems, and headers. Since the type of fabric that 118" goods usually comes in are normally very slippery and hard to work with, **you eliminate puckered seams.** Consequently, the draperies hang nicer, due to lack of seams and puckering.

- **Unless you make overlaps for opening the drapery in the center, you will have a continuous, uninterrupted, seamless drapery.**

- **There is never a *possibility* of seam breakage with seamless goods.**

Sheers

Make sheers into one-way pull panels:

Try to avoid making sheers into pairs. When sheers are made into pairs, you will have four layers of fabric laying over each other. If the drapery fabric is especially sheer, the overlapped area becomes very noticeable, and will stand out visually. **Make drapery or sheers a one-way pull for a consistent, continuous look.**

Some customers insist on being able to look through to the outside from the middle of the drapery or sheer. You may end up changing a few one-way pulls to pairs, if you do not check with the customer and find out if a finer looking drapery is preferable, or is the ability to look out from the middle of the drapery favored.

If the customer is more concerned about the drapery's looks and hanging ability, they will opt for the one-way pull. After a few years of hanging, and being drawn open and closed, sheers that are pairs tend to separate. The sheer's leading edges will not fall completely straight any longer; the closer the leading edges get to the hem, the farther they *"snake back."*

Sheers need to lay-over the hanger for a few weeks:

Always let sheers lay-over the hanger for two weeks after they are made, if possible. Sheers need the weight of the fabric, folded onto itself, to set the pleats and make the folds uniform. If it is a rush job, explain ahead of time to the customer that sheers will not hang quite as uniformly, since they will not be allowed much time to hang-out over the hanger.

Bunch or fold sheer fabrics up:
Bunch up or fold sheer fabric, several times, to get a true perspective on the color. If you forget to do this, you may get a call from your customer saying these sheers are not peach, they are pink. The pleating and the folds laying on top of each other, give you a completely different view of the color. The color of the sheer is the color the sunlight coming in is going to change to when filtering through the fabric into the room. Always beware of the color name. If it says apricot-haze but looks off-white, it is sure to appear apricot when folded up and fabricated.

Sheers or Drapery that Hang Badly

Some of the seamless sheer fabrics that are available are stiffer and do not hang as nicely after they are fabricated. You will not always be able to determine how each fabric is going to cooperate ahead of time, from a small swatch.

If you receive complaints that the sheers or drapery are not falling in nice folds, first **determine if the drapery or sheers have a double-folded hem, and weights at regular intervals.** The hem may be reworked and lined for weight, and weights may be inserted at regular intervals.

Notice if the grain of the fabric is even horizontally and vertically. Has the leading edge been stretched? If the answer to these two questions is yes, the drapery will have to be remade.

Depending on the fabric and the reason the drapery are hanging poorly, **your installer may be able to correct the hang problem by the use of steam or sizing.**

If all else fails, **have memory-stitch tape or bead-chain inserted at the hem to help correct the hang problems.**

Length Fluctuations in Fabrics

Most fabrics will fluctuate in their length stability. Fabrics breathe and absorb moisture and humidity. Therefore, fabrics shrink up and get shorter, stretch and get longer, depending on the moisture and humidity levels in the air. The normal variance is about 2 — 2½ percent of the finished length of a drapery.

- **Tightly woven fabrics will hold their shape much better than an open-weave or loosely woven fabric.**

- Instruct your customers to have tolerance of small fluctuations in lengths of draperies. **No fabric is completely stable.** A completely stable fabric is a very dull fabric with no interesting texture to it.

- **Fabrics breathe and absorb moisture and, therefore, will shrink and stretch as the weather changes.** A 3 percent change in a length of 108" (or 3") is normal, depending on the fabric used.

- **Double-hemming at the hem of a drapery will help minimize length fluctuations by providing weight for the drapery.**

Discussion to Have with Your Customer About Casement Fabrics

If your customer selects a casement type of fabric that does not have a lockstitch design incorporated into it, to keep the fabric stable you need to remind your customer of the following:

Resin finishes have not been applied to this fabric to help stabilize the fabric. If the manufacturer had done so, the weave would have a flattened, rough texture and the dyes and color of the fabric would be diffused. Since this finish has not been applied, **this fabric will probably fluctuate in length**, depending on the weather and the humidity levels. As the humidity increases, the drapery will get longer, possibly even resting on the floor; as the humidity decreases, the drapery will probably get several inches shorter. This will happen throughout the lifetime of the drapery.

This is not a defect of the fabric, but an inherent characteristic of this type of fabric. The workrooms work to minimize the problem, but are unable to completely eliminate the problem of length fluctuations. If you feel this will really bother you, then I suggest you reselect to a more stable fabric that will be more resistant to fluctuating in length.

Insulate Against the Elements by Using Fabrics at the Windows

Airspace between the glass of the window and the window treatment will provide some insulation and sound absorption, due to the dead air trapped between the two layers. The air is prevented from circulating. **The more layers of window coverings, and the more effectively you select the window treatments, the better the insulation can be.**

Some treatments will trap more air between the layers then will other treatments. If you select a fuller drapery that projects from the wall 3½", you have more air space than an I.B. mounted miniblind.

- **Lined drapery are more insulative** than unlined drapery.

- **Natural fibers in cold climates will bulk up and prevent heat loss** at the windows, due to their bulking up.

- **Tightly woven, opaque fabrics** that are light in color will reflect the sun's rays.

Matching Patterned Fabrics

Patterned fabrics usually have a straight across horizontal match, rather than a drop match. In other words, the print pattern will match up at the selvages, if lined up correctly. A drop match is when the repeats are staggered at the selvages and you have to drop the fabric half a repeat to match the pattern up. Some fabrics are drop matched to make the design on the fabric appear larger. Drop matched patterns are found usually on narrower width fabrics.

Categorizing Fabrics

Fabrics fall in categories depending on the weight of the fabric;

Very thin fabrics:	*Primarily used for sheers, sheer-type window treatments, and some fabrics for linings and trimmings (banding, ruffles).*

Batiste

Sheer fabric consisting of 100% polyester or polyester blended with rayon or cotton. Batiste has fine-quality construction with a soft hand and a high count of yarns used.

Batiste is more opaque than voiles or ninon and has a cloudy appearance that allows some light to filter through. This fabric is recognizable by the readily, apparent lengthwise streaks. To see the true color, hold several thicknesses together. When selecting the color, it is better to go one shade lighter, rather than one shade darker.

Batiste will provide more privacy than a more translucent voile sheer. At night with the light on, you would still be able to see through the fabric from the outside.

Marquisette

This is a thin, sheer, transparent, fine fabric with a leno weave. Composed of polyester, glass fibers, nylon, rayon, acetate, acrylic, silk, cotton or blends, and combinations of these fibers.

Ninon

A very sheer, voile, transparent, smooth, fine fabric used for sheers. Woven in a plain weave, open mesh with a smooth surface. Ninon has a crisp hand. Usually of 100% polyester. May also be made of rayon, acetate, nylon, or other synthetic fibers. Silk used to be used for ninon.

Organdy Fabric which is thin, stiff, crisp, and airy. Organdy is an almost transparent cotton, sheer fabric, closely woven of fine yarns in a plain weave. Finishes for this crisp, starched hand will not wash off.

Voile This fabric is a thinner, sheer, mesh fabric made by using highly twisted yarns and a variation of the plain weave. Voile is soft, lightweight, similar to ninon, but with a crisp, drapable hand due to the tightly-twisted, fine denier yarns. Generally 100% polyester.

Lightweight fabrics: ***Used for drapery and window treatments, lighter-weight upholstery, and accessories.***

Antique satin The antique satin family is a broad one, covering satins woven with slubby surfaces and textures also. Very particular customers are hard to please with the use of slubbed, textured fabrics. They will not hang smoothly and appear very puckered. The use of steam usually worsens the situation. Pressing stretches the fabric; if you are a company that cares about your reputation and customer goodwill, you end up remaking the drapery to a smoother fabric.

Sharp pleats cannot be achieved with this fabric. If you can get antique satin fabrics to fall fairly nicely, it will hang in rounded folds which tend to billow out.

Beware of using antique satins with slubs, particularly if the draperies are to be replacement draperies. This is especially true where the original draperies are hanging on the windows and you can see they are very nice-hanging draperies, although ready to be changed. The customer, who may not be a drapery expert, has looked at those draperies for years and will see the difference in the sharpness of the new drapery's pleats, and in the way the new drapery fall and hang in general.

Review the *Satin* section above; antique satin fabrics are composed of the same fibers. Antique satins are actually a spin-off of the satin family.

Broadcloth A plain weave fabric, plain or printed with the fill threads of a finer denier and quality (combed Pima cotton, usually) than the warp threads. Usually of cotton or cotton blends.

Challis Very soft, lightweight fabric which has a beautiful, soft hand. Challis is usually woven of a twill or plain weave. This type of fabric is usually quality printed in patterns of beautiful colors. Challis is usually rayon, wool, or cotton and rayon blends.

Chintz Polished cotton or chintz fabric that has been glazed with a resin finish. Chintz will wrinkle easily, so is a poor choice for treatments that need to be functional.

Many choices of finishes may be applied to achieve the highly polished sheen. If wax glaze or starched finishes are used, they will wash out. The durable finish is resin and will not wash off. Recommended cleaning method is dry cleaning, to retain most of the applications applied for the shiny-surface finish. Steam will mark the finish, if used. Usually made of 100% cotton.

Faille This fabric is known for its horizontal-flat ribs, soft hand, and good draping qualities. Faille has heavier fill than warp yarns, which gives it the ribbed effect. May be 100% silk, rayon, acetate. Should not be subjected to heavy use.

Gingham A light to medium-weight checked, plaid, or striped patterned fabric. Woven in a plain weave. Usually, made of cotton, cotton and rayon, or cotton and polyester.

Homespun A course, loosely woven fabric, that is woven with a rough texture that resembles hand-woven fabrics. Homespun is made up in a plain weave but is made of uneven yarns, with small slubs of other yarn colors, woven in. Medium in weight, homespun may be cotton, wool, rayon, or blends of these fibers. Also called crash, hopsacking, or monk's cloth.

Linen

Flax or linen is a product of the flax plant. Linen has a stiff hand, will not soil rapidly, has a natural sheen, and is smooth in surface texture. Linen fabrics have poor resistance to wrinkling. May have finishes to help resist the wrinkling problems. Commonly combined with rayon and cotton when used in casement fabrics or textures.

Moire

A fabric that is also referred to as wood-looking or water-marked-looking fabric. Moire fabric is at its best tied back when used as drapery. If the customer is not extremely particular, the drapery will be reasonably nice and free hanging. Sharp pleat for drapery cannot be achieved with this type of fabric. The drapery will fall in soft, billowy folds when made into drapery. This fabric is very elegant, sophisticated, and *"top drawer."* There are variations and spin-offs of the traditional moire patterns, available in a range of styles. Beautiful colors are available in this type of fabric.

Moire is actually a finish that is used on silk, acetate, rayon, cotton, nylon, or cotton and acetate blends. This finish is applied by passing the fabric between rollers, engraved with the moire pattern, that heat press the pattern into the fabric. When light shines through the fabric from behind, the moire design has a tendency to disappear.

When subjected to heat and moisture, as in bathrooms, moire fabric is not a very stable fabric. This fabric should be used in a treatment where unevenness will not be readily noticeable, as in a balloon and Austrian shades or valances, or in stationary panels, tied back.

Moire fabric has the tendency to pucker at the seams, and for the lining to slightly show at the bottom of the drapery (compensate for this tendency by making the lining shorter). Moire fabrics should not be subjected to heavy use.

Muslin

Any plain weave cotton fabric ranging in weight from very sheer to very heavy may be termed muslin. Usually 100% cotton fabric, but may be blended with rayon or polyester. Comes in a variety of grades. The better grades have little sizing added.

Silk

An expensive, natural fiber made from the fibers of silkworms. Silk fabric is available in many weights. Silk fabric may be raw silk, which is silk wound directly from several cocoons, with only a slight twist added. Silks made from lightly twisted yarns are less shiny and lustrous than fabrics made of tightly twisted yarns. Silk has a luxurious appearance with a natural, deep luster to it. Silk may be dyed to beautiful colors, but will fade from sun or light shining on the fabric.

Sateen

These fabrics have a smooth, sleek, shiny face, while the back of the fabric is dull. The sateen weave is used for the weaving pattern — floating, fill yarns over warp yarns, creating a lustrous finish. Made to imitate satin fabrics. The original satin fabrics were made of silk. Because of cost, today the fabric is made of cotton, rayon, or acetate. Used for linings and decorative uses.

Satin family

Satin is a lustrous fabric woven with floating yarns. The satin family has many variations in fabrics and weights, from soft to stiff. Basic solid, antique satin comes in 100+ colors. The selection of these colors is generally based on the colors in fashion at any given time. This fabric is a good, inexpensive, basic fabric with a multitude of uses. Sharp pleats can be achieved with this fabric. One of the most common fabrics. This whole family is known for its luxury looks and the fiber content almost always consists of two-thirds rayon and one-third acetate. The rayon gives the fabric its luster and a wide color range. Acetate is used to add strength and durability. Should not be subjected to heavy use. The satin family of fabrics have sunlight-resistant backings. To protect and last from the sunlight's harmful rays, line these fabrics.

Shantung

A plain-weave fabric that is woven with slubby textured fill yarns. This fabric has a slightly lower luster than basic satin. Usually composed of polyester, rayon, cotton, or combinations of these fibers. Should not be subjected to heavy use.

Taffeta

This is a fine, plain-woven fabric which is smooth on both sides, usually with a sheen on its surface. Taffeta may be printed, plain, striped, checked, plaid, or woven with uneven yarns. Taffeta comes in various weights, and is known for its rustly hand and body. Should not be subjected to heavy use.

Medium-weight fabrics:

Used for medium-weight drapery and window treatments, upholstery, and accessories.

Brocade

Fabric with a rich, fairly heavy hand. Brocade fabric is made with a jacquard weave. A jacquard weave is an all-over, interwoven weave. Generally the fabric is woven in raised designs of flowers and figures, with contrasting colors and surface textures. The surface of this type of fabric is a prominent, raised effect rather than a flat surface with an embossed appearance. The background may be a satin weave, twill weave, or other combinations. Brocade consists of silk, rayon, and nylon yarns with or without the addition of gold or silver metallic yarns. Should not be subjected to heavy use.

Cretonne

Plain-weave, printed fabric with (usually) larger designs. This is an unglazed, cotton type of fabric. May be used for slipcovers and most other decorative uses.

Foam-backed fabric

A fabric which has been laminated or bonded to a backing of polyurethane foam by heat, pressure, or adhesives. Foam-backed drapery fabric is usually hard to find. This type of fabric does not look custom and hangs very heavy and awkwardly. Many customers who like to wash their own drapery and like the insulative qualities of an attached foam lining (one piece) will ask for this type of fabric.

Refer them to readymade at the local department store or switch them to a much higher quality, separately lined drapery with thermal-suede lining. These drapery will have to be dry-cleaned but will be a much finer end product for the customer.

Hopsacking

A loosely woven, coarse fabric, usually in a basket weave. Usually made of cotton, rayon, linen, or blends of these fibers. Also called monk's cloth, crash, or homespun.

Mohair

Fabric woven from Angora goat's hair. Known for its coarse hand, silky look, and lightweightness. Mohair gives fabrics a fluffy look.

Open-weaves or casements

Loosely woven fabrics, also referred to as casements. Known for its loosely woven designs and open areas.

Open-weave fabrics or casement fabrics have a reputation for shrinking or growing longer in length, depending on the humidity in the air. See the section on *Length Fluctuations in Drapery.* Today, some of the fabrics have been improved by the incorporation of the use of lock-stitch designs in their weaving. Real open-weaves are hard to find today. A fairly sharp pleat may be achieved, depending on the evenness of the other textures in the fabric and the openness of the design of the fabric.

Some fabrics may require a lining, which defeats the purpose of the open feeling casements or open weaves provide. A very bulky casement fabric mounted on a regular traverse rod is not a wise selection for a floor to ceiling treatment, since the pleats are bulky. With bulky pleats, there may not be enough clearance to traverse the drapery back and forth. To correct the problem, use a decorator rod and line the drapery. Lining will eliminate the need for the header to be doubled and the decorator rod will allow room for the pleats to fold back and forth.

Open-weave or casement fabric is generally more casual in its look and feel. The exceptions to a more formal look would be the casement fabrics made of shiny yarn, off-white or white.

Serge

An even twill-woven fabric with the diagonal wale showing on both sides of the fabric. Usually made of cotton or rayon, or a blend of the two.

Textures

Fabrics with all-over, plain-even textures or have designs woven in them similar to open-weave fabrics. These types of fabric are not loosely woven, nor do they have any open areas in the weave. Textures usually make very nice hanging drapery. Many of the newer textures combine a solid stripe with textured-patterned stripes. Usually made of cotton, rayon, acrylic, linen, and blends.

Heavy weight fabrics:

Used for some heavier drapery and window treatments, upholstery, and accessories.

Boucle

French term meaning "curled." This type of fabric has a knotted, looped, or curled surface texture. Boucle may be woven or knitted and may be made of synthetic or natural fibers. Should not be subjected to heavy use.

Brocatelle

Cross-ribbed, heavy drapery and upholstery fabric with jacquard figures and designs raised in high relief.

Canvas

Coarse, heavy cotton fabric, woven in a plain weave. Heavy weight duck is also called canvas.

Damask

Fabric which has jacquard-type (elaborate floral and geometric) patterns, a flatter surface to the fabric than brocade, and is generally reversible. Damask has a firm hand and a glossy look. This fabric is available in different weights with the heavier weights, generally used for drapery. This fabric is difficult to achieve a smooth hang or look. Damask should always be lined to improve the draping characteristics and to protect from the sun. When sunlight shines through damask, the woven pattern appears to wash out or to lighten up in color. Damask usually consists of linen, cotton, rayon, or silk, or a blend of these fibers. Should not be subjected to heavy use.

Denim

Heavier cotton fabric, woven of twill weave or plain weave. Denim is woven with colored warps and white fill threads. May be found in stripes and patterns.

Duck

A tightly woven, medium-to-heavy cotton fabric of plain or ribbed weave. Also called sailcloth. In its heavier weight, similar to canvas fabric.

Frieze

Fabric usually used for upholstery that has a hard hand to it. Frieze has a rough, raised texture.

Laminated fabric

Fabric lamination is the process of laminating fabric to paper or other material with heat, adhesives, or binding agents for wallcovering applications, upholstery, custom shades, or vertical louver vanes.

Matelasse

A woven fabric of the jacquard weave, with a double face to it. Matelasse has an unusual quilted, puffy-raised texture. Coarse yarns are interwoven into the fabric face making the surface very puffy. Used for upholstery.

Monk's cloth

Heavier cotton fabric that is woven in a basket weave, usually used for upholstery. Also called hopsacking, crash, or homespun.

Needlepoint   An upholstery fabric found usually on chair seats or in other accessories. Needlepoint is an embroidered design with yarn on needlepoint cloth or other coarse fabrics.

Pile fabrics   Fabrics with warp yarns covered with a surface of cut-pile yarns. Rows of cut pile give even, uniform surface to this type of fabric. The yarns on the surface of the fabric are made to stand up due to the use of mechanical finishing equipment. These types of fabrics are commonly found in suede cloths or simulated fur fabrics.

Plush or velour   Upholstery fabric with a very soft hand, that has a longer, cut-pile height than velvet, but is less densely woven, usually in a satin or plain weave.

Sailcloth   Sailcloth is a tightly woven, durable cotton fabric. Sailcloth is similar to canvas fabric. Also called duck.

Tapestry   Machine made tapestry is fabric with designs woven in with the jacquard weave of cotton, wool, or other fibers. The design is woven in with the use of colored-fill threads. The backside of the fabric is in stripes from the floating yarns. Tapestry historically was handwoven fabric with scenes incorporated into it.

Ticking   A tightly woven, heavy cotton fabric in striped patterns of white with another color. Usually a twill weave, but may be found in a sateen weave.

Tweed   Fabric that has a soft hand but a rough, masculine texture. Tweed fabric usually has flecks of other colors in it. Tweed areas may be found in stripes and plaids.

Velvet   A short-piled fabric with warp yarns covered with a surface of cut-pile yarns. Rows of cut pile give even, uniform surface to velvet fabrics. The weave is either of twill or plain weave. Velvets are rich appearing with a smooth surface and are more expensive. Velvets are heavier fabrics generally used in colder climates.

                       Velvet is manufactured by weaving two faces of the fabric together, and then shearing them apart to create two fabrics. Velvet's pile may be chemically dissolved in areas, to create designs on the fabric. Velvet may also be left with the loops uncut. The pile may also be pressed flat to make panne velvet, or the pile may be a combination of cut and uncut pile, to make patterns and designs. This is a napped fabric that requires that all cuts must be made in the same direction. Velvet is generally made of silk, rayon, or cotton. Should not be subjected to heavy use.

Velveteen   Similar to velvet but with a much shorter-pile surface. Velveteen has a more lustrous surface than velvet does. Velveteen is a napped fabric that requires that all cuts must be made in the same direction. Should not be subjected to heavy use.

Life Expectancy and Wearing Ability of Fabric Window Treatments

Life Expectancy

Life expectancy of window treatments depends on many factors. The following is a list of elements and conditions that affect interior fabrics and materials:

- **What fibers are used** in the interior fabric.

- Whether the window treatment is **lined versus unlined.**

- **How often the treatment is operated** — pulled open and closed, pulled up and down.

- **Whether the windows are tinted.**

- **What the exposure to the sun is:** north, south, east, west.

- How much smog the treatments or other materials are subjected to.

- **Exposure to nicotine.**

- **Average temperature inside and outside** of the home or building.

- **How often** the treatments are **maintained and cleaned.**

- **Heating source** in the room or building.

- Whether or not **a fireplace is used in the same area.**

- **Exposure to greasy cooking or moisture.**

- **How much abuse** the treatments are subjected to by children and pets.

Due to the many conditions the treatment *may or may not be subjected to,* it may be difficult to give your customer an accurate answer on how long the treatment or other interior material will last. Each of the above areas is covered thoroughly within this book. See the index for location of information.

Elements that Deteriorate Window Coverings

Unprotected window coverings have enemies both inside and outside the home that deteriorate them and shorten their life. These enemies include the sun with its ultraviolet light, oxidation, nicotine, humidity, and water damage.

The Sun and Its Effects on Window Coverings

The biggest enemy that window coverings have is the sun. The sun, if left unchecked, will rapidly deteriorate *most* window coverings. Drapery fabrics, especially, will be severely damaged if protective devices are not utilized. Any other fabrics in the sun's path, such as fabric on furniture, carpeting, and wood furniture will also suffer irreversible damage.

Some of the ways to protect an investment in window coverings and other interior fabrics are:
- Tint the windows.

- Addition of lining for drapery and other window coverings.

- Use of an undertreatment under the drapery or other O.B. mounted treatment, such as blinds and shades.

- Fabric or metal awnings added to the exterior of windows, especially windows with southern or western exposure.

- Obstruct the sun from hitting affected windows from the outside by the incorporation of outside shrubbery and trees into the landscaping.

- Drapery or undertreatments should be drawn shut or pulled down on sunny days to protect interior furnishings, in addition to window treatments.

The sun provides three enemies that shine through the windows daily. They are ultraviolet light, heat, and glare. Not only is the summer's sun harmful, but the winter sun reflecting off of snow is also harmful.

Sun damage is also known as sun rot. Sun rot will affect window coverings and drapery in several ways. Fabrics of window treatments and drapery are affected by fiber deterioration; chemical changes in color, from ultraviolet light; fading; and thread breakage at seams of drapery. If left unprotected, woven woods will also fall apart from sun deterioration in a very short time.

Windows with southern or western exposure are particularly in need of extra protection. Window coverings incorporating the use of fibers such as in fabrics and woven woods, if left unprotected, the fibers will rapidly deteriorate and have a very short life. Vinyl P.V.C. vanes in vertical blinds are also known to warp and twist at hot windows.

Windows with northern or eastern exposure will also allow sun damage, but not to the same extent.

Chemical action on certain dyes will cause the color to change. This may affect only one color of many on a printed fabric or stripe, or may affect the whole drape. Colors most frequently affected in this manner are red, yellow, and yellow-green. If the fabric selected is vat or solution dyed, these dye methods will reduce the chance of chemical changes in their color.

Fading is a very obnoxious problem with the ultraviolet light from the sun. Fading of the fabric may show up while the window treatment is still hanging on the window, or may not show up until the treatment is cleaned. Upon examination of the drapery or other treatment, you may find the leading edges very faded. Fading will readily show up on both front and back of the fabric. The folds that fall nearer the glass will be very faded, probably shredded, and deteriorated. The fabric will easily tear with the slightest pressure. Yellow streaks may also show up in the folds from the exposure to sunlight.

Deep-colored fabrics will fade from constant exposure to sunlight. This will occur especially if the drapery or treatment is not lined. On windows with southern or western exposure, you are safer in using white or off-whites for the base fabric color.

Drapery may suffer thread breakage at the seams, and have loose seams. The fabric may otherwise still appear in good condition. The thread used to sew the drapery may not be as strong as the base fibers of the fabric. Many times the seams may be restitched and the treatment rehung at the window.

If the lining shreds up from the sun shining constantly on the treatment, or shows up after the treatment is cleaned, there are a couple of remedies. The treatment can be relined if your customer really wants to live with the same treatment for years to come. The lining may also be clipped out of the drapery, very close to the edge at the leading edges and the header. Use the treatment, unlined for a period longer, until the base fabric fades and falls apart.

Solutions for windows with southern and western exposure:
- Sell protective undertreatments mounted I.B., close to the glass.

- Recommend good quality linings for drapery and other treatments.

- Select drapery fabrics with fiber content that is less affected by the sun.

- Use liners whenever available for hard-window treatments.

Oxidation

Oxidation is produced by exposure to fireplace fumes, natural gas fumes, furnaces, or a close location to a busy street. Traffic exposure results in exposure to automobile exhaust and fumes. These elements will deteriorate and discolor window treatments. When fabrics are in contact with these components, and when they are combined with oxygen and humidity, acid is formed on the fibers. Fabrics absorb the chemicals formed. If acid is allowed to sit on the treatment, the acid will deteriorate the fibers.

Gases and fumes in the home will also cause certain colors to change colors. Colors, especially affected are blues, greens, and colors with blue dye in them.

Nicotine

Nicotine will stain and discolor fabrics. Nicotine stains, nicotine film, or discoloration may never be able to be removed. People who smoke heavily indoors may not want to buy expensive fabrics, or want to add lining to their treatments, because the fabric is going to become stained before the sun is going to deteriorate the fibers. **Selling an indoor smoker a darker color, will be the foremost answer to preserving the fabric's looks** from nicotine stains as long as possible. Frequent cleaning of the treatment will also prolong the life of the fabric and help keeping some of the nicotine removed.

Humidity

Humidity is an element that will especially affect fabrics in the loose-weave family. Drapery will grow in length during periods of high humidity, and get shorter in length during weather that is very dry. Fabric manufacturers have worked on improving this situation. To help keep fabrics stable in length, lock-stitch weaving has been incorporated into the weaves of the fabrics.

Water Damage

Water damage to fabrics at the window may occur due to leakage around the windows or condensation sitting on the window glass. Condensation may result in water-marked or discolored areas on some fabrics. Water-marked areas may not show up until the treatment has been cleaned. Fabrics especially affected are those in the antique satin and satin families. This type of stain will not be removable. Selection of linings that resist water will help improve this situation.

Shrinkage

Fabrics may shrink during washing or dry cleaning. Every interior item that you custom make should be dry-cleaned. The only exception are sheers that may be washed, *carefully*. Dry cleaners that work with decorating fabrics know the correct methods to use for certain fibers to help prevent shrinkage. Review the section on *Dry Cleaning*.

Make a note on every sales slip and label every fabric item that you sell as to the correct cleaning method to use for the most favorable results. It is a federal law and requirement that you *do* provide the fiber content for fabrics. Once you locate the fiber content, it is easy to write down the proper cleaning method (listed next to the fiber content, usually). You are also limiting your liability if the customer incorrectly maintains the item and comes back to you later, unhappy. This information is found on your fabric samples and on the information sheets provided by your manufacturers and vendors.

Techniques for Prolonging the Life of Fabrics

Some of the techniques for prolonging an interior fabric's life are:

- **Line the draperies or window treatments.**

- Select **more durable fabrics.**

- **Vacuum draperies and treatments regularly,** so dirt does not become imbedded in the fabrics or treatments.

- **Dry-clean** items, **as needed.**

- Use of **applied tinting to windows.**

- The **addition of undertreatments** under drapery treatments.

Fabric Wearing Ability

In general, the more you use the fabrics the faster they are going to show wear, or the shorter their life is going to be. If you take precautions against the sun, especially the windows subjected to southern or western exposures, you will broadly lengthen the life of the fabric. All the above-named elements in life expectancy of window treatments, apply *especially* to fabrics.

Applied stain-resistance finishes are going to aid in the removal of any stains and spots on fabrics. They will only help in removal, not prevent every stain. These finishes are especially necessary for lighter-colored fabrics. Always promptly remove spots and spills from fabrics and carpets when they occur, to help ensure the stain's ability to be removed.

Lined Drapery and Window Treatments

Lining of draperies and window treatments has many advantages. *These benefits far outweigh the extra cost for fabrication, lining, and dry cleaning.* Most fabrics work well with the addition of a lining. Most fabrics hang nicer with a lining.

There are a few fabrics and window treatments that hang better and are less bulky without a lining. These fabrics are composed of a fiber content that is more sun resistant than most drapery fabrics.

Some of the fabrics that are best used unlined for drapery are: canvas, denim, muslin, and taffeta (be sure to use an undertreatment with taffeta to protect the fabric).

Years ago, fabrics were much heavier than they are today. This is especially true for the fabrics in the satin family. Today, heavier drapery fabrics are very hard to find. When and if you do find them — they are very expensive. Drapery were almost always interlined, in addition to being lined. Drapery were top quality and very, well made; made to last many years. Heavier fabrics, interlinings, and linings were used to cut down on possible drafts coming in a room around windows. Today, as in years past, **window treatments are used for insulation.**

The reasons to add a lining to drapery and window are outlined below. Review these reasons with your customer when resistance to lining of the drapery and window treatments is expressed:

- **Lining improves the appearance of the drapery** by adding body to the drapery fabric. Some fabrics become limp when hanging at the window over a period of time. Drapery that is lined is a much nicer quality, more luxurious drapery.

- **To achieve the best-hanging drapery possible.**

- **To keep the drapery looking its best, for a much longer period of time.**

- **Makes drapery appear fuller and more custom looking.**

- **Less-expensive fabrics appear more expensive looking.**

- Line drapery if your customer plans to stay in their home four or more years, because the **energy savings** from having the drapery lined will offset the cost of the lining.

- **Line drapery with a southern or western exposure,** especially if the drapery fabric is from the satin family. You can only expect, at most, a four-year life at these exposures if you do not line the drapery here. Intense **sun will quickly deteriorate and fade the drapery fibers.** After cleaning, they will shred up and fall apart.

- Line drapery to help make a cold room warmer, or a warm room cooler. **Lining will cut down on drafts** getting in a room around drafty windows. **Overall insulation can broadly be improved.**

- **A long life is expected or needed from the drapery.**

- **If you are using a deeper fabric color that you want to protect from fading, and also do not want to see that color from the exterior of the home,** especially from the front of the house. You may also choose to add an undertreatment that is kept in a down position most of the time, to alleviate the color from the interior fabric showing on the exterior.

- **To get more of a true color of the fabric selected.** When sun shines through fabrics it may add a tint of yellow to the fabric. The fabric may actually be a tint of another color. You may not visually see the other color until the drapery is made up, and is hanging in folds, with the sun shining through the fabric. Then a tint you never dreamed the color was, is apparent. Beware of fabric color names, although the fabric may not look like apricot blush, this is a sure tip-off that this fabric is peachy-pink, although you see it as off-white.

- **Most housing and condominium associations in developed tracts, townhouses, and condominium complexes will have in their homeowners association rules that you must use only white or off-white window coverings from the exterior of the home.** With the use of a lining, the window coverings may be any color, as long as the outside color is white or off-white.

- **Lining provides privacy.**

Reasons Not To Line Drapery

Sometimes customers will have real reasons not to want to line the drapery. Some of the legitimate reasons are noted below:

- **The customer may be fixing up the house to sell.** The prospective buyer will probably not notice that the drapery are not lined. The drapery will probably retain their crispness long enough for the customer to live in the house for a period of time. The customer may not feel the extra cost for the lining will be realized in profit on the sale of the house.

- **The customer may be draping a large expanse and be very weak physically, or may be arthritic. The extra weight of the lined drapery, may be too much for this customer.** Recommend undertreatments or window tinting to preserve the drapery fabric.

- **Due to having limited wall space on either side of the window, a very tight stack may be required.** Lining on drapery does take up more room. If foregoing the lining, sell the customer undertreatments or window tinting to protect the drapery.

Points to Remember About Lined Drapery

Below are listed some important points to remember about lined drapery:

- **Lined drapery is fabricated with a single hem on both the lining and the drapery, rather than a double hem.** This allows the drapery to hang well in combination with the lining at the folds. Casement fabrics for drapery that are lined will still require a double hem.

- **Try to purchase lining in the same width as the drapery fabric.** By selection of the same width fabrics for both the lining and drapery fabric, the seams will line up. You **prevent** the possibility, when the sun shines through the two fabrics, that the seams from the lining will show through to the face drapery fabric. If the seams should show through, they will show up in different areas than the drapery fabric seams. If you may not purchase the lining in the same width as the drapery fabric, then select an opaque lining that the sun will not easily penetrate and/or an undertreatment for under the drapery that can be closed, to eliminate this problem.

- **If you are using a fabric that is a different width than the lining, calculate separately the two different yardages needed. This is to prevent the possibility of ordering too little or too much lining fabric.**

- **Always hold up the lining fabric and the self-fabric of the drapery, to get a good idea of how the two fabrics will hang together.** If you are using a lightweight fabric with a heavier lining fabric, they may not hang well together. If it is necessary to use two *incompatible* fabrics together, mount the lining on a separate traverse rod than the drapery, and make it a separate draw. If the fabric is heavy with the lining light to medium weight, then they are probably going to work well together.

- **Hold up the fabric and the lining selected together in front of a window,** if in doubt at all about the two colors and how they will work together. Always consider, does the customer want an ivory base behind this drapery or a white base? Ivory lining will make a loosely woven drapery or lightweight fabric more yellow in color. White will make these fabrics more white.

- **White lining will get dirty faster,** since it is white, is rubbing against the window and the screen, and needs to be cleaned more often than ivory lining. White lining is always the lining color choice for homes that are white on the exterior.

- **If you use a lightweight drapery fabric with a lining other than off-white or white, the color of the lining may show through the drapery fabric and tint the drapery fabric to that same color. A tint of yellow may also be added to the fabric when the sun shines through the fabrics. Sell white lining when the fabric is white or has a white background.** If you must use a colored lining, and the fabric is thin, interline the drapery in white flannel.

- **Line all draperies within the same room.** Sometimes customers will want to line only one drapery due to privacy or exposure problems, etc. The unlined drapery will hang differently from the lined drapery, appear different in color, opaqueness, amount of light coming through the fabric, etc. Lined drapery within the same room as unlined drapery are going to appear very different. On the exterior of the home, the color and the fabric is also going to appear different.

- After many years, despite having a northern or an eastern exposure, **linings will deteriorate and fall apart from exposure to the sun, dirt, nicotine, smog, fumes and other elements. Over-cleaning draperies more than necessary will also deteriorate them and shorten their life as well.** Linings do have a limited life. After the lining has started to shred up, the customer may choose to invest more money into the draperies and have them relined. The reason why a customer would elect to do this is that if they want to use them for more years to come, and if the drapery fabric will stand up to do it. The customer may also clip the deteriorated lining out of the drapery, as close as possible to the edges of the drapery fabric at the back of the header, and at the side hems. The lining is then removed and the drapery used unlined for a period of time.

Types of Available Lining Fabrics

Lining fabrics come in a wide range of heaviness and styles to fit the range of needs that consumers have today. An overview of the different types are listed and summarized below:

- **Polyester and cotton blend linings** — These types of linings hang softer and wrinkle less than other linings. This type of lining varies in weight from very thin to medium weight. Available in 48", 54", and 118" widths.

- **Sateen linings** — Usually composed of 100% cotton. Sateen lining is long wearing, nice hanging, but will wrinkle. Sateen lining comes in various degrees of quality. Generally, sateen lining is lower quality than drapery sateen. Sateen is available in neutral pale shades or whites. Available in black for use as a light-blocking interlining. Available in 48", 54", and 118" widths.

- **Roclon linings** — Roclon lining is also known as water-repellant lining or Rain No Stain lining. If you should have water leakage around the windows, the water will bead up and roll off, not penetrating the lining, not staining the lining or the drapery. You will probably receive many requests to do replacement draperies for customers who had leaky windows and did not select this type of lining for their drapery (they may not have known about it) initially. Composed of 100% cotton, with added finishes for performance, shine, and smoothness. Roclon linings are long wearing, come in colors, and may wrinkle. Available widths are generally 48", 54", and 118".

- **Designer linings** — This group of linings are linings that are printed in small prints, geometric designs or stripes, roller printed on pastels or off-white shades of fabrics. Available colors are usually tone-on-tone colors, or white applied on pastels whites, or off-whites shades of fabrics. Designer linings are more expensive, but very classy. Unfortunately, they do not readily show up since they have a subtle pattern. If the liner is placed at front windows, or other windows that are viewed closely from the outside, then the pattern will be noticed. Designer lining fabrics may be used as drapery and other decorator fabric ideas to create beautiful bedspreads and bedroom ensembles using different fabrics combined for the many accessories in a bedroom. This type of lining is composed of polyester, cotton, and rayon or 100% cotton or polyester and cotton blends. This lining is water and stain repellant and wrinkle resistant. Widths available are generally 48" and 54".

- **Colored linings** — Colored linings are usually used under laces or open-weave type fabrics where you want the color to show through. This is a very decorative, interesting window treatment idea. The color of the lining will show on the exterior of the home. Mount under treatments under the drapery to camouflage the color from the outside. Composed of 100% cotton, polyester, cotton blends or polyester, cotton, and rayon blends. Available widths are usually 48" and 54".

- **Thermal-suede linings** — This is an insulating lining. Thermal-suede lining keeps rooms cool on hot days (if the drapery is closed) and is also able to keep rooms warmer on cold days. Thermal-suede lining is a heavier lining, harder to open and close for people who are weak or arthritic. Drapery will not hang quite as nicely with this lining, but most customers will not notice the difference and would prefer the added insulation benefits to help cut down the utility bills. If the customer seems particularly discriminating in manner, or if you observe by looking around the room that they are very meticulous, or if the customer expresses to you that they are more concerned about having the nicest hanging drapery possible, select another lining.

- **Blackout linings** — This type of lining is the answer for customers who have trouble sleeping, or who want a "total blackout environment" for the room when the drapery is drawn. Blackout lining is insulating also, but has a very heavy, poor hand.

    This type of lining may be attached to the drapery as a lined drapery, or may be a separate liner on a separate rod to pull as needed. Sometimes workrooms are not careful when fabricating a separate blackout liner to be used behind drapery. If not careful with needle selection, they will leave pinholes all along the leading edges of the blackout liner. When the sun shines through the completed liner, the pin holes are magnetized many times their size and appear very large. Workrooms need to use a smaller-gauge needle or remove the straight sewing needle from the three- or-four cord overlock machine to remedy the situation. This lining has a tendency to wrinkle.

- **Reflective linings** — Reflective linings are medium weight, woven in twill or satin weave fabrics, coated on one side with a metallic or white finish that protects draperies by reflecting sun and heat.

Separate Liners

Linings may be mounted separately on a separate rod from the drapery. Many lining fabrics may be used this way, but generally linings installed separately are blackout linings or thermal-suede linings — see above. **The preference in hanging the lining off a separate rod is usually desired by a customer who wants** to have a light, sheer drapery or other light drapery during the day, with the choice of having a darker room, more insulation, or privacy when desired.

Basically, the use of sheers and lined drapery as an overdrapery perform the same function. The lined drapery is on the top instead of on the bottom as a separate liner.

Separate liners that pin on the back of draperies:

Sometimes your customer will insist on having unlined drapery, and when the drapery is completed, they find that they needed a lined drapery. The customer may have purchased an existing home that came with quality unlined drapery, and they would like them to last for awhile. The reason may be the amount of sunlight that filters through the fabric, an objectionable color showing on the exterior of the home, or the room may be too cold. You may be at the customer's home helping them with other windows and you are asked what can be done to alleviate this problem. Pinning a separate liner to the back of an already fabricated drapery will go a long way toward a partial solution for some of the problems that arise.

Available on the market is a separate liner to pin on the back of pleated, unlined drapery to give more privacy, insulation, or to protect the drapery. Pin-on liner can be attached by slipping the buttonholes, which are fairly strategically placed (to correspond to an average pleated drapery in the placement of pleats), over the already in place drapery hooks.

This type of lining is a flat lining fabric with a casing at the top, hem at the bottom, and is finished at side seams. The casing at the top has buttonholes placed at the same intervals as pleats on drapery. This is very easily fabricated, or is available readymade in standard sizes through your larger department store catalogues. If your customer purchases these liners readymade, they will be limited to standard sizes, which line up with readymade drapery sizes. Standardized sizes may be made shorter by rehemming or made wider by sewing panels together.

Care and Maintenance of Fabrics

Dry Cleaning

Always instruct your customers to select a drapery dry cleaner rather than a clothing dry cleaner when choosing a dry cleaner for decorating items and window treatments. Regular dry cleaners do not always know the proper handling of decorating fabrics. Many times, drapery, top treatments, and linings (that are not very old) are mishandled, ruined, and handed back to the customer with no recourse. If the drapery falls apart from the strong solvent used at the cleaners and come back a shredded mess, you still must pay for the dry cleaning. Now, your customer also needs to replace the drapery.

Drapery dry cleaners will usually guarantee that the drapery will not shrink in length more than 1". They will not even take the drapery if there is any evidence that the drapery or other decorative item will not make it through the dry cleaning. They deal with drapery and other decorating items all day long and know how certain fibers and linings need to be treated, and which drapery to even attempt to clean due to deterioration of the fabric. They may give a guarantee that the fabric will hold up through the cleaning. An experienced dry cleaner is going to make a very accurate guess about the fabric's outcome by examining the fabric before proceeding.

Always include the fiber content on the face of the sales contract. The laws say that you must do so, and you are passing your liability on possible mishandling of the fabrics by the cleaners by doing so. The customer can tell or show the cleaners the fiber content of the fabric before the drapery or other items are cleaned. The dry cleaner can proceed accurately on the proper cleaning method for the item, due to having correct information on the fiber content.

Dry cleaners who attempt to dry clean items in questionable condition — those appearing very dirty, worn, sun-damaged, stained, etc.— should not be held responsible for the quality of the end product. They will usually speak up and tell you that they do not know if they will come out well and will probably require a signed disclaimer from the customer before proceeding. They are making an educated guess in some situations and when given the authorization to go ahead with the job can only attempt to clean the items satisfactorily.

Fading in the folds and creases of drapery will sometimes show up after the drapery have been dry-cleaned. Deterioration of fibers due to harsh sun exposure where the sun hits the folds is the reason for this.

Drapery need to be dry-cleaned every couple years or so, depending on how dirty the environment is and the elements they are exposed to as listed in the *Life Expectancy of Window Treatments* section of this book. If there is very little exposure to any of these elements, dry-clean as infrequently as possible.

Dry cleaning items too frequently, results in drapery that do not last as long as ones which were cleaned only as needed. The dry cleaning process weakens the fibers due to use of strong solvents.

Dry-Clean Only!

When writing up a sales contract, **always** include in writing on the sales contract that these drapery or other fabric items are **dry-clean only**. Always **verbally** read this fact to the customer when verbally reviewing the whole sales contract with them. Technically, some fabrics such as sheers are washable and will be laundered at the dry cleaners in some cases. You can **tell** the customer, "yes, this fabric probably could be hand washed, or laundered on a delicate cycle in the washing machine. Depending on how carefully they are handled, will determine the finished result of how the drapery or treatment will look after being cleaned."

Remind the customer that you must write **dry-clean only** on the sales contract regardless of how the customer chooses to care and maintain the fabric items. Every item sold to a customer made of fabric should have a label attached to the item stating that this item is to be dry cleaned. Have labels made up for this purpose. You do not want to be responsible for negligence due to the customer wrecking a very expensive item because of improper cleaning methods.

If drapery are handwashed, pleats must be hand dressed while still wet. This is done so the buckram in the drapery will not get all folded up and permanently wrinkled. Shrinkage will probably occur. Fabrics especially effected are cotton and cotton-blend fabrics.

When fabrics are washed, applied finishes, which give the fabric a better appearance, will wash off the fabric. Since the customer is making a large investment, it is always preferable to safeguard the looks of the drapery or other item as you would for any expensive piece of clothing and have them dry-cleaned.

How to Remove Dust from Drapery and Top Treatments

Dust needs removing from drapery and top treatments often. If allowed to sit on the fabric, dust will weaken the fibers. To remove dust from drapery, simply fold top of drapery header up evenly, leaving hooks intact. Place the top of the pleated-up bunch into a lingerie bag and tie the top of the bunch and the bag together with a string. Place the drapery in the dryer, on the air cycle (use no heat). Tumble the drapery in the dryer to remove dust from the fabric.

To pull the dust out of drapery fabrics, vacuum drapery and other fabric window treatments with vacuum attachments or a small hand-held vacuum cleaner, while up on the window, regularly. Do this about every six months or so, depending on how dirty the environment is.

Part 5

Measuring and Planning the Job for Window Treatments

Accuracy in Planning the Job

*Always be as accurate at you can be when planning the job. Check your addition and pricing of everything going into the job **twice**,* before announcing the price to the customer. Try to work off a worksheet that lists the essential parts of the job. Working off of a worksheet that lists the various parts for fabrication and installation *makes it hard for you to skip major items* such as fabrication costs. *Always thoroughly review all style and fabric selections, and hold all proposed selections of window coverings up to the window before finalizing the selections. If possible, allow the customer to see fabrics in their home during the day and in evening lighting. Always double-check all measurements **before** leaving the customer's home,* after the sales contract has been signed and reviewed. You will have taken time to absorb the job, and need to double check your original impressions on the measurements.

Misfiguring the Job

The worst telephone call you will ever make to a customer is the one where you call them up and say, "I misfigured the amount on your order. I am short on the amount of money $425. There is no possible way I can place the order without your authorization for the extra money. I have figured I can cut the amount down to $375. That is as low on the price as I can go. I am very sorry, and feel very badly about this, but there is nothing I can do. Will you authorize the extra amount?"

As a decorator, *you will lose about one-third to one-half of the customers who had intended to buy here.* Customers have the tendency to have buyers' remorse on items that they did not plan to purchase right away. They feel they may have rushed into it; the price seems too high; friends and neighbors hear they placed an order with you, and tell them they could have gotten it at a lower price from their source. They ask *themselves* if this the style they really want now and will want two years from now, etc. *Many excuses for canceling are running through their mind.* The three-day right to cancel seems *like eternity* to any sales professional. Many customers exercise their right to cancel after all your time and effort. They *will* cancel, just as you get all the paperwork completed.

You are giving the customer another reason to cancel, by calling him or her up and saying that you misquoted the price. The customer probably thought the original price seemed too high to begin with. You were able to convince them that the benefits surpassed the expenditure, and finally got them to sign on the dotted line.

Now, any problem you present to them which gives them a possible way out *will be used by the customer to put the order on hold, to speak with their spouse, shop around a bit more, or just put the purchase off until a future date.*

If you find that you have *misfigured and misquoted* the price, use the techniques in the section on *Techniques to Use to Cut the Price Down,* to find a way to *cut the price down* without calling the customer and *losing* the job. *These techniques* allow you to absorb the shortage anywhere you can. *After applying these techniques, if you still have a shortage, then try to absorb the balance by not making as much on the job.*

If you are still quite short on the money to cover the job, consider lowering your commission rate if you have to. It is better to earn *something,* learning from your error, than to call the customer, lose the job, and *not get paid at all* for the time, effort, and grief you have already invested in the job. When we *pay* for our mistakes, we tend not to repeat the mistake again.

Realize, if you are short on money for the job, you will have removed *any cushion* of profit for errors and problems with the job. The money is not going to be there for any extra calls by the installer, and for reworks and remakes, so it is imperative that the job is remeasured by the installer before proceeding. Explain the situation to the installer — possibly he or she will not charge as much for this remeasure, due to the slim margin of profit.

Many times, after giving a customer an estimate, they respond *unfavorably* since they had no idea what window coverings or other custom items for the home cost.

Sometimes they react unfavorably because they have already received other prices from other companies for similar, or what seems to them to be comparable items. Actually what they probably got a bid on was in fact a much less-expensive, lesser-quality product, fabric, a smaller size, shorter length, less fullness, less-expensive top treatment, unlined version versus your lined version, etc. You realize this, but your customer can really only see that your price seems high for what they perceive as being the same look.

There are ways to trim the price down, if this seems to be the situation you are in. *Remember, some of the ideas work only for the customer who does not seem particularly discriminating and especially particular.* If the customer falls into the particularly discriminating and especially particular category, let the other company have the job. Remind the customer, *"you get what you pay for in the decorating business,"* and then leave. *Let the other company have the headaches and problems to be resolved with that customer, when the products arrive and they are not up to the quality of what that customer perceived he or she was going to get.*

Consistency Within Related Areas of Rooms

Within related areas of rooms, keep drapery and other window coverings consistent in selection of lengths, fabrics, window treatment selection, and styling. Top treatments may be fabricated in variations of each other, if necessary or desired. Keep a consistent and related theme. Use tailored styles with other tailored styles, shirred styles with other shirred styles.

Keeping consistency is **especially necessary when spaces are open and flowing together.** Many homes will have sliding-glass doors or French doors in the middle of the wall, with two short windows on the same wall. The window treatments will look best if *all* are full-length, rather than two short treatments and one full-length treatment. **Exceptions to this rule are** window-seat situations, bookcases, and other architectural features that will prevent you from keeping all lengths consistent.

It may become necessary for you to vary the lengths of the treatments that you are planning. **If you are working with a fabric or other treatment with a horizontal repeat, the repeat needs to fall at the *same level* all around the room, *regardless* of the length of the treatment.**

Keep all drapery consistent in height around the room. Be careful when planning treatments where some are O.B. mounted doors and others are to be I.B. mounted treatments. **If the treatments are different heights at the top, you will not achieve eye-flow around the room.** The answer is to keep *all* the treatments O.B. mounted and keep the height the same for all of the treatments.

If it becomes *necessary* to I.B. mount some of the treatments, then finish off the irregularity of the heights by placing a top treatment at the same height all around the room. The top treatment should be planned to cover the tops of all windows, hardware, and the tops of any I.B. mounted treatments. Additionally, it is essential, to make the length of all the valances the same. To decide what is the correct measurement for the length, measure from the highest point to be covered, on the highest window, down to the lowest point to be covered, on the I.B. mount or the lower treatment. Add 3"— 4" into the window to cover hardware and tops of the lower treatment.

Keep all heights of drapery rods consistent. When a room steps down or up to another level, and other windows are on the upper portion of the room, plan all the rods at the same level throughout the area. Plan step-down area treatments longer in their length to compensate for the differences.

All drapery rods or treatments should have the same projection out from the wall. The same projection should be used, even if some windows in the same space do not have an undertreatment. This rule holds especially true if the windows are on the same wall.

Lining needs to be consistent within the same space of the rooms. *Some* customers will want to economize on lining some of the windows. They may have different exposures within the room on different windows; want less privacy or light to filter in at some windows; or desire a filtered view for some windows, and may not want to line some of the drapery. They are making an error, because the lined drapery will appear *very different* in color, body (of the fabric), amount of light filtering through, opaqueness, and in the overall way the drapery hang. Additionally, the exterior of the drapery from the outside of the home will appear different.

Unfortunately, many customers will insist on making windows within the same areas dissimilar heights, different lengths, etc. If you do not go along with their ideas, you may end us losing the job. Satisfy their requests, as they will never be happy making the treatment full-length, if what they really wanted was a short treatment. The customer will call or come back, unsatisfied. You will end up reworking the treatment shorter, which is what they wanted in the first place.

Using these design guidelines will avoid a piecemeal effect, or a look that has been put together piece by piece, as the mood strikes the owner. Your objective is to have a professional-looking job, that when you gaze around the room, you see consistency and unity that flows within the related spaces. Friends, relatives, and associates will see the finished treatments. They will also want to use your services for themselves, supplying you with the very best lead you can possibly have, a referral from a satisfied customer.

Windows and Window Dressing

Windows and their functions:

Windows are provided to give light to a room of a home or building. Windows display views, provide ventilation, may be *dynamically* decorated, and may become the focal point of a room.

Properly planned and selected window treatments:

Properly planned and selected window treatments can emphasize architectural details and features. Window treatments can also take attention away from, or cover up, architectural features that the customer wishes *were not there.*

Form follows function for faultless decorating:

Form and function are the two most important rules to consider when decorating and planning window treatments. What is the look you are trying to achieve; will the window treatments be functional and easy to operate? For good design, you want to consider the proportions of the window and all the windows in relation with each other. Additionally, you need to consider what you are trying to achieve in style and design. The purpose in dressing windows is to filter and screen the amount of light coming in, minimize heat and air-conditioning loss, have sound control, to be able to have nighttime privacy, and to soften up the harsh lines of bare windows.

Window Terminology

Apron The flat wood trim portion of the window casing below the sill.

Arch window A window that is vertical at the sides and bottom and curves upward at the top.

Awning window A window that has horizontal sashes (that hold glass), and opens out to the exterior of the wall. Since this window opens out, rather than in, it is not a difficult window type to treat.

Bay or bow window A window that creates a curved or angled alcove area in the wall. If the area is angled with two or more windows, it is called a bay window. If the window is curved around the area, it is called a bow window. Bow windows are usually nonmoveable windows. Window seats are frequently used in combination with these types of windows. You are somewhat limited on the treatments you may put on either types of these windows.

Casement window
A swinging, double or single, sashed window. May swing into the room, or out of the room. The windows that swing into the room, are more limited in the way they can be treated. The treatment needs to be mounted right on the sash, or must be mounted so it completely clears the window when the window is opened and closed. The outward swinging windows usually have a crank that must also be planned around when treating the window.

Casing
The part of the window that fits flat onto the wall area (usually of wood). Sometimes has a molding around it. Also called the frame of the window.

Half sash
Divider point, where the bottom half and the upper half portion of a double-hung window meet, usually in the middle of the set of windows.

Jamb
The interior frame of the window opening, into which the window sash sits. This is the recessed area of the window opening.

Mullion
Divided areas between individual panes of glass.

Sash
Wood or metal frame that holds the window glass.

Sill
The narrow interior ledge that lies horizontally at the bottom of a window.

Function of windows
To supply light to an interior space; provide ventilation; create a focal point; display a beautiful view; and may be dressed to provide privacy.

Considerations of Window Treatments and Windows

When planning window treatments, there are certain factors to consider before planning the appropriate window treatment for the customer's needs. Some of the main points to consider are:

- **What the exposure of the window is** — north, south, east, west? Windows that face south and west will need to be covered during the hottest parts of the day. On windows with northern or eastern exposures, use treatments that will let in a maximum amount of light.

- **How cold or hot** does the weather get in the climate the window treatments are to be used in? Does the window have excessive cold or hot air coming through it?

- Will the **rays of the sun** *be used* to **warm** the room?

- Is the **view** the prime consideration? Or, is how **beautifully done** the windows *are*, the prime interest?

- Does the customer want to completely cover the window or ensure coverage of the window at only certain times of the day for **privacy**?

- Is **noise** inside or outside a factor to consider?

- Is **light control** of prime importance?

- Is the customer concerned with **saving** as much **energy** as possible with their selection of window coverings?

- Is the proposed treatment **easily operated**, on windows where *this* function is very important? While it may be hot during the day, the customer may want to open the window at night to let in a cooling breeze.

- Is the fabric or treatment selected very **durable**? Is this customer and their family likely to give the proposed treatment and fabric much wear and abuse?

- Is the **color, pattern, and texture** *right* for the theme of the room?

- Does the **style of the treatment suit the lifestyle of the customer, family, and the style of the room?**

- Is everyone involved happy with the selection of fabric and treatment?

- Plan **all the windows which are visible from the same angle outside the home to have a similar style and exterior color.** Line the window treatments with a similar colored lining.

- If planning to use **multiple layers,** will the **windows be easily opened,** or will the windows *ever* be opened? Will enough light *still* filter through to suit the customer?

- Which side should the controls to operate the window treatments go on? Which side should the treatment draw to when opened? Will the treatment stack high enough overhead for taller people to walk under? Will the treatment clear the top of the window?

- Oversized drapery and sheers can camouflage poorly placed windows with odd proportions. If the window came complete with skimpy moldings, cover them up. Simple treatments outside mounted, finished off with a simple valance would be the solution, if the customer wants to keep the styling very simple.

Some of the solutions to the above problems are outlined below:

- **Fabrics and wood window treatments absorb sound and are very insulating.** The more layers of *these* used, the quieter the room will be.

- **Reflective treatments** such as those with aluminized backings and reflective shades will **reflect the sun off the window.** They will keep the room warmer in winter and cooler in the hot summer months. At night reflective treatments may be pulled up to let the breeze in.

- **Measure a tight fit for I.B. mounts. A tight fit will help keep the heat in during the winter and the heat out during the summer.**

- Use **clear glass for solar heating.**

- Suggest to your customers to have **two sets of window coverings,** if the climate in the winter and summer months are extremes from each other. They may have different requirements for their windows in the summer and winter months.

- It is preferable to **stack-off the window glass with window treatments for ventilation, air flow, and views.**

- On **windows with northern exposures,** plan treatments that will **allow as much light as possible to filter through.**

- On windows with **southern or western exposures;** plan to **minimize the amount of light filtering through.**

View windows or architecturally beautiful windows:

Some windows have wonderful views, or are designed so attractively that the customer may feel these windows are *best* left uncovered, without a window treatment. These windows need window treatments to control the amount of sun flooding in, the amount of heated air escaping through the window, the amount of air-conditioning escaping through uncovered windows, the cold air coming in during the winter, and to take care of privacy needs.

When planning for view windows, try not to incorporate too many layers which will *obstruct* the view. Try to frame the view *like* you frame a picture.

Make the window stand out:

Pull attention to the window treatment you are planning by selecting colors, patterns, and textures that will stand out and cause attention to be focused on the window.

Keep the view as the focal point:

Keep the view as the focal point by having window treatments stack-off the window when opened. Select plain, neutral colors that are as close to the wall color as possible, and use subtly textured fabrics. Following these guidelines will keep the view as the focal point, rather than the window treatments as the focal point.

Maintain privacy while decorating view windows:

Many people want to maintain privacy, while still being able to fully enjoy their view. Achieve this by installing blinds, or any type of shade, that will pull up and tightly stack together when opened. Some window coverings, such as woven woods, Duettes, and some shades will pull down from the top. Vertical blinds are very light, airy, and take a minimum amount of space to stack, so are ideal for view windows. When the vertical slats are tilted open, they are hardly noticeable.

Layered treatments:

The use of layered treatments will grow with the *awareness and need* to save energy. Since adding window treatment layers works very well with the design of the treatment, aesthetically, adding layers has grown as an important window fashion, look.

Layered window fashions that are functional in energy savings are here to stay. Even the simple use of a lone undertreatment or shade needs to be finished with the use of some type of valance. Customers may change the valance periodically, for a different window look. The use of stationary panels and a valance to frame the window has grown in popularity. Stationary panels work well with some climates where the customers *want the look* of a lot of style and layers, but do not want to spend money on *unneeded*, extra fabric widths, and do not need to weatherize the windows, as required in harsher climates.

Window Dressing

The important points to consider when dressing a window are:

- **Materials and fabrics.**

- **Style** of the treatment.

- **Type and style of the window.**

- **Functionality of the treatment** — does it need to be opened and closed?

- **Proportion** .

- **Line.**

- **Color.**

- **Pattern and scale.**

- **Location of the window and its orientation** (north, south, east, or western exposure).

- **The most professional and better proportioned-looking treatments are going to appear rectangular rather than square in shape.** If you stack-off the window with the treatment, the treatment is going to appear more square than rectangular. You will have decreased, rather than accented, the height.

- Casement window treatments should be made to go to the floor in length. Length gives them height.

- Puddled drapery were brought into style to keep heat from escaping out the window. They were also popular because they prevented the harsh elements from outside from filtering into the room.

- If you need to contrast the lines of the drapery with other furnishings that have predominantly straight lines, tie drapery back with tieback holders or tiebacks.

- **A finished window treatment is one which has a top treatment or decorative rod to finish it off.**

Simpler is usually better:

If you want to avoid many problems, use the keep it simple (KIS) principle for the fabrication process. You will get your delivery faster *and* with fewer problems. As a designer or decorator, you love to create and design, and may not want to follow this advice. You will end up learning the hard way.

Using color on the outside of the home:

Many homes, townhouses, condominium complexes, or commercial situations have homeowner association rules or leasing guidelines that will not allow any color showing on the outside of the building, other than white or off-white.

Many violators have been fined and forced to remedy this situation. These situations may be remedied by relining the drapery, adding honeycomb shades, pleated shades, or mini blinds in a white or off-white exterior color. Pin-on liners, a liner usually found in larger department store catalogues, may be slipped on the back of the drapery over the existing hooks. Any white shades or blinds that are added will generally have to remain in a closed or down position. Opening the blind or shade would reveal the offending treatment's color.

Note: Remember, when ordering striped mini blinds, unless you can get duo-tone (white on the exterior side of the slats), you will also have the striped, colored effect from the outside the home or building.

It usually looks unattractive to see any color other than white, off-white, or the aluminized-backing color (appears whitish-gray) from the outside of *any* home or building.

Discuss placement of the window treatment:

Make it a practice to always hold the measuring tape up, discuss the placement and lengths of all top treatments or drapery, discuss how wide you should make *each* window treatment, how much of a wall extension to add on each side, how much room stacking is going to take up, how far projections from the walls are going to be, etc.

Practicing your planning and measuring this way will prevent *many* remakes and reworks, while keeping your clientele happier. Many customers have trouble visualizing. Some customers are very hard to please. They think you will correct the situation if they do not end up liking the way items have come out. A designer or decorator cannot afford to give up his or her commissions making design changes for an indecisive customer. Larger companies that will absorb the remakes and reworks cannot afford the unprofitability of these situations. Make it very clear *how you are planning the job.* Discuss with your customer each and every aspect of the job. *Have the customers make decisions on each point.* **Take notes.** Record the notes on your worksheet, and then put them in writing on the sales slip.

Your customer will not be able to come back to you and say, *"You decided that, I didn't. You chose the placement, style, fabric, color."* When of course, *you and the customer selected these elements together.*

Never make *these* decisions on your own. *Unless you do not mind changing these decisions*, when your customer complains that they do not like what you have selected. You will be blamed, because *you* were the one who picked the elements out, or planned them that way.

Grain of fabrics:

The grain of fabric on drapery fabrics should go in the *same direction* as the grain of the sheers, undertreatments, top treatments, etc. **Example:** never use an antique satin with a horizontal slub or thready look, with a sheer that has a vertical, thready look. Consequently, never use a vertical, striped texture with a sheer that has a horizontal texture running across it. Always carefully look at the fabric swatches. **The swatches *as they are facing you* are the direction that the fabric is going to lay on the window, unless you railroad the fabric (turn the fabric sideways).**

Dyelots vary in color:

Remind your customers that different dyelots do vary slightly in color. Order *all* like fabrics or needed companion print fabrics to be used in the same room at the same time. Note on purchase orders to the supplier that the fabrics are to be *"cross-matched"* to each other. List the purchase order numbers of the other cross-matched purchase orders, on all of the purchase orders.

When *guessing* at a correct measurement for a particular item, realize that should you incorrectly guess a size and the item should have to be remade, that other matching fabric items in the room may also have to be remade, if you are unable to closely match the original dyelot. You could end up remaking the rest of the room to match the one item that you incorrectly guessed the measurement for, due to unavailability of a closely matching fabric. *This does happen* and will *eat up all the profits* for the job and probably several others.

It is better to make something *too big* (unless it is certain top treatments such as cornices, where the only remedy is to remake them) and be able to rework the item (cut it down, reuse the same fabric) than to have to remake *a too-small* item.

Show fabrics under the same lighting conditions:

Make sure your customer sees fabrics, carpeting, and any other decorating items, in the lighting conditions the items will be used in. It is preferable to see fabrics during the evening hours in addition to the daylight hours. Colors do change and appear different during different lighting conditions, from day to night, and *in* different *types* of lighting.

You *are* taking a chance when loaning your samples to the customer to be viewed both day and night. The customer may and probably will go shopping with your samples, to see if they can get a better price from a competitor. **Customers almost always take your samples and price compare them, when you loan them carpet samples.** Drapery is much harder to compare item-to-item, due to the many more factors involved in price comparing. Other hard window coverings are not going to be to hard to compare, though. If you lend your samples, **try hard to get a signed sales slip and a deposit from the customer, first.**

If you do not get a signed sales slip and the customer wants to show their spouse, or see the sample at night, insist on having it back the next day. Explain to them you need the sample *first thing in the morning*, for your next call. This way, they *can* show their spouse and *are* able to see it at night. Let the customer know, when they are ready to make purchases of other items elsewhere, while waiting for their order to come in, to come into the studio and *check* the sample out for the day, as needed. At that point if they shop around, you *have placed* the order, and it is *too late* for the customer to cancel.

Pleat up with your fingers fabrics that are to be lined and hold them up to the window with the selected lining fabric, behind the self-fabric. Many off-whites with just a bit of sunlight coming through them will appear yellow or orange. Hold the fabric up to the wall next, and again note the color. **Be sure to pleat up the fabric to see what color is in the folds.** Fabrics will sometimes take on a completely different color. Orange or yellow may appear and fall in the folds of the fabric against the wall, which you will *never* notice until you pleat up the fabric. Pay attention to the names of the colors on the various fabrics being considered. If it says *"pink glow,"* and you do not see a hint of pink, chances are when it is pleated up *you will see pink* in the folds.

Any time a customer calls up and says, *"This isn't what I ordered,"* grab the original sample you sold the fabric or carpet off of, and head over to their home. You do not want any installer turned away that has to be rescheduled later, because your customer *forgot* what they ordered. The installer will charge you a trip charge for the return trip, *for the customer's mistake*. Large areas of carpeting and fabrics look different from the small swatch you showed of the carpet or fabric when you were making the sale. Carpeting installers notoriously roll the carpet out, outside in the sunshine. The color looks completely different outside in the sun than in the dimmer light or different lighting of the home.

Custom Products:

Reinforce to your customers that you are responsible for correct measurements, guarantees on the products, fabrication, workmanship quality, guidance on suitability, and selection of products for their situation and needs. *But, custom products are made to fit individual customer's windows, in their selection of fabric, color, and style. These selections are not returnable due to the customer not liking the selected style, color of the treatment, length, or anything else that was decided by the customer.*

Always reinforce to the customer exactly what they are going to receive. Reinforce and review with the customer before leaving the home, after making a sale, what the two of you have planned and decided to be the right course of action to take.

*After confirming in writing a **complete** description of the job, any changes after the three-day cancellation period by the customer, will cost the customer money.* Any changes that cost your company money to change will have to be charged to the customer.

Multi-layer treatments are expensive:

When bidding on jobs, avoid treatments that require expensive custom fabrication labor charges, *if* cost is a main factor with you obtaining the job. Elaborate multi-layer treatments with ruffles, jabots, ruching, banding, insets, etc., are very expensive in labor and time.

For a sumptuous effect, you need to use yards and yards of fabric. The fabric needs to be lined, and in some cases, interlined. Some elaborate treatments require hand-finishing and hand-sewing.

If cost seems to be a big factor, and the customer wants top treatments, that are interesting and exciting, suggest treatments that take less labor and money, to look elaborate. Try a treatment such as an unconstructed valance, swaged on a pole rod with stationary panels and a soft-pleated shade for privacy.

Lengths for Window Treatments

Use the following guidelines when planning drapery lengths for various rooms:

Living room/dining room	Full length.
Master bedroom	Full length.
Family room, secondary bedrooms	May be made short, if desired, depending on the treatment you are planning. Full-length drapery and vertical-type treatments are nicer looking when made full-length.
High windows with a large amount of wall space, beneath (generally found in bedrooms or family rooms)	Make the window treatment short. A shutter, sheer, drapery, or shades fabricated in the same color as the wall will help camouflage this type of window.

Other windows

You will probably want to make short, depending on each situation. If the windows are in bathrooms, laundry rooms, kitchens, or the study, make short, or I.B. mount the treatments.

How to Treat All Types of Windows

Arch windows

These windows have horizontal sides and bottoms and are curved at the top. See the section on *Arch-Top windows*. Try to accent the shape, rather than selecting a rectangular or square treatment. Use fabric sunbursts mounted on a frame, arch-shaped shutters, pleated shades, Duette shades®, woven woods, stained or leaded glass. Another alternative is to treat only the bottom squared or rectangular area of the window, leaving the top uncovered, enjoying the window as the architect intended, with maximum light coming through.

Awning window

This window is usually three or more horizontal sashes holding glass, that open out of the room to the exterior by the turning of a crank. Plan your treatment around the crank, or have your customer buy a crank made for mini blinds (much flusher in style, available at the hardware store).

Bay windows

Three or more windows set at angles with each other, that project outward from the room. These are usually double-hung, with the middle window, normally stationary. They are planned similarly to the corner window. Usually a place for a dramatic type treatment and the focal point of the room.

Preferably, do not place a top treatment across the top on the outside of the bay window. To do so is to *cut the bay window area off* from the rest of the room, rather than incorporating it into the room.

Sheers are more desirable to use on a bay than heavier, full draperies. Heavier drapery will overpower a bay window, and cover the side windows, with their stacking. Use the heavier drapery in smaller, stationary panels and the sheers or other undertreatments, for the larger areas of a bay window.

Bow windows

These windows are similar to bay windows because, they form a recessed area within a room. Instead of being angled, they are curved. Use fabric treatments to treat a curved window. The bow window will eliminate any use of a hard treatment, due to its curved shape.

Casement windows

In-swinging, hinged windows that swing into the room; or out-swinging, swinging out of the room. They are operated by hand or by crank.

These are harder windows to treat with less options available on styling. Shutters which also swing into the room, mounted over the casement windows, are a wise selection for this type of window.

Otherwise, *drapery must clear the window when stacked back, along with any top treatment selected clearing the top of the casement window,* so the window may open and close without getting caught in the hinges of the window. The projection of the crank must be allowed for in the clearance of the treatment; or have the customer get a crank made for mini blinds, available at hardware stores.

R.T.B. treatments, hourglass treatments, blinds, shades, or woven woods may be attached to the window frame itself, swinging open and closed with the window. Any hard undertreatment should be ordered with hold-down brackets to keep the treatment fastened down when the window is opened or closed.

If the window opens out of the room or building, *it is also important to clear the glass area, when stacking-back* (with whatever treatment you select). This helps keep the window treatment cleaner from the dust and dirt blowing into the room, and to allow for maximum ventilation.

Clerestory windows

These windows consist of a small window placed near the ceiling, usually in an un-usual, slanted shape that follows the roof line. They are intended to be left untreated with a window treatment, to allow light to come into the room.

Corner windows

Two windows which butt together, or come close to butting together at a corner. Treat a corner window situation as two windows that are planned together, to flow together with each other.

Excellent way to treat is with, two one-way traverse rods butting and passing in the corner. If there is wall space between the two corner windows, than treat the two windows as pairs, butting and passing each other. If you leave the wall space *exposed* between the two windows, it will not be as effective.

See the *Measuring* section under *Corner Windows* for an in-depth evaluation on how to properly plan out corner windows for window treatments.

Doors with windows, French doors

Doors with windows and French doors have panes of glass framed by a casing. See the section on *French Doors*. R.T.B. treatments of all types, hour-glass treatments, shutters, blinds, and shades may be mounted *right* on the swinging doors. Any hard window treatment, will need hold-down brackets to keep the treatment fastened down when the window is opened and closed. As with casement windows above, French doors or other doors with windows may have overtreatments mounted on the outside of the doors, if the overtreatment clears the door, when stacked back.

Stationary panels mounted at the sides of the door, free hang or tied back, may have to come into the door a bit and work best with doors that swing to the outside.

Top treatments and valances over the top of the treatment, will finish these doors off. Any top treatment must be planned high enough to clear the door, swinging into the room so as not to get caught up into the door when opened and closed. If the door swings out of the room, then stacking-off and clearance at the top of the door, are less important considerations. Go with what looks the best. The treatment should still come close to clearing at the sides, to show the doors, and should be high enough at the top for a tall person to freely pass through.

Dormier windows

These windows are placed so they tunnel the light into the room. This happens due to the wall areas right next to the windows that create an alcove. Since there is limited wall area, you need to use a shade or blind type of treatment that pulls up and down, with a top treatment or a shutter. If you use side panels or full drapery, they are going to take a majority of the window's space to stack-off. Cafe treatments that leave the middle areas exposed also work rather well.

Double-hung windows (sash)

Double-hung windows are extremely common windows. They may be opened from the top or from the bottom. They may be cut up with small panes on both the top or the bottom, or may just have one, large pane of glass for each of the top and the bottom areas. Double-hung windows are easily made larger in appearance by stacking-off the drapery or vertical blind horizontally. Stacking-off will allow the view to be unobstructed, as this type of window is not very wide.

Any treatment added above should not obstruct the window from the top. The treatment should have the ability to be pulled up above the window for maximum exposure of glassed-in area of these small windows.

Using a top-down treatment will allow the top to be free, while ensuring privacy across the bottom of the window.

Double window

A double window is two or more windows that are set side by side, using the same connecting outer frame on the outside and the same window sill. Treat this window as if it were one window. Measure from the outside of the outer frame on each side to the opposite, outside frame on the other side.

Glass walls or sliding doors

This type of window is an energy waster. This may or may not be sliding glass doors to gain access to and from the house, or may be large walls of glass to visually let the outside come into the home or building. Usually found on modern homes and commercial buildings.

Undertreatments should be able to clear easily the glassed-in areas when pulled up or down. If the undertreatment is an energy-saving type of treatment, then you can use stationary panels with a top treatment to frame the glass area, giving the appearance of a full drapery, stacked or tied back.

If the climate is a very hot or cold one, your customer will probably welcome the use a full-functioning, insulative drapery (with a thermal-suede lining) that will stack-off the glass areas.

If the glass area is a sliding door, plan the drapery or verticals to be a one-way pull, to pull with the direction of the way the door opens. An addition of a stationary or *"dead"* panel at the opposite side to the stack-off area on a one-way pull may be employed to give a balanced, stacked-off appearance when the drapery is stacked back.

If the drapery or vertical may be made wide enough to stack-off, plan them to be nicer-looking pairs, rather than one-way pull panels.

On a sliding door or any other door opening, any treatment planned should be high enough in height to allow a taller person to pass through, without bending their head down. The treatment should also be wide enough to allow a wide person to pass through.

Sliding French doors are treated like sliding doors. All treatments are mounted on the wall, to the sides of the sliding door, and mounted to clear the door above.

Jalousie window

This window is similar to an awning window, except that the glass is not framed in a sash but is actually *just* horizontal strips of glass that open outward by turning a crank. Allow clearance for the crank for any treatment you may plan for this type of window.

Multiple windows on same wall

See the section on *Two or More Closely Placed Windows on One Wall*. Multiple windows may be treated as separate units, or as one large unit. The drapery treatment may be hung in a series, or the overdrapery may be made to cover the whole expanse. The undertreatments, if hard window treatments, may be broken up into multiple units. Unless the expanse is quite large, over five feet, try to make the undertreatments in one piece, *if* the overtreatment is in one piece.

Break up the treatment and treat the windows separately. A beautifully related, overall treatment is a great way to accent this type of window. Each window may have stationary panels tied back over an undertreatment. The window treatments butt-to the next drapery unit, forming an hourglass effect across the wall. If the windows are narrow enough (so the rod is completely covered with the panels at the top), you may want to forgo the top treatment. A top treatment would tie the whole unit together and make the treatment complete.

Picture windows

This type of window usually frames a view on the front of the house. Picture windows generally have one large, fixed pane of glass, with smaller windows on each side, which have the ability to be opened.

If your customer needs privacy, or if the view is not very nice, plan a hard undertreatment for versatility (to take care of privacy and view needs, under the overtreatment). A versatile hard treatment will also allow you to leave the overtreatment in place and untouched at all times.   Another solution is an overtreatment that may be traversed open for air flow and viewing out when needed, and traversed closed for privacy, when needed.

Your customer will probably not want to spend the extra money to stack-off this already wide window, unless they are striving to make the window appear larger in size. If they do not stack-off of the window, the air flow will be obstructed, due to the window treatment stacking on the smaller side windows.

Slanted windows

Slanted windows usually follow the slanted roofline above them. They may take up the whole wall, or only a portion of the wall. There is usually a horizontal mullion dividing the slanted top from the bottom, rectangular section of the window. The bottom portion of the slant may or may not be a sliding door. The upper section of the window is non-moveable.

Slanted windows are difficult windows to treat. Try to leave the slanted portion of the window alone and uncovered, to allow light in. If your customer is *really* having a problem with light and sun control, then pleated shades, Duette shades®, or blinds may be used. These hard window treatments will incur heavy surcharges.

Drapery may be planned to cover the whole window. The drapery must be straight and non-distorted at the top slant. This is difficult to do, as the top of the drapery on a slant is folded and pleated up, on the bias.

Templates are required for ordering. Whatever you select to place on the slanted portions of the window will need to be consistent with the bottom portion of the same window, and any other windows within the same room.

Small windows placed high up the wall

These types of windows are placed high up on the wall to allow light and air to come in. Regardless of the drapery on the other walls in the same room, you are dealing with an odd type of window that will appear different, even if the window is treated the same as the other windows in the same room. Plan to make the oddly placed window in a treatment such as wood blinds, shutters, or shades. Select a color that is a close match to the wall color of the walls. You want this window to perform its function, not stand out and fade into the wall unnoticed. If you are using a neutral undertreatment on the other treatments in the same room, use that same undertreatment. A tiny, short drapery in the same room as full-length ones will not relate to each other. The placement of shutters on these windows is an excellent alternative.

Tall, vertical windows

Tall, vertical windows look outstanding with floor-length verticals and drapery. Under-treatments, mounted with an I.B. mount, with full-length drapery that draws open or is stationary, and tied-back panels are good combinations for this type of window. Fabric shades of all types are naturals for these kinds of windows.

Ranch-style windows

These wide, horizontal, three-sectioned, short-in-length windows (usually located high up on the wall, with very odd proportions), look their very best when treated with shutters. Short drapery may also be used, if the color is light, to avoid drawing attention to the odd proportions. Full sheers and drapery, full-length, will help cover up and camouflage this type of window.

Windows on the same wall

Windows on the same wall, closely spaced together, are going to look nicer if they are treated as separate units, rather than one large unit. Treating the windows as one unit will give you the square effect, that is better avoided.

How To Determine the Price to Charge
for Any Fabric Interior Treatment

Below is a listing of the steps you need to go through to arrive at correct pricing for any custom product you are selling:

- Decide **which fabric** is to be used. Determine **how much fabric** is needed. **Multiply the fabric yards times the fabric price per yard.** Include **extra fabric needed for any repeat. Take** any **discount** on the fabric at this point.

- Select **what style of treatment** you are fabricating.

- Decide if the treatment is **to be lined.** If lining is to be used, **multiply the yards of lining times the lining price per yard.**

- Determine **what size and measurements** to fabricate the treatment in.

- Calculate the **fabrication price on labor, from your fabrication price list.** Multiply the fabrication price times the amount of widths of fabric to be used.

- Are there any **other labor or fabrication charges** that should be charged for the particular treatment or situation you are planning?

- Is there an **extra charge for trim**, or are *any other* fabrics to be used for trim?

- **Calculate each element individually,** according to the correct price to charge for each item. **Figure each layer, and all the charges separately,** *then* add all of the figures together for each layer. Your customer may want to change or eliminate one of the layers. If you have planned and figured the layers separately, it is easy to change them.

  Take any sale discounts on each individual item. Do this by first determining the retail price. Take the percentage that the item is on sale for, multiply the percentage off times the retail price of the item (50% off becomes .50). Next, subtract the resulting number from the retail price to determine the sale or discounted price. You will not want to discount the fabrication labor or the installation under normal circumstances.

  To keep everything clear, **always price out the original price. Draw a line through the original price, and write the discounted figure next to it.** When you go back to double-check your figures before quoting the price to the customer, it is easy to see if you have already taken the sale discount, *if* you have the original price noted and crossed out, with the sale price next to it.

  Example: The fabric your customer is interested in is 40% off the retail price of $24 per yard. $24 x .40 = a discount of $9.60 per yard. Subtract $9.60 from $24 to arrive at a $14.40 sale price per yard. 29 yards is needed for the window treatment you are planning. 29 yards x $24 (regular retail) = $696. Now, multiply $696 x .40 = 278.40. Subtract $278.40 from $696 to arrive at your sale price for the fabric of $417.60.

- Decide **what hardware is needed** for the treatments you are planning. Add up all required hardware.

- **Figure installation charges. Include remeasure. Keep installation charges separate from other charges, because they are not sales-taxable.** Installation charges are found on the installation price list. Multiply the installation charge, per item or width, times the number of items or widths you have planned.

- **Add *all* the figures up. Keep the installation figures separate, until you add the tax.** Now add in the installation.

- Review and **double-check your figures** before quoting them to your customer.

- **Close the sale.**

- **Write up the order, being very specific and complete.**

- Thoroughly **review the** whole **job and sales slip** with the customer.

Working with a drapery or soft window treatment price chart:

- Some studios work off a chart for drapery and soft window treatments that have the fabric, lining (if you are using the *lining chart* of the fabric price, per yard), fabrication, and the installation already figured in. *Use* the price listed, under the retail price, per yard for fabric, according to how many widths needed and the finished length desired. Take the discount off this price for any sale price and add in any hardware and tax.

These charts are planned for normal drapery hems and headers of 18". If you are planning a wide rod pocket that requires you to add 30" to the finished length for hems and headers, you are going to require more fabric. See the *S.O.R.* section to see how to figure the extra yardage needed and how to charge your customer accordingly.

To use the chart, you would add in the additional amount of yardage needed for the finished length, subtract 18" (pretend you were using a normal hem and header, so your chart pricing will still work for your circumstances), and use the resulting amount (for chart purposes only) for your new finished length. Use this same formula when adding horizontal repeats, needed for finished length.

Example: You are planning a drapery with a gathered rod pocket top, with six widths of fabric needed, to achieve 300% fullness. The drapery will have a finished 86" length. According to the chart on *Specifics on Planning Rod Pocket Treatments* in the pole, rod section of this book, you need to add 30" to the finished length for hems and headers. The chart you are working with for drapery has only 18" added in for hems and headers. You need to *adjust* the price to take care of the additional yardage needed. There are two ways for you to proceed.

1st method: Take the 86" **finished length;**, add 30" to it for the hems and headers for the particular rod you want to use. 86 + 30= 116". Next, subtract 18" for a drapery with a *"normal"* hem and header allowance. 116" — 18" = 98". For the purposes of using the chart, use 98" as your new finished length.

2nd method: Using the same situation as noted above, take the 86" finished length. Determine the difference in yardage from 18" to 30" (the amount allowed in your yardage chart, versus the amount you need to do the job). 30" — 18" = 12". 12" is ⅓ of a yard. Multiply ⅓ of a yard x the amount of widths you are using. As noted in the example, you need 6 widths of fabric. 6 widths x ⅓ = 1.98 yards, or 2 additional yards needed to accommodate this rod pocket treatment.

Using a chart when additional fabric is required for repeats:

You have determined that your printed fabric with a horizontal repeat of 16" will need 8 widths of 54" goods, and the desired finished length is 96". You are using a pleated header for the drapery.

1st method: Determine the new cut length using the directions in the *Determining Horizontal Repeats* section of this book. Figure the cut length of the drapery; 96" + 18" = 114". Divide the cut length with the repeat amount (16"). 114" divided by 16" = 7.13 repeats. Round up this figure to 8 repeats. Multiply the amount of repeats times the repeat size. 8 x 16" = 128". Subtract the normal chart hem and header amount of 18" from the multiplied, repeat amount. 128" — 18" = 110". The resulting number is the length to use for chart purposes for **charging the customer, only.** 110" is the correct finished length to use for your chart purposes, in this example.

2nd method: Use the same procedure for figuring repeats, as immediately above; figure the repeat for the fabric as needed. Using the new cut length of 128" as shown above, subtract from 128" the cut length for a plain fabric of 114" (the normal plain fabric cut length, for a finished length drapery of 96"). 128" — 114" = 14". **The resulting number will be the difference in yardage needed for a printed fabric, with a repeat of 16" per width. Multiply the resulting difference times how many widths of fabric are required.** 14" x 8 widths = 112". 112" divided by 36" = 3.11, (round up slightly) or 3¼ yards of additional fabric needed for an 8-width drapery with a repeat of 16" and a finished length of 96".

How to Determine the Price to Charge
for Any Alternate Window Treatment

Below is a listing of the steps you need to go through to arrive at correct pricing for any alternate or hard window custom product you are selling:

● Determine **which sample of hard window material** is to be used.

● Decide **what style** of window treatment you are fabricating.

● Decide if the window treatment is **to be lined.** Some hard window treatments have liners available.

● Decide what **size and measurements** to use to fabricate the hard treatment.

● Determine the **price of the item,** corresponding to the sample selection, style, and measurements.

● Are **any other options** for the hard window treatment to be included? Check the *Hard Window* section in this book to see available options for hard window treatments.

● Are there any **other labor or fabrication charges** that should be charged for the particular treatment or situation you are planning?

● Is there an **extra charge for scalloped edges, trim,** or are any other fabrics to be used for trim?

● **Figure each element out individually** according to the correct price to charge for each item. **Figure each layer, and all the charges separately,** then add them all together. Your customer may want to change or eliminate one of the layers. If you have planned and figured the layers separately, it is easy to change them.

Take any sale discounts on each individual item. Do this by first determining the retail price. Take the percentage that the item is on sale for, multiply the percentage off times the retail price of the item (50% off becomes .50). Next, subtract the resulting number from the retail price to determine the sale or discounted price. You will not want to discount fabrication labor or the installation, under normal circumstances. Unless you are selecting an option for a hard window treatment, the fabrication labor prices are built into the hard window price. Use the vendor's price list for the extra option charges.

To keep everything clear, **always price out the original price. Draw a line through the original price, and write the discounted figure next to it.** When you go back to double-check your figures before quoting the price to the customer, it is easy to see if you have already taken the sale discount if you have the original price noted and crossed out with the sale price next to it.

● **Figure installation charges. Include remeasure.** Keep installation charges separate from other charges because they are not taxable. Installation charges are found on the installation price list.

- **Add up all the figures.** Keep the installation figures separate, until you add the tax. Now add in the installation.

- Review and **double-check your figures** before quoting them to your customer.

- **Close the sale.**

- **Write up the order, being very specific and complete.**

- Thoroughly **review the** whole **job and sales slip** with the customer.

Techniques to Use to Cut the Price Down

- **Sell unlined drapery instead of lined drapery.** If the sun exposure is southern or western, it may be less expensive to add a less expensive hard treatment under the drapery.

- **Compare the price difference for drapery fabrics, between using a heavier cotton or a cotton-blend fabric, unlined, versus a lined-satin or lightweight fabric that requires a lining.**

- **Use a less expensive vendor or source with better pricing, possibly with a slightly lower quality product.**

- **Switch your customer to a less expensive type of fabric.** Try plain fabrics instead of a print, or plain-woven types rather than jacquard types.

- **Cut down the fullness on fabric items.** End up using fewer widths of fabric, cutting down fabrication, lining, and fabric costs.

- **Use 54" goods rather than 48" goods.** Use wider fabric, so you need less fabric than the original plan. You may end up paying slightly more for the wider goods, but overall, you use *fewer* widths, coming out *way ahead* in money saved.

- **Use seamless sheers instead of seamed sheers.** These will be much better hanging, nicer looking, seams will not show or pucker, and there is not a possibility of the seams ever coming apart after the thread they were sewn with deteriorates from the sun. **Seamless sheers always hang nicer and in all ways are a higher-quality sheer for your customer.** Only when *very short* draperies or top treatments are planned, will it probably work out on to be less expensive to use 48" goods. Calculate the job using both fabrics to see which is the better buy.

- **Use floating sheers under a wall-to-wall drapery or similar situation.** Plan the sheer measurements to go 12" on each side of the window opening. If made to fit wall-to-wall, the sheers will drag against the overdrapery every time the drapery was opened and closed. This also avoids a complaint from the customer that the drapery and sheers are mounted too close together.

- **Use stationary panels instead of a full drapery.** *Especially* if top treatments are also planned. The top treatment will cover the bare rod in the middle, or the abruptly ending stationary-panel rods. If the customer wants to use a very expensive fabric, this is *an especially effective* way to cut the price down. Use less expensive undertreatments for privacy to pull closed at night. Smaller panels tied back look better and take up less of the window than larger panels tied back. They will probably *never* be untied and *used* to traverse back and forth.

- **Do not stack draperies off the windows.** Plan the extensions on each side of the window at custom's basic amount — 5" on each side of the window. The drapery will stack, mostly on the window. Review section on *Drapery Stacking. Not* stacking the drapery off of the window will work well, unless there is a beautiful view, or your customer wants full visibility or maximum air flow from the window. This will be *considerably less expensive* than planning the drapery wide enough to stack-off the window.

- **Use less expensive top treatments,** such as a basic French pleated valance, all types of gathered-on-the-rod valances, rod top-and-bottom valance treatments, pouff-style top treatments, and wraparound top treatments.

- **When planning top treatments with drapery under them, plan the drapery to go only 5"-6"** *above* **the window,** rather than the true custom way of doing it — planned at 3½" below the top of the top treatment.

- **Allow customers to install their selections.** This will work well with *handier* customers and some of the more basic treatments and hard window coverings.

- **Have customers make use of some readymade hard window products or other window coverings on the market** — suggesting these when you are completely out of the ballpark on the price. This may allow you to at least get *part* of the job, the *more custom* portions of the job, or may free up money from less important rooms for custom treatments in the more important areas of the home.

- **Sell the customer the fabric to make their own top treatments and other accessories, to go along with the drapery you are selling them.** A bit of profit on the fabric sale is better than no sale at all. The customer may want a total look, not just drapery, and cannot afford to go custom for *all* the top treatments and accessories.

- If the customer wants a lots of trim and banding extras, but is not willing to pay the extra labor charges, suggest they add the trim themselves. The customer may never bother to do it, but you will not lose a sale because these added charges make the price sometimes *prohibitive.*

- Add cords and tassels to wraparound top treatments, to give a very rich effect. Wrap the cord around the top treatment in the same direction the top treatment flows.

- **Make use of the toppers available** from several sources, **for low-cost alternatives to finish off those hard window coverings in the secondary, less-visible rooms of the home.**

- **When planning vertical blinds,** *remember* that free-hang slats or vanes are considerably less expensive **than inserted vanes in plastic holders.** Some customers prefer the *look* of the free-hang slats with chains and weights to the inserted types. Other customers perceive that inserts are more durable, like the effect of them, and will insist on having the inserts over the free-hang types.

- **Have the customer incorporate wall stenciling,** rather than wallpaper everywhere.

Customers shopping around or those who want to spend as little as possible:

Many times after arriving at your customer's home you are informed by the customer that they are going to get more prices, or want to spend as little as possible. They may not have indicated this to you when you were working with them in the studio, and you thought your visit to their home was *to merely finalize* the fine points of the sale with the planning and measuring.

Any clues that the customer gives you about price comparing or not wanting to spend much signal you to employ the techniques below on cutting the price down.

Keep the Overlap and the Return the Same Size

Have the drapery fabricated with the same size return as the size of the overlap — the first pleat to the leading edge of the drapery. When the drapery fades in the center, at the leading edges, your customer may *exchange and reverse* the faded overlap portion of the drapery to the side areas where the returns are now. If they do this, it will keep the drapery looking much nicer for a longer period of time. This will be most effective when there is a top treatment over the drapery, the drapery are traversed open during the day, or when you are using stationary panels, so the six-inch expanse from the leading edge to the first pleat will not be as obvious.

Tied-Back Drapery

If your customer wants to have the drapery tied back, have them leave the drapery tied back, rather than letting the drapery loose and retying the drapery repeatedly. They will end up with limp, wrinkled drapery, from all the handling, rather than a quality, custom-made appearing treatment.

Add an undertreatment to take care of privacy needs. Later, after the drapery has been cleaned and pressed, *for a different look,* the customer may then choose to leave the tiebacks off.

Stationary Panels

Due to high fabric prices, labor prices, double-paned windows, and exceptional views, customers prefer a lighter look at the window — especially in mild climate areas. The use of stationary panels has really caught on. Stationary panels are the method of adding accent panels that have the appearance of drapery, but will not draw. Your customer does not end up paying for yards of fabric that remain tied or pulled back, and never get traversed across the window. Stationary panels appear to be drapery stacked, or tied back. In essence, they are merely panels of fabric — usually 1½ panels to 2 panels of fabric on each side of the window — just enough fabric to accent the window with a framed, rich look.

1½ panels or widths of 48" fabric on each side of the window is the most common application of stationary panels for your average-sized windows. On wider windows, use 2 panels (or widths) of 48" fabric on each side of the window, to balance the heaviness of the window. If you are using 54" wide fabric, you can get away with one panel (or width) of fabric on average-sized windows; 1½ widths on each side for wider windows. Model homes (trying to cut every corner) usually use one skimpy-appearing panel of 48" goods on each side of the window.

Use this formula to plan how wide to make the stationary panels in proportion to the overall width of the window: Plan each stationary panel to be ¼ — ⅓ of the overall width of the window treatment.

Stationary panels are mounted on stationary rods and will not draw. They may be pleated or gathered on the rod. Top treatments hide the abruptly ending rods and finish off the treatment. Placement over bathtubs or showers is the only place to even consider letting the rods end (better yet, use a top treatment to finish the treatment) abruptly in mid-air without a top treatment.

Stationary panels actually look much nicer than a full drapery, tied back. A full drapery uses yards and yards of extra, unnecessary fabric, cuts down the view and the air-flow of the window. A full drapery tied back takes up so much of the window, you can hardly see out. The leading edges on the drapery (if the window is fairly wide), when tied back, *will almost come up to the level of the tieback*, and will look very unprofessional. When you do sell **full drapery or stationary panels intending to be tied back, specify on the workorder, "flat-fold" drapery.**

On your workorder, note that these are stationary panels, and request cut-to-measure utility rods. The installer will cut the rods to fit the panels on the job. Charge the customer by the foot, for the rods — usually about $1.50 — $2 a foot, plus the installation charge.

Drapery or Curtains?

Drapery are heavier fabrics **usually lined, pleated, and hung up by hooks.** Drapery may also have a rod pocket and be nontraversing. The main point is the weight of the fabric. If the fabric is not very lightweight, it is considered to be a drapery rather than a curtain. If made out of *"sheer"* or lace types of fabric, they are called sheers. They are called sheers whether they are constructed with a rod pocket or are pleated like a drapery.

Curtains are generally lighter in weight, unlined, and have a rod pocket or casing at the top, to slip over a pole rod or another type of curtain rod. Curtains do not traverse and must be drawn back by hand. Use is favored when undertreatments are used and the curtains will not be handled. Curtains are primarily used in kitchens, bathrooms, and secondary bedrooms. Usually washable.

Rod Pockets and Headers

Rod pockets should always be double, folded in the rod pocket and the stand-up header areas. Double folding gives more body and depth to the rod pocket, and to the stand-up headers — instead of two layers of fabric (if lined, four layers), you have three layers (lined, six layers). Using only two layers is more economical, but produces a much limper end-product for the rod pocket and header.

Stand-up headers above or below the rod (in the case of a rod-pocket sleeve) may vary in size from ¼" up to 5" depending on the body of the fabric selected. If the header is too wide and the fabric very limp, the header will flop over.

Buttonholes for rod-pocket drapery:

For pole rods with decorative finials at the ends, when you are using curtains or drapery gathered up on the rod, plan for fabrication for the drapery or curtain to have buttonholes set in. Set the buttonholes in at the same number of inches as the return point or the projection point from the wall of the drapery panel. **The buttonhole allows the finial to slip through the rod pocket and still allows your drapery to have returns at the sides.**

- Note on the workorder for the workroom to sew vertical buttonholes on each side of your drapery panel at the return point or projection point out from the wall of 3½", 6", or 9".

- Charge your customer for each buttonhole. Fabrication charges are listed in your fabrication price list.

Hems and Headers

Hems and headers are like rod pockets: they need to have their fabrics double-folded for body, weight, and depth. The hem is made single-folded when used in combination with a lining that also has a hem. An unlined drapery needs the weight of the double-folded hem to help it hang nicely.

Hems are usually 3½" — 4" deep; headers are usually 3½" — 4", depending on the workroom. Pleats of headers are the full width of the header, 3½" — 4", and are bartacked at their base.

Pleated header styles may be termed French pleated, triple pleated, etc.

Gathered Sheers Versus Pleated Sheers

The advantages of pleated *over* gathered sheers are many. Pleated sheers overlap in the middle, if they are made a pair. Gathered sheers can only meet in the middle. Pleated sheers hang uniformly, can traverse open and closed as needed, and tend to be more significant.

Both types of sheers can usually (depending on the fiber content) be handwashed or washed on a delicate cycle with mild detergent.

If pleated, the pleats need to be hand dressed while still wet. The top of the sheers with the hooks intact (if pleated up uniformly) may be placed in a lingerie bag and tied shut, preventing the hooks from snagging the fabric of the sheers.

Seamless Fabrics or Railroaded Goods

Railroaded goods are wide-width, imported European seamless goods from 115" to 118" wide. Railroaded goods are turned on their side or fabricated in the opposite direction from 48" goods. The width becomes the length. A sheer or drapery out of 118" fabric can be made as wide as needed (or as wide as the bolt of fabric is) without a seam. Railroaded goods may be pleated or fabricated with a rod pocket. Unless you make the sheer or drapery into a pair, there will not be any seams or overlaps in the middle of the drapery.

Seamless goods are usually lightweight and sheer, or are loosely woven fabrics.

Points to remember:

● The use of seamless goods will generally result in a **lower cost** than will the use of 48" goods.

● You **cannot exceed a finished length for a pleated drapery of 100"**. The extra 18" is needed and used for the hem and headers.

● There are **no seams across the width of the draperies.**

● Seamless goods are **easier to fabricate and work with in the workroom**, because the workroom only sews the edges, hems, and headers. Since this type of fabric is usually very slippery and hard to work with (in either 48" or 118" goods), you **eliminate puckered seams**. The draperies end up hanging nicer, due to lack of puckering and lack of seams.

● Unless you make overlaps for opening the drapery in the center, you will have a continuous, uninterrupted seamless drapery.

● There is **never a possibility of seam breakage and puckering** with seamless goods.

Sheers

Try to *avoid* making sheers into pairs. When you make them into pairs, there will be four layers of fabric, laying over each other. If the drapery fabric is especially sheer, the overlapped area becomes very obvious and stands out. Make drapery or sheers one-way pulls for a consistent, continuous look.

Some customers insist on being able to glimpse through to the outside, from the middle of the drapery or sheer. You may end up changing a few one-way pulls to pairs if you do not check with the customer before fabrication and determine if the finest obtainable looks are preferred, or is the ability to look out from the middle of the drapery favored.

If the customer is more concerned about the drapery's looks and hanging ability, they will opt for the one-way pull. After a few years of hanging and being drawn open and closed, sheers that are pairs tend to separate at the leading edges. The leading edges will not fall completely straight. The closer they get to the hem, the farther the leading edges *"snake back."*

Always let sheers lay over the hanger for two weeks after they are fabricated, if possible. Sheers need the weight of the fabric folded onto itself to set the pleats and make uniform folds. For rush jobs, explain ahead of time to the customer that the sheers will not be *quite as uniform* in their hanging, since they will not be allowed anytime to hang out over the hanger.

Always bunch or fold sheer fabric up several times to get a true perspective on the color. If you forget to do this, you may get a call from your customer saying, *"These sheers are not peach, they are pink."* The pleating and the folds laying on top of each other give you a completely different view of the color. The color of the sheer is the color the sunlight coming in will change the color to, after filtering through the sheers. Always beware of the color name. If it says apricot haze, but appears off-white in color, it is sure to appear apricot when folded up into pleats.

Sheers or Draperies that Hang Badly

Some of the seamless sheer fabrics that are available are quite stiff and will not hang very uniformly and nicely when they are fabricated. You will not always be able to determine how each fabric is going to cooperate, from viewing a small swatch of the fabric. Heavily slubbed fabrics are notorious for poor hanging ability. If you have a seemingly particular customer, sell fabrics that have an evenly woven texture with a soft-flowing hand.

You may receive complaints that the sheers or drapery are not falling in nice folds. If the sheers or drapery are hanging poorly, first determine if the drapery have been left tied back for the time the installer recommended after installation. Next, determine if the sheers or drapery have double-folded hems and weights at regular intervals.

Steaming and fabric (wrinkle releasing) sprays may help solve, hanging problems.

If steaming or fabric sprays do not completely correct the hanging problem, or if the fabric may not be steamed, have memory-stitch tape or bead chain inserted at the hem, to help correct the hang problem.

Measuring and Planning the Job

Measuring Accurately and Consistently

One of the most important elements in planning of window treatments is measuring accurately.

Always *start* the measuring process with the first window to the left as you walk into a room. Proceed with each window clockwise around the room. If you always work in this direction, your installer will know what goes where, if you should forget to list the room on the workorder. *It is an industry standard to work clockwise around the room in planning, measuring, and installing of window treatments.*

Use a 25'- 30' steel tape measure that can be held rigidly for about 7'. **Always show your measurements in inches,** *unlike floorcoverings, which are shown in feet.* Inches are converted to yards when ordering fabric.

Turn to page 197 and 198 for diagrams on how to measure and the basic types of installations.

Variances in Measuring

Depending on where you are employed, *how tight* you want the drapery on the rod, *who* is instructing or working with you, etc., you will find that *the amount to add* for the returns, overlaps, and the stacking formula, *may vary* by about an inch, either way. *A slight variance is not a big concern.* The advice given here is adapted from *considerable* experience and education received in this field using four different methods. The following formulas and methods work well; other methods you *may discover* may also work.

As the formulas are presented, *note the range given.* It is left up to you to decide to go with adding the larger number, the smaller number, or somewhere in between. *If you add more, you get a looser fit; if you add less, there is less room to work with,* if there is a slight discrepancy in the workroom's fabrication, the customer's walls, the possibility of your mismeasuring, and how close you want to come in length without touching the floor (usually ¼"). Add *too large of an amount,* and you may have to rework the length.

The opposite problem is that the drapery may not stack-off as planned, *if you have not added enough.* On the other hand, if you subtract too much the item will be too short. *These are rules for you to adapt to the individual situation using your best judgement and the guidance of your installer and workroom.*

The Three Lengths Needed When Planning Window Treatments

There are three basic window treatment lengths: **the vertical length** of the window treatment, **the width** length of the window treatment, and the **length of the projection of the return. Refer to page 197 (end of this chapter) for diagrams on how to measure.**

Note on wall extensions of windows: Drapery, vertical blinds, woven-wood drapery, and other drapery-like treatments, *require* **a minimum of 4" — 5" on either side of the window; 4" — 5" above the window; and 4" — 5" below the window for O.B. mounted treatments.** This amount is the requirement to achieve a custom fit, to ensure privacy, and to avoid light leaks.

Vertical length: **Measure from where the rod is to be placed down to the desired length.** This may be floor to ceiling; 5" above the window down to the floor; 5" above the window to 5" below the sill; *or* this length may be the measurement of the length of the window treatment needed for I.B. or O.B. mounts.

Width length: **The width or bracket-to-bracket measurement of a window treatment is the width of the window's inside or outside frame to the other side of the window's inside or outside frame, *and* any additional allowances for extensions,** as shown below.

Add a minimum of 4" - 5" on each side of the window width for extensions. To add *less*, will allow the side hems to show from the outside of the home or building. Also, *there will* be no guarantee of coverage at the sides of the drapery from light leaks. For a standard mount you may want to stack-off the window and add ⅓ to ½ more width to the original measurement. Review the *stack-off* section.

Note: If the window ends within 8" of a corner, *it is preferable* to take the treatment all the way to the corner for a nicer, more finished appearing treatment. This will allow the customer to easily arrange furniture within the room and will also create a treatment that flows, rather than creating a chopped-up look.

Projection length: **Measure how far *out* from the wall the treatment needs to sit to clear any undertreatment, cranks, and other obstructions.** This projection allows the treatment to move *freely* side to side or up and down. *This is your return size.*

Bracket-to-Bracket Measurements

Bracket-to-bracket measurements are the measurements from the tip of one side of the rod or treatment to the tip of the *other side* of the rod or treatment.

For all windows *strive* to add a minimum of 4" - 5" on each side of the window. Using this as a minimum figure, add amount needed to completely stack the treatment off the window, or make the treatment wall-to-wall.

The **horizontal width** of the window treatment **must always be made wider than the window width.** Making a treatment wider makes the treatment look richer, fuller, more expensive, and helps avoid privacy and light-leak problems. Some windows will allow only a few inches extra in width on each side. Depending on the window placement and your customer's needs, the amount of extra width you need to add will vary.

Since you add extensions of 4" - 5" on each side of the window for wall extensions, or up to ½ or 50% more of the window width for stacking the treatment off the window, this bracket-to-bracket measurement is *never* the same measurement as the window measurement.

Example: Window I.B. measurement is 36" wide. You are only going to add the standard 5" on each side of the window (standard mount) for this treatment.

36" + 10" (5" extension on each side of the window x 2) = 46". **Your bracket-to-bracket measurement is 46".**

Projections and Returns

Projections are the depth of the drapery rod, headrail, or other window treatment, from its **face point, or part that projects the furthest out into the room** (as in vertical slats rotating) **back to the wall.** *All* O.B. **mounted window treatments have projections out from the wall.** *Not all O.B. mounted treatments are available with returns.* Refer to page 198 for diagrams on basic types of rod installations and return amounts to use.

Standard rod projections:

	Projection	
Single treatment	3"	On a rod with a 3" projection; the drapery is ordered with a return of 3½".
Double treatment	6"	On a rod with a 6" projection; the drapery *may be ordered* with a 6" or a 6½" return.
Triple treatment	9"	On a rod with a 9" projection; the drapery *may be ordered* with a 9" or a 9½" return.

Returns:

Returns are the side sections of the drapery or other treatment which cover the projection (of the side of the rod, headrail, board, etc.) out from the wall, of drapery and other window treatments. **Most drapery treatments and top treatments have returns.**

Return exceptions:

- Drapery that are one-way pulls which have returns *on one side* only.

- *Some* corner situations, where the returns *are not added in,* when the drapery butt-and-pass each other.

- *Some* wall-to-wall situations.

- Replacement drapery where the drapery were *originally planned without returns,* and the customer wants the replacement drapery planned the same way.

- An undertreatment under an overtreatment which does not have returns because the overtreatment's returns cover the sides of the undertreatment.

Ninety-seven percent of all drapery jobs will have returns on *one* side or *both* sides of the drapery. If the return is not planned for the end of the drapery, the drapery will end with an overlap end hanging out from the wall, exposing the interior of the drapery, the side of the rod, and the drapery cord. Drapery without returns end with a flat overlap (no pleat at the corner, as drapery with returns have), and will *"snake"* out at the sides, instead of uniformly hanging, and hugging the sides of the rod and drapery, as pleats at the corners of drapery do.

The returns on all traverse rods (regular and decorative) **will vary with the projection used.** If the rod has a 3½" projection, you will double this for a pair to equal 7" or 8". On a one-way pull drapery which has only *one* return, you will add 3½" or 4" (for a little extra slack). If the projection is 6", you will *double* that for a pair; *use singularly* for a drapery with only one return. If the return is 9" you will *double* this number for a pair; for a one-way pull use only one return.

Note: When planning a return for an I.B. mount, you need to allow at least ½" space on each side of the interior width, for the return to slide in.

Note: When planning for the returns on an *extremely shallow or tight wall situation,* allow an area of 1" on each side of the wall, for the installer to mount the brackets for the return.

Note: When planning returns, always allow 3" *between layers* of the window treatments, to be able to properly traverse and operate treatments.

Returns sizes *will vary* according to the amount of layers of undertreatments and their corresponding individual projections that are O.B. mounted on the same windows.

Single drapery

3½" return or returns. A single drapery may have an undertreatment mounted I.B. on the same window. An I.B. is mounted on the inside of the window, barely protruding beyond the wall level. An I.B. mount generally *will not interfere* with an overdrapery with a 3½" projection and return.

Double treatment;
double drapery,
overdrapery
a top treatment

6½" return/returns for or overdrapery and 6" returns for top treatments. An underdrapery *does not have* returns under an overdrapery, as the single layer with returns will cover the sides of the underdrapery. For an over-drapery *under* a top treatment, add returns for the overdrapery.

Triple treatment;
usually top treatment,
other undertreatments

9" return for the top layer, generally a top treatment. Use 6" - 7" for the second drapery and sheers or layer; use 3" - 4" for the bottom layer.

Specifications for returns on the workorder:

On the workorder when specifying return size, it is also necessary to specify which return you are referring to. Use the abbreviations below when specifying which return you are referring to.

L/R   Both, left and right panels receive returns; as in a pair of drapery.
L   Panel, to receive the return on the left side.
R   Panel, to receive the return on the right side.
O   No return/returns for the panel or the pair; as commonly found in underdrapery.

Plan single overdraperies with larger returns for ease in adding future treatments:

Always ask the customer who is purchasing an overdrapery without an undertreatment if they would like you to make the returns 6" instead of 3½", so in the future an undertreatment may be easily added.

It will be difficult, when the customer calls you back later, to add an undertreatment under a shallow return of 3½". You will only be able to add a blind, shade, or S.O.R. (sheer on the rod, with a narrow return). Even an S.O.R. treatment will rub against the overdrapery when the overdrapery is drawn open and closed. Additionally, since you have *subtly suggested* (and planted a seed for a future purchase) an undertreatment to the customer to add at a later date, that customer will probably want to add the underlayer later, and give you a future sale.

Overlaps

Overlaps are an allowance in width of a drapery, that overlap each other in the center, which allow the drapery to close tightly. Overlap measurements do not vary with each situation, they are *always* 1½" on each side; 3" for a pair (center open), or 1½" for a one-way pull. For a one-way pull, the overlap extends 1½" to the side.

Note: If more than 1½" is used for each side of an overlap, the drapery will sag, hang poorly, and lean forward when the master carriers overlap.

Add the overlaps to the returns; to the face-width of the window treatment to arrive at the finished width needed for ordering.

As you become more familiar with overlaps *and* returns, you will either add 10", 11", or 12" to the face width of the drapery for *both* the overlaps and the returns. Adding a number that encompasses both the overlaps and the returns will cut down on the confusion of planning individual overlaps and returns every time. *The variance in the amount to add* depends on the tightness of the fit that you or the company that you work for wants you to use.

Note: Be sure to state whether the drapery is a **pair or a panel** in the appropriate box on the workorder.

Example: The drapery pair is planned to be 46" wide. You have already extended the treatment 5" on each side of the original window measurement of 36". You now want to add the overlap amount for a pair, which is 3". The returns needed, are 3½". Note that examples and two formulas are shown on how to add the return in. Both are correct procedures and answers.

46" + 3" (overlaps) = 49". 49" + 7" (3½" returns for each side) for the returns = 56". **56" is the finished width for the pair, if you want a tight fit.**

Or, 49" + 9"(3½ returns for each side + 2" slack for the face-width) = 58". **58" would also be correct for a drapery that has a loose fit — more versatility and range in its fit.**

Finished-Width

The finished width measurement is the **face width of a drapery**, after pleating. Finished width is the size of the drapery; after the sides of the drapery are hemmed, **the returns and overlaps are added in and after the wall extensions beyond the window are added in. This is the finished width of the drapery; the size in width necessary to do the job.**

Example: Your window size is 86". Add in 5" on each side of the window for a standard mount. The desired bracket-to-bracket measurement is 96"; after adding in the wall extension of 5" on each side of the window.

86" + 10" (2 wall extensions of 5", each) = 96". 96" + **overlaps and returns** of 12" = 108". **Your finished width is 108".**

Stack-Back

Many customers have wonderful views and may not want anything to obstruct their visibility. Some customers have more extreme feelings about obstructing their views than other customers.

When you want to stack-back or off a window, you want to be able to clear or nearly clear the window when the drapery or other treatment are open to allow you to see out or let in maximum light and air.

If economy is a main factor, stacking-off the window may not be the right course of action to take. The extra fabric, fabrication, installation, and extra rod length will cost proportionately more money, so make sure your customer really wants to open that window up for the view.

The stack-back area is the amount of area that the drapery, when pulled back or when opened, takes up.

The formula for figuring stack-back varies with several factors: the type of rod, type of fabric selected and its heaviness, and any lining selected and its heaviness.

To completely stack-off the window, take the window width measurement and add at least 33% to 50% more width to the window width measurement.

If you are using a regular traverse rod, measure the window width and add 33% more to the width measurement. Add 33% more whether the fabric is fairly lightweight or if the fabric is unlined or lined.

To double-check the above formula, note that *each width of 48" fabric needs approximately 6" in stacking space, per width.*

- **Sheers are going to take the least amount of stack-back space;** about 33%, if mounted on a regular traverse rod.

- **A lined drapery will not be as tight stacking** as an unlined drapery.

- For drapery hung ff of **decorative rods, you need to add up to 50% more in width for stacking-off.** If you are using decorator rods with rings, the rings take up more space than hooks on regular traverse rods. You will need to measure the window width and add 50% more for the stack-off width to the window width measurement.

- If the **fabric is heavy,** or has a thermal suede or blackout lining to be mounted on a regular traverse **rod, you will need to add up to 50% more** width to the window width.

- **The fuller the drapery is, the more room needed for stack-off.**

Note: If the drapery are a pair, then half of the added stack-back will fall on each side of the window.

Note: If the drapery are a one-way pull, then the whole amount added will fall **on one side only** — the side you have chosen to extend over on the wall for stacking area. You will additionally need to add an extension on the other side from the stack back area of 4" - 5" to ensure privacy and coverage. This amount is added to also ensure that the drapery hem will not show from the outside of the home or building.

If there is almost no room on the small extension side (opposite side to the stack-off side), you may only be able to add an inch or so. Explain to the customer, since there is not a return on this side, and very little room for an extension, there may not be complete privacy and there may be light leaks *on that side.* You never want to add less than 4" - 5", *if you have the wall space.*

Note: The above formula for adding stack-back of 33% - 50% allows in coverage for each side of the window of the drapery to fall 4" into the window, which allows the sides of the window casings to be covered up.

Example: The window width is 54". You have selected an antique satin fabric to be lined with a heavy thermal-suede lining. Your customer wants to be able to completely clear the window to see the view. Take the 54" width and add 50% more, or 27". If this is a pair, you would end up with 13½" on each side of the window (divide the extra width amount added for stack-back in half, to arrive at this figure). The drapery, when pulled open, will be able to clear the window and sit in that 13½" area of the wall, allowing maximum view, light, and air circulation.

In the above example, if the drapery is a **one-way pull**, the same formula applies. The difference is, **when the drapery is drawn open, the full 27" stack back area is on one side only. Now add an extension for the opposite side of the stack back area.** See above for an explanation of this additional amount.

Next, add in the overlaps and returns to arrive at finished width.

Number of Widths

Number of widths are the **number of single panels of fabric widths (45", 48", 54", 60")** **pleated or gathered up to make up a finished width of drapery or other fabric treatment.** Use the *Determining Fullness Chart* to determine widths needed for your particular job.

When planning the amount of widths needed for a single window in a room, after dividing the widths into the finished width, if you should end up with a split width on a one-way pull situation, it is preferable to go ahead and absorb the extra ½ width into the overall finished width (larger and closer pleats). If you should cut the questionable width in half, the ½ width will only be wasted and your customer has paid for *all* the fabric, the labor charges for fabrication, and installation for the full width.

For a *single* window by itself in a room, the extra fullness that the drapery may have will not be noticed. If you *try* to absorb the extra fabric on one odd window in a room of multiple windows, that window is going to *appear* fuller than all the others. **If you order balance pleating on the workorder, the workroom will cut off the excess fabric.**

Standards of Fullness for Fabric Window Treatments

Since fabrics come in varying widths, the width of the fabric will vary after it is pleated or gathered up. **The fuller you make the drapery, the more stack space the drapery is going to take up.** Immediately below is a listing of the guidelines to use when planning fullness for a fabric window treatment.

- **200% fullness**   For separate liners behind drapery, or for economical drapery.

- **250% fullness**   Custom drapery, economical sheers.

- **300% fullness**   Custom sheers, gathered drapery, gathered top treatments.

Note: Most jobs you are planning should fall into the categories of 250% — 300% fullness.

If it is a less important window that is to be lined, you may want to plan the drapery fullness at 200%. Two hundred percent fullness would be less expensive for your customer, for the amount of fabric needed, for the fabrication, and for dry cleaning costs.

You may want to go fuller than 300% fullness for gathered sheer fabrics, or lightweight, unlined, gathered top treatments. Depending on the *look* of fullness desired, and the weight of the fabric, it is possible to go up to six times the fullness, or 600% fullness. This would be a rare circumstance, considering the price of fabric today.

Gathered S.O.R or R.T.B. treatments:

If you are planning a gathered S.O.R, R.T.B., or hourglass treatment, you may choose to make the treatment fuller. Depending on the fabric selected and how exaggerated your customer wants the gathered effect or the hourglass treatment to be, **the fullness may be varied.** Below are the fullness guidelines for these treatments.

Fullness:	minimum	medium	very full
Sheer fabrics	300%	400%	500%
Lighter-weight fabrics	300	400	
Medium-weight fabrics	300		

Determining Fullness Chart

Below are custom fullness guidelines to estimate how many widths of fabric are needed to cover the needed overall width of the window treatment. **Pleat or gather the fabric up to the desired fullness.**

Decide what the face width of the treatment is to be. Add any overlaps and returns to the face width, to arrive at the finished width. Find the appropriate fullness needed with the fabric width you are using. <u>Divide</u> **the number shown in the chart below, into the finished width of the treatment, to arrive at the widths of fabric to use to cover the finished width of the window treatment or drapery.** As shown in the examples, and discussed in the *Determining Yardage Needed* section, determine the cut length and multiply the cut length by the widths. Add in any repeats. Divide by 36" to determine the amount of yardage needed for the treatment.

Regular weight fabric:

Fabric width	200% fullness	250% fullness	300% fullness
45"	20"	16"	13"
48"	22"	18"	14"
54"	24"	20"	16"

Railroaded goods:

Fabric width	200% fullness	250% fullness	300% fullness
118"	Divide the finished width needed by 16" to arrive at needed yardage.	Divide the finished width needed by 14" to arrive at needed yardage.	Divide the finished width needed by 12" to arrive at needed yardage.

Note: As shown in the above chart, there is some variance in how full you may make the fabric window treatment. If it is a luxury job or a very particular customer, always use the fuller amounts.

If the customer is stressing to you to keep the price down on the job, or is saying that they are happy with what is up (which is fabricated with less fullness) then use the lesser fullness amount to help cut the price down.

Pleats Per Width

For custom full drapery at 250% fullness, figure that you will have five pleats, hooks, or need five rod rings per width, for each 48" drapery width. Less full drapery or narrower fabrics will require a few less pleats, rings, or hooks, per width. Consequently, fuller widths or wider fabrics will require a few more pleats, hooks, or rod rings per fabric width.

Consistency in Fullness

When planning a room with more than one drapery, plan all the drapery in the same room, and (preferably) throughout the house, to have the same amount of fullness.

All drapery and treatments in the same room *must have the same degree of fullness* to appear the same. If you do not keep the same amount of fullness, the amount of light filtering through the fabric will vary, the hanging ability of the treatments will be different from one unit to the next, and the widths of the pleats will vary in the distance apart from each other, with each drapery. To achieve uniform fullness, follow the following guidelines:

Determining equal fullness for all drapery in the same room:
● **Measure the window widths.**

● **Add all desired wall extension allowances** on each side of the window.

● **Add** in the overlaps and the appropriate **returns** for the situation.

Take the resulting figure, divide by the fullness factor above for fullness that corresponds to the type and width of the fabric you are using. **Example:** the window is 48" wide. The fabric is a lined 48" antique satin on a decorator rod. The drapery pair is to stack-off the window, and the customer is planning to add sheers later. Because sheers are to be added in the future, you need to use a wider, 6" return for the drapery. Therefore, add 48" for the window width, plus the amount needed to stack-off the window, which you have determined to be 24" (lined drapery with a decorator rod, you need to add 50% for stack-off). Now, add the overlaps of 3", plus the returns of 6" on each side, or 12". This totals 87". Take the 87" and divide by 18" (or what fullness factor you are using) to arrive at 4.83 needed widths. Round this number up or down to the nearest width. In this situation, you round up to 5 widths.

Do this formula for all windows in the same room. If a number should come out uneven, where you have ½ a panel on one window in a room where you are trying to balance the fullness with the other windows, that is acceptable. The workroom will end up splitting this ½ panel, if the drapery is a pair (realize, you are creating more seams, and on ¼ panels — a ½ panel, split for a pair — this may allow a *seam* to show in the center of the pleat. But, it may be more important that the fullness is balanced).

If you are doing *only one* window in the room, it is a one-way pull, and the fullness comes out split between one width and the next; either round the number up, or round the number down — going up or down to the closest width.

Do not split widths when you have only one window in the room. You would end up throwing the fabric away, instead of making a nicer, fuller drapery with it.

The easiest remedy is to extend the odd-width window bracket-to-bracket measurement out to a wider width (if there is enough wall area to do this). This will work *if* your customer *does not care*, that the window has more wall extension area than the other windows in the same room.

Balance Pleating

If there is more than one window within the room, and mathematically, the number of widths is not falling exactly even for the amounts of widths needed for all the windows; when you are determining the fullness, indicate *"balance pleat"* on all workorders for the same fabric within the same room. The workroom (when balance pleating) will make all the drapery evenly pleated, with the same amount of fabric used in the pleats. The pleats will be evenly spaced for all drapery in that same room. The workroom does this, even if they have to cut the widths down to do so.

Extend or make narrower the width of some of the window treatments, to work their sizes out more evenly.

Remember to order balance pleating when there are multiple windows in the same space. Order balance pleating especially if the customer is very particular and the windows actually are on the same wall, or butt-to each other in a corner situation.

Printed Fabrics and Split-Widths

Always try to **use full widths of fabrics for window treatments when using printed fabrics.** The vertical repeats should fall in full widths, and full repeats, all around the room. If necessary, make some windows narrower, or some windows wider to achieve this.

If you do not use full widths of fabric when planning printed treatments, you will end up with a half width on one window, because the window size is slightly off a full width. The odd width will also end up overlapping the split width on top of the other split width, at the center of the *other* panel of the drapery. Your customer will notice the pattern is split in half. The pattern will not match up to the opposite split width, because they are overlapping. You will lose 4" in the overlap, and lose 3" for the two leading edges turned back. The pattern is now *off* 7" in the center of the drapery.

If you cannot avoid splitting the widths, due to the windows being very diverse in their measurements, and you are unable to make the treatment smaller or larger to accommodate the difference, **use the split widths *at the sides* of the window treatment, rather than the middle of the treatment.** When you glance around the room (if there are other windows in the same fabric), you will notice, especially on large repeats, that the window does not look the same. The sides are split widths, while the other windows are full widths. The full, vertical pattern repeats will fall in different areas than the other draperies within the same room.

Finished Length

Finished length is the desired **finished length of a drapery or treatment after the hems and headers are added in and finished off.**

Example: On a drapery, this is the point from where the top of the drapery is going to sit, slightly above the rod, to the desired length, ¼" — ½" off the floor, 5" below the sill, or other determined length.

Cut Length

The cut length of a drapery is the finished length, plus the double 4" hems, and double 4" heading allowance, **which is usually 18" for pleated drapery and valances. Work with the chart** *in the rod section under Specifics on Planning Rod-Pocket Treatments,* for rod pocket amounts to add. Now add in the allowance needed for fabrics with repeats. Review the *Determining Horizontal Repeats* section for information on how to calculate fabric repeats. Add the finished length, hems, and header amount needed, and the repeat allowance, to determine the cut length.

Note: For all gathered styles of drapery, refer to the chart *in the rod section under Specifics on Planning Rod-Pocket Treatments;* **add the take up amount needed for the rod you are planning. Rod pocket, styles also require more fabric in length to be added for the header. Refer to the chart for needed amounts.**

Note: Record on the workorder for the workroom that you need a rod pocket of 3¼" wide and two buttonholes at the 3½" return — if your returns are going to be 3½".

Example: Finished length is 94½". You are planning a job using regular, pleated drapery with standard hems and headers.

94½" + 18"(hem and header allowance) = 112½". **112½" is your new cut length** using fabric without a repeat.

Another example: Finished length is 84" for the drapery. The job you are planning is using a wood-pole rod, with a gathered rod pocket. You will be using plain fabric, without a header above the rod. Referring to the chart for wood-pole rods in the hardware section, note that you need to add take-up of 1¼". When the fabric is gathered up on a pole rod, the treatment's length *gets shorter* by 1¼". Note also that you need to add 30" to the finished length for double hems and double headers, because a rod pocket *requires* more fabric in length than a pleated header does.

84" + 1¼" for take-up = 85¼". 85¼" + hems and headers = 115¼". **115¼" is your cut length** for your 84" drapery to be mounted on a wood-pole rod in a fabric without a repeat.

Another example: Finished drapery is 96". You are planning a job using a double 4½" rod with a 3" header to stand up above the double rod. Note from the chart in the hardware section that you need to add take-up for this style of double rod of 1". You also, must add 6" additional fabric for the header (front of the header, 3"; back of the header, 3"), and need to add 35" in length for the fabric to accommodate the wide, double rod pockets and hems.

96" + ½" take-up = 96½". 96½" + 6" for headers above the rods = 102½". 102½" + hems and headers of 35" = 137½". **137½" is your cut length** for your 96" finished length drapery, with a double 5½" rod pocket, and stand-up 3" header, in plain fabric.

Note: Make a note on workorder for the workroom and installer that you need two rod pockets 5½" wide, each.

Determining Yardage

The number of yards needed is determined by first planning out how many widths are needed for the treatment, multiplying the widths needed by the cut length (with any repeat added in), and dividing by 36" (yards). Using this formula will give you the exact yardage needed for ordering and charging your customer.

Always *round up* to the nearest yard, or *add slightly more* fabric. Allow for bad cutting and flaws in the fabric. If the fabric is flawed, you may still be able to work around the flaws. The fabric should always be visibly inspected before cutting and sent back to the supplier if the flaws cannot be worked around.

Fabric suppliers usually allow you a few extra inches more than you have ordered. Do not ask for *just* a new cut if the fabric is flawed, as the dyelot may be different. **Send the whole piece of fabric back and request another unflawed piece** *before you proceed to fabricate other items in the same room, in other cuts of the same dyelot* (you may have requested a piece of the same dyelot to be drop shipped to the bedspread fabricator for a matching bedspread or quilted yardage).

Example for determining yardage on a *plain* **fabric: The finished width of the plain, lined, antique satin drapery is 96"; the cut length is 118".** Determine the widths for custom fullness, or 250% fullness for this 48" fabric to be 5.33, by reviewing and using the *Determining Fullness Chart.*

Since the resulting width is a split one, and *below* ½ of a width, you are able to **round the number down** to 5 widths, rather than going up another width, to 6 widths. If the resulting number falls above the ½, or .50 mark, round up to the next width. If the number would have been 5.68 widths, you would have needed to **round the number up**.

5 widths x cut length of 118" = 590". 590" divided by 36" (yards) = **16.39 yards. Round the number up to 17 yards.** *If not possible to round all the way up to 17 yards, since you are trying to keep the price as low as possible and are using a very expensive fabric, order 16.50 yards or 16½ yards.*

Order the same amount of lining fabric as the drapery fabric, if the self-fabric is plain, with no extra fabric figured in for a repeat. If the repeat has been figured in, refigure the self-fabric without a horizontal repeat to determine the lining yardage.

<u>Another example using a *repeat* fabric:</u> Your customer has selected a **54" printed fabric with a 27" horizontal repeat** to be made up in a **lined, pleated, overdrapery with a finished-width of 88", and a return size of 6" on each side. The finished length is to be 84".** Review the *Determining Horizontal Repeat* section, below.

The finished width of 88" was determined by taking the window size of 62" with an extension of 5" on each side. 62" + 10" = 72". Next, add 72" in width + 16" for overlaps and returns of 6" for each side = 88". The **cut length is 102"** (finished length of 84" + 18" for standard hems and headers for a pleated drapery). Now you need to **determine the extra fabric needed for the repeat. 102" divided by the repeat of 27" = 3.77 repeats. Round 3.77 up, to a repeat of 4. 4 repeats x 27" = 108". 108" is your new cut length.**

Divide the amount to use for the fullness desired for a 54" drapery with custom fullness of 250% into the finished width of 88". After reviewing the *Determining Fullness Chart*, the correct figure to use for 250% fullness with a 54" wide fabric is 20". **88" divided by 20" = 4.4 widths of fabric.** Again this figure falls below the .50 point on the balance of the widths needed. Round the number down to an even 4 widths of fabric.

4 widths of fabric x 108" cut length with repeat = 432". 432 divided by 36" (yards) = 12 yards. 12 yards would be the exact amount you need. It is preferable to add an additional ½ yard to the 12-yard amount.

Next, **plan the lining yardage.** Lining generally is of plain fabric, without a repeat. **The original cut length above was 102",** before we changed it to a new cut length with a repeat of 108". 4 widths of lining (always try to use the same width lining fabric as your face fabric) x 102" = 408". 408" divided by 36" = **11.33 yards of lining fabric. Round up to 11.50 yards or 11½ yards of lining.**

Determining Lining Yardage

The amount of lining yardage that you will need to order will be the ***same as the amount of fabric needed if the self-fabric is plain, without a repeat.*** If the face fabric has a repeat, calculate the yardage separately, using the formula *for figuring with a repeat fabric* shown in the example immediately above.

Some linings will have a repeat and will need to have the yardage determined the same as you would for a self-fabric with a repeat (designer linings).

Always **try to use the same width lining fabric as the self-fabric you are lining.** If the particular lining you desire is unavailable, in the same width as the self-fabric, figure the lining and the self-fabric *separately,* using the *Determining Fullness Chart* to determine the amount for the appropriate widths.

Linings for drapery are fabricated 1" shorter than the bottom of the drapery, to keep them from showing from the front of the drapery.

Determining Horizontal Repeats

Even the smallest horizontal pattern repeat should be pattern matched. From a distance, even a small, mismatched pattern readily shows up. *All* treatments in the same fabric within the same space should match up with their repeat placements. *The object is to achieve eye flow around the room.*

Always place printed fabrics of the same fabric in the same room or space on the same workorder, or make large notes stating, *this workorder 32456 cross matches with 67897 — <u>all repeat placements, must match each other</u>.*

Decide *where* you want the pattern repeats to fall in the drapery or other window treatments that are to be fabricated. ***All like items need the repeat to fall in the same spot within the same room or space.***

Most workrooms place the full repeat just below the pleated area of the drapery, or in the case of top treatments, will center the repeat, vertically and horizontally. On short drapery, the repeat is placed about one inch above the hem, at the repeat's most visible point.

When you need the **pattern centered in the middle of a treatment, you will need to order an extra full repeat in addition to the extra repeat yardage you have planned.** This extra amount of fabric ensures that the workroom has enough to get the first cut centered; then every cut after the first cut will follow the regular repeat formula.

If you combine short and long drapery together within the same space, plan all the repeats within the same room or space to line up just below the pleats. *Combining short and long drapery in the same space is not the nicest looking idea,* so do this only if necessary, due to interfering obstructions such as heating units or window seats.

To determine cut length with fabric that has a horizontal repeat:

Take the horizontal repeat amount (which is found in the fabric description provided by the fabric supplier, or is printed on the fabric cap); divide the pattern repeat into the normal cut length (finished length plus hems and header added together). *Round up the resulting number to the next whole number.* Multiply the whole number times the horizontal repeat size (noted on the fabric sample or specification sheet) to arrive at the correct cut length to order. *Never split the repeat when planning the extra fabric needed for the repeat; work in full repeats.*

The additional amount of fabric needed to match the repeat *must be added in and charged to the customer at the time of making the bid on the job.* The extra fabric may be substantial or minimal. Always work with full repeats, *never* split them.

Example of how to figure repeats: A 66" cut length divided by a fabric with a horizontal repeat of 15" = 4.4 repeats. Take the number, if uneven, as in this case, and **always round up to the next whole number or full repeat.** Round 4.4 repeats up to 5 repeats in this example. 5 repeats x the repeat size of 15"= 75". The cut length for this repeat is now 75". For plain fabric without a repeat, the cut length would be 66" (includes hems and header allowance).

> 66" *normal* cut length divided by a repeat of 15" = 4.4 repeats. Round this number up to 5 repeats. 5 repeats x 15" = 75". 75" is the new cut length.

Another example: You are planning a drapery in a printed fabric. 114" is the *normal* cut length needed. The fabric you have selected has a repeat of 24". The hems and headers for the finished length have been included in the 114" cut length figure.

> 114 divided by a repeat of 24" = 4.75 repeats. Round up the number to 5 repeats. 5 repeats x 24" = 120". 120" is the new cut length.

The Three Vertical Lengths for Drapery
and How to Measure for Them

The three lengths for drapery are **sill length, apron length, and floor length.** There may be other variations of these lengths, due to air-conditioning units built into the wall, heating vents obstructing, and other architectural additions.

Always discuss the rod placement with your customers and make sure you are both in agreement before proceeding to measure.

Sill-length drapery	Mounted ¼" — ½" off the sill.
Measuring	Measure down from 4" — 5" above the lintel to the top of the window sill. Mounting above the lintel allows the rods, heading, and pins to be concealed. Deduct ¼" - ½" of this length measurement, for clearance, to determine finished length.

Clearance	Sill-length drapery should clear the sill by ½". This amount of clearance looks nice, and the drapery is prevented from rubbing on the sill, which subsequently will soil and wear out the fabric from the abrasion.
	The top of the drapery will sit ¼" above the rod.
Above the window or to the ceiling?	If there is less than 12" of space between the top of the window and the ceiling, take the measurement and placement for the drapery all the way to the ceiling and then down to the top of the sill; deduct ¾" for regular fabrics to 1" for loosely woven fabrics.
Make returns deep enough	Make the returns of the drapery deep enough to compensate for the sill that may be sticking out into the room. If the returns are made *deep* enough, the drapery will *freely* traverse back and forth.
Should the hard window treatment rest on the sill?	Determine by talking with your customer if the I.B. hard-window treatment should rest on the sill. Customers do vary in their preference. *The complaint about the hard* treatment resting on the sill is that the blind or shade bottom rail marks up the paint of the sill. Their complaint when the blind or shade does not come down and rest on the sill is that there are light leaks and they have less privacy.
	Look around at the other hard window treatments in the home to see if they rest on the sill, and make yours the same. The new treatment's fit will be judged against the existing treatments. If the treatments you are planning are made up to fit differently, you will probably be requested to change yours.

Apron-length drapery

	Mounted 4" — 5" below the apron.
Measuring	Measure from 4" — 5" above the lintel, to a point 4" — 5" below the bottom of the apron of the window, to arrive at finished length. Measuring from this point prevents you from visually observing the hems and header of the drapery from the outside of the home or building.
	The top of the drapery sits ¼" above the rod.
Casement windows	When there are not sills, aprons, or trim on windows, measure above the window 4" — 5", and below the window 4" — 5". You may also take the rod to the ceiling and down to 4" — 5" below the apron.
*Notes for **all** apron-length drapery*	Make sure to make the return deep enough to compensate for the sill that may be sticking out into the room, so the drapery will freely traverse back and forth.
Underdrapery	Underdrapery need to be planned ½" shorter than overdrapery.

Floor-length drapery

	Mounted ½" minimum off the floor.
Wall mount above the window	Measure 4" — 5" above the window or lintel to conceal the pins, rods, and the back of the header from the outside. A point at 4" — 5" above the window usually gives nice proportions to the window, additionally. Measure from this point to the floor and deduct ¼" for clearance.

Above the window or to the ceiling?	If the distance from the top of the window or lintel is less than 12", start the treatment from the ceiling.
Clearance	The top of the drapery sits ¼" above the rod, and the ¼" — ½" clearance off of the floor equals ½" — ¾" total clearance.
Underdrapery	Underdrapery need to be planned ½" shorter than the overdrapery.
Carpet and pad	Deduct for carpet and pad if they are not installed yet. If the customer does not have samples of the pad and the carpet, and the drapery are to be floor-to-ceiling, sell the job to be hand-hemmed in the home. Another alternative is to sell the customer a top treatment with the drapery mounted from 5" above the window to 3½" below the height of the top treatment. The height of the drapery may easily be adjusted underneath the top treatment.
Unstable fabrics mounted above the window	Deduct an extra ½", so drapery will be mounted ½" off the floor to allow for fabric fluctuations.

Decorative rod, with an underdrapery

Make the underdrapery the same length as the overdrapery. The sheer rod is held in the bracket with a higher hook set. The hook set projects the rod up, which places the sheer higher and naturally shorter at the bottom hem.

Second-story windows

You will not want to observe the back of the headers, rods, or hooks from the outside first story of the home or building. The top of the header should be 7" above the window or lintel to ensure coverage for second-story windows.

Floor-to-ceiling treatments

Measure three to five places for the length. Take the smallest length measurement and deduct 1". If you are using a measuring stick and want tight clearance for the length, you may deduct ½". When you take only a minimal clearance, you are taking the chance that you may have to rework the hem shorter if the drapery comes out ¼" too long — and the hooks cannot be adjusted at the header since this will cause the header to rub against the ceiling.

When measuring for floor-to-ceiling drapery, start at one side of the drapery; run the tape up to the ceiling or to the top of the wall, and hold down to the floor tautly (walk the tape down to the floor). Measure to the top of the carpet or floor. Note the measurement, and measure this length again two more times (measure in the middle and again at the opposite side of the drapery placement). Take more length measurements if the drapery is too be made very wide. Ceilings and floors are not always straight. You will want to take the smallest measurement of the three length measurements.

Length fluctuations

If the length measurements vary more than ½", inform the customer that the floor is uneven, and note this conversation in your notes, in addition to noting on the sales slip. When the drapery or other treatment gets installed, you want to be protected when the customer says the window treatment is longer in places, or is uneven.

The drapery may be hand-hemmed in the home. Hand-hemming is an optional charge, and will help obtain a drapery that appears even in length, in an uneven wall and floor situation. The customer may take you up on having the drapery re-hand-hemmed, after they see how uneven the drapery came out when they are installed. Note on the workorder for the installer and in your records that hand-hemming was suggested, and declined (if this was the case). You and your company will not want to end up paying for hand-hemming, if the installer sends in the request for the hand-hemmer to come out and correct the situation, to make an unhappy customer happy. If you discussed the situation with the customer, they will pay for it.

If the drapery are hand-hemmed, or you have the drapery fabricated longer on one side than the other, when you draw the drapery back together, the drapery's now wavering hemline will probably drag in spots and have a very uneven appearance when stacked-back against each other. The leading edge is obviously going to appear longer or shorter then the folds next to it. If the drapery will be drawn open frequently, this is the way to go to help correct the situation.

Note: a wall mount at the ceiling will help correct length fluctuations more than a ceiling installation will. The rod may be tighter to the ceiling at one end then the other. If the rod is moved down to 5" above the window, you will probably not be able to notice that the installer has mounted one end higher than the other. If you add a top treatment to go straight over the crooked rod, you will not notice at all that the rod is crooked.

Wall Mount

Use a wall mount whenever you can. It is the stronger installation method, over a ceiling mount. If the customer has had a ceiling installation previously and you remove the old hardware, you will probably need to go with another ceiling installation, due to the unsightly appearance of the area under the rod. Review section under *Removal of Existing Hardware and Removal of Existing Hardware, for Acoustical Ceilings* for more information.

Clearance

The drapery sits above the rod ¼". The clearance is ¼" above the drapery to the ceiling; clearance at the bottom of the drapery is ½" to ¾".

Underdrapery

Underdrapery need to be planned the same length as the overdrapery. The underdrapery sits higher on the rod underneath than the overdrapery does.

Unstable fabrics

Ceiling mount, or on the wall at the ceiling, deduct an additional ½".

S.O.R.
(shirr-on-rod)

For an O.B. mount:
Measure the width of the existing rod or the desired width of the treatment. It is desirable to have a minimum of 4" of wall extension on each side of the window. Measure the length of the existing treatment; or from the top of the existing rod or rod placement of new rod (4" - 5" above the window) down to 4" - 5" below the window. Add ½" for take-up for shorter lengths of curtains and drapery, 1" take-up for longer lengths.

For an I.B. mount:
Measure the width across the top of the I.B. frame of the window; measure the length for the I.B. on each side of the window. Use the shorter of the two lengths, and order the length for the I.B. in the same length as the actual length measurement. When the drapery is shirred up on the rod, the length will draw up and be shorter. Using the actual length measurement will give you the correct clearance off the sill that is needed.

R.T.B.
(rod-top-bottom)

For an O.B. mount, using existing rods:
Measure the width across the top of the existing rod; then measure the length. For a standard rod pocket, measure the length from top of the rod on one side and check the length again on the opposite side. Add 3" to this length for headers above and below the rod and take-up.

For an I.B. mount, using existing rods:
Measure the width of the I.B. area. Measure the length of the I.B. area in three places, recording the shorter of the three. Note what size rod pocket is used or what size the existing rod is. Note this information on the workorder. Record

measurements exactly on the workorder. Add ½" for take-up to shorter lengths, 1" take-up to longer lengths.

For an O.B. mount, when rods are not up:
Measure the width desired, adding 1½" on each side of the window glass; measure the length of the window glassed area, and add 5" to the length measurement for the rod pockets and take-up.

For an I.B. mount, when rods are not up:
Measure across the top and bottom, using the narrower I.B. width measurement; measure the I.B. length on each side, using the shorter I.B. length, and add 1" to length measurement.

Additional Length Points

• When planning draperies, keep in mind that you will not want to observe the back of the hem or header from the outside of the home. Make the header and hem a minimum of 4" above the window or lintel and 4" below the window. 5" is the preferred amount to add for the hem and header placement for a standard mount.

• Drapery **should be 7" above the window or lintel when placed under a top treatment** for a quality installation. 5" is the minimum placement above the window to use under a top treatment. A 5" amount under a top treatment should only be used under certain circumstances and is not a standard to use regularly. The bottom of the drapery pleats will barely be covered when a person is sitting down near the window treatment.

• Drapery planned to hang below decorative rods, including top treatments hung on decorative rods, need to be planned 2" shorter than regular drapery, so they are able to hang below the rod.

• Under normal planning conditions, drapery planned to hang under a top treatment should be planned 3" shorter in length, with the underdrapery planned 3½" shorter than the finished length of the total window treatment. Draperies actually need to hang under traverse rods to freely traverse and stack-back. Always deduct at least 2" off the drapery length to achieve this. The extra 1½" (preferred) allowance is to allow for the top treatment board width. Draperies that sit under top treatments should be planned to have an even pin or hook set.

R.T. or S.O.R. (Rod-Top or Shirred-on-the Rod) Treatments

R.T. stands for rod-top. S.O.R. stands for shirr-on-the-rod — as in a rod pocket needed for sheers or drapery that gather or shirr-on-the-rod at the top). The rod pocket is only designated for the top of the treatment with the use of either of these abbreviations on a workorder to the workroom.

Depending on the fabric selected and how exaggerated your customer wants the gathered effect of the treatment to be, **the fullness may be varied.** Below is a listing of the fullness to consider when doing this treatment.

Fullness:	minimum	medium	very full
Sheer fabrics	300%	400%	500%
Lighter-weight fabrics	300	400	
Medium-weight fabrics	300		

How to plan an R.T. or S.O.R. treatment:

- **Order the finished width needed.** This is the size you need when the fabric is gathered up. **Determine the widths needed** for the fullness and fabric you are using for the treatment. Refer to the *Determining Fullness Chart.*

- **Specify the finished length.**

- **Specify the rod pocket and header sizes.**

- **Determine extra take-up needed for the length:** If the fabric is tightly gathered and relatively full, add ½" for lighterweight fabrics to ¾" for heavier fabrics for take-up. Check your hardware chart for take-up for corresponding rods. Or, specify for the workroom to plan in the take-up for you.

- **To determine cut length:** Add 16" for the hem and rod pocket for a 1" rod pocket. Add 30" for a wide rod pocket. 30" would be enough to cover a double 4" hem, and a double 5½" rod pocket, with a stand-up header up to 3" deep. Check the *Specifics on Planning Rod Pocket Treatments* chart for the corresponding rod you are using for amounts to add for hems and headers.

- If your studio works off a chart that has the fabric, lining (if using the lining chart), fabrication, and the installation already figured in, just take this price, take the discount for a sale price, and add in any hardware and tax. Add in extra yardage, if you added more than 18" for hems and headers.

These charts are planned for normal drapery hems and headers of 18". If you are planning a wide rod pocket that requires you to add 30" to the finished length for hems and headers, you are going to require more fabric. You may determine this extra fabric two different ways. Follow the examples below to figure the extra yardage and consequently the extra money to charge your customer.

Example: You are working off a chart for a lined fabric at $18 per yard. You need 5 widths of fabric. You are planning an 84" finished length drapery with a wide rod pocket. You need to add 30" for the hems and headers, not the 18" that the chart allows you.

First method: Subtract 18" from 30" to arrive at 12". Multiply 12" x 5 widths of fabric = 60". 60" divided by 36" (yards) = 1⅔ yards. You simply charge your customer for an extra 1⅔ yards.

Second method: Take your finished length of 84". Add to the 84" the extra 30" for hems and headers. Now subtract the normal hems and headers of 18" from this figure. You now have a figure of 96". On your chart find the "finished length" of 96". Although, you are going to make the drapery or other treatment 84" in length, you need to charge your customer as if you were making the treatment a 96" finished length, due to the additional yardage needed.

84" + 30" = 114". 124" — 18" = 96". 96" is the correct length to work with on your chart.

Wide Rod Pocket Treatments

When planning wide rod pocket treatments such as the 4½" styles, pole-top treatments, or a curtain rod pocket treatment of any type, ask the customer if they want the stand-up ruffle-header above the rod. Depending on the fabric, with the header or without the header, are both good-looking treatments. Find out your customer's preference.

Hourglass S.O.R. (Shirr-On-Rod) or Pleated Treatments

Hourglass style panels, tied-back, work only on evenly sectioned windows. The hourglass panels in the center areas should end up on the sectioned areas of the windows, or on the wood posts or wall areas between the windows.

- Extend the side panels only 2"-4" beyond the trim of the window. This amount keeps the side panels balanced with the center panels.

- Sheers used as undertreatments should be traversed open and closed minimally. If they are drawn regularly, they will get hung up with the tied-back panels.

Notes about tiebacks for hourglass treatments:

- When working with tiebacks and determining a tieback's measurements, it is somewhat confusing, since what is commonly perceived to be the *length*, is actually the tieback's width. What is generally perceived to be the *width*, is actually the length of the tieback.

- A tieback for an hourglass treatment is usually ⅓ of the size of the window width.

- An hourglass tieback needs to be ordered with Velcro attached to its back-tabs.

- Unless specified, an hourglass tieback will not come with crinoline interlining.

- Figure the tieback by one of the two methods outlined below.

   First method: Divide the face width of the window you are planning by .33. Use the resulting ⅓ figure for the face width of the tieback.

   Second method: Determine the face width of the tieback by holding a tape up to the proposed tied back area. Decide how wide you want to make the tieback.

   Next: After using one of the two methods outlined above, multiply the face width desired x 2 (for the back of the tieback) + 2" (for the Velcro, overlapped area in the back of the tieback). Now, figure the *"length" (up and down width)* desired for the tieback.

   For examples of these two methods, see below in the *Stretched Hourglass* section.

R.T.B. (Rod-Top-and-Bottom)

Rod-top-and-bottom is the meaning of the term R.T.B. The drapery or sheer is fabricated with a rod pocket at the top and another at the bottom. R.T.B. is the way to note this type of fabrication on the workorder for the workroom.

Depending on the fabric selected and how exaggerated your customer wants the gathered effect of the treatment to be, **the fullness may be varied.** Refer to the chart above under *R.T. or S.O.R. (Rod-Top or Shirred-on-the Rod) Treatments* for the fullness to consider when doing gathered treatments.

- When ordering R.T.B. treatments, always **order the gathered-up width,** or the size the widths you have planned will be gathered to. This will be the finished width.

- Always **specify** the **finished length.**

- **Specify the rod pocket and header sizes.** Unless specified, R.T.B.'s are fabricated with 1" rod pockets, top and bottom.

- Unless you have figured the take-up yourself, **specify on the workorder for the workroom to figure the take-up and the tension needed for the treatment.** Otherwise, you may have a short R.T.B. The back of the rod pocket *will show* from the exterior, because take-up was not figured in.

- **Add, 15" minimum for hems and header for a 1" rod pocket** (double folded), **with a ¼" header top-and-bottom. Add 30" for double-folded, wide-rod pockets.**

- **Note:** When measuring for an R.T.B. or an hourglass treatment for a door, or an O.B. mounted window where you are also planning to have headers above and below the rod, **the header is going to need so many inches. The rod pocket needs to be planned high and low enough to prevent the rod pocket from showing from the exterior of the door or window. You also have take-up for this type of gathered treatment.** Take-up is planned at ½" to 1" above and below the rod pocket. **This amount needs to be planned in, to ensure that the rod pocket will not be seen from the exterior.** On doors, you generally have limited space; trying to keep the treatment in proportion can be a challenge.

    Example: The door you are planning an R.T.B. treatment for has a glassed-in length of 76". You are planning an hourglass panel with a 2" stand-up header above and below the rod. The rod pocket is a standard one, of 1½".

    76" + 2" + 2" (headers, for top and bottom) + 1½" + 1½" (rod pockets, top and bottom) + ½" + ½" (take-up top and bottom)= 84". 84" is the correct finished length to order for this R.T.B. treatment.

    Note: after arriving at the correct finished length, hold your tape back up and decide if this length appears too heavy. If it does, shorten the header above, below, or both above and below, to lighten up the treatment.

Stretched Hourglass Treatments

All stretched hourglass treatments are **contoured in shape.** The sides are slightly scooped out; the bottom and the tophems are shaped. A tieback, with velcro attached at both ends for the middle, needs to also be ordered on the workorder.

A header above or below the rod *may or may not* be desired for this treatment.

Notes about hourglass tiebacks:

- When working with tiebacks and determining a tieback's measurements, it is confusing because what is generally perceived to be the length, is actually the tieback's width. What is generally perceived to be the width, is actually the length of the tieback.

- **A tieback** for an hourglass treatment **is usually ⅓ of the size of the window width.**

- An hourglass tieback needs to be ordered with **Velcro attached to its back tabs.**

- Unless specified, an hourglass tieback **will not come interlined with crinoline.**

- **Review the *R.T.B.* section above,** as the fullness and directions for measuring, directly apply to all hourglass treatments.

- You must **specify rod pocket sizes for top and bottom.**

- Specify **header sizes for both top and bottom;** you may not want to make them the same.

- Specify to **the workroom to take allowances for take-up and tension.**

- Hourglass **fabrication requires extra charges** to the customer for the extra contouring needed.

- **Plan the tieback** by one of the two methods outlined below.

First method: Divide the face width of the window you are planning by .33. Use the resulting ⅓ figure for the face width of the tieback.

Second method: Determine the face width of the tieback by holding a tape up to the proposed tied back area. Decide how wide you want to make the tieback.

Next: After using one of the two methods outlined above, multiply the face width desired x 2 (for the back of the tieback) + 2" (for the Velcro, overlapped area in the back of the tieback). Now, **figure the *"length" (up and down width)*** desired for the tieback.

Example using first method: The face width of the window is 18". Divide 18" by 3 = 6". 6" x 2 + 2" = 14". 14" is the correct *"width"* to order. The length you have decided on is 2". On the workorder, specify a tieback of 14" x 2".

Example using second method: You hold the tape up and decide that the face *"width"* of the tieback looks good at 8". 8" x 2 + 2 = 18". 18" is the correct *"width"* to order. The *"length"* you have decided on is 3½". On the workorder you will specify a tieback of 18" x 3 ½".

- **Charge** the customer **for the tieback;** also adding Velcro may be a surcharge.

- **Order the extra fabric needed for the tieback.**

- Hourglass treatments may be I.B. mounted on spring tension utility rods or wide curtain rods, or O.B. mounted with all types of curtain rods.

- **Add 30" to the finished length for the contouring, hems, and headers** for an hourglass treatment.

Reverse Hourglass Treatments

Reverse hourglass treatments are a *reverse* treatment of a regular hourglass treatment. They require two tiebacks instead of one tieback. The difference is, the treatment is made a pair rather than a panel. The installer installs the hourglass treatment in reverse. The original leading edges of the pair are mounted on the sides, with the contoured area aimed to the center. The contoured area scoops out the middle of the reverse hourglass treatment. Each tieback ties back one panel, to the side. When correctly mounted, a diamond shape is formed in the middle of the treatment.

When ordering this treatment, follow the guidelines above under *R.T.B. and the Stretched Hourglass Treatment* sections for the guidelines for fullness, planning, ordering and amount of extra fabric to add. Note on the workorder *"Reverse hourglass, to be made a pair; include two tiebacks, without Velcro."* **Charge the additional charges for the extra tiebacks and fabric.**

Measuring for a Double Drapery Treatment

A double drapery treatment is installed on a double traverse rod with a double, common bracket.
- Use a **3½" projection for the underdrapery.**

- **Do not add in returns for the underdrapery.**

- Use a **6" projection for the overdrapery.**

- **Overlaps are used on both draperies.** Determine if both drapery are pairs, one-way pulls, or a combination of a one-way pull for the underdrapery and a pair for the overdrapery. Plan overlaps for each drapery according to their situation.

- As shown in the above chart, **the underdrapery needs to be made ½" shorter than the overdrapery.**

Measuring for Wall-to-Wall Window Treatments

Measure wall-to-wall window treatments by running your tape to one end of the wall, butt the end of the tape against the wall, and walk the tape across the room. Divide this width in half, *if the window appears centered.* Check and observe if the middle of the width measurement falls in the middle of the window. If there is a variance of 3" or more, make the pair an offset pair. Review the *Measuring for an Offset Pair* section for information on measuring for offset pairs.

If the window falls approximately in the center of the wall, then take the total measurement from wall to wall, and **deduct ½" for the traverse rod size.** Take this deduction so the return of the drapery can slip in the outside of the bracket next to the wall, with the return's ¼" of fabric on each side.

If you are using a top treatment with the wall-to-wall drapery treatment, the boards will take up an additional ½" area (of the space) on each side. **Deduct 1½" on each side for the traverse rod and drapery width, or 3" total.** Order the top treatment 1" smaller in width, so the top treatment may slip into the area with its padded boards. Be sure to **note on the workorder,** *"this is the maximum width, it is a wall-to-wall installation."*

Measuring for Sheers on a Wall-to-Wall Situation

On a wall-to-wall situation with sheers, it is preferable to float the sheers. Floating sheers is to plan the sheers to measure only 12" on each side of the window opening. When the sheers are traversed, they are anchored and will not move beyond that point. With floating sheers, the rod is made the same length as the overdrapery, and mounted in the common bracket with the overdrapery. The traverse cord is located under the overdrapery at one end of the traverse rod.

If you would like the sheers to stack-off the window, then use the ⅓ width amount for stacking-off the window, adding just enough to stack-off the window under the overdrapery (½ of the ⅓ = 1/6 for each side of the window, in stack-off area).

When you float a sheer under an overdrapery, you are eliminating or cutting down the problem of the sheer dragging against the overdrapery, every time the drapery is open and closed. Static electricity builds up with manufactured fabrics and will cause the sheers to cling to the overdrapery every time the drapery is traversed. This clinging will annoy all customers and look as bad from the interior of the home or building as the exterior. The sheers will then have to be readjusted by hand to get them to hang freely. The answer to this problem is to allow a large enough return or clearance, so there is room between the two layers. Use a 6" return for the overdrapery, 3½" return for the underdrapery.

By floating the sheer, you are also doing your customer a favor, by charging them only for sheers that cover 12" on each side of the window opening, instead of going wall to wall. The customer will not end up paying for excess fabric under overdrapery that they never see.

Order the same length rod as the overdrapery, for floating sheers. When writing up the workorder, it is a simple mistake to glance up at the size of the sheer and order a rod the same size. Make yourself a big note on the worksheet to order the same size rod as the overdrapery, so the installer does not take out the wrong size rod. If the installer takes the wrong size out, chances are they will go ahead and install the shorter rod under the wall-to-wall rod. Your customer will receive a nicer installation, when both rods fit into the same end brackets.

The installer will install lock slides on the rod track to prevent the floating sheers from sliding into the window area unanchored.

Measuring Existing Traverse Rods

If you decide to go ahead and use the existing traverse rods after reviewing the section on *Hardware and Reasons to Change Existing Hardware,* then follow this guideline for measuring the existing rods that are already mounted.

Existing traverse rods:

Measure the width of the existing rod tip to tip. Measure and note the return size. Divide the width measurement in half and see if the overlap of the rod or existing drapery fall in the middle of the drapery.

If the drapery is an offset pair, review the *Offset Pair* section. Measure the length from the top of the rod to the carpet or floor and deduct ¼"-½".

Measuring for Decorative Rods

When determining decorative rod sizes or bracket-to-bracket widths, **add an additional 1" to each side of the bracket-to-bracket measurement, for a total of 2" for a pair, to allow for the immovable rings on the ends of the rod.** Add this measurement to the bracket-to-bracket measurement, but do not change the rod size to include this allowance. Review the *Hardware and Decorative Rods* section before proceeding to plan a job with decorative rods. Note the information on finials and how much room they take up (generally 6" on each side) and correct placement for this type of rod.

If your customer insists on placing the decorator rod right at the ceiling, measure floor to ceiling and deduct 3½" for the finished length of the drapery. This measurement includes the extra amount the rings need in extra space to traverse, and the additional space they take up above the rod.

Decorative rod treatments look best if the drapery have a looser fit in their width. Add an additional 1" in the width of a one-way panel, or 2" for each pair of drapery.

Note: When measuring the width of decorative rods, *add or allow* **an extra 2" on each side if a one-way pull, or 4" for both sides of a pair** (beyond the tip of the return bracket, in width) when measuring for the immovable rings on the end of each side of the rod. This amount must be added whether you are working with new rods or existing rods. If you fail to do this for existing rods, the drapery will not fit. If you fail to do this for new rods, the installer will have to mount the new rods 2" narrowed in width on each side of the window.

Measuring existing decorator rods:

Measure the **width** of the rod from the tip of the return bracket across to the tip of the other return bracket, and note the following information. **When measuring the width of existing decorative rods, remember to** *add or allow* **an extra 2" on each side if a one-way-pull, or 4" for both sides of a pair** (beyond the tip of the return bracket, in width) when measuring for the immovable rings on the end of each side of the rod. If you fail to do this for existing rods, the drapery will not fit.

The correct **length** to make the new drapery may be determined by **measuring from the top of the carrier or the top of the end-bracket to the floor. Do not deduct anything from this measurement.** If the existing rod is mounted with "F" brackets, as with sheers, take the length measurement in the same way, and deduct ¼".

Measuring for Offset Pairs

To plan a for draperies with an off-centered window, your customer needs to make a decision. Either the drapery can be centered to the wall, or the drapery can be centered to the window. If the drapery is planned to fall in the center of the wall, the overlap area will fall in the center of the wall, not the center of the window. If the drapery is centered to the center of the window (which is the preferred method) the drapery, when shut, will have the overlapped area off-center to the room. When the drapery is open and stacked-back, the window will be framed evenly, although there will be more fabric on one side than the other, when stacked-back.

Making the drapery a one-way pull takes care of the situation somewhat. You will not really notice that the window is offset when the drapery is drawn back, but a one-way pull is not nearly as attractive looking as a pair of drapery.

Off-centered windows are a very common occurrence, especially in bedrooms. Decide with the customer the placement of large pieces of furniture. Use the furniture placement as the guideline for which way you should go in off-centered window situations.

Discuss this situation with your customers every time it comes up. There is not a perfect solution, either way you plan the windows. If you do not discuss the problems and pitfalls of either solution and do not allow the customer to make the final decision on which way they want to go, the customer is going to call you with a complaint. They are unhappy with the overlap off-centered in the room, or they do not like the way the drapery does not overlap in the center of the window. Either way you will get a complaint, as the customer does not realize there is not a perfect solution to this problem.

If you elect to go one way on your own, making the decision without discussing this situation with your customer, you will have to rework or remake the drapery when the customer complains that they do not like it. Let the customer make the decision in the first place.

To center the drapery to the room, decide where you want the drapery to go by measuring. **Find the center of the room;** this is where the middle of the drapery will fall if the drapery is centered to the room. Measure out from the center area of the room on one side to see how wide you want the drapery to be. You may elect to go just beyond the window or wall-to-wall. *There will be a difference in the amount of wall space on each side of the window, and on an even pair the overlap will fall to the center of the room.*

When drawn open, the drapery will stack in an even pair, uniform in the amount of fabric stacked-back on each side. **The drapery will be lopsided in appearance inside and outside the room.** If you are measuring for a wall-to-wall installation, review the section *Measuring Wall-to-Wall Window Treatments* in this section, on how to proceed.

To center the drapery to the window, measure out from the center of the window to how wide you want the treatment to be on each side. When the drapery is drawn open, the drapery will open evenly from the center, but will have more fabric on one side than on the other, when stacked-back. **This method will look the best and allows the overlap to fall in the center of the window.** You will need to label and preferably sketch the individual panels' placement on the workorder for the workroom and the installer.

Add in the overlaps and returns needed to achieve finished width.

Drapery Hung-in-a-Series

Drapery hung-in-a-series is planned for windows closely placed together. This is a good solution when you want to cut down on the amount of separate panels used, to create a more professional looking treatment. By eliminating and combining the sides (which normally butt together) and their returns, the drapery openings are all eliminated, down to the overlaps in the center and at the sides of the drapery. Usually, drapery hung-in-a-series is used on pairs when you want to cut down the number of panels, but still have the panels draw open from the middle. Typically, the rods are still hung as regular pairs. The drapery is drawn by reaching under the drapery from the center, and pulling on the traverse cords.

Drapery hung-in-a-series is a term that means the same as a multiple draw. Select this type of treatment when you want to combine some of the pairs into panels within the room.

This technique allows the drapery that are pairs to open as pairs. This treatment combines the side returns (where other drapery butt-up against each other) to be combined in one piece. Because you eliminate the sides butting against each other and the pleats turning the corner against each other, you end up with a much nicer looking treatment. Place the draw cord on the side that does not combine the units together, so you are able to get to the traverse cord. A motorized track is also a solution to this situation.

Determine the measurements and the widths needed (*especially for the main panel of the treatment*) **before showing your customer printed fabric that may not work with this situation.** The reason is: if the widths work out with a split-width or panel in the series using a print, the printed panel will be split down the middle, splitting the pattern repeat in half. If a pair is used in an odd number of split-panels, the panel of the repeat of the print will be split and overlap, losing 6" (with the hems of the leading edges and the overlap) in the middle of the drapery. Since you lose 6" of the pattern (and this is the only panel you split), the split panel will appear quite different. If you should figure the widths using 48" goods and come up with this dilemma, refigure the goods using 54" wide goods. This may be the answer to your quandry of having to split a patterned width. Decide the best course of action to take before getting your customer excited about a fabric that you *cannot use* in their situation. If the customer insists on using that fabric, then plan the treatment as best you can, discuss the situation with the workroom, and draw a diagram to show how each panel is going to fall around the room.

Note: Many customers will have this system all ready in place and just want replacement drapery.

Measuring Swinging Doors

On French doors, doors with glassed-in upper areas, or any other door with windows that have door knobs, measure 1¼" - 1½" in width on each side of the glassed-in area. Measure this way even though the knob may protrude into your measured area. Depending on the fabric or material, the installer can trim most shades or blinds around this knob area while out on the site installing the treatment.

Always request hold-down brackets for hard treatments to be installed on a swing door or window to keep the treatment firmly fastened down from movement when the door or window is opened and closed.

Unless vertical blinds have a track on the bottom, they are not suitable selections for mounting on a door. Verticals may be mounted above the door and far enough over on either or both sides so they stack-off of hinged areas of the door when drawn back.

Corner Windows

On corner window situations where two windows butt or nearly butt together, **the best way to treat them is with two one-way pulls that butt and pass at the corner.**

When butting the rods, you do not want them to actually butt together, but just appear to butt. If they were to actually butt together, the two corner edges of the drapery that met in the corner would *"snake back"* allowing poor privacy, light leakage, and additionally, the drapery would not hang straight.

Selection of hardware is crucial here, if you want to achieve a tight corner without privacy problems and light leakage. The best rods you can select for traversing are the basic heavy-duty traverse rods. They will move smoothly, the side drapery may be butted close, and they will allow a nice, tight fit at the corner.

If you were to make these treatments into two pairs, when the drapery is open the drapery will take up the whole corner in stack-back. Your customer will not be able to see out, dust will blow on the drapery when the window is open, and there will be little air flow.

Pair rods, used in corner situations without a top treatment, are a better installation when mounted in the ceiling. If the rods are one-way pulls, mount them in the wall near the ceiling if you want a ceiling-hung look.

Top treatments will be easy to plan or much more difficult, depending on the top treatment you select. Some top treatments, like any of the gathered styles, are adaptable to most situations. Top treatments such as cornices, swags and cascades, Austrian valances, and balloon valances are constructed separately and are mounted on their individual boards. They are also priced as two top treatments rather than one, where other top treatments that can be made to take the curve in the corner are priced as one top treatment (even if they have two separate boards mitered together at the corner).

Rods for top treatments or for drapery for corners may be bent at the home by the installer. Doing the bends on site, in the home, allows the bends to be placed *exactly* where the bends should be placed.

Cornice boxes, swags and cascades, Austrian valances, balloon valances, etc., have high and low points, gathered sections, swags, etc., that need their accent points or areas to fall right in the corner where the other section butts against it. This can be achieved with a remeasure by the installer and a careful diagram of the walls and all measurements on the workorder for the workroom.

There is always a chance that one of your measurements will be misinterpreted by the workroom, resulting in a remake. Optimistically, the error could result in a rework at a much lower cost to you instead. A rework may happen if the type of top treatment with the error may be reworked. Careful planning here is the key for unadaptable top treatments in corner and bay window situations.

The accurate solution to properly plan and measure complicated top treatments is to have the installer cut the cornice or other top treatment boards for the workroom while remeasuring the job. Cutting of the boards by the installer, while on site during a remeasure, will eliminate questions from the workroom that will come up if in their view you have not taken completely accurate measurements. The installer cuts the boards, labels them in sequence with the customer's name, and the workroom fabricates the top treatment for the boards.

To correctly plan and measure for this situation, have the rod and drapery facing the front of the home or building go all the way to the corner. The rod on the opposite side should be planned so it *"butts to"* the other rod, 1" away. This is at a point 3½" out from the wall for the bottom underdrapery; or 6" out from the wall for an overdrapery. Measuring this way will allow you to come close to the other drapery, while still allowing enough room for the drapery opposite to it to have its fabric slip in and go all the way to the corner. If you use this method, you will achieve privacy and avoid light leaks in the middle. This is called a *butt-and-pass*, and looks nice from both the inside and the outside of the home or building.

Your customer will probably want to stack-off on each side for a view situation and for ventilation. So include the stack-off area, if it is desired.

To plan this situation, take the front window and plan it as a normal window in measuring the width; figure any stacking, extensions, appropriate overlaps, and add *only one* return. This would be the return that is opposite to the corner.

Since you are butting the drapery to the corner, you do not need the interior corner return. The opposite drapery will intersect 3½", or 6" into your front-facing drapery. The side window cannot go all the way to the corner, and must butt against the front window drapery and rod. You will not use a return on the side of the drapery that butts up against the front drapery here, either.

If you are using only a drapery without any other under or overtreatments, simply figure the side drapery as if it is going all the way to the corner, and deduct 3½".

If you are planning a job with underdrapery and an overdrapery, the job becomes slightly more complex. Plan the first layer of the underdraperies, as shown above, and then proceed to plan the overdraperies and any top treatments.

For the second layer of the corner situation, take the front window's original measurement in face-width, and deduct 3" from this width measurement. You are now out from the wall and the corner 6", not 3½" as you were when you planned the first layer. Add in the appropriate overlaps and the new return size. Take the side's face width for the first layer, and deduct 3" from its face measurement. Add the appropriate overlaps and new return size for the new layer.

For the third layer proceed the same. The differences are, you are now out from the wall 9" at the corner and do not use overlaps for a top treatment. Therefore, subtract 3" more from both of the second layer's face-widths, and add in the new returns of 9" for each side.

Walk yourself through every step in the example below to get step-by-step information, understanding, and to get comfortable with how to plan corner window situations.

Example: The corner situation we are working on has two windows that butt together, about 1" apart at the corner. The front window is 64" wide with only 24" of stack space available at the side, since the fireplace is placed in an adjoining position. The opposite side window to the left is 48" wide with 24" of available wall space for stacking off the window. You are using regular traverse rods for both the under and the overdraperies. Your customer wants to use a straight cornice, that butts together in two sections at the corner.

Front Window
The front window is the window to start with.
64" face width, divided by ⅓ = 21.33". Since we have available 24" to the fireplace, we fall within our allowance. Instead of just adding 21.33", leaving a **small amount of wall space exposed** at the fireplace, we will want to **use the full 24" available.** Plan and measure this first window as you would any regular window, with the exception of not using a return on the side of the window that goes to the corner. 64" + 24" = 88" face width measurement.

• **88" is the face width measurement for the first layer or undertreatment in this example.**

Take the 88" front window, face width for the first layer or underdrapery and add in the overlap of 1½" (3" if it were to be a pair). **Do not use a return for the underdrapery, since we are using an overdrapery.** 88" + 1½" = 89½" finished width measurement.

■ **89½" is the finished width for fabrication for the underdrapery or first layer for the front window.**

For the second layer for the front facing window, take the face width of 88" and subtract 3". **Subtract 3" because this is the second layer, 3" farther out from the wall and corner than the first layer.** 88" - 3" = 85" is the face width measurement for the front window.

• **85" is the second layer face width measurement for the front window used in this example.**

Take the 85" front face width for the second layer or overdrapery and add in the overlap (in this case 1½") and the return. We are out from the wall 6", so the return is 6". 85" + 1½" + 6" = 92½" finished width measurement.

■ **92½" is the finished width for fabrication for the overdrapery or second layer.**

For the top treatment for the front window, subtract 3" more from the second layer's face width, since we are now out from the wall and corner another 3", or 9" total. Refer back to the second layer or overtreatment face width, above, for the face width measurement of 85". 85" - 3" = 82" face width for the top treatment for the front window.

● **82" is the third layer, or top treatment face width for the front window in our example.**

Take the 82" face width for the third layer and note the return for the one side. Depending on the style of the top treatment, the return size may or may not be added in. For pleated valances or gathered valances, add the return in. For any other fancy top treatments that need to go through the top treatment or *"fancy"* division of the workroom, you will not add the return in, but will note its size in the appropriate box on the workorder when ordering.

■ **For pleated or gathered valances, the finished width with the return added in is 82" + 9" = 91", for the finished width for the third layer for the front window. If the return is not to be added in, then your finished width is 82" with the 9" return noted on the workorder. The workroom will fabricate the top treatment with a face width of 82" and a return of 9".**

Side Window

The side window to the left is 48" wide, with 24" of stack space available. 48" divided by ⅓" = 16". Again, rather than leave a small strip of wall exposed, why not cover it up? 48" + 24" = 72". **Measure all the way to the corner and subtract 3½", since you are not able to go all the way to the corner, but must back off and butt-to the front windows rod and drapery 3½" back.** 72" - 3½" = 68½" is the face width measurement.

● **68½" is the face width measurement for the side window's undertreatment or first layer in this example.**

Take the 68½" side window face width for the first layer or underdrapery and add in the overlap of 1½" (3" if it is to be a pair). **Do not use a return for the underdrapery, since it has an overdrapery.** 68½" + 1½" = 70" finished width measurement.

■ **70" is the finished width for fabrication for the underdrapery or first layer.**

To arrive at the second layer's finished width for the side window, again take the face width and subtract 3". 68½" - 3" = 65½" is your face width for the second layer for the side window.

● **65½" is the second layer face width measurement for the side window used in this example.**

Take the 65½" face width for the second layer or overdrapery for the side window and add in the overlap, in this case 1½" and the return. You are now out from the wall 6", so the return is 6". 65½" + 1½" + 6" = 73".

■ **73" is the finished width for fabrication for the overdrapery or second layer.**

For the third layer for the side window, subtract 3" from the second-layer, side window width measurement since you are 9" out from the corner and the wall. Refer back to the above measurement for the second layer of 68½". 68½" - 3" = 65½" for the side window face width measurement.

● **68½" is the side window face width measurement in this example.**

Take the side width measurement and add in the return for the one side only. Refer to the information in the third-layer top treatment on arriving at the finished width to see if you want to add the return into the finished width or just note its size on the workorder.

■   **In the above example, for pleated valances or gathered valances, the finished width with the return added in is 68½" + 9 = 77½" finished width for the third layer of the side window.**

If the return is not to be added in, then the finished width is 68½" and the appropriate return of 9" is noted on the workorder. The workroom will fabricate the top treatment with a face width of 68½" with a return of 9".

This is a long example for you to follow step-by-step, so you can really gain an understanding of how to plan and measure corner windows accurately. Note in the next section on *Bay Windows that* they are planned using similar methods. Once you understand how to do a corner window, you easily grasp bay windows also.

Bay Windows

Bay windows, when beautifully decorated, naturally become the focal point of the room. Many types of top treatments are useable and desirable on bay windows. *To ensure* that the job will go in the first time, the most successful treatments to do for bay windows are any of the gathered rod pocket types, mounted on rods. With this type of styling, there are no boards to cut, there are no pleats to miss the corner, nothing to line up perfectly at the corners. The curtain rods are bent by the installer, and will usually get installed without any problems.

You certainly can do treatments such as the box-pleated valance, swags and cascades, Austrian valances, cornices, balloon valances, etc., but you must definitely get all the needed measurements and have a conversation or a visit with your installer at the site of the bay window before ordering and submitting the workorder to the workroom for fabrication. These are the hardest windows to cover without any problems arising.

Stationary panels tied back or free-hanging, with an undertreatment combined with a top treatment, are nice combinations for bay windows. Stationary panels will not take up nearly as much room as a full drapery, stacked-back will. With bay windows, you do not have *any* excess room, therefore you have to make the most of a small, angled situation.

Stationary panels can be repeated with the same undertreatment all around the room. Your customer may want to forego the stationary panels for the rest of the room and use only the undertreatment with the same or a similar top treatment style out of the same fabric.

Other bay window drapery planning points to consider:

●   Overdrapery that meet in the middle of a bay window, that are a full traversing pair, will block the side windows when stacked-back.

●   Three pairs of overdrapery, one for each window of the bay, when drawn open will take up the whole corner area on each side of the bay window.

●   For over- or underdrapery, one center pair with two one-way pull panels for the side windows (one-way pull, stacking toward the room on each side) will help to free up a portion of the corner.

●   **Stationary panels used for the overdrapery, tied back or free-hanging, will take up a small amount of room and keep the bay from appearing too heavy, while accenting the bay to the right degree.**

●   **The following is the nicest looking solution for underdrapery on a bay window, when you are planning the use of three rods which butt-together at the corners or a rod set incorporating three traverse areas on the same rod.** Use stationary panels for the three panels of the overdrapery and make the underdrapery a one-way pull. This leaves the underdrapery seamless in appearance without any overlapped areas showing. The large center window will pull either right or left, and the side windows pull to the room side on each side.

- **The preferred solution for underdrapery when using one traverse rod bent at the corners, or a rod set with one traversing area on one rod,** is to make the underdrapery a one-way right or left, and leave the drapery in one traversing panel to traverse across the whole width of the bay window. You will not want to open this unit often. This underdrapery will hang uniformly and look very nice for the life of the fabric.

When measuring and planning for bay windows, you need to **measure the windows two ways** and determine the angles at the corners.

The first method is used *to show on your workorder the exact measurements of the bay window, and how it lays on the wall area.*

The second method is used to show *how you arrived at the measurements you are using* to order the treatments. Additionally, any question that the workroom may have concerning the measurements, when planning the fabrication of the treatments, can be easily checked against the bay window's actual measurements. How to determine a bay window's angles is discussed here, below the measuring information.

Measure the exact height; distance above the window to top of the bay. **Measure all angles of the bay** from tip of the wall corner, to corner of the interior of the bay; from the interior corner to opposite interior corner; from opposite interior corner out to the tip of the wall corner. **Measure the flat wall areas,** rather than the trim on the window areas. **Record these measurements exactly, and draw an accurate diagram of the particular bay window you are working on.**

Next, take any coins out of your purse or pocket. Place the coins 3½" out from the wall at every corner, and other various intervals. If you are adding a top treatment or an overdrapery, or both, do the same with the next set of coins 6", and then 9", out from the wall. **Note, the area is getting much smaller, as the area does with corner window situations.**

Take two of your business cards, place one at the corner and the other at the adjoining opposite wall at the same corner. Place each card against the wall, and overlap ½" of the end of each card over each other at the corner to create the bay's angle for that corner. Staple the cards together to show the bay's wall angle. Flip the cards over and double check that the opposite side matches up with the same angle. Either make up two sets, one for each corner or mark on the face of the cards that this is a right corner angle, and then mark on the opposite of the other card, that this is a left corner angle. You may want to send the cards in to the workroom with your workorder or you may want to take a protractor and measure the degree of the angles and write the degree of the angle on the workorder.

Because of the difficulty in doing bays, unless you are extremely accurate and determine all measurements shown above, have the job remeasured.

Many installers *prefer* to bend rods for bays rather than waiting and taking a chance that the bay window rod set that was ordered will end up actually fitting. The installer can use stock hardware and bend the rods to the needed angles, right on the job.

Drapery *can* traverse around bends and turns, whether it is rods that the installer has bent for you, or rods that have been made up for bay windows. Bay window traverse rods will not be the smoothest moving traverse rod that you have experienced. It is preferable to use a sheer for the underdrapery that will not be opened and closed frequently, with stationary panels that will be left alone.

For complicated corner and bay windows, have the installer cut the cornice boards and other top treatment boards at the time of the remeasure and deliver them to the workroom. This practice will eliminate questions that the workroom will have. The installer labels the boards in sequence, with the customer's name, and then turns the boards over to the workroom to fabricate the treatment on the same boards.

Window Seats with Bay Windows

If the customer wants a cushion made for the window seat area of a bay and you are planning a treatment without a top treatment, determine the depth of the cushion, and measure from the top of the bay at its ceiling point, down to the cushion and deduct 1" for clearance of the drapery.

If the bay window is to have a top treatment with the cushion, determine the depth of the cushion. Again, measure from the top of the bay at its ceiling point down to the top of the cushion, and deduct 3½" for clearance to fit under the top treatment. Some bay windows have shallow wall areas above the glass area to their ceiling. In this situation, you may be able to deduct only 2" to eliminate or lessen the amount of the header showing from the outside.

Cafe Curtains

Cafe curtains are non-traversing drapery used as a tier. Cafe curtains can be planned to control light, air, and views. Covering the lower portion of the window allows privacy for seated people, while allowing light to come in the upper uncovered portions of the window.

Cafe curtains may be used singly or in multiples. If the drapery or curtain covers the window in horizontal sections, rather than in one piece, they are considered to be cafe curtains.

Cafe curtains may be made to overlap in the center or meet, depending on the type of rod selected for use. The header may be shirred, scalloped, attached by rings, be pleated, or have simple tab tops that slip over the rod.

- **Determine the length** of the cafe curtain. The length is normally at its best when placed at any visible horizontal point on the window. Horizontal points would include horizontal paned areas of paned windows. The rod should cover the wood strips or metal strips of the panes, and any locks to the window.

- **Exact placement needs to be noted on the workorder** for your installer. If you fail to note this information for the installer, exact placement will only *be guessed* at during installation.

- When planning cafe curtains, **always add 1" per width to the finished width to accommodate the extra fabric needed to cover the window.** If you do not add extra width, the cafe curtain, when slipped back and forth, will not stay in place over the window. Extra slack for the width must be added in.

- When planning a double-cafe treatment that is meant to overlap on top of each other, the top cafe portion should be planned long enough to cover the top of the bottom cafe curtain's pleats. The projection of the top cafe curtain should be longer than the projection of the bottom cafe curtain.

- If the cafe curtain is mounted on a decorative traverse rod, the unfinished portion of the back of the rod and the cord running through the back of the rod, will be visible from the exterior of the window. This will look especially unsatisfactory on front windows, where the back of the rod is visible as you walk up to the window by the door.

Draperies Over a Bathtub or Shower

Accent draperies over a bathtub or shower may be fabricated as full panels or stationary panels tied back over the shower or tub, lined or unlined. The self-fabric of the drapery may be lined in plastic to prevent water from penetrating the drapery fabric. The drapery may be free-hang or tied back. The panels may be gathered or pleated.

Fabricate the plastic liner separately from the drapery and install on a separate rod, or attach the plastic liner like a lining to the drapery.

Plan the drapery using one of the following three methods. Make the drapery the full width of the tub or shower and tie it back all to one side (the drapery appears a bit wide, most of the time, with the leading edge coming up very short on one side); make the full-width drapery a pair (better); or use narrow stationary panels, tied back or free-hanging on one or both of the sides of the shower or tub. This is the nicest looking solution, when used with a top treatment. Stationary utility rods will abruptly end in mid-air and look strange; the abrupt, unfinished look of the treatment will be apparent, unless you cover the panels with a top treatment.

Grommets or large eyelets can be attached at the top of drapery panels to finish off the top hem.

Fabrics to match the room's window treatments may be plastic, laminated for a different effect and will be a drapery fabric that water will not penetrate.

A short, lambrequin styled valance is a nice finishing touch to a shower curtain over a tub or shower. Make the valance short, about 12", cut to the same width as the shower curtain, and finish off at the top and bottom. Apply the grommets separately to the valance and the drapery panel, or together as one unit with the shower curtain. If you apply one set of grommets together with the shower curtain and the valance, the valance will hug the body of the drapery panel tighter and appear to be one unit, rather than separate units — if the grommets were attached to the valance and drapery panel separately.

Draping Arched Interior Areas

When draping arched interior areas, whether you arch the drapery or make it straight across, line the drapery panels. Use the same self-fabric for the lining; a contrasting drapery fabric, that goes with the decor in the room facing the lining; or a lining fabric. When you walk in or out of the room, you want to see a nice fabric on both sides; not an unlined drapery panel.

Existing Wood Cornices and Overdrapery with 3½" Projections

While decorating homes, you will receive common requests to do almost impossible installations. Many older homes have existing wood or venetian blind cornices that are heavily bolted into the walls. They may have existing drapery mounted to them already, or have venetian blinds attached.

You will get requests to add sheers under the existing overdrapery, or to add draperies over the existing venetian blinds that are mounted under the existing cornice. Another common request is to add both new sheers and drapery under the 3½" projection of the existing cornice.

Other customers will have existing overdrapery mounted on traverse rods with projections of 3½". They will request you to add sheers under the existing overdrapery.

Adding over- or underdrapery or other items in these situations is nearly impossible. The customer will usually not want to get rid of the architectural cornices that came with the home, or the *"perfectly good"* venetian blinds with the cornice attached.

You do not have enough room to add another layer of sheers, blinds, or drapery inside a 3½" return. If you attempt to add the second layer, **the drapery will always drag against the sheers or blinds, every time the drapery are opened and closed,** wearing and soiling the drapery.

There is only enough room to add rod pocket sheers, if the customer insists on keeping their existing cornices or set-up of existing rods. The rod pocket sheers may have only very short returns. Another alternative is to add an overdrapery mounted on a curtain rod that will not traverse.

When you come across these situations and conditions, it is preferable to replace *everything* and start over; or walk away from these jobs and avoid the potential complaints you are setting yourself up for from these faulty conditions.

Special Effects

Puddled Drapery

Puddled drapery are a very traditional way to treat drapery. Originally, drapery were puddled to cut down on drafts coming in windows. It is a very interesting effect. Realize that this is not the treatment for a customer who is not going to be willing to *redress* the drapery after each vacuuming.

There is always the risk of a careless customer getting the fabric caught in the vacuum cleaner, a small child stepping on the excess fabric and pulling the rod out of the wall, and excess dust collecting on the fabric portions which lay horizontally on the floor. This effect also costs your customer more money for fabric, but will alleviate any mismeasurement of the length.

To plan drapery that are to puddle up on the floor, add 12"-18" extra to the finished length. If you want a conservative puddle (is there such a thing?), add 12"; if you want to exaggerate the puddled effect, add up to 18".

Bishop Sleeves

Bishop sleeves are another popular effect to add *flare* to your window treatments. Bishop sleeves are held in place and never let down. Bishops sleeves may be pouffed out in one or two places in the length. They may be made slightly pouffed or very full. The amount of fullness depends on the effect you are trying to create. To pouff the bishop sleeve out slightly in only one place is more conservative than to pouff the drapery out fuller in two places. **Listed in the first three points are specifications for planning a slightly pouffed bishop sleeve tied in one place; a slightly pouffed bishop sleeve tied in two places;** and a *fuller* **bishop sleeve tied in two places.** Depending on the fabric selected and the fullness desired, in addition to how many tied back areas you want to include, adapt these guidelines to your individual situation.

- For a bishop sleeve with a **slight pouff tied in one place, add 6" to the desired length** of the drapery.

- To plan bishop sleeves to pouff out slightly **with two tiebacks in two places, add 12" to the desired length** of the drapery.

- To plan bishop sleeves **to pouff out fully with two tiebacks in two places in length, add 20" extra for the length.**

- **Determine how many tiebacks are needed** — one for each ballooned-out section.

- **Make the tiebacks short in length.** The tiebacks need to tightly hold the bishop sleeve's ballooned sections in place.

To order and plan the tiebacks for fabrication:

For 1½ panel widths on each side — use a 12" length for the tieback, for an unlined panel; 15" length, for lined panels **+ the return size.**

For 2 panel widths on each side — use a 15" length for the tieback, for unlined panels; 18"length, for lined panels **+ the return size.**

Two, Three, or Four-Cord Shirred Headers

Two, three, or four-cord shirred headers are headers which are formed by having shirring tape sewn in the back of the header. The header has small cords running through its width, across the top of the drapery, or lengthwise to the shirring tape.

When the cords are pulled (two, three, or four cords, depending on the heading style desired) all at the same time, you will achieve a smocked effect. Many different valances, shade styles, and top treatments may be shirred up this way to add needed fullness and to finish off the top edges of a treatment in a beautiful manner. The finished treatment is stapled, or Velcro is attached to its mounting board.

Beauty-Pleat Drapery

Beauty-pleat drapery are drapery that hang in nice, rounded folds and stack back fairly tightly. Beauty-pleat drapery are attractive and do not use nearly as much fabric as custom drapery do. They hang off of a rod that traverses, with a spring inserted, through the top of the rod pocket of the drapery.

Unless your installer is particularly experienced in installing and reinstalling replacement beauty-pleat drapery, do not sell them. If the customer will not let you switch them to the type of rods you sell, encourage them to look in the yellow pages and find a company that specializes in beauty-pleat draperies.

Although the system *appears* simple to you visually, an inexperienced installer can spend the bulk of his or her day trying to *reinstall* the spring in the top of the drapery correctly. This is a great way to alienate your installer.

Top Treatments and Fabric Shades

Valances and Top Treatments

A valance is a horizontal, decorative pleated or gathered top treatment placed over the top of windows or drapery to finish off the window treatment. Top treatments may be used alone or with many layers of undertreatments. The *term* top treatment refers to all valances and top treatments.

All top treatments will conceal hardware and the top of an undertreatment's headrail and pleats. Top treatments can improve a window's awkward proportions, add width, and give height to a window and a room. If the window is placed low on the wall, a top treatment will give the window height. Top treatments and undertreatments can add width to the window and its area, by extending the window treatment in width on both sides.

Top treatments add warmth, character and interest to a window. They also have the capability of making a window the focal point within a room.

Top treatments may be styled to echo other design elements within the room and be made up in a coordinating fabric to help pull everything together.

Planning a Top Treatment Over an Undertreatment

How to plan the addition of a top treatment:

- **Select the desired top treatment design.**

- **Calculate face width** to clear the hardware and undertreatment. Top treatments need to be planned wider than the drapery or undertreatment that they are fabricated to fit over. **An additional ½" on each side is sufficient for most soft-sided top treatments** (those without boards for the returns), with the option of going wider if you prefer.

  If the top treatment is **hard-sided**, as a cornice is, you need to plan the top treatment **1" wider on each side** than the drapery or undertreatment, so the top treatment will be able to slip over the top of the undertreatment.

- **Determine the projection** or return *needed* to clear the undertreatment. Allow a deep enough return, so the undertreatment will freely traverse or pull up and down underneath.

- **Measure the minimum short length needed for coverage.** See guidelines below to figure the length. Make sure the shortest point of the top treatment will not leave the drapery pleats exposed, the top of the window exposed, or the headrail for undertreatments exposed. If you have extreme length, differentials in the short points and the longer points of the top treatment, the overall coverage of the top treatment is affected.

- Top treatment's **lengths must be planned above swing areas of doors or casement windows.**

- **Drapery planned under top treatments need to be planned at least 2" shorter** than they would be planned without a top treatment. This is so the drapery will hang under the rod and freely traverse and stack-back in uniform folds. The basic rule is to deduct 3" from drapery, deduct 3½" for underdrapery from the total treatment length to allow for the board-width area that is needed. The drapery should be ordered to have an even-pin or hook setting.

Select the fabric before you select the style of the top treatment:

Decide which fabric you are going to use before finalizing the style or the shape, and style the top treatment will be fabricated in. The style of the top treatment should follow the style of the fabric.

The larger the pattern of the fabric, the fewer alternatives available with the style of the top treatment.

Other top treatment points to consider:

When planning top treatments and the top-point placement for top treatments, look around the room. Consider if there are any design areas, architecturally, that have height, tall furniture, or any other distinguishing element within the room or space that already has an established height. If there is, this would be the height to continue with your top treatment placement. You do not want a chopped up appearance for the room. It is favorable to continue the *flow* that present elements have already started.

Look for distinctive architectural lines or motifs within the space or furniture. Is there a treatment that you could plan that would echo or pick up these lines that are already present? Repetition is a very effective design element.

If there is not a distinctive point to echo for the height of the top treatment, then it is preferable to plan the top treatment for placement at the ceiling. You may make the top treatment lower at 90" or 87". Keep in mind that 84" is *usually* about 5" above the window in most homes.

The header of the drapery or the hardware of the undertreatment needs to be hidden from the outside of the home, so the drapery generally needs to be 84" minimum length. The top treatment needs to sit 3" higher, with 3½" higher preferred. The drapery or undertreatment should ideally be made 3½" below the top treatment's height. **Only in rare cases, when you are really trying to keep the price down, place the top treatment at the ceiling and the underdrapery or undertreatment at 84".**

Top treatments made with a dust cover across the top and with hard sides at the returns, such as cornices, can only be placed at the top of the wall in the room. They are not able to be placed up on the slanted ceiling area. Consequently, it is better not to place these treatments in particular all the way up to the top of the wall, but at a point about 7" above the window opening. This placement will look much better than the gap that will occur if you proceed to place the cornice or another similarly planned top treatment at the top of the wall.

If your customer is insistent on placing a cornice up on the slant of the ceiling, then use a similar treatment such as a lambrequin in place of a cornice that can be mounted on a 1" by 2" wood board up on the slant. **Most top treatments may be placed up on the slant as long as they may have soft returns, and can be mounted on a 1" by 2" board.**

If the top treatment is to be mounted on the ceiling due to having a slant-top cathedral ceiling, it becomes necessary to mount the top treatment to the ceiling on a 1" by 2" board. The installer will cut the board at the job site to fit the situation. Note on the workorder for the installer to supply and cut the board on site.

If you are planning a bay window and install the top treatment straight across on the outside of the bay window area, you will make the bay window appear to be a separate area from the room. This can be effective in some instances, but you will generally want to treat the angles of the bay with top treatments that bring that area of the room into the room.

Some bays have a drop-ceiling. If you treat the bay with a top treatment that is somewhat lower in height, the area is going to appear *different* and lower. You may want to plan a wide rod pocket single- or double-stack valance for these windows and proceed with the same fabric in a different, related style on the other windows in the space.

Rooms with moldings next to the ceiling will need the top treatments to go all the way up to the molding, or be placed several inches below the molding to keep the molding visible.

If some windows within a space are fairly close together, with or without I.B. or O.B. mounted undertreatments, consider making the top treatments in one piece rather than chopping them up and making individual units. If you do make them in individual units and are planning a pleated or other type of top treatment that may be affected, the pleats on pleated top treatments, or any other styling at the corners, will butt up against each other at the returns, not giving as nice an effect as is possible when making the top treatments in one piece.

On corner windows, this same rule holds true. If you are planning a style that can be made in one piece, it is preferable to do so. Rods can be bent, or boards cut in two pieces, and the valance can be fastened to flow around the corner. Many treatments can be done this way: pleated valances, gathered valances, Austrian valances, sleeve valances, etc. Check with your workroom or your installer if in doubt.

Supply exact measurements of both walls and diagram the situation on the workorder. Plan the treatments as shown in the chapter on *Measuring* and the section on *Corner Windows*. Top treatments need to be made so the pleat or other decorative point falls in the middle of the corner.

Top treatment delivery:

Any top treatment over 144" is a difficult to deliver item. If the top treatment must be mounted on a board while at the workroom (such as swag and cascade types of styles), the delivery may be impossible or may incur special charges. You should probably select a style that the installer can mount on a board while in the home.

Additionally, take note of any oversized top treatment or other item to be installed on the second story of a home. Take the time to inspect to see if you are able to get the top treatment in the house and up the stairs easily.

Top Treatment Styling and Fabric Considerations

If the fabric is plain, but has an obvious grain to it, **many top treatments will require that the fabric be railroaded in the opposite direction from the direction of the drapery underneath.** Railroading the fabric for the top treatment will show an obvious directional change from the top of the window treatment to the bottom.

Some fabrics are not going to allow you to railroad them and will need to be seamed rather than railroaded. The seams should be placed at the shallow point of the top treatment, rather than at the long point of the top treatment. To achieve this placement, you may end up wasting a bit of fabric.

Other points:

- **Seams should always be placed at both sides of a top treatment rather than in the center of a top treatment.** Seams should be placed equal distance from the center, on each side.

- **Always place the largest pattern within a pattern, in the center of the top treatment or other treatment. Strive to place the largest pattern on the ends.** You should **end the treatment with ½ the pattern at the middle, on each end of the top treatment.** This is the point where the return breaks back to the wall.

- To achieve the most effective looking treatments, **there should also be an odd number of long points in the style of the treatment.**

- **Adding banding at the bottom of valances** is decorative, but **will cause the valance to flare out** rather than hang in nice folds. Always add the appropriate labor charges and extra yardage needed when you do add banding.

Workorder Points to Note for Top Treatments

Top treatments are ordered by face width only, with the returns noted on the workorder. Do not include returns in the face width measurement, unless the top treatment is a regular French-pleated style (just like drapery pleats) or is a gathered style.

If you are planning a French-pleated style or a gathered style, do not write up the top treatment in the top treatment fancy *area*, of the workorder. Order in the drapery section of the workorder, as you would for drapery.

For top treatments to be mounted on boards, write on the workorder, *"Supply boards for the top treatment."*

Draw diagrams and note wall measurements *exactly* on the workorder; difficult situations, such as getting a pleat or other decorative design point to fall exactly in the corner of a treatment, may be achieved by the workroom and the installer.

When writing up the workorder for cornices or other top treatments with repeats in the design of the top treatment (not a pattern repeat of the fabric), the box on the workorder that states "multiple repeats" refers to the repeat of the top treatment design.

"Feature stripe" on the workorder, refers to applied banding. You will need to specify the placement, width, etc. On top treatments, always discuss and draw a rough sketch of the finished product and placement, to make sure the workroom understands what you want.

Cord welting can be made the same color as the face treatment or can be made a contrasting color. Specify and order the appropriate choice. Again, discuss any applied design with your customer.

Gathered Valances

Gathered valances are usually 300% in fullness. Gathered valances require more fabric than a conventional pleated valance. Gathered valances are softer, more feminine, and romantic. They may have a country type of a look, depending on the rod pocket size, type of rod, amount of ruffling, and header styles.

Gathered valances may have very wide rod pockets and be mounted on the Kirsch Continental® rods, or be mounted on pole rods; or may have a small rod pocket, and be mounted on a regular curtain rod. Rod pockets also vary in styling. Depending on the look desired, they *may or may not* have a stand-up header above the rod. Styles without the header tend to be more elegant and cosmopolitan; styles with the header have a more casual and country feeling. The header may be made very large — up to 4", or very short — ¼". Depending on the fabric selected, and how much body and stiffness it has, will determine how high you may go with the header and still have it stand up, rather than topple over.

Rod pockets below the valance may also be added for a stretched look. This type of valance may only consist of a wide rod pocket; or it may consist of two- or three-rod-wide rod pockets stacked together.

Note on the workorder what size rod pocket you need. Allow enough slack in the size, for the rod pocket to fit over the rod and record what size the headers are to be. If you are using a rod pocket sleeve style, note the size of the header above the rod and the size of the header below — making them *different* sizes can be a great look.

Many looks and styles may be derived from this basic valance. Also, many different rods of all types may be used to mount these valances: narrow rods, wide rods, pole rods, etc.

When planning wide rod pocket valances, such as the 4½" styles, pole-top treatments, or curtain rod pocket valances of any type, ask the customer if they want the stand-up, ruffle-header above the rod. Depending on the fabric, with the header or without the header are both good-looking treatments. Find out your customer's preference.

Planning Rod Pocket Sleeves

To plan any rod pocket sleeve for fabrication and fabric needed follow the guidelines below:

- Determine the size of the wide rod you will be using — 2½" or 4½" wide.

- Decide the size of the header or ruffle to sit **above** the rod pocket sleeve, if you want a header or ruffle. Review the *Rod* section for this type of rod to see what the maximum width of the header above the rod is. Limper fabrics need to have a shorter header.

- Select the size of the header or ruffle to sit *below* the wide rod pocket sleeve, if you want a header or ruffle. The header below the rod does not need to be the same size as the header above the rod. It is very attractive to make the header below the rod longer in length.

- Add up these three measurements. Now double this measurement, add seams allowances of 1", and *ease* of 1" or more, so the sleeve can easily slip over the rod. If you forget to add the ease, and make the sleeve the same size or almost the same size as the rod's diameter, you will never get the sleeve on the rod.

  Example: You have decided to use a 4½" wide rod. The header above is to be a deep one of 3". The header below the rod is to be 5".

  4½" + 3" + 5" = 12.5". 12.5" x 2 = 25". 25" + 2"(seam allowances) + 1" (ease) = 28". 28" is your cut length for a 4½" rod pocket sleeve with a 3" header above, and a 5" header below.

- **Allow for any pattern repeat of the fabric.** Figure the cut length with a pattern repeat the same way you do for any drapery or top treatment. Review the first example below. If the repeat size is larger than the original cut length, the cut length you use is the repeat size.

  Example: The cut length in the above example is 28". The fabric you have selected has a repeat of 16". Divide the cut length of 28" by 16" = 1.75. Round 1.75 repeats up to 2 repeats of 16". The new cut length is equal to two 16" repeats, or 32".

  Example: The cut length in the above example is 28". The fabric you have selected has a repeat of 29". Your new cut length is 29".

- **Rod pocket sleeves need to be made with 300% fullness for most fabrics, to look effective.** For sheer fabric it is more custom looking to make them even fuller.

  To determine the number of widths of fabric needed, take the rod width, face measurement, and add in the returns. Divide by the fullness factor found in the fullness chart. Take the resulting number and round up or down to the closest whole number.
  To figure the yardage: Take the amount of widths needed, and multiply the cut lengths by the widths. Divide by 36" (yards) to arrive at the amount of yardage needed. Since we have figured *exactly* the cut length needed to achieve fabrication of the sleeve, round up the yardage to the next ¼ yard.

  Example: We need 7 widths of 48" fabric to have 300% fullness for the rod width we are going to cover for the above example with a cut length of 28".

  28" cut length x 7 widths of fabric = 196". 196" divided by 36" = 5.44 yards. Round up the yardage ¼ yard. 5.69 or 5¾ yards is the correct amount to order in this example.

- If the sleeve is being made to cover the center area of a **lined**, shirr-on-the-rod drapery panel, and the back of the rod is visible from the outside the home or building, you also need to line the sleeve, rather than just fabricating it, double in the self-fabric.

Pouff Valances

A pouff valance is a variation of a gathered valance. The valance is made longer — a minimum of 12", to almost double the desired finished length. A separate rod pocket is sewn in at the bottom of the valance. A curtain rod or steel rod is inserted, and the valance is pulled up from the back of the valance to the desired finished length. Because of the fullness and abundance of length pulled up under in the back, the valance automatically pouffs out without any need of tissue paper or padding, which pouff valances with less fullness require.

Pouff valances are usually made 300%-400% fullness, depending on the heaviness of the fabric; a very sheer fabric is going to need to be 400% fullness.

Single Stack 4½" Wide Top Treatments

When placing a single stack 4½" valance at the ceiling without a header above or below, the total treatment will be only 5" deep (5½" rod pocket, gathered on the rod = 5"). If the single stack treatment is added over pleated drapery at this height, the bottom of the pleats of the drapery will show. Use a double-stack or triple-stack (2 or 3 single stack 4½" treatments, stacked together) at this height instead.

If you were placing the valance at 64" height or less, you may get away with a single-stack valance of 4½" mounted over pleated drapery. You are not looking up under the valance as you do when it is mounted at ceiling height.

Board Mounted Top Treatments

Most top treatments will be mounted on boards, unless they are gathered on the rod styles. Boards are mounted to the wall or ceiling with the use of angle irons.

For board-mounted valances, dust caps are used to cover the top of the top treatment. Dust caps help prevent air-conditioned and heated air from flowing out of the window, thus lowering energy bills. Dust caps also help protect the top treatment from dust and dirt.

Insist on the use of Velcro to fasten the top treatments to the boards for quality top treatments, rather than the installer and workroom preferred method of stapling the top treatment to the board. Staples will show, rust (depending on the home or building location), and cause customers to *question* you about the quality of the job.

Top treatments should not be installed any lower than 2" above the top of the rods. A top treatment should sit 3"-3½" above the drapery rod or undertreatment headrail for proper hang and flow of drapery or undertreatment underneath.

Planning Lengths for Top Treatments

When planning a top treatment over an undertreatment, you will want to plan the top treatment long enough so the top of the undertreatment or pleats of the undertreatment are not visible from anywhere in the room.

This is done by planning the length at the shortest point to hang at least 4" down over the undertreatment. This will prevent you from seeing the top of the window area, trim, and the base of the pleats underneath. Unless someone is sitting right under the top treatment, the coverage should be planned so you will not easily see under the top treatment.

If the customer objects to the top treatment coming down into the window 4", give them the option of making it shorter. Inform the customer that making the top treatment shorter will not *ensure* coverage. Record this information on the sales agreement and in your notes, *to cover you* for their possible future complaint call about the coverage.

A top treatment length must also be in proportion to the width of the window treatment. A very wide window is going to require that the top treatment is longer in length than a narrower window.

Most valances and top treatments should be planned at a minimum of 14" in length for a free-hanging valance. If it is a narrow window with a pleated or gathered valance with a narrow rod pocket, you can get by with 12" in length. Another exception would be rod-pocket sleeves over a wide rod pocket — which really have a narrow, stretched, cornice effect.

Some customers will try to get you down in the length to 9" or 10". If you make the valance this short, the valance will not hang uniformly. **12" minimum length and weight is needed for correct hanging ability on a pleated or gathered valance.**

You may sell as short as an 8" valance *if* you have the valance self-lined and hemmed with a handkerchief or rolled hem. A standard 4" hem is not going to hang well on a length under 12".

To achieve accurate *coverage* in length with a top treatment, follow the guidelines below for minimum lengths for the corresponding projections:

3" projection   Top treatment should drop down into the window area 4", with a **minimum of 2"**.
Top treatment should be 13" in length, with a **minimum length of 11"**.

6" projection   Top treatment should drop down into the window area 5", with a **minimum of 3"**.
Top treatment should be 14" in length, with a **minimum length of 12"**.

9" projection   Top treatment should drop down into the window area 6", with a **minimum of 4"**.
Top treatment should be 15" in length, with a **minimum length of 13"**.

In addition to the above coverage guidelines, **for top treatments to look well-proportioned, they need their overall length to be in proportion to the width of the top treatment.**
To achieve proper proportions, make the top treatment 1/6th or 1/7th (for a very wide top treatment) of the length of the drapery. Apply both rules when planning the length of top treatments.
Another formula to check for proper proportions; the height or length of a top treatment should be of a scale equaling 1½" for each foot of window treatment length (from the top of the desired window treatment placement to the floor) for a shaped or flat valance. This amount will go up to 2½" per foot, for a total length of a top treatment for gathered top treatments, festoon types, etc. Jabot length should be figured even longer.

Measuring for valances and top treatments:

For measuring information, refer to the above section on *Planning a Top Treatment Over an Undertreatment* and *Planning Lengths for Top Treatments*.

Pleated Valances

French pleated valances require the least amount of fabric of almost all top treatments. The exceptions would be cornices and lambrequins.
French pleated valances are usually mounted on a board, but can be mounted on a rod.
These type of valances are **very tailored, transitional in design, and will go with almost any decor.** Many people have had them, and replace older pleated valances with new pleated valances.
Mount French pleated valances, on a decorator rod 5" above the window for a fresh, new look.
Box-pleated valances are flat, box pleated and mounted on boards. This type of valance is **more tailored**, with the design of the valance capable of variations. Tab-tops may be added, the box pleats may be spread out *quite* wide, or the pleats which are normally hidden underneath may be reversed, and appear on top.

Pleated and Shaped Valances

When planning and ordering fabric for pleated, shaped valances, or shaped valances, order and figure the widths of fabric and convert to yardage as you would for drapery.
When working with any valance that is shaped, price out and figure the yardage from the longest cut length, disregarding that the valance is shorter in the middle. If the fabric has a repeat, it must match up. Making some of the widths shorter originally will complicate matters. Some workrooms work with cutting all the widths the same length initially, and then shaping the valance after the side seams are sewn. Always order full cuts of the longest points of the valance for the whole valance (imperative on fabric with repeats).
With all types of pleated valances you use the 4" header and 4" hems, unless the valance is self-lined. (doubled, same fabric on both sides, with no hem).

Tapered Top Treatment Valances

Tapered valances should not exceed 120" in width, and should not be narrower than 48". If the valance is under 48", plan a simple, straight bottom or a curved valance. Plan the cuts for determining cut lengths from the long point of the tapered valance. The workroom will cut all the lengths the same and then make the tapered cut, after the widths are stitched together. This is necessary for pattern matching, especially.

Self-Lined Valances

Self-lined means lined with the same fabric as the self-fabric. A self-lined valance is made like a sack. The fabric is folded in half and seamed, with the seam running the length of the folded fabric.

Yardage for a self-lined valance is planned by determining the widths, multiplying the widths times the cut length (for a self-lined valance), and dividing by 36" (yards) to arrive at yardage needed.

The cut length is determined by doubling the finished length and adding 10" to the resulting number. If a repeat must be figured in, double the finished length, add the 10" figure; determine the extra, repeat yardage needed; then add in the extra yardage for the repeat.

Decorative valances are almost always self-lined. Check with the workroom, if in doubt before ordering the fabric.

Cornices

Cornices are padded, flat, valance-type top treatments mounted over a board. Many variations can be had in shaping at the sides, top, and the bottom. Insets, ruching, cording, various braids, trims, banding, singled or doubled, are used. If the fabric is not railroaded, seams will show, especially in light, solid colors. Lightweight fabrics will also allow the seams to show through. Always try to select a fabric that can be railroaded. You do not need an unhappy customer that will not come back for repeat business because they are unhappy about their cornice's seams showing.

If the fabric cannot be railroaded and the window is any wider than 39", your cornice will have vertical seams. In a light-color fabric, especially white, seams will show badly. Seams will show through any light-colored fabric that is lightweight.

Cornices need to be at least 14" in length to look well planned. To properly plan the correct length, make the cornice 1/6th of the total length of the overall treatment.

Cornices are usually fabricated out of ⅜" plywood with all corners glued and nailed. 1" x 3", 1" x 6", or 1" x 9" dust caps and returns are used, depending on the undertreatments used, underneath the cornice. A layer of padding, self-fabric, and lining are applied and blind-tacked so the staples are not visible.

When ordering cornices, remember that the cornice must fit over any undertreatment or drapery. Therefore, the cornice measurement must be larger in length and in depth (return) to do so. 1½" on each side is the correct amount to add to the length. The depth is determined by what undertreatments are used underneath the top treatment.

When you place an order for a cornice, the measurement you ask for is the inside measurement of the wood frame. If the cornice is to go wall-to-wall, specify this fact to the workroom so that they will not exceed the width of the requested face width.

A cornice's shortest point should not be shorter than 3" into the glass area of the window. You can get away with 3" rather than 4" for other valances, because cornices are flat rather than pleated, gathered, or swaged; *where* the fabric may not *lay flat* across the bottom, tightly hugging the window.

Since many cornice styles are curved or cut out, **the longest measurement will come into the glass even more.**

If you design your own cornice style, remember that **the side corners of a cornice must come down or descend on the sides (longer points of the cornice) to create a finished look** rather than curving up at the sides, with the longest point in other areas of the cornice.

Crown, pagoda, arch-top styled cornices:

For cornices that have a crown, pagoda, or arch-top, where the top *flares up* higher than the top of the return, deduct 10" off of the underdrapery length. Since the top section is higher than the top of the return, the drapery need to be 3½" shorter than the top of the return. This usually works out to be 10" shorter than the top of the face of the cornice, in a crown, pagoda, or arched up design.

Lambrequins

Lambrequins are similar to cornices; they are also flat, but do not have boards inserted in the fabric in the front drop, or in the side drops (returns) of the treatment. **They are considered a soft cornice.** Lambrequins are usually mounted off a board at the top of the treatment and may be straight bottomed, scalloped, or have other designs across the bottom.

Lambrequins should be installed on a board, but may be installed with a rod pocket to be mounted on a curtain rod or a pole rod.

Flat, soft treatments such as lambrequins have the tendency to waver in and out when they are hung up, and require interlining to help keep them flat. Styles with pleats added will also help correct this tendency to waver.

Determining the Yardage for Cornices and Lambrequins

Determine the yardage for **railroaded** cornices or lambrequins by measuring the face width, plus the returns; add in an additional 12" for cutting and wrapping around the board. Add any extra fabric needed for the repeat to be centered. The fabric's design needs to be placed in the middle of the cornice or lambrequin, if the fabric has a repeat.

Some fabrics cannot be railroaded. Their designs go in one direction only. To change the direction of the fabric's design would look absurd, or changing the direction would prevent the top treatment's fabric from matching the pattern of the underdrapery or undertreatment underneath.

If the fabric cannot be railroaded and must be seamed for a cornice, always make sure the customer realizes this. Give them the option to change to a different railroadable fabric, or a different top treatment style.

To figure the yardage for unrailroaded cornices or lambrequins that must be seamed, measure the face of the cornice plus the returns and add 12" for cutting and wrapping around the board. Determine the widths needed by taking the above measurement and dividing the width of fabric you are using into it, to arrive at the amount of widths of fabric needed. Next figure the cut length. Cut length is the finished, longest length, plus 12". Figure in the extra needed yardage for any repeat. Multiply the cut length times the widths needed and divide by 36" (yards) to arrive at the yardage needed. Round the yardage up to the next ½ yard.

Any repeats on cornices or lambrequins must be perfectly matched at the seams, since the fabric will lay flat. Quilting the fabric will decrease the possibility of the seams showing.

With some fabrics that are railroaded in *another* direction from the underdrapery, undertreatment, or from that same fabric used elsewhere in the same room, the railroaded item may appear *different* in color from the other fabrics, due to a different reflection on the fabric. You can decrease this problem by placing contrast welting between the two fabrics where they come up against each other.

Welting for Cornices and Lambrequins

Cornices need the addition of welting to give them a finished appearance. Since lambrequins are similar to cornices, welting will also help give them a finished appearance.

You may use single, double, or triple welting to finish off cornices. The welting may be in a contrast color, or may be in a cut-out area, inside the face of the cornice, framing a contrast, decorative area. When selecting contrast welting, finish the top of the cornice or lambrequin, with the self-welting of the fabric to be used in the cornice or lambrequin face. Check with your workroom to see if making the top edge welted is standard with them. Use the contrast welting at the bottom of the cornice, a few inches up from the bottom, or in the cut-out areas of the cornice. Contrast-welting placement across the top tends to make the cornice more casual in appearance, in feeling, and makes it look inexpensive.

Lambrequins look very finished with the addition of trim at the bottom, rather than welting. You may decide, if working with a lambrequin, to forego the finish welting at the top of the lambrequin. Lambrequins appear simpler in design than cornices, and therefore can get by without additional welting.

Remember to place an order for the contrast-welting fabric. **Plain welting should be cut on the bias to lay evenly,** and requires additional fabric. **Shirred welting is usually cut on the straight grain.** Shirred welting needs to be made up in light- to medium-weight fabric to lay well.

When figuring how much additional yardage to order for welting, never order less than 1½ yards of fabric. To order less would ensure frequent seams in the welting across the treatment.

Ordering Cornices and Lambrequins

When ordering cornices or lambrequins, you need to supply the workroom with the following information on your workorder:

- **What design** has been selected for the cornice or lambrequin. Use sketches if you are selecting or designing an unusual design. The workroom will work out the design in proportion to the width and length you have ordered, and plan other cornices and lambrequins in relation to each other on any corresponding windows within the same room.

- **Face width measurement.**

- **High point of the length.**

- **Low point of the length.**

- **Return size.**

- Determine **what type of welting, contrast, and self-fabrics are to be used.** Review the above information about welting. Contrast welting may be added at no additional charge, but additional fabric must be ordered for **any** contrast or self welting.

- **Note and sketch any placement of design detail and trim.**

Other points:

- Top-boards and returns of cornices are generally ¾" pine.

- Face-boards of cornices are generally ⅜" plywood.

- Any area on boards not covered by the self-fabric is covered with a lining fabric.

- White or off-white gimp is used to finish off edges at the back of the board to give a beautifully finished look to the cornice on both sides.

- Any cornice that is over 144" is hard to deliver. An extra charge will be charged if delivery is possible. You may need to select a different style that the installer can mount in place on the boards in the home.

Cantonnieres

Cantonnieres are also very similar to cornices. They are a three-sided treatment that also has a padded board structure. Cantonnieres come down the sides of the window area and hug the sides of the undertreatment. They may only come partway down on the sides or may go to the floor. Cantonnieres may have shaped designs on the interior edges, or may be shaped in a gentle curve, or a rectangle.

Cantonnieres are a beautiful window treatment. You can get very imaginative and architecturally change the room, create alcoves within the room, etc. Well-planned cantonnieres in a room give the appearance that the architect planned them in with the original room layout.

Planning Cantonniere Treatments

- **Decide what the minimum face length and width** to cover the area is to be. Placement at the ceiling is the preferred placement. With placements lower than the ceiling, placement should not be lower than 9" above the window. The cantonniere should go down to the floor in length, or 6" below the sill of the window.

- **Any cut-out areas needed**, such as moldings, chair rails, or base boards, must be drawn out on a template and accompany the workorder to the workroom. Check with the workroom for the extra charges to be charged for the cut-outs.

- Cantonnieres **over 45" in length for 48" goods, or 51" for 54" goods, will not be able to be railroaded.** For non-railroaded goods, if the width exceeds 34" for 48" wide goods, or 40" for 54" wide goods, the cantonniere will have to be seamed vertically.

    Seams may be placed at the point where the board folds back on the return, or placed so you can accent the seams with welting.

- **Pricing and determining amount of yardage needed:** Measure the width of the cantonniere, add the returns to the width; determine how many widths are needed; determine the finished length. Add an additional 10% of length to the finished length and any additional yardage needed for the repeat to determine the cut length. Multiply the cut length times the amount of widths and divide by 36" to determine amount of yardage needed for ordering and to charge the customer.

- When ordering the cantonniere from the workroom, use the guidelines outlined above in the section for *Ordering Cornices and Lambrequins* and apply the appropriate information to ordering cantonnieres.

Austrian Valances

Austrian valances differ from Austrian shades since they are shorter in length and are a top treatment. They do not pull up or down, and also do not have returns. Austrian valances look their best fabricated in lighterweight fabrics.

The width of the top treatment needs to be slightly wider than the mounting board, to accommodate the depth of the boards that the Austrian valance is mounted on.

You may vary the look of the Austrian valance by varying the width of the swags from a narrower swag to a wider swag across the face of the top treatment, on wider windows. Austrian valances used without ties look very elegant on a wide window, with the swag areas about 12" wide apart. If the ties are also to be used with the swaged areas, then placing the swag areas about 15" apart on wider windows looks very balanced and proportionate.

Returns on a swag treatment need to be made in *similar proportions*, to the width of an individual swaged area. **Example:** if the top treatment is to be 48" wide, and you decide to make each swag across the Austrian valance 8" wide (48" divided by 8" = 6 swag areas), then the return can be made *slightly smaller or slightly larger* than the 8" swag size and still look very similar. You may make the return from 6½" (which also allows for the extra board depth) to 9" deep.

To determine how much fabric is needed in *widths* for an Austrian valance: Allow one width of 48" wide fabric for every 30" of face-board width, **including** the returns.

To determine cut length: Determine the finished length and multiply by 3 for sheer-weight fabrics, by 2½ for light- to medium-weight fabrics, or by 2 for medium-weight fabrics and add 18" for hems and headers.

Austrian Shades

Austrian shades differ from Austrian valances because they are made to fit the whole length of the window. They usually fit I.B. in the window if used with other treatments, are able to be drawn up off the window, but require much stack space, and do not have returns.

Austrian shades are decorative shades which hang off of special hardware mounted above the window. They gather up in swaged or scalloped areas when hanging down into the window. Austrian shades scallop up at the bottom and are usually finished off with trim or a ruffle at the hem.

Important points to remember:

- Header should be a two- or four-cord header for operating purposes.

- There are **no returns** on shades.

- **Specify cord position** on workorder.

- Austrian shades are usually mounted on a 1" x 2 or 2½" board with a chain pull on a reel.

- The projection on an Austrian shade is usually 2" deep, but may be ordered deeper.

- **Plan in pattern repeats** for pattern matching.

- **Trim or ruffles may be added; add appropriate labor and yardage.**

Austrian shades perform one function: beauty. You will not want to sell these to be raised and lowered all the time. They are made to be left alone, elevating them only occasionally. When raised, Austrian shades will take up a large stack space, due to the amount of fabric and fullness required to give them a luxury look. Sheer and lace fabrics are your best fabrics for an Austrian shade, to allow you to let light in, and still be able to see out.

Austrian shades may be ordered with an Austrian valance separately, or mounted to the front of the same board the shade hangs off, to finish off the treatment if they are not going to be used in combination with other treatments on the window.

Measuring for Austrian Shades

O.B. Mounts:

To measure for an O.B. mount: measure the width to be 4"-5" beyond the window area on each side. You need this additional amount because an Austrian shade has no returns. Using an overtreatment such as stationary panels and a top treatment will ensure privacy.

To determine finished length, measure from 4" above the lintel or top of the window, and down to a minimum of 4" in length. Any length shorter than 4" below the sill will not cover light leaks or ensure privacy, due to the way Austrian shades scallop at the bottom.

I.B. Mounts:

To measure for an I.B. mount: measure the width from where the board will sit. Deduct ½" from this overall measurement. When measuring the length, remember that privacy and light leaks are not going to be taken care of when mounting an Austrian shade with an I.B. mount. Measure top to bottom for the length, deduct ¼" from this length measurement. Finished length is the length from the top of the shade to the bottom of the trim or ruffle, if any.

To determine how many widths of fabric are needed for an Austrian shade: Allow one width of 48" wide fabric for every 30" of face width.

To determine cut length: Determine the finished length and multiply by 3 for sheer-weight fabrics, by 2½ for light- to medium-weight fabrics, or by 2 for medium-weight fabrics, and add 18" for hems and headers.

Balloon Valances

Balloon valances look like balloon shades, but are non-functional and much shorter in length.

The width of the top treatment needs to be slightly wider to accommodate the depth of the board which the Austrian valance is mounted on.

Balloon valances make up best out of lighterweight fabrics with some body to them. Once your installer dresses them, you want the fabric to retain the shape.

Points to consider when planning balloon valances:

- If you ruffle a balloon valance, the valance has the tendency to droop.

- Specify what type of header: shirred, three- or four-cord; 2½" or 5½" wide rod pocket; 3" pole-rod pocket; 1½" rod pocket for **balloon valances** only (non-functional).
- Tailored styles of balloon valances must be lined.

- **Valances need their return sizes *specified*** for the workroom.

- **Plan in pattern repeats** for pattern matching.

- **If trim, banding, or ruffles are added, add appropriate labor and yardage.**

- **Do not make balloon valances more than 120" wide.**

Balloon Shades

Balloon shades are shades capable of being raised and lowered. They hang in pouffy sections, either very gathered or more tailored.

Points to consider when planning balloon shades:

- If you ruffle a balloon shade, the shade has the tendency to droop.

- Header on **shades** should be a two- or four-cord header for functioning purposes.

- Tailored styles of balloon shades must be lined.

- There are **no returns** on shades.

- **Specify cord position** on workorder.

- Shades are generally mounted on a 1" x 2 or 2½" board with a chain pull on a reel.

- The projection on a balloon shade is usually 2" deep, but may be ordered deeper.

- Balloon shades may be ordered with a separate balloon valance, or the valance may be mounted to the front of the same board that the balloon shade hangs off. Mounting the valance to the front of the same board the balloon shade is mounted on finishes off the treatment when the balloon shade is used by itself.

- **Plan pattern repeats** for pattern matching.

- **If trim, banding, or ruffles are added,** add appropriate labor and yardage.

Measuring for Balloon Shades

O.B. Mounts:

To measure for an O.B. mount: Measure the width of the shade over 4"-5" beyond the window area on each side. You need this additional amount because a balloon shade has no returns. An overtreatment such as stationary panels and a top treatment will ensure privacy.

To determine finished length, measure from 4" above the lintel or top of the window, and down to a minimum of 4" in length. Anything shorter than 4" below the sill is not going to cover light leaks or ensure privacy — because of the way balloon shades scallop or curve up at the bottom.

I.B. Mounts:

To measure for an I.B. mount: Measure the width of the area where the board is going to sit. Deduct ½" from this overall measurement. When measuring the length, remember that privacy and light leaks will not be provided for when mounting a balloon shade with an I.B. mount. Measure top to bottom for the length, deduct ¼" from this length measurement. Finished length is the length from the top of the shade to the bottom of any trim or ruffle.

Roman Valances

Roman valances are a very simple, tailored type of valance that hang in folds. There are several variations in the types of folds available for Roman valances and Roman shades: flat folds, rounded folds, reverse folds.

The best fabrics to use for Roman valances are **fabrics with body, stiffer cottons, and canvas.**

- **The width of the top treatment needs to be slightly wider than the board,** to accommodate the depth of the board that the Roman valance is mounted on.

- **To determine the yardage needed for a Roman valance,** measure the width and add a minimum of a 6" allowance (more for wider windows) for the joining of the widths and side hems. Measure the desired length and add 25% more length to arrive at finished length. Add in 18" for hems and headers. The hems are smaller here, but the excess of the 18" will be used to make horizontal, reverse tucks at 6" intervals on the shade. These tucks have rings attached to them on the back of the valance which, with cords running through them, will hold the tucks at a folded point. The tucks will allow the valance to fold up into 3" folds.

- **Valances need their return size specified.**

Roman Shades

Roman shades are fabric shades that hang in folds. They will draw up the window, due to special hardware, into accordion pleats. When the shade is down, the shade will hang in straight, neat, tailored folds.

Roman shades are practical, functional, and are very tailored in appearance. There are several variations of Roman shades available: flat folds, rounded folds, and reverse folds; with the Roman valance and its variations, they are very popular.

The best fabrics to use for Roman shades are: fabrics with body, stiffer cottons, and canvas types.

Roman shades are fabricated on the same principle as Austrian shades. They do not have the gathered fullness and have flat folds instead. Roman shades may be ordered with a separate Roman valance, or may be fabricated with a valance attached to the front of the same board the shade hangs off, to finish off the window treatment if the Roman shade is being used alone on the window.

Points to consider when planning Roman shades:

- **To figure the yardage needed for a Roman shade:** Measure the width and add a minimum of a 6" allowance (more for wider windows) for the joining of the widths and side hems. Measure the desired length and add 25% more length to arrive at the finished length. Add in 18" for hems and headers.

  The hems are smaller here, but the excess of the 18" will be used to make horizontal reverse tucks at 6" intervals on the shade. These tucks have rings attached to them on the back of the shade, which with cords running through them will raise and lower the shades. The tucks will allow the shade to fold up into 3" folds.

- **Roman shades have no returns.**

- Roman shades are mounted on a 1 x 2" or 2 ½" board headrail with a chain-pull, on a reel.

- **On a large window,** it is preferable **for ease of use to use multiple shades** nearly butting against each other, rather than one large hard-to-use shade. These shades will also take a bit of room to stack when pulled up.

Measuring for a Roman Shade

O.B. Mounts:

To measure for an O.B. mount: Measure the width to be 4"-5" beyond the window area on each side. You need this additional amount because a Roman shade has no returns. An overtreatment such as stationary panels and a top treatment will ensure privacy.

To determine finished length, measure from 4" above the lintel or top of the window, and down to a minimum of 3" in length. Anything shorter than 3" below the sill is not going to cover light leaks or ensure privacy.

I.B. Mounts:

To measure for an I.B. mount: Measure the width of the area where the board is going to sit. Deduct ½" from this overall measurement. When measuring the length, remember that privacy and light leaks will not be provided for when mounting an Austrian shade with an I.B. mount. Measure top to bottom for the length, deduct ¼" from this length measurement. Finished length is the length from the top of the shade to the bottom of the shade.

Swags and Cascades

Swags (festoons) and cascades are very elegant, classic window treatments. Swags and cascades may be used alone, or in combination with other undertreatments such as sheers and full drapery or side panels. The cascades which are placed at the ends of the top treatment may be placed on top of the last swag, or placed underneath the last swag. Many styles of top treatments incorporate cascades within their design.

The softer the fabric selected, the better the hanging ability of the swags and cascades treatment. When planning swags and cascades, realize that parts of the treatment will be on the straight grain, while other parts will be on the bias. Plain antique satins, moire fabrics, solid fabrics, and small all-over, patterned fabric are going to be your best fabric choices. Some florals will work if their patterns are not obvious stripes and one-way, directional prints.

Patterned fabrics may be cut across the grain, but will not hang as nicely as a fabric cut on the bias.

Points to consider when planning swags:

- **If the swag is more than 24" in length,** you will end up with **diagonal bias seams that show,** especially in solid colors.

- **If you use 48" wide fabric, and the swag is over 32" wide in width at the top, the swag will have to be seamed with a bias seam;** with the possibility of the seam slightly showing in the areas that are not overlapped. Swags almost overlap to the middle of each other; therefore, the seams are fairly camouflaged.
  For better proportioned swags, make them 40"-55" wide (wider for wider windows).

- When supplying measurements of swags to the workroom, **always supply the shortest point of the swags** — where they will cross each other at the bottom. This is necessary because this is the point where you must cover all hardware, pleats of the drapery, and the top of window frames. **The shortest point should be a minimum of 3" into the glass of the window, with the longest points coming down farther into the window.**

- **Swags can be fabricated in odd or even number of swags.** The **odd-numbered swags** are the **more traditional and familiar,** or the well-known look. You may choose to have a larger-center swag in the middle on the top or on the bottom.

- **With an even number of swags, you can only have them overlap one on top of each other, all the way across the width, with swags the same size.** This is a **more modern or transitional** effect.

- If you place the center swag on top, making it larger or the same size as the other swags in the same treatment, the treatment has the effect of coming toward you.

- If the placement of the center swag is on the bottom, the treatment has the effect of receding away from you.

- **For a swag that is 24" in length at the shallow point, plan 3 yards of fabric for each swag and 3 yards of fabric for each cascade. If the swags are to be self-lined, plan 5 yards of fabric for each swag.**

- Swags are usually 4"-6" shorter, at the shortest point, than the overall long point in length.

- **Swags are fabricated lined or self-lined.**

Planning odd-numbered swags:

When planning how many swags to have, figure that the bottom layer is a swag almost meeting another swag, side-by-side. The top layer is the other swags placed on top, slightly spread, meeting each other. Therefore, you take the total width desired; divide by 40"-55" (for wider-in-width windows), keep working with the above approximate numbers until you come up with the number in width, that will give you an odd or even number of swags(whatever you prefer in styling) for the bottom layer. Now, decide if the odd number of swags is to be on top or on the bottom. Double the number of swags you arrived at for the bottom layer, minus one swag, **regardless** if it is to be an odd or even number on the bottom layer.

Planning even-numbered swags:

Take the total width desired; divide by the 40"-55" figure to arrive at an even number. Now, double the figure to arrive at how many swags your treatment will have for that width. They will each overlap right-to-left on top of each other, or left-to-right on top of each other. Specify on the workorder which way you want them to overlap.

Balance out all swags in size as closely as you can within the same room or space. Make some windows smaller or larger to achieve a balanced measurement for all.

The workroom plans and determines the fabrication of the swags, but you must know how much fabric to order to charge the customer, and to make fabrication possible.

Points to consider when planning cascades:

- **When planning the length of the cascades, they should be ⅓ or ⅔ of the length of the overall treatment; or go to the floor** for good design proportions. **36" is a good length, proportionately, for most windows.** If the cascade's long point is placed at the ½ point of the total length of the whole treatment, you will cut your treatment in half, visually.

- **Cascades are generally made 10"-15" wide in finished width.**

- **Cascades are fabricated self-lined or lined.** You may want to line the cascades with a contrast fabric to show up where the underportions of the cascade show.

- Cascades may be used with other types of formal top treatments mounted on boards.

Specialty Windows

Slant-Top Windows

When planning a fabric window treatment for a slant-top window, always add 30" to the finished length. Figure the pattern repeat after you add the 30" to the cut length, then add any additional yardage needed for the pattern repeat.

Slant-top drapery need to be hand hemmed in the home to achieve an even hemline.

Vertical blinds may be used for slant-top windows or angle-top incline windows. When ordering vertical blinds, supply the vertical supplier with the width of the blind; the long side of the vertical blind — right or left side; and the short side of the blind — right or left side. You will need to price the vertical blind out at the longer-side length, and add the surcharges for the slant-top window. Slant-top verticals and angle top verticals will probably not traverse open and closed (depends on the manufacturer's system), only pivot to let light in.

Slant-top treatments that traverse, whether it is a drapery or a vertical blind, will always be very ugly when drawn back. The small side will stack to the large side, and depending on how much of a slant the window has, may be 4' off the floor when drawn open. Your customer will only want to draw the window occasionally, probably when they want to clean the windows. Verticals are a good choice because the customer may rotate the slats for large amounts of light to come in without pulling the vertical back.

On a slant-top sliding door that is full length, vertical blinds or drapery would be a very poor choice. If a full-length vertical or drapery were drawn back for opening, the short side would be 4' off the floor at the opposite side, or would not traverse from the long side to the short side, due to having 4' of vanes or drapery fabric puddling up on the floor.

If your customer wants to use verticals or drapery in this situation, split the slanted top separately from the bottom, sliding-door portion, and treat them as two units, using the same vertical material or drapery fabric. A hard top window treatment may be selected for the slanted-top portion instead of using the same drapery or verticals as the lower areas. This will work especially if the hard top treatment is used elsewhere in the room as an undertreatment.

Effective pleated valances that are made for slant-top or angle-top windows are made the same finished length the *whole width*, rather than starting short at one end and gradually getting much longer at the other. Request that the workroom make the header on the bias, instead of making the hem on the bias, to have a nicer hanging valance.

All types of gathered valances are very effective, framing slant-top or angle-top windows. A simple, wide rod pocket, single or double, over an undertreatment or without any other treatment covering the slanted areas, can finish these windows right off. Incorporate any top treatment selected elsewhere, within the same room.

Always use the longest point for pricing, add the surcharges, have the windows remeasured, make a template for the slanted portions, and request on the workorder for the installer to bring a ladder for remeasures and installation of high windows.

Measuring Slant-Top Windows

To measure slant-top or slope-top windows, follow the sequence outlined below:

- **Measure the longest point** and the **shortest point** in length.

- **Draw a sketch** of the window and **record** these **actual measurements.**

- **Measure the width** of the area to be covered.

- **Measure across the slope-line where the drapery or other treatment are actually going to sit (measure parallel to the floor). Measure the slope line, as it slopes from tip to tip. Record both of these measurements.** The first measurement is important when you are determining whether the item to be fabricated will be operable, or if the slanted-top portion is to be left uncovered. The second measurement is for treatments that will be mounted to completely cover all areas of the top of the slope window.

- If this is to be an O.B. mount, measure the area available above the window. Ideally, 5" will be available.

- When pricing out the job and planning the yardage needed, **determine the price to charge and yardage needed, from the longest points of the window.**

If your customer has a slanted-top window that sits above another window with wall space between the two, split the horizontal wall area in two sections and take ½" of the area for the lower treatment and ½" of the area for the upper, slanted portion. Each section may be opened independently of the other, when sun and light control is needed. They may be opened with a long wand, motor, or long cord to operate the upper window.

Your customer may want to cover only the bottom portion of the slanted window. Plan a treatment to go across at the break-point (where it starts to slant up) between the upper and lower windows. Planning the job this way will give you the same amount of wall space around the upper window as you have around the lower window, for maximum effect.

Be sure there are places to mount center supports, if the window is very wide. Measure from the middle beam between the two windows and down. You may measure from the top of the beam or the middle - whichever you decide will look the best, to the floor. Deduct 1" for clearance off the length.

You will encounter some customers, due to privacy or sun problems, who will want to cover the whole top and bottom areas of the slant-top windows. Covering both sections will give height to the room. Drapery that are made slant-top will need to be hand-hemmed in the home.

Make a template for any slant-top treatment you are planning. Templates provide the workroom with a pattern and a guide to fabricate the treatment with. Vertical blind treatments do not require templates.

Arch-Top Windows

Two-, three-, or four-cord shirred drapery may be attached to a board cut in the shape of the outside area of the window. This board should be at least 1" thick, preferably thicker, to give the drapery depth. This board should be covered with the same fabric as the drapery, as the board will show slightly from the sides.

Any drapery planned for an arch-top window should be planned with a finished length from the longest point from the drapery, plus 18" for cut length and any additional repeat yardage needed. The drapery will be hand-hemmed in the home after the drapery is mounted. Hand-hemming will incur extra charges to your customer.

Rods are available now that can be bent and mounted inside or outside of an arch-top window. The drapery is gathered up on the rod like a regular curtain rod and mounted to the contours of the arch-top window shape.

A full-length drapery must be mounted on the outside unless the window and I.B. window frame goes full length to the floor. A very effective treatment can be achieved if you do have an I.B. window frame that does go to the floor; by mounting the rod I.B. and having the window frame, frame the I.B. mounted drapery. Unfortunately, this type of arch-top window is rare.

Most arch-top windows have the arched area separated by wood and drywall from the lower window portion; or the arched-top is directly above the square or rectangular window that stops short from the floor several feet. You can plan the arch-top treatment and the window beneath it together as an I.B., but can only go as long in length as the window length. To achieve a full-length drapery, you need to O.B. mount the treatment and take it full length to the floor.

Sunburst Fabric Treatments

Sunburst treatments can be mounted as an I.B. or an O.B. mount. Sunburst treatments may be tailored or have ruffled edges. They may be mounted to a board or to a bendable curtain rod, that easily bends to the shape needed.

Ruffled edge styles that are mounted on boards may be fabricated so they fasten with Velcro to the boards and may easily be removed for ease of cleaning. The tailored styles are mounted by stapling to the board; therefore, tailored styles have to be cleaned, as any hard to remove top treatment is, in place on the wall.

The sunburst treatments fabricated on rods, with a rod pocket, may be easily slipped off the rod for cleaning. This type of sunburst treatment may be fabricated *with or without* a ruffled edge above the rod pocket, to give it a more tailored or frilly effect.

Sunburst treatments can be fabricated with the use of a rosette made of fabric (frilly or more tailored); a large, covered button; with the addition of *nothing at all*, where all the fabric comes together in the middle, bottom area. **If a rosette is to be fabricated for a sunburst treatment, ½ yard must be added for each rosette. For treatments using a covered button, slightly round up the yardage — ⅛ yard (4") is all that is needed additionally for a large covered button.** Add in the extra fabrication charge for rosettes or covered buttons.

Fabrics for sunbursts should be sheer types of fabrics. Some of the fabrics suitable for this treatment are: laces, sheers with stripes, batiste-weight sheers, designer linings, and very sheer, ninon types of fabric.

Always make a template for the workroom to fabricate the sunburst treatment off of. Request for the installer to bring a ladder on the workorder and add the workroom's fabrication charges for sunburst treatments.

Determining yardage:

Use the following formula to plan and order fabric for a sunburst treatment for 48"-54" fabric: double the height of the treatment; add the width of the treatment; multiply by 2½; divide by 36" (yards) = yardage needed.

Example: A 60" wide window with a 48" height at top point of the treatment, to be fabricated out of 48" fabric. This is a tailored style, with only a covered button used to finish off the treatment;

48" x 2 + 60" = 156". 156" x 2½ = 390". 390" divided by 36" = 10.83. 10.83 yards needed. Round the figure up to 11 yards. Order 11 yards of fabric for the above example.

118" Fabrics:

If the fabric you are using is 118" railroaded goods, use the following formula to arrive at the yardage needed for ordering: 118" fabric; double the height of the treatment; add the width of the treatment; and divide by 36" (yards) = yardage needed for ordering.

Example: 72" wide window with a 42" height at the top point of the treatment, to be fabricated out of 118" wide goods. A rosette will also be fabricated to finish off the treatment;

72" x 2 + 42 = 186". 186" divided by 36" = 5.16 yards. Round up to 5.25 yards. Add ½ yard for the rosette. 5.25 + .50 = 5.75 yards. Order 5.75 yards of fabric for the above example.

Other Types of Sunburst Treatments

Other treatments for treating the arch-top portion of the window would include: custom-made shutters mounted either I.B. or O.B. on the window, pleated shades, Duette shades, or woven-wood treatments.

Shutters:

Shutters may be made with horizontal wide or narrow vanes that start out quite narrow in width at the top, and progress down to the width of the horizontal width of the arch-top window area.

Sunburst style shutters are another option with the shutter look. This style accentuates the arch-top window rather than covering it up and camouflaging it. Again, the shutters may be made with wide or narrow vanes, with the wide vanes creating a beautiful treatment. The frame of the shutters would be stationary, while allowing you to control light by rotating the vanes.

Pleated shades or Duette® shades:

Pleated shades or Duette shades may also be fabricated for arch-top windows in a sunburst style. These may be I.B. or O.B. mounted, but would be stationary, immovable selections. These are effective if the same window covering is used in the window area below the arch, as well as the same undertreatment used elsewhere within the same room. Depending on the pattern and fabric selected, the amount of light filtering through will vary.

Woven woods:

Woven woods can be made to the shape of the arch-top area. The woven wood would lay flat, and simply be shaped at the top in an arched fashion. Woven woods would give you a horizontal effect, contoured to the arch shape, and would be completely immovable. Woven woods would be a heavy selection for a window intended to emit light. Depending on the selected pattern, very little light will filter through. There are some patterns that quite a bit of light may come through; even more light than sheer fabrics, from the pleated shades collections.

How to Make a Template

Accompany with templates any odd-shaped workorders for windows such as arch-tops, octagons, slant-tops, or circular shaped windows.

Make a template by placing thin paper over the window, tape the paper in place, and trace around the paper. If you use thin paper, the light will shine through, easily outlining the window underneath.

If the treatment is to be an I.B. mount or an inside mount, then indicate this on the workorder and on the template in large letters. If the treatment is to be on the outside or O.B. mounted, then trace around the window shape in the depth of the outside wall area that is to be covered, while the paper is still attached to the wall.

Trace the depth of the wall area that is also to be covered, while the paper is still attached to the wall. This will ensure that you do have enough wall space left all around the window for the depth that you want to use. Take into consideration any other treatments that you are adding, and where they will sit below or above this same window. Allow for these treatments and make sure all parts will fit well together. This is especially important in the case of slant-top or arch-top treatments, where you have the lower drapery or window treatment butting right up to the upper, slant-top or arch-top treatment. By using this technique, you double-check your available wall space.

You may need to get up on a small ladder or step stool to make the template. If you do not make the template while you are at the home during the in-home visit, charge the customer for making the template; send a workorder to the installer to remeasure the job and make the template.

If you add both the remeasure charge and the extra template charge to your customer's bill, you are taking the chance of losing the job if your customer is shopping around. Making a template is very easy to do, so consider making them yourself.

Tiebacks, Jabots, Banding and Trim

Jabots and Ties

Jabots are pleated portions or flat portions of fabric, placed on top treatments as accents to hide seams, hide overlapped areas, or are placed at corners of corner windows to hide the top treatment where it butts together.

Jabots are usually self-lined but may be lined, especially where their color visibility from the outside the home is a concern.

Ties are smaller in width, flat sections of fabric to accent the top treatment or to hide seams. Ties may be fabricated in a contrast fabric, or the *lined area* of the tie may be lined in a contrast fabric. They may be flat-shaped, bell-shaped, or be an inverted bell style (looks like the back of a man's necktie).

Tiebacks

Tiebacks are strips of fabric with a buckram interior that hold drapery back, exposing some of the window. Tiebacks encompass the drapery that they are holding back and may be mounted at different heights for different design effects. Tiebacks are used for style and design, to see the view, or to let light and air in a room. When the drapery is tied back, it forms a graceful curve.

Tiebacks can be made in a full range of fabrics, styles, combinations of fabrics, and may be made to match the drapery or the top treatment of the same window. Tiebacks should be cut on the bias of the fabric (some fabric's designs and the effects you want to create will not allow you to do this) to lay nicely. Cord and tassel-type tiebacks are also used in a corresponding or accenting color of the window treatment.

Some of the different styles tiebacks may be fabricated in are: straight, straight with welted edges, straight with banding, straight with an arrow-shaped return, curved with welting, contoured with no welting, with a ruffle on both edges, contoured with welt edges, contoured with ruffle on bottom edge only, tapered (wide in the middle, narrower at ends), tapered with welted edges, tapered with banding, shirred with jumbo cord inserted, braided, styles with ruching (gathered inlay portion of design), lap tie, bow styles, one-cord shirred, two-cord shirred, four-cord shirred; fabricated to match headers of wide rod pocket styles of window treatments; jumbo cord with ruffle on one side.

The use of carson holders is standard with tiebacks. These are plastic holders that project the tieback out from the wall, at the sides, to prevent the drapery from being smashed down.

When ordering drapery that is to be tied back, specify *"flat fold drapery"* on the workorder.

Note: When working with tiebacks and planning a tieback's measurements, it is *confusing* because what is generally perceived to be the length, is actually the tieback's width (the *long* part of the tieback); what is generally perceived to be the width, is actually the length of the tieback (the *short* part of the tieback).

Tieback Placement

Tieback placement depends on the effect you are trying to achieve. You should consider design rules when placing the tiebacks to maximize your window treatment's design.

Place tiebacks ⅓-⅜ of the distance down from the top of the treatment for a younger, today-looking treatment; or place the tiebacks ⅜ up from the floor or the bottom of the window treatment, for a more traditional effect. Placement in the middle of the treatment will cut the window treatment in half, visually.

Planning Tiebacks

When planning tieback width, realize you may want a tighter or a looser, wider tieback effect. In the formulas below are included the tighter, younger, more today-looking style's formula first and followed with the more traditional formula, second. You need to determine which way to go, depending on your customer's personality, age, style, etc.

Tighter styled tiebacks:

One way to plan how wide to make the tiebacks for fabrication of a tighter styled tieback is to take the extension area that you added beyond the window for one side; add 4" for the area that extends into the window area; multiply by 2 (this takes care of the backside of the tieback); add one return of the drapery (tiebacks use only one return) to arrive at the correct length for each tieback to be fabricated in.

Example: You have just planned a pair of drapery that are to stack-off the window. You have already figured stack-back would be 15" beyond the window on each side. The return of the drapery is 3½" deep.

15" + 4" (tieback area that extends into the window) = 19". 19" x 2 = 38". 38" + 3½" = 41½". 41½" is the width for the finished tieback, for fabrication purposes.

Wider, looser tieback style:

Another way to arrive at the correct length **to fabricate a wider, looser tieback style is** to take ½ the finished width of the drapery; multiply times 2; add the return. This will give the correct width for each tieback.

Example: The finished width of the drapery is to be 48" wide. The return is 6" to allow for the sheers with a projection of 3½" mounted as an undertreatment underneath. ½ of 48" = 24. 24" x 2 = 48". 48" + 6" (return) = 54". 54" is the correct width to order for the tieback.

Example: You are planning a one-way pull panel 78" wide that needs only one tieback. The return is 3½" deep. ½ of 78" = 39". 39" + 3½" = 42½". 42½" is the correct width to order for the finished wider, looser tieback.

Note on workorder: Specify the length (short point) of the finished tieback. If you do not note it, the workroom will determine the length for you, and it may not be proportionally correct to go with the look you are planning. Plan the length in proportion to the size of the window. 3½" to 4" for a wide window; 2½" for a smaller window.

Specify on workorder: The quantity of left, right, or center tiebacks you are ordering. The workroom makes up the tiebacks in the direction that they are going to be installed. Name the style and number of any that you are planning; draw a sketch if the style is unusual, and specify the width and length.

Centered Tiebacks

Centered tiebacks are usually used on windows that are in an hourglass design. The windows at the sides are tied back with carson holders, slanted down, and any panels (combined over two adjoining windows to eliminate seams) in the center are tied back horizontally with a tieback. The only way that the tieback may hold the panels together in the center is horizontally.

The horizontal tiebacks appear very different from the tiebacks at the sides of the drapery treatment, because they are aimed in different directions. Also, the horizontal tiebacks almost never want to stay put; they are constantly having to be readjusted, due to their tendency to slip down. They may be pinned in place to the drapery.

The best remedy for this imperfect situation is to make all the drapery pairs with the appropriate returns that butt against each other for all of the windows. Now, make each pair of drapery two tiebacks. Each tieback will be slanted downward like the one next to it, and you have eliminated slippage problems.

The one drawback is, the drapery pairs are butting against each other at the return point. There are two sets of pleats touching each other at this point, on each pair of drapery. If the window treatment is to be finished off with a top treatment, then this is not a negative point. If you are using the drapery by themselves, then consider if the different angles and slippage are more of a drawback to the customer than pleats coming together at the top of the drapery.

Planning Centered Tiebacks for Hourglass Treatments

Notes about hourglass tiebacks:

- A tieback for an hourglass treatment is usually ⅓ of the size of the window width.

- An hourglass tieback needs to be **ordered with Velcro attached to its back tabs.**

- Unless specified, an hourglass tieback **will not come with crinoline.**

- **Charge the customer for the tieback;** also, adding Velcro may require a surcharge.

- **Order the extra fabric needed for the tieback.** If a standard hourglass tieback is needed in a contrasting fabric, order and charge the customer for a minimum of one yard of fabric in the contrasting color. If a style other than a standard tieback style is desired, you will need additional yardage.

- **Plan the tieback by one of the two methods outlined below, or use the method immediately beneath these two examples for planning** *a tighter styled tieback.*

  First method: Divide the face width of the window you are planning by .33 and use the resulting ⅓ figure for the face width of your tieback.

  Second method: Plan the face width of the tieback by holding a tape up to the proposed tied back area and decide how wide you want to make the tieback.

  Next: After using one of the two methods outlined above, multiply the face width desired x 2 (for the back of the tieback) + 2" for the Velcro overlapped area in the back of the tieback. Now figure the "length" (up and down width) desired for the tieback.

  Example using first method: The face width of the window is 18". Divide 18" by 3 = 6". 6" x 2 + 2" = 14". 14" is the correct *"width"* to order. The length you have decided is 2". On the workorder, specify a tieback of 14" x 2".

  Example using the second method: You hold the tape up and decide that the *"face width"* of the tieback looks good at 8". 8" x 2 + 2 = 18". 18" is the correct *"width"* to order. The *"length"* you have decided is 3½". On the workorder you will specify a tieback of 18" x 3½". ·

  To plan centered tiebacks for a tighter style: take the wall area measurement between the adjoining windows and add 4" of area into each window's glass on each side. Multiply times 2, and add an overlap area for the tiebacks to overlap each other in back of the tieback of 2".

  Example: planning center tiebacks for a tighter style: You are working with an group of windows that you are using an hourglass treatment across the group of windows. Between every two windows you have wall space or space from one window's glass to the next window's glass of 6".

  6" (wall space) + 4½" + 4" (area into each window's glass on each side) = 14". 14" x 2 = 28". 28" + 2" = 30". 30" is the correct tieback width to order for a tighter tieback style. Specify on workorder "attach Velcro to each end of tiebacks."

Another method to use to plan the correct length of the **centered tieback for a looser, wider tieback style is:** Take the rod width of the pair of drapery, where a centered tieback is to be used; add 1". This is the same measurement as the panel width from the middle, overlap area from the middle of the window and panel, to the next middle of the window and panel (this panel is to be encompassed in a centered tieback). Specify, *"attach Velcro to each end of tieback"* on workorder.

Example: The individual finished width for each window in question is 60". 60" also happens to be the width from center of one window to the next center of each adjoining window. 60" + 1" = 61". 61" is the correct width to order for this looser tieback.

Determining Yardage for Tiebacks

Depending on the style of tiebacks you are planning, the yardage *needs* vary.

In general terms, for plain tiebacks, one yard of fabric is needed to make four tiebacks, 4" long by 46" wide, if made on the bias.

Tiebacks that are cut on the straight grain, due to the design of the fabric or the effect you are trying to achieve, one yard of fabric will make four tiebacks 4" long by 32" wide.

Determine and add extra fabric needed, for individual design effects.

Trim

The use of trim on window treatments adds color, style, personality, contrast, outlines, and also accents the treatment. Plan trim selection at the time of selecting fabric and window treatment style.

Place trim swatches on fabric swatches to see if they are in the same scale as the fabric's design (if the fabric has a pattern or design). Check for correct color selection. Be sure that the trim is large enough to accent the treatment and is also able to make a statement from across the room.

Trim comes in a variety of styles: tassels, fringe, braid, gimp, ribbon types, banding, braided fabrics, cording, welting, etc. Additionally, there are variations of all that are listed here.

For more information on welting, see the section in this chapter on *Welting for Cornices and Cantonieres.*

- Flat, braid styles of trim look best when placed up from the edge 1" or so.

- Trim may be glued on, machine stitched, or hand stitched. Most trim that is attached in a custom workroom will be glued on. The trim will stay on with careful handling by the dry cleaners.

- There is a charge to sew or glue on trims from the workroom in addition to the cost of the trim needed per yard, or the fabric needed to make the trim per yard.

- If fabric rosettes are planned, allow ½ yard for *each* rosette.

Planning Banding and Trim

To plan banding or trim labor and yardage needed, determine the lineal feet of the areas to be covered with the trim or banding. If the banding or trim are to be placed on the leading edges, determine the finished length of the drapery, and add 10" for each cut needed. If the banding or trim is to go on the bottom hem of pleated valances or drapery, you will multiply the amount of widths used in the valance or drapery by the fabric width, to arrive at total inches. Divide the inches by 12" to arrive at lineal feet needed. Convert the feet to yards by dividing by 3' for ordering purposes. Your workroom may use yards or feet for labor charges.

When selecting banding, always try to select a fabric similar in fiber content as the self-fabric of the drapery or top treatment. This will ensure and enable the cleaning ability of the fabrics. The fabrics are similar and may be cleaned using the same solvents.

Determining Yardage for Banding

Below are the formulas needed to determine how much extra fabric is required for banding in various situations. When using banding you want to have as few seams as possible. Never order under 1½ yards; too many seams will be needed and detract from the finished effect.

To figure how much width you need for the width of the banding: determine the finished banding width and multiply x 3 for the width of each strip needed.

To determine banding for leading edges only:

- Determine cut length of drapery and divide by 36" (yards).

- Determine cut width of the banding by multiplying the finished width x 3 (amount of extra yardage needed in width for each strip of banding).

- Decide how many strips of banding will be needed; versus the cut length of the drapery. Do not make the length, seamed strips less than 1½ yards long each (there will be too many seams).

- Follow the examples below to clearly decipher in your mind how the correct yardage is arrived at.

Example: You are planning two pairs of floor-to-ceiling drapery. The finished length is 96". The finished banding width of the strips are to be 3½" wide. You are working with 48" wide fabric. 96" + 18" (hems and headers) = 114" cut length of the drapery. 114" divided by 36" (yards) = 3.17 yards.

Now, determine the width of the banding in yardage. 3½" wide banding x 3 = 10½" wide.

Since you are making two pair of drapery, and your fabric is 48" wide; 4 strips of banding 10½" cut width = 42" *needed* in the width of fabric.

You will make your banding seamless, the full length of the drapery. You will need to order one length of fabric at 3.17 yards long or 3¼ yards. You will end up with only a 6" scrap of fabric by 3¼ yards long.

If you were only doing one pair of drapery, you could take the length of the banding and divide in half, with a seam on each length of banding to save on yardage.

Example: 3¼ yards of banding needed, if seamless — this gives you waste of 27" of fabric by 3¼ yards long. Cut this in half, with one seam on each banding strip. 3¼ yards divided by 2 = 1.62 or round up to 1⅔ yards. If you only need two strips of banding with a cut width of 10½" wide, order 1⅔ yards of extra fabric.

To determine banding for bottom edges only:

- Triple finished width of the banding. Multiply this tripled width by widths of the drapery or valance. Divide by 36" to determine yards needed.

Example: The valance is going to need 7 widths of fabric. The desired width of the banding is 2¾". Multiply this size 2¾" x 3 = 8¼". 8¼" x 7 widths of fabric = 57¾" of fabric. Divide 57¾" by 36" to arrive at 1.60 yards of fabric. Round this figure up to 1¾ yards of fabric needed to cover banding for 3" x 7 widths of fabric.

Determine the correct labor charge for the application and the fabrication of the banding by the workroom:

• Depending on the workroom, labor may be calculated in feet or yards. Either divide the cut length needed by feet (12"), or by yards (36") to arrive at lineal feet or lineal yards. Multiply your workroom's labor charge x feet or yards to calculate the labor charge.

Determining Amount of Yardage Needed for Ruffles

A quick and easy formula to determine yardage needed for ruffles, whether the ruffles are hemmed, shirt-tail ruffles, or self-lined ruffles, up to 4" deep: plan ½ yard of fabric for every 36" of lineal feet of ruffle needed.

Use the above formula for calculating labor for banding to calculate labor for ruffles. Determine the lineal feet or yards of ruffling and multiply by your workroom's labor charge in feet or yards.

Problems that Arise with Custom Window Coverings and Interior Fabrics

When decorating and working with fabrics, problems do arise. Some of the *common problems* that arise *daily* with the planning and fabrication of custom window products are outlined below:

Flawed fabrics

Fabrics and window coverings with flaws are a very common problem. This is one of the biggest hold-ups a designer or decorator will encounter. The fabrics were supposedly inspected before they left the manufacturer, and the workroom did not check the fabric before cutting and making up the item. Always work with a workroom that is *willing* to inspect all fabric before cutting it. You will have *bought* the fabric if you cut it — flawed or not. Some flaws will not show up until the light hits them. As soon as the window treatment gets hung, the sun shines through the fabric, and your problems begin.

At best, you will end up with a nuisance with the vendor making it right. They will want to replace the flawed section only. You may run into trouble matching the dyelot. The rest of the room's fabric may be in perfect condition, and they are willing to replace the one flawed panel.

You get stuck remaking the whole room at your expense because you are unable to match the dyelot. Always insist on an inspection at the workroom before cutting the goods. If they will not do it, then *you* will have to do it.

Ship the fabric to your studio to ensure inspection before delivery to the workroom. This inspection will take time. But, if you do not inspect the fabric, the expense of the problems that will arise, in addition to the time it takes to correct the problem, and the anger of the customer, makes it worthwhile.

Puckered seams

Sheers are famous for this problem. Since the advent of 118" goods, this problem has decreased. Beware, when pricing out a short drapery in 48" goods versus using the slightly more expensive 118" goods. You may end up with some waste, but you eliminate the possibility of puckering at the seams. There *may or may not* be a slight increase in cost. **Calculate the job both ways** before making a decision to use narrower goods. Paying slightly more in cost for the preferable 118" goods must be weighed against the cost to you for service calls, reworking time and reworking charges.

Wrinkling

Many drapery when fabricated arrive with wrinkles. These wrinkles may be formed by staying on the hanger too long; from being packed in a box for shipping (if not made locally); the fabric may have been wrinkled before they were fabricated, becoming more obvious when hung up at the windows. Sometimes, no matter what you do, you will not be able to get the wrinkles out of the fabric. A steamer in the hands of a professional installer will usually solve most wrinkled fabric problems. Some fabrics will not take the steam and will be even more wrinkled after steaming.

Fabric relaxing sprays are another alternative to this problem with some fabrics. An experienced installer is going to know the *best* technique to remove wrinkles, for the type of fabric he or she is working with. The use of steamers and fabric relaxant sprays are standard equipment of this trade.

Nonmatching patterns

Patterns on fabrics may not be able to be matched up horizontally from one panel to the next panel, or from one drapery to the next drapery.

Vertical pattern repeats may not be able to be fabricated to match the pleats. Sometimes this may not be possible to do if the pattern used is less than 12".

Enough extra fabric must be provided to ensure fabric matching on horizontal and vertical matches. See section on *Figuring Pattern Repeat* for formula to do this. Some fabrics have a pattern which drops farther and farther down on each cut. If the pattern drops only slightly on the fabric, try to work with the fabric. If there is a large variation, over ⅝", send the fabric back to the vendor. Reselect the fabric if the vendor cannot provide fabric true to its match. If the match is slight, match the fabric for all cuts from the top of the drapery, rather than the bottom. As you look across the width of the drapery, note that the pattern falls farther and farther down on each succeeding width.

Reworks

Length corrections are the most common rework. Designers and decorators forget to take the allowances necessary in length. Fortunately, most length corrections can be reworked.

Many problems with window coverings and drapery *may be solved* by reworking the window covering or drapery. Some of the problems that can be solved in this manner are outlined below:

- **Adding extra widths of fabric to drapery, some valances, and top treatments.**

- **Making most window treatments smaller.** Exception: some of the more intricately made top treatments.

- **Changing unlined drapery to lined drapery, or changing lined drapery to unlined drapery.**

- **Repleating the drapery header, because it was fabricated a few inches too narrow or too wide.**

- **Repleating the header to place pleats to the back of the pleats,** rather than to the front of the pleats.

- **To unpucker seams.**

- **To remove and replace a flawed panel with an unflawed panel.**

- **To lengthen too-short drapery.** On drapery that are too short, up to 4" may be added to lengthen the drapery. This is done by facing the hem. Facing the hem keeps the double hem and the weight it provides for good drapery hanging ability.

- **Shorten too-long drapery.**

Remakes

Always get the same dyelot for all the fabrics to be used, in the same pattern or fabric. Make sure you have ordered enough fabric. Make the drapery long enough. You can cut down drapery that are too large, but *it is difficult to make something too small, larger.* One error here will cause you to remake everything in the same room, in the same fabric, if the same dyelot or a close match are unavailable.

Pleated Shades may be Lengthened up to 5%:

Pleated shades may be lengthened up to 5% of the shade's length. This is done by removing the bottom-rail cap, on the opposite side from the cord lock; then carefully loosening the knot, without retying it completely, and pulling the shade down to the correct length.

Measuring for I.B. and O.B. Mounted Treatments

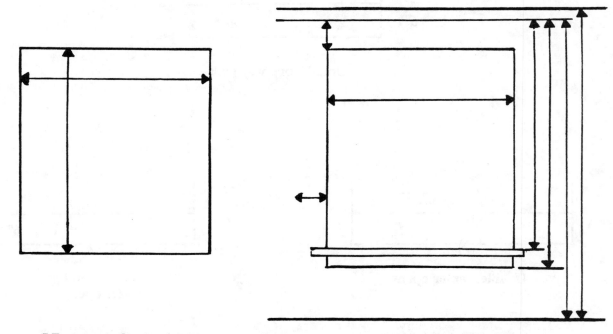

I.B. mounted treatments   O.B. mounted treatments

Types of Installations

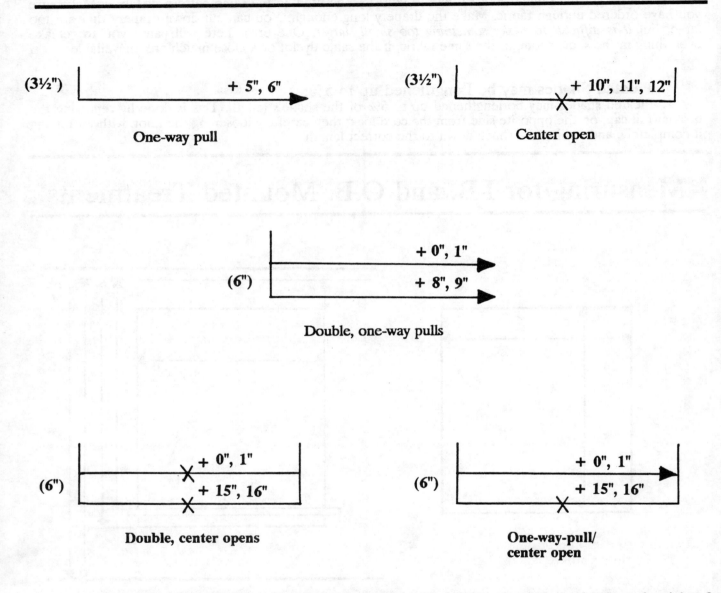

Add overlaps and returns to drapery rod face widths. The amounts to add are shown to the right of each diagram, for the various installation situations. The return size noted to the left of each diagram is *included* in the overlap and return amount shown on the right. *Do not add the return amount shown in addition to the overlap and return amounts.* It is shown only for informational purposes.

Add the lesser amount shown for the overlaps and returns, if you desire a tighter fit in width. Add the larger amount shown to achieve a more versatile, looser fit in width.

Part 6

Drapery Rods, Hardware, Fabrication, and Installation

Rods and Hardware

There are many different type of rods available on the market for different applications. Some rods are available to fit the exact need, others need to be adapted or conformed for the individual requirements. The Kirsch® line of hardware and rods is a dependable, long-lasting quality and an industry standard. Generally, existing hardware that is made by Kirsch® is reusable.

The reusable exception would be decorative rods that have received constant, hard use. Decorative rods need to be replaced, rather than reused. The customer will buy new draperies to be mounted on a worn-out decorative rod, and spend more money later for trip charges and rod installations to change the rod that should have been changed initially when the new drapery were sold to the customer. Review the sections on *Decorative Rods* and *Existing Hardware* for what to look for when the reuse of existing rods and hardware is questionable.

Curtain and Pole Rods

Basic Curtain Rods

Curtain rods are rods which use rod pocket style drapery or curtains to slip over the rod. When the drapery or curtain is slipped on, the rod is covered up. When the rod pocket is slipped over the rod, the fabric is bunched up, and the curtain becomes gathered up — if enough widths of fabric have been used for the width of the curtain or drapery.

Curtain rods have changed in recent years. They enable us to achieve formal, elegant, or country looks, when beautiful fabrics are combined with or without stand-up headers.

Rod pocket treatments are the easiest treatments to fabricate. These types of treatments are also the most reasonable types of treatments available to sell to your customers. You can select a beautiful fabric, slip it over the rod and end up with a fabulous looking window treatment or valance. If the treatment is planned in a beautiful fabric with style, rod pocket treatments do not appear simple to make.

Curtains or drapery may be hung on separate rods mounted under traverse rods or other curtain rods. They may also be hung off the same bracket, if proper hardware selection is done in the planning. Curtain rods with a 1¼" projection may be mounted under a traverse or curtain rod with a 3½" projection. Any hard treatment or other window treatment I.B. mounted in the window has the ability to be used with a curtain rod that has a projection of 2".

Valance rods for gathered-on-the-rod treatments, or pin-on treatments, may be used over single- and double-traverse rods. To use over a single-rod treatment, the clearance for the brackets and the returns should be 6". To use over a double-traverse rod, the clearance of the valance rod should be 8¼".

- Headers or rod pockets shirr over the rods, hiding the rod completely.

- Curtains or gathered drapery treatments may be used as over- or undertreatments.

- Curtain rods are available in clear plastic for use with lighter-weight lace and sheer fabrics.

Curtain rods vary from small, round rods to flat, wide rods 4½" deep. They come in a variety of styles and may be used single, double, or triple. Different projections are used to accommodate the different layers of the treatment.

There are two drawbacks to curtain rods. One is that curtain rods *do not traverse* like a traverse rod. They are a stationary treatment that needs to be left alone, unhandled. If the curtain or drapery needs to be drawn back, the drawing back of the drapery has to be done by hand (handling and soiling the drapery).

The other drawback to curtain rods is that the panels *may only butt together*, and will not overlap. Your customer's privacy may suffer or there may be a light leak from the butting together point of the panels.

Wide Curtain Rods

Wide curtain rods or the Kirsch Continental® rods are like any other curtain rods, except they are deeper from top to bottom. This extra depth gives a shirred heading that looks like a valance. Pockets should be fabricated 5½" for the 4½" rod and 3" for the 2½" rod for ease and ability to slip the rod pocket over the rod.

The wide rods may be used for gathered drapery panels. They may also be sewn in a sleeve fashion for valances. Two rods may be mounted one above the other for extra depth and to achieve an elegant effect.

- Wide rod pockets in the 2" or the 4½" size will also give a very different look to tiered cafe curtain styles.

- You may order the brackets with a ¾" projection to be used on doors and undertreatments.

- Sash rods project ¼" and are used for treatments to be mounted on doors.

Rods with 3½" projection *are for use alone* or over undertreatments that are inside mounted, or over curtain rods with 1¼" projections. A 3½" wide projection will also accommodate anything O.B. mounted, close to the wall (not for use with vertical vanes that are 3½" wide vanes). You need to allow a 2" clearance between the layers of the different treatments.

For rods with the deeper projection of 4½" to 5½", a projection bracket may be used over single or double traverse rods, verticals, or any undertreatment, including single-wide rods that have a depth of less than 2" - 3½". Special brackets are available for Pricilla type treatments.

Spring Tension Rods

Spring tension rods fit inside the window frame. Spring tension rods do not use brackets. The rods have springs inside of them that hold the rods under tension and in place.

Spring tension rods come in different weights, depending on the width of the window, and may be used under a rod return of 3½".

Cafe Rods

If a standard cafe rod is used as the underdrapery with overdrapery, you will not need to change the bracket projection. It will be 2½"-3½".

If the cafe rods are used for a tiered effect, you will want the bottom tier to have the smallest projection. Progress up to the maximum clearance with the subsequent tiers, according to the amount of tiers you are using on the window.

Crescent-Shaped Curtain Rods

A crescent-shaped curtain rod is the rod used for window treatments that arch up on top in the center, and also arch up at the bottom in the center. Interesting treatments may be created with the hem arching up in the middle. The arched-up area depth comes in proportion to the size of the rod selected. Crescent-shaped rods are available in two widths: 1" and 2½".

- Use crescent-shaped rods for simple, tied-back curtains, rod pocket draperies, or gathered, rod pocket valances with an arched-top effect.

- Crescent-shaped top treatments may be used over regular traverse rods.

- Order the crescent-shaped top treatment or drapery to be made straight at the bottom and top, allowing the rod to do all the curving up on its own.

- This is another very *reasonable* type treatment to sell to your customer; when fabricated in beautiful fabrics it looks fabulous.

Pole Rods

Pole rods are used with curtains or drapery that have rod pocket tops. The rod pocket slips over the rod, gathering the fabric up on the rod, if enough widths of fabric have been planned.

When treatments are shirred on pole rods, the heading of the treatment takes on a rounded effect, different from the other flat curtain rods.

Pole rods may be used with the addition of rings. The rings may be either sewn on flat panels for a less full look or sewn on pleated-up panels for a pleated drapery effect.

Rings will not slide over rod supports, so part of the treatment becomes stationary if the rod is mounted with supports.

Pole rods have standard returns up to 3½". Pole rods may be used over many types of undertreatments, but may require you to use elbows or "F" brackets, if the return required will be larger than 3½". Wood-pole brackets are not adjustable.

Many pole rods have elbows available for use in returning the treatment to the wall. These types of elbows were previously unavailable, and give the treatment a much higher quality effect, especially in the hanging ability of the treatment. The treatment also looks more professional with the sides covered, rather than leaving the sides exposed with the sides of the treatment flaring out.

If the pole rod you prefer does not come with elbows, have the workroom place a buttonhole at the desired, return projection point, out from the wall. You will need to specify the placement for the buttonhole at 3½", 6", 9", etc.

Pole rods come in a variety of styles and materials such as plastic, wood, metal, dowel, simulated wood, brass, copper, chrome, wrought iron, tree branches, and P.V.C. plastic. The various styles may or may not have decorative end finials.

Wood-Pole Rods

Wide-width, wood-pole rods without center supports such as rods used with cafe curtains will dip and bow when the rod is mounted to go across an expanse of window. There is not a center support to hold the rod in place. The rod will dip down and the drapery or top treatment will be longer in the center.

On very wide windows with real wood-pole rods, the rods are very difficult to keep straight even with supports. This is the nature of wood — the rods come crooked from the manufacturer. Always discuss this with your customer so they will not be surprised or upset when their rods arrive and this is the situation. It might be better to use less expensive simulated wood decorative rods.

Specifics on Planning Rod Pocket Treatments

Below are the specifications needed to properly plan rod pocket treatments, with the specific rod selected. Always double-check by referring to this information affecting the rods and fabrication.

Spring-tension rods
Diameter — ⅝", **circumference** of the rod — 1¾".
Rod pocket size to order for fabrication — 1½".
Additional **take-up** to add to drapery length for **one** rod pocket — ½".
Additional **take-up** to add to drapery length for **two** rod pockets — 1".
Heading size, **minimum** — 0".
Heading size, **maximum** — 2".
Maximum rod width without support — 24"
Minimum I.B. area to mount — ¾".
Available projections — 0".
Amount of fabric to add to finished length for cut length, for **single** rod pocket — 18" (plus any pattern repeat).
Amount of additional fabric to add to finished length for cut length, for **double**-rod pocket — 0".

Valance/oval rods
Diameter — ⅝", **circumference** — 1¾".
Rod pocket size to order for fabrication — 1½".
Additional **take-up** to add to drapery length for **one** rod pocket — ½".
Additional **take-up** to add to drapery length for **two** rod pockets — 1".
Heading size, **minimum** — 0".
Heading size, **maximum** — 2".
Maximum rod width without support — 24".
Available projections — 2½", 4" — 5", 6" — 7", 8".
Amount of fabric to add to finished length for cut length, for **single** rod pocket — 18" (plus any pattern repeat).
Amount of fabric to add to finished length for cut length, for **double** rod pocket — 23" (plus any pattern repeat).

Oval curtain rods; sash, door rods
Diameter — ¾", **circumference** 1½".
Rod pocket size to order for fabrication — 1½".
Additional **take-up** to add to drapery length for **one** rod pocket — ½".
Additional **take-up** to add to drapery length for **two** rod pockets 1".
Heading size, **minimum** — 0".
Heading size, **maximum** — 2".
Maximum rod width without support — 30".
Available projections — ¼".
Amount of fabric to add to finished length for cut length, for **single** rod pocket — 20" (plus any pattern repeat).
Amount of fabric to add to finished length for cut length, for **double** rod pocket — 25" (plus any pattern repeat).

Custom heavy-duty, oval tracks
(for wider expanses)
Diameter — 1", **circumference** — 2½".
Rod pocket size to order for fabrication — 1¾".
Additional **take-up** to add to drapery length for **one** rod pocket — ¾".
Additional **take-up** to add to drapery length for **two** rod pockets — 1¼".
Heading size, **minimum** — 0".
Heading size, **maximum** — 3".
Maximum rod width without supports — 60".
Minimum I.B. area to mount — 1".
Available projections — 3" — 6".
Amount of fabric to add to finished length for cut length, for **single** rod pocket — 20" (plus any pattern repeat).

Amount of fabric to add to finished length for cut length, for **double** rod pockets — 25" (plus any pattern repeat).

4½" wide curtain rods

Diameter — 4½", circumference — 9½".
Rod pocket size to order for fabrication — 5½".
Additional **take-up** to add to drapery length for **one** rod pocket — ½".
Additional **take-up** to add to drapery length for **two** rod pockets — 1".
Additional **take-up** to add to drapery length for **three** rod pockets — 1½".
Heading size, **minimum** — 0".
Heading size, **maximum** — 3".
Maximum rod width without supports — 60".
Minimum I.B. area to mount — 1¼".
Available projections — ¾", 3½", 6".
Amount of fabric to add to finished length for cut length, for **single** rod pocket — 30" (plus any pattern repeat).
Amount of fabric to add to finished length for cut length, for **double** rod pockets — 35" (plus any pattern repeat).
Amount of fabric to add to finished length for cut length, for **triple** rod pocket — 40" (plus any pattern repeat).

2½" wide curtain rods

Diameter — 2½", circumference — 5½".
Rod pocket size to order for fabrication — 3½".
Additional **take-up** to add to drapery length for **one** rod pocket — ½".
Additional **take-up** to add to drapery length for **two** rod pockets — 1".
Additional **take-up** to add to drapery length for **three** rod pockets — 1½".
Heading size, **minimum** — 0".
Heading size, **maximum** — 2".
Maximum rod width without supports — 48".
Minimum I.B. area to mount — 1¼".
Available projections — 3" — 5".
Amount of fabric to add to finished length for cut length, for **single** rod pocket — 30" (plus any pattern repeat).
Amount of fabric to add to finished length for cut length, for **double** rod pockets — 35" (plus any pattern repeat).
Amount of fabric to add to finished length for cut length, for **triple** rod pockets — 40" (plus any pattern repeat).

Brass and wood pole rods

Diameter — 1½", circumference — 4¾".
Rod pocket size to order for fabrication — 3¼".
Additional **take-up** to add to drapery length for **one** rod pocket — 1¼".
Heading size, **minimum** — 0".
Heading size, **maximum** — 3".
Maximum rod width without supports — 60".
Minimum I.B. area to mount socket — 1¾".
Projections available 3" — 4".
Amount of fabric to add to finished length for cut length, for single rod pocket — 30" (plus any pattern repeat).
Specify placement of buttonholes at returns if brackets and finials are being used.

Decorator pole rods

Diameter 1⅜", circumference — 4½".
Rod pocket size to order for fabrication — 3".
Additional **take-up** to add to drapery length for **one** rod pocket — 1".
Heading size, **minimum** — 0".
Heading size, **maximum** — 3".
Maximum rod width without supports — 40".
Available projections — 3" — 6".

Amount of fabric to add to finished length for cut length, for single rod pocket — 30" (plus any pattern repeat).

Specify placement of buttonholes at returns if brackets and finials are being used.

Traverse Rods

Overlaps

All traverse rods (regular and decorative) overlap in the center 1½" on each side. The overlap extends 1½" on one side only, for a one-way pull. When ordering drapery for a center open, add 3" for a pair, and 1½" for a one-way pull for the corresponding overlaps. See the *Measuring* section for more information on overlaps.

Returns

The returns on all traverse rod (regular and decorative) will vary with the projection used. If the rod has a 3½" projection, you will double this for a pair for a total of 7" or 8". On a one-way pull drapery which has only one return, you will add 3½" or 4" (for a little extra slack). If the projection is 6", double the amount for a pair (12"); use the amount singularly for a drapery with only one return (6"). If the return is 9" you will double this amount for a pair (18"), and use only one return for the one-way pull (9").

Add the overlaps to the returns planned above and to the face width of the window treatment to arrive at the finished width needed for fabrication. See the *Measuring* section for more information.

Drapery Hooks

Hooks are used to attach a drapery to the drapery rods. One hook for every pleat is needed. If required, hooks can be moved up or down to adjust drapery length and hanging ability.

Hook weight should correspond with the type of treatment and the weight of the treatment to be installed. Workrooms usually stock a few types of drapery hooks. Workrooms will pin hooks on almost everything they fabricate, if you *specify* the desired hook set.

Hook set

Hook set varies with the type of rod used, installation placement of the rod, whether it is a single or a double treatment, and the style of the window treatment.

A hook set is figured from the top of the hump or curve of the hook to the top of the finished drapery pleat.

Hook set specifications:

The specifications for hook set for various rods, installations and types of different treatments are listed below:

		hook set
Wall-mount installation, with a regular traverse rod	—	1¾"
Ceiling installation, with a regular traverse rod	—	1½"
Decorative rod (finial type)	—	½"
Decorative rod with elbows	—	¾"
Double, regular traverse rods; wall mounted		
Overdrapery	—	1¾"
Underdrapery	—	1½"

Double, regular traverse rods, <u>wall-mounted</u>; under a top treatment, mounted at or on the ceiling

Overdrapery	—	1¾"
Underdrapery	—	1⅜"

Or, note on workorder that both underdrapery and overdrapery receive an *"even pin"* or hook set.

Regular traverse rods; mounted at the ceiling, on the wall

Overdrapery — acoustic ceiling	—	1⅜"
Overdrapery — smooth ceiling	—	1½"
Underdrapery	—	1½"

Double, regular traverse rods; mounted on the <u>ceiling</u>

Overdrapery	—	1½"
Underdrapery	—	1½"

Decorative rod, combined with regular traverse rod

Overdrapery — decorative rod	—	½"
Underdrapery — traverse rod	—	1¾"

<u>Underdrapery, mounted on regular traverse rods needs to be made the same length as the overdrapery.</u>

Two decorative rods, used together

Overdrapery	—	½"
Underdrapery	—	½"

Decorative rod with elbows, and traverse rod

Overdrapery — decorative rod	—	¾"
Underdrapery — traverse rod	—	1¾"

Rod Supports

Rod supports need to be installed every 48" to 60". The variance in the distance depends on the weight of the rod. One support needs to be installed in the center, to give the rod the support it needs when weighted down with a drapery or a curtain.

Types of Rod Installation

There are three types of rod installations. **The three types and where to mount them are listed below:**

Wall mount   4"-5" above the lintel or top of the window.

Wall mount, near ceiling   Top of the rod is placed 1" below the ceiling.

Ceiling mount   Rod is installed into the ceiling (a wall mount is preferred whenever it can be done, as a wall mount is a stronger installation) or installed to the **top** of the lintel in an I.B. mount.

Basic Traverse Rods

The most common rods are the basic traverse rods, which open and close draperies by pulling a cord that runs through the traverse rod. The drapery stack to the sides, or side of the rod. When the drapery is closed, drapery cover the rod so no part of the rod is visible. When the drapery is open and a top treatment is not used, the uncovered rod areas will show. If the room is painted off-white to closely match the white rod, a visible rod will not be as offensive. If the room is a contrasting color, use a decorative rod or a top treatment to cover the rod. Regular traverse rods are available in simulated wood-grain colors and finishes to match wood or paneled walls. They are only a few dollars more and should be used if a top treatment will not be used to cover the rod.

For proper hanging and privacy, **all pair rods have carriers that overlap in the center** (carriers may be moved to another area of the rod, for off-set pairs).

Traverse rods are either one-way pull rods or center-open (pair) rods. One-way pull rods can be either left-to-right, or right-to-left, pulls. The cord will be on the same side as the return, unless specified to be a reverse draw, available for an extra labor charge. When a reverse draw is drawn open, the cord mounted to the wall is exposed. If you leave the placement of the cord in the normal manner, under the return, the cord is hidden under the stack-back of the drapery and never seen.

One-way pull, traverse rods are usually used on sliding doors, corner windows, or any window that the customer wants the drapery to completely stack off the window to one side.

On a center open or a pair rod, the cord may be placed on the right or the left. Each side of the pair of drapery may also be made to open independently of each other (some customers request this for sun control or want privacy on one side). Again, this is an option at an extra labor charge.

Always discuss with your customer and record on the workorder which side the customer wants the cord to be mounted on with a center-open rod. If they are willing to pay the extra charges and desire a reverse draw or a installation, where each side of the drapery will open independently of each other, then request on the workorder for the installer to do this. On 99 percent of all your orders, the subject of reverse draws and independent draws will never come up.

Traverse rods may be wall mounted or ceiling mounted. It is usually preferable to wall mount the rod at the ceiling, *on the wall*, as this is the *stronger* installation method for traverse rods.

Projections for traverse rods:

- If you are planning a **curtain** to be mounted under the drapery, you will plan the return at 4" — 5". Both curtains and drapery share the same brackets.

- If you are using an **underdrapery** under the overdrapery, plan the brackets and returns at 5½" — 6½". One set of brackets will hold both rods.

- If you are planning a drapery over an undertreatment that is a hard window treatment other than verticals, plan the bracket return at 4½" for clearance.

- If you are planning an overdrapery over vertical blinds, plan the bracket and returns of the drapery at 4½" — 5½".

Conventional traverse rods come in sets of adjustable lengths, or the installer will use cut-to-measure rods, selecting the right brackets and hardware to go with the individual situation. Adjustable brackets are included in sets for returns from 3½"-4½". An optional bracket for 6" and 9" returns is available.

If the installer works out of a large workroom that stocks hardware, you may not need to individually order frequently used hardware. If you are planning something unusual, you will have to order the hardware, when you order the fabric. Some installers will need hardware for each job ordered, regardless of how often the same hardware is used, or how common the hardware is. Use your hardware manual for ordering and looking up the rods for pricing and sizes, as needed. Be very accurate in ordering the appropriate hardware, so you do not to hold up the order because of incorrectly ordered hardware. If in doubt, always discuss correct hardware selection with your installer.

Corner and Bay Windows

You may use single or double curtain or traverse rods sets especially made for corner and bay windows. The installer may also use cut-to-measure rods.

If you use the sets for corner windows, each side will adjust from 28" — 48". If you need a wider rod than this, butt single, wider curtain or traverse rods at the corners. Your installer may also accurately determine where the bend of the rod should be, and bend the rod for you at the job site on the day of installation.

If the corner windows are using **one-way pull rods, wall-mount** them above the window or on the wall, near the ceiling. If the corner windows are using **pairs** of drapery without a top treatment, you will get a better installation if the rods **are ceiling-mounted**, in this instance.

For bay windows you may use single or double curtain or traverse rod sets made especially for bay window situations. Each side adjusts from 18" — 42". The center area adjusts from 36" — 63". If you need wider rods than these, use standard rods, butted together. It is hard to order a bay window rod set and get it to fit accurately. It is preferable, and usually less expensive, for the installer to use cut-to-measure rods that they may bend in the proper points at the installation site. There are extra charges for each bend made, but the rods will end up fitting and usually be less expensive than the specialty bay or corner-window rods.

Motorized Drapery Rods

Like most everything else, motorized drapery rods have come down in price. Motors have become more compact, have been improved, and are quite sophisticated. Motorized rods are ideal for high windows or large expanses of glass. Today, motorized rods can be as low as $200, with motors for more complex drapery treatments running in the range of $500-$750.

Once the motor is going to be incorporated into the treatment, drapery can be opened and closed from long distances away from the home or building. Drapery can also be programmed to open and close in response to the amount of light coming in the window, with the use of a remote control and sensors.

Decorative Rods

Decorative rods are made of real wood, brass, other *"real"* materials, or are simulated to look like real materials. Simulated materials will not deteriorate, tarnish, or warp. Simulated materials are less expensive than the real material and look adequately authentic.

Drapery is attached by rings that slip over these rods, and traverse back and forth. Because of the ring width required, these types of rods need more stack-off space.

With a decorative rod system, only the master rings slide. The rings immediately above the master carrier of the rod are fastened to the traverse cord. Master rings pull the drapery back and forth. The other rings are hooked to the drapery and follow the master rings when pulling the drapery.

Decorative rods open and close draperies when the cord that runs through the rod is pulled, like a traverse rod. Drapery mounted on a decorative rod have a ½" hook set, so they may hang below the rod — showing the decorative features of the rod, whether the drapery is open or closed.

Decorative rods are decorative and require no additional top treatment to finish them off. This is the rod to use when you want to simply accent the room, and want to keep the price down at the same time.

Valances may be hung off the decorative rod instead of a drapery rod, by using a regular traverse rod for the undertreatment. Double decorative rods may be used with drapery and sheers for a different effect. The use of "F" brackets (there is an additional charge for each "F" bracket — mounted every four feet) must be used at regular intervals if a decorative rod has any other undertreatment mounted on a rod underneath.

Decorative rods come in varying diameters, usually 1", 1⅜", up to 3". People generally prefer the wider rod unless they have a small window with a lightweight drapery.

All decorative pair rods have overlapping master carriers. They overlap 1½" on each side of the master carrier; add 3" for the overlaps for a pair, and 1½" for a one-way pull.

Decorative rods come in sets of pairs only, but are easily adapted to a one-way pull, right-or-left, with an additional labor charge. Each side may also be made to open independently of each other.

Rod placement:

Decorative rods look their best mounted above the window, 6"— 8". The drapery would sit 4"— 6" above the window in this position.

Placing decorative rods against the ceiling hides them rather than accenting them. The rings must project above the rod about ½", and if the rod is at the ceiling the rings will not be able to project up. The end result is the rod will have to be lowered, and the drapery to be installed will be too long by about ¾".

Another formula to figure the **rod placement** is to measure floor to ceiling and subtract 3½".

Measuring for the width of a decorative rod:

When measuring for the width of a decorative rod mount, the finials will take up about 6" more room on each side of the drapery treatment. Therefore, the length of the rod is considered to be the rod area that the drapery will occupy; the distance from the outside ring to the outside ring of the rod.

The outside rings of a decorative rod are stationary and immovable. To take care of the immovable rings on the ends, **when planning decorative rod size or bracket-to-bracket width, add an additional 2" on each side for a one-way pull. Add an additional 2" to each side for a pair rod.** The ring slides do not touch the rod except from the back; therefore, there is not a possibility of the rod becoming scratched up. Rings may be removed or added for fuller or less full drapery.

Decorative rods come in sets in a variety of adjustable widths. The width of the rod is measured from one side end ring to the opposite side end ring. The finials, usually an additional 6" on each side, are not included in this measurement. Plan for the rod to be about 12" longer in width than the face width of the drapery. Allow room on each side of the drapery to accommodate the additional room needed.

Realistically, because of the extra amount of space needed on each side of the drapery, many window situations cannot use decorative rods. Many homes and buildings will have room on one side and not the other. They can be butted against the wall — without the finials — leaving one finial on one side only, or no finials at all. This is not the best-looking idea. If all other windows in the space work with both finials intact, and you have only one or two windows that you need to remove one or both finials to make it work, go ahead and remove the finials for those exceptional windows.

Decorative rod projection and return size:

Brackets included in sets will accommodate returns of 3½" to 4½". Any larger returns will need "F" brackets to accommodate the returns. "F" brackets accommodate undertreatments by sharing the bracket with them. By using this bracket, not only will both the rods be supported properly, but the headers of both drapery will be aligned properly to each other. "F" brackets need to be installed every 40" for proper support. Charge the customer for the correct amount of "F" brackets, as they are expensive.

If the decorative rod is being used over an O.B. mounted undershade or blind (not vertical), set the overdrapery returns at 4½".

If you are using a curtain for the undertreatment and want to avoid the "F" bracket charges, you will need to use a stock utility rod or curtain rod for the curtain with its own individual brackets and supports.

For use with underdrapery, set the returns on the overdrapery at 6½"— 7½". For use over vertical blinds or other undertreatments that have more depth, if the 7½" clearance will not accommodate the situation, special brackets are available for added clearance.

Sheers or underdraperies mounted on a traverse rod to be used with an overdrapery with a decorative rod, need to be made the same length as the overdrapery, since the sheer actually sits higher on the traverse rod underneath than the drapery will sit on the decorative rod.

Existing Decorative Rods

If you are planning a job using existing decorative rods, always count the number of rings on the existing rod. **You will require five rings per width of 48" fabric. If there are not enough rings,** ask the customer if they have any more in a drawer or the garage that had been removed during the rod installation. If the customer does not have any extra rings, and if the existing rod is not a brand that you carry, and can *readily* order more rings for — **give the customer the responsibility of going out and finding more rings. The other alternative: simply replace the existing decorative rods.**

Customers are often resistant to replacing existing rods. **Decorator rods that have already lived through one set of drapery are usually ready to be replaced.** They are just not as sturdy as plain, heavy-duty traverse rods, which may live through several drapery lives. The decorative rods may look okay, but are an installer's nightmare. Frequently, they will fall apart as the installer installs the new drapery. The new drapery may be of a different weight than the original drapery and will not pull the same, resulting in customer complaints.

Insist on selling the customer new hardware; or put in the sales slip, *"new hardware was suggested — customer accepts responsibility of usability of existing decorator rods."*

A couple of years later, if the rod survives the installation of the new drapery, the rod will have to be replaced and now the customer faces additional installation costs and hassles.

Measuring Existing Decorator Rods:

On existing decorative rods, the proper length to make the new drapery may be determined by measuring from the top of the carrier or the top of the end bracket, to the floor. Do not deduct anything from this measurement. If the existing rod is mounted with "F" brackets, as with sheers, take the length measurement the same way and deduct ¼".

When measuring existing decorative rods, remember to add (or allow) an extra 2" to **each side** of the rod. For a one-way pull rod, add 2" to one side only. For a center open or pair rod, add 2" to each side of the rod.

Top Treatment Boards

Top treatments are usually fabricated and mounted on the board with tacks, staples or Velcro before they leave the workroom.

Basic pleated valances and variations of these are shipped separately, unattached to the boards. The installer may cut and cover the boards or the workroom may send them with the order. The installer will staple, tack, or attach the valance to the board when he or she arrives at the installation site.

Boards come with a dust-cover board across the top to give a quality, finished appearance.

All boards should be covered in white or off-white lining fabric to give a nice appearance during installation and for finished, quality looks.

Boards which are mounted downstairs, where the top of the boards may be viewed from upstairs; should be covered in the same fabric as the drapery. If the top of the boards are covered in plain lining fabric, the fabric will show, stand out, and be noticed. Order extra fabric to cover the boards in the same fabric as the treatment, when this situation applies.

- Velcro may be used and added for an extra labor charge at the workroom to attach the valance (and some top treatments) to boards, rather than stapling. Some customers feel stapling looks very low quality and is offensive.

- When planning a job that is going to require the use of boards, make the boards 1" wider than the rod width or the drapery or headrail of the undertreatment.

- All valances must be fabricated with the same size returns as the return size of the boards to be used.

- **If the valance is going to be six or less inches from the ceiling, then plan the valance to go all the way to the ceiling to achieve a better-looking treatment.**

- Boards get installed separately from the rods. The rod may be mounted to the top of the board, but is usually mounted to the wall, behind the face of the board.

- The top treatment or valance should come down into the window 3" — 4".

- Top treatments mounted on boards independently from the undertreatments may be easily raised and lowered if the customer is unhappy about the placement.

Reasons to Change Existing Hardware

Below is a listing of the reasons why your customers should be encouraged to change their existing hardware:

- **Most installation problems occur with the use of existing drapery rods. Many rods, especially decorator rods, will not survive the *reinstallation* of new drapery on them.** Decorator rods, if opened and closed frequently, usually need to be replaced with the drapery as they really only last through one drapery life.

- **The new drapery will probably be heavier,** using more fabric, lining, etc. **The old rod is not going to pull and feel the same as it did with the old drapery.** You will get a call saying the installer did something to the old rod, and now it will hardly work.

- **Rods wear out.** Slides and glides wear with the weight of the drapery. Interior parts in rods get sharp edges on them, from use. These sharp edges fray the drapery cords as they slide over the sharp edges. **Any new cords, restrung to replace the old cords, will also slide back and forth over the sharp edges, wearing the new cord out.**

- **Parts may be missing or need to be changed.** The brand of hardware you carry may not be interchangeable with your customer's old hardware.

- **Dirt, dust, and sand get into the interior of the rods.** If the rods are located in a humid climate, the rod parts become gummy. Gummy rod parts wear down the other parts.

- **If the rod was installed by the customer or some other non-professional installer, it is probably not straight.** The rod projections may be incorrect and uneven from one side to the other. You may be able to adjust the return brackets, but you probably will not be able to adjust the support brackets.

- **There may not be enough rings for the existing decorator rods.** To complicate matters further, *you may not have access to or know who* manufactured the rod that the rings are needed for. You end up sending the customer out on a neverending quest, looking for rings.

If the customer is still resistant to changing the existing hardware, tell him or her the installer will **decide if they are able to use the existing hardware when they come out for the installation.** Have the installer come prepared with the correct hardware, and a sales slip with the hardware charges on it, ready to be signed and paid for by the customer, *if their hardware is found to be unusable.*

If the customer is going to paint before the treatments are to be installed, have them remove the old rod, and fill all holes in the wall. When the new rods are mounted or the old ones remounted there will not be any old holes to show in the area of the newly mounted hardware. See the section on *Existing Holes in Walls and Ceiling from Old Hardware.*

The installer will remount the old rods (at a small remounting charge for existing rods) or replace the old hardware with new hardware. **When the installer does the remounting or replacing of the old rods, rather than the customer, the rod placement for the new window treatments are ensured to be correct and made to fit the window treatment.**

Always note on the sales slip when new rods are declined, *"new rods were recommended. The customer accepts responsibility for the use of the existing rods with the new drapery."*

Existing Hardware that Appears to Be in Good Condition

Many times, the existing hardware will be in good enough condition to reuse. Although **most length and fit problems occur with the reuse of existing rods,** some customers just will not consider replacing what appears to be perfectly good hardware. Below is a list of points for you to consider, *to reasonably determine if the rod or hardware actually, is reusable.*

- Is the rod **evenly mounted** on the wall?

- Does the rod appear to be in **good mechanical shape?**

- Is the rod securely mounted, not pulling out of the wall anywhere? Are the rods **mounted securely to hollow walls** by the use of molly bolts?

- Does the rod have **enough center supports** to support the new drapery selection? Is the new drapery going to be heavier, therefore making the rod pull differently?

- **Note whether the rod is a center open or a one-way pull.** Is the rod **the proper set-up for the new drapery?** Is it a one-way pull, when you need a pair? Is the rod set up to be an off-set pair, when you need an off-set pair? Any rod conversion will cost the customer money in labor and part charges.

- Be sure to **notice** when planning new drapery treatments **if the drapery are off-set pairs.** The drapery may be only slightly off-set and not noticeably visible. If you do not check the old drapery when you are selling the customer new drapery, the new drapery will not fit the existing rods, without modification of the rod or the drapery. This would require repleating and possibly adding an extra width of fabric to the drapery, if the same dye lot is available. If fabric in the same dye lot *is not* available, a remake of all the draperies in the same space will become necessary.

  It is much simpler and less expensive to change the rods to even pairs. But if the customer is used to the evenness of the off-set pairs on their windows, they will not be willing to settle for even pairs on their uneven walls — unevenly framing their windows.

- Does the existing rod **have the correct projection?**

- **Is the rod properly placed** for stacking-off the windows — if the customer now wants to stack-off? Is the customer happy with the existing placement of the rod?

- Is the existing rod's **cord frayed?** This tells you that the parts in the headrail are worn and sharp — the rod needs to be replaced.

- Are the **cords dirty?** There is a labor charge for restringing. The customer can almost purchase a new rod for the charge of restringing the old rod.

- If using existing rods, **you must determine proper hook set for the new drapery.** If the existing drapery are still up, measure the hook placement. If they are not, measure the drapery placement to be ¼" above the rod and note visibly, where the top of the hook will fall within the nylon slides, in line with the drapery header. Usually, this will be 1½" or 1¾".

- **Always give a price for the drapery with replacing the rods.** Give the customer a price for the new hardware, even if you have discussed it with the customer and the customer has vetoed the idea. They may not realize how inexpensive the rods are. Review the reasons it is a good idea to replace them again with the customer. If the customer still declines the new hardware, record in your notes and on the sales slip, *"the customer has decided to use existing rods, replacement was recommended."*

Restringing Existing Rods

Many customers want to restring old rods due to frayed or dirty drapery traverse cords. **Restringing old drapery rods is almost as expensive in labor charges as what new rods will cost.** Frayed cords usually mean worn, sharp parts in the rod's headrail. **These sharp parts are fraying the cords.** The fraying of the cord by sharp parts will also happen to the new rod cords, *if the cords are replaced in the same rod.* **Insist on new rods,** as you do not want to receive a call from this customer telling you that you use inferior cord, since the cord was replaced a few months ago and is already fraying or wearing out.

Removal of Existing Hardware

Depending on your place of employment, there may or may not be a charge for removing old hardware for your customer. If there is a charge, determine if the customer would probably want to save money by removing their own hardware. If you think they will want to do their own hardware removal, bring up the removal charge and discuss it. If the customer seems very price conscious, always give them the option.

If you can see that the person will not want to bother with it, do not even mention removing their own hardware. Just add the removal charge into your quoted price.

Note: When you mention many extra charges, people get turned off.

If the installer is to do the hardware removal, be sure to note on the workorder that the installer is to remove the old hardware, so the installer can allow enough time for the removal.

Existing rods heavily bolted to the wall:
Sometimes you will encounter rods that are hung with many bolts intricately fastened to the wall. **Require your customer to spend the time removing these rods and other hardware, rather than your installer. Do not make it an option, at an extra charge, to remove these rods.** The installer will end up hours later, exposing damaged walls — after prying the rods off of the walls. The installer will end up repairing the damage at his or her expense. Who do you think is going to catch the grief? Installer removal of hardware is not an option in this situation.

Existing Rods Mounted into Acoustic Ceilings

Beware of existing rods mounted into acoustic ceilings, where the ceiling has been sprayed with acoustic, since they were originally mounted. The rods *become part* of the ceiling in your view.

If an installer attempts to remove the rod, the *immediate* surrounding area of the acoustic ceiling will come down with the rod. Your installer and your company will end up having to respray the whole ceiling for your customer! In this situation, always use existing rods. If the customer insists on a new treatment where new and different hardware is needed, **the customer is the one who must remove the old hardware**, period! Explain the situation to the customer and let the customer take the responsibility and risk for doing their own removal.

Existing Holes in Walls and Ceiling from Old Hardware

When planning new window treatments and hardware, try to cover holes made by old rods and hardware with the new treatment. Ask the customer if they are planning to repaint and plug the existing holes, if the new treatment is going to be lower or narrower. If you do not discuss this problem area with them, do not be surprised when the customer acts shocked that you did not plug the holes and do the touch-up painting for them!

Ceiling holes and track lines on acoustic ceilings are a real problem for the customer. Once existing track is removed, if the new treatment is not the same height (to the ceiling), as wide as the existing treatment, with at least the same projection, the customer will have to respray the ceiling (time, hassle, and expense). Better to spend money on a beautiful window treatment that covers the problem instead.

Children's Safety and Window Treatment Cords

If you are on an in-home visit and note there are small children living in or visiting the home, you need to instruct your customer to take precautions with the window treatment cords. Small children have strangled from these cords. The cords that the children have strangled on were either fastened to the wall or looped. Keep small children away from these cords and keep these cords out of reach of children. Tie or hang up the cord, near the top of the treatment. Instruct your customer not to place cribs or playpens near the windows as this additional height will help children reach the cords.

Children have died and nearly died because precautions were not taken with the cords hanging down within a child's reach. Your company, you the designer or decorator, and the product's manufacturer can and will be named in the lawsuit if an unfortunate mishap should occur. If you see any evidence of small children, thoroughly discuss this area with your customer.

Techniques to alleviate this problem: fasten the cord itself onto the window covering with a clamping device; wrap or tie the cord to itself; or use cord cleats to wrap the cord around itself and mount to the top of the drapery.

Fabrication

Custom Drapery Fabrication Standards

- **Headers and bottom hems are double folded on unlined drapery. On lined drapery, a single-folded header is used** because of the addition of lining. Addition of the lining results in four layers of fabric at the header.

- **Crinoline in the header is heavy-duty buckram** and is dry-cleanable. Washable crinoline may be requested for fabrics such as washable sheer fabric or other fabrics the customer is insisting on washing.

- **Headers are 4" wide.**

- Lining at the header will be lined up to the top of the drapery.

- **Bottom hems are 4" wide on unlined drapery, 3" wide on lined drapery.**

- **Bottom hems are blind stitched** unless an open-weave fabric is to be used.

- Lining hem will line up with the drapery hem. The lining hem will actually be 1" shorter at the bottom edge than the drapery bottom edge.

- **Side hems are 1½" wide and blind stitched.**

- **Seams are overlocked stitched or serged.**

- **All seams are hidden.** This is done with placement of the seams to the back of pleats.

- **Covered weights are added at all seams and corners.**

- Corners are squared and mitered.

- Corners are closed by bonis or handstitching.

- Pleats are tacked once at their base.

- **Vertical-pattern pleating is done on request, when possible.** With prints having vertical-pattern repeats, matching patterns around pleats may not be possible. Any repeat less than 12" cannot be accommodated. If vertical-pattern pleating is possible, **seams may not be to the back of the pleats in places on the drapery.**

- **Horizontal-pattern repeats are lined up horizontally** and are preferably tabled from the top rather than the bottom. Some workrooms match them from the bottom of the drapery rather than the top. Some fabrics have repeats that will not match up, cut-to-cut. The repeat will be off slightly on each repeat, so the cuts will not match up. The repeat will fall farther and farther down on each repeat.

- **Balance pleating will be done on request.** This is done for all drapery used in the same space. Balance pleating ensures that the pleats and fullness of the drapery are the same distance and fullness, guaranteeing all the drapery will look the same.

- **Drapery pins or hooks are added to the drapery, according to the pin or hook set specified** by the designer/decorator on the workorder.

- **There may be slight length variations on custom drapery up to ½" in length and 1" in width of the fabricated drapery.** Loose-weaves may be 1" shorter in length. For floor-to-ceiling measurements, **specify on work order *"must be exact in length."*** This indicates to the workroom that a ½" tolerance cannot be accommodated.

- **Drapery is pleated up, hung over a hanger, and covered in plastic** ready for installation.

- **Drapery may be flat-folded,** upon request. Flat folding is preferred for shipping, curtain styles that are finished flat, etc.

- **Drapery care labels** should always be sewn onto the drapery to ensure proper cleaning of the drapery or other item. Care labels are also important to release you from liability, if the drapery or other item is improperly cleaned.

Typical Fabrication Price List

Unlined Lined

Basic Charges:
```
Pleated drapery 20" — 100" in length....$7.00   9.00  per width
Pattern Pleating and matching............4.00   extra per width
Pleated drapery 100" — 161"..............4.00   extra per width
Pleated drapery with 5" hems or headings...50   extra per width
Pleated velvet or fiberglass drapery......4.00  extra per width
Drapery using blackout, or heavy linings...75   extra per width
Drapery, interlined...........................  11.50 per width
Drapery out of loose weave fabric..........50   extra per width
Fabric-overlay drapery........................  11.50 per width
Beauty-pleated drapery....................7.00   9.00  per width
Shirr-on-rod; rod, top and bottom........4.50   6.00  per width
Double, rod-pocket top...................3.00   extra per width
Hour-Glass Panels + tieback..............7.50   9.00  per width
```

Fancy, miscellaneous:
```
Drapery pleated, top and bottom..........4.00   extra per width
Pleated door panels, top and bottom......6.50   8.00  per width
Three- or four-cord shirred heading......10.00  12.00 per width
Slant-top drapery, up to 120"............17.00  24.00 per width
Slant-top drapery, over 120".............20.00  27.00 per width
Arch-top drapery/valances, mount on rod..23.00  25.00 per width
Arch-top drapery/valances, with frame....27.00  29.00 per width
Scalloped-top drapery/valance (no pleats)10.00  12.00 per width
Scalloped cafe with pleats................5.50   6.00  per width
Box-pleated drapery/valance...............7.00   8.00  per width
Pleated valances, up to 20"...............5.50   6.00  per width
```

Unlined Lined

```
Rod pocket sleeve........................4.00      per width
Pouff valance............................6.00  7.50 per width
Balloon valance..........................4.50  5.00 per foot
Balloon shade............................4.50  5.00 per sq.foot
London shade.............................4.50  5.00 per sq.foot
Roman shade..............................4.50  5.00 per sq.foot
Scalloped styles of pleated valances.....5.00  5.50 per width
Pleated valances, self-lined.............5.50  6.00 per width
Pleated valances, on boards..............4.00 extra per width
Slanted-top valance......................6.00  8.00 per foot
Cascades or abots.......................20.00 23.00 per pair
Floor-length cascades or jabots.........30.00 extra per pair
Ties for swag or Austrian treatments.....9.00      each
Swags, up to 5'in width.................26.00 33.00 each
Swags, over 5'in width...................2.00 extra per foot
Austrian valance, up to 22" in length....4.50  5.00 per foot
Austrian valance, over 22" in length.....5.50  6.00 per foot
Austrian shades, with cording............7.00 10.00 per foot
Lambrequins, up to 28" in length.........5.00  5.50 per foot
Lambrequins, over 28" in length..........6.50  7.00 per foot
Cornice box, fabricate, straight........30.00      per foot
Cornice box, fabricate, all other styles.40.00     per foot
Recover existing cornice + trip charge..22.00      per foot
Cornice, lined for sheer fabrics.........9.00      per foot
Sunburst, up to 60"wide, with frame....125.00      each
Sunburst, 60" — 96" wide, with frame...175.00      each
Rosettes................................25.00      each
Grommeted shower curtain.................6.50      per width
Tieback, straight and plain..............5.00      each
Tieback, with welting....................9.00      each
Tieback, contoured or tapered............7.00      each
Tieback, ruffled; add ruffle charge and..1.00 extra per foot
Table skirt, up to two widths of fabric.25.00      each
Table skirt, more than two widths.......35.00      each
Table skirts, fancy; check with workroom......
Table runner............................ 35.00 each
Dust ruffle, twin.......................50.00      each
Dust ruffle, full.......................70.00      each
Dust ruffle, queen......................85.00      each
Dust ruffle, king......................100.00      each
Pillow shams, plain, corded, flanged....20.00      each
Pillow shams, ruffled, add ruffle price per ft.
```

Trimming:
```
Fabricate ruffles........................5.50      per foot
Fabricate banding........................1.50      per foot
Sew on banding...........................2.75      per foot
Hand sew on trims........................4.75      per width
Machine-sewn trims — sides/bottom hems...2.25      per width
Machine-sewn trims — top of drapery......3.00      per width
Glue on trim, banding....................4.00      per width
Sew on rings and hooks...................2.75      per width
Reinstall pins........................... .60      per width
```

Miscellaneous:
```
Remakes and repairs......................5.50      per width
```

```
Hand hem in the home + trip charge........8.00          per width
Press and fanfold.........................2.50          per width
Fanfold only .............................1.25          per width
Sew on Velcro, includes Velcro...........8.00    extra per width
Sew on shirring tape, includes tape.......5.00          per width
Covered-beaded weight (includes shot tape)4.00   extra per width
Memory stitch (drape rite tape with s.tape3.00   extra per width
Snap-tape mounting........................4.00          per width
Tack strip................................1.50          per width
Covered boards for valances, lambrequins..4.00   extra per foot
Relining drapery..............................    9.00 per width
Reinstall pins............................ .50          per width
Cutouts..................................35.00          each
Trip charge to pick up cornice..........25.00    extra
```

Linings (available through the workroom):
```
Shop lining, satin sheen..................4.00          per yard
Thermal suede lining......................6.50          per yard
Black-out lining..........................7.50          per yard
```

If you ever have a question on a treatment that does not fall unquestionably into a certain category, call the workroom.

Installation

Installer Selection

As a professional decorator you endeavor to project a high-quality image and do quality jobs. Professionally completed projects will generate referrals, bringing you more business. To perform quality jobs, you need your installation support person to meet certain qualities and standards. These standards for installer selection are outlined below:

● A neat, clean appearance.

● Ability to communicate with a positive attitude to customers, while projecting a professional image.

● Each installation should be done in a professional manner with a positive attitude projected to the customer about the decorator/designer's ability, and the company they are representing. An installer should never say anything negative about the company he or she may be subcontracting for. An installer should never say anything that may indicate the decorator/designer is inexperienced or, *"not very good,"* regardless of the problems that may arise.

● A well-stocked installation van or truck ready to meet challenges, which may and will come up at any given time.

● An installer should attempt to complete the installation and *always* dress the window treatments on the first visit to the home. If there is a small problem that he or she must correct or remedy while at the home, they should do so quietly without calling it to the customer's attention. The installation goal is to get the job in on the first visit. The C.O.D. money may then be collected, or the billing may be started on the credit card.

● The installer should attempt to collect part of the C.O.D. money on incomplete jobs, if possible. Write up a large job on **several** sales slips. This is the correct procedure. If one sales slip is completely installed and the other is incomplete, the billing should be started on the completed sales slip. If the collection is C.O.D., the C.O.D. money should be collected for the completed sales slip, without any delay.

If a large job is placed all on one sales slip, and one tieback is missing, some customers will try not to pay you for the rest of the items completed. They will hold up all the money due, until they get that tieback. The installer should make an attempt to get some money, anyway.

- If a serious problem should arise, the installer should strive to do what can be done that day. Any paperwork that must be generated to complete the job should be written up that day, preferably while the installer is still on the job — so nothing further will be missed.

- Find an installer who *will* work with you on mistakes or problems that arise. The installer should promptly attempt to correct the problem and educate you on how to prevent the problem. If you are informed and shown what you are doing wrong in your planning, you will not keep repeating the same error on all subsequent, similar jobs.

- Find an installer who is willing to remeasure. The installer should also be willing to review any jobs you feel need reviewing, and also examine the paperwork. The installer should be paid a remeasure fee for remeasures. Consider this the same as buying insurance. The remeasure is to find and correct any mistakes or problems, before ordering materials or starting the fabrication.

- Always try to work with the same installer or installers. They get to know your *"look"* and style. If you should forget to write special instructions, or the instructions are worded ambiguously, and the installer cannot understand what you mean, they probably will interpret correctly what you want, since they do jobs for you regularly.

- Your installer should have business cards to hand to the customers upon their arrival.

If you are an inexperienced designer/decorator, make it a point to ride along for a couple of days with an experienced installer. You will gain much insight into what installers go through during the installation, and the extra engineering they have to do to get an incorrectly planned window treatment installed.

Always treat your installer with respect and always make positive comments about him or her, even if they have angered you. They can give you a hard time if you do not work in a professional manner with them. They also make mistakes, as you do. Try to correct these mistakes, together, as quickly and as painlessly as possible.

Installation Tools

Below is a list of the tools and parts installers use in hanging window treatments:

Tools
Rachet screw driver   12" screw driver
6" screw driver   25-30' tape measure
A pair of dikes   Measuring stick
Hand steamer   Hexhead socket
Jiffy steamer, 4 qt., 120 volt

Parts
Box of molleys   Box of plastic plugs
Box of 3/4" #6 screws   Box of 1/4" #6 screws
Box of T-cup hooks   100 yards regular duty 3 1/4 cord
Can of silicone lubricant   Can of spray to release wrinkles

Installation Price List

Installation:
```
Minimum installation.....................40.00
Remeasure ...............................35.00
Trip charges to outlying areas (confirm)15.00 — 25.00  extra
Installation of blinds, shades..........2.25          per foot
Installation of drapery.................2.50          per foot
Installation of drapery, over 100"...... .75    extra per foot
Installation of drapery rods only.......2.50          per foot
Take down existing hardware.............4.00          per window
Install tiebacks........................4.00          each
Installing into concrete...............10.00    extra per window
Restringing of customer's old rods.......2.00         per foot
Readymades, press/fanfold/pin/install.. 15.00         per width
```

Miscellaneous:
```
Delivery to a customer's home...........25.00
Trip charge.............................25.00
Making template for odd windows........30.00          each
Record rods............................10.00    extra each
Bend custom rods.......................10.00          each bend
Flip master carrier.....................7.00          each
Glue Velcro to top treatments/boards.....4.00         per foot
Cut down woven woods, shades, blinds....15.00         each
Install or reinstall pins................60            per width
```

Rods/hardware usually available through the installer:
```
S.O.R rodding — oval tube, with brackets.2.00         per foot
Utility rodding.........................2.00          per foot
Door rods...............................2.00          per foot
Custom heavy-duty traverse rods.........4.00          per foot
Custom heavy-duty traverse rods, walnut..5.50         per foot
Basic decorative rods, broken package price..
Basic decorative rings..................1.00          each
F brackets..............................7.00          each
Wood pole rods.........................15.00          per foot
Cafe rods, brass........................4.00          per foot
Valance boards, covered.................3.50          per foot
Carson holders for tiebacks.............5.00          each
```

Order all other rods and accessories through your hardware supplier. Check with your installer to see what they carry in stock.

Installation Planning

Upon the completion of the fabrication of decorating items, your customer should be scheduled for an installation date by telephone a couple of days ahead of the available installation date.

If a customer cannot be reached after repeated attempts by telephone, a postcard should be sent to the customer, requesting them to call the studio or the installation clerk to be scheduled.

At the time of the installation scheduling it is preferable not to give any time of arrival to the customer. The installer needs to review paperwork and look at all the different locations for installations for the whole day, before deciding what is the preferred plan of action and itinerary to take. Some customers are going to insist on times after 3:30 P.M. or before 11 A.M. Note these priority times for the installer. Tell all the customers that the installer will call them the morning of the installation and give them an approximate time.

Installation persons that are knowledgeable about how much time to allow for each installation item, and how much time to allow for removal of the old hardware, may want to arrange the schedule for the installer. They should plan the quickest route to take, to take care of all the calls for the day. Again, only an approximate time of arrival should be given — the installer never knows what they will run up against during installation.. This is especially true if he or she has not previewed the job before the installation date. Matters get done quicker or slower, depending on the problems that do or do not arise. Installers also need to take a lunch break.

If information on the workorder projects that the customer is to remove the old hardware, provide missing rings for existing rods, or that the customer will not be there for the installation, etc., this information should be reviewed by the person scheduling the installation with the customer. They should review exactly what the customer is to provide or do, before the installation date. This is a good time for the scheduling person to ask what the nearest, larger cross streets to the installation site are, and to note directions for difficult locations.

Some customers will prefer to give you a work telephone number so the installer can call them at work when they are ready to leave to go over to the home. This is preferable to some people, rather than waiting around all day for the installer to show up.

This is the time to remind any customer with a C.O.D. stamped on the workorder that the installer will need to pick up the C.O.D., and what the amount is, the day of the installation.

The day before the installation date, or the morning of the installation, the installer should call the customer and give an approximate time of his or her arrival. He or she can confirm difficult directions to the home at this time. Again, the customer should be reminded of the C.O.D. amount due **that** day, and the amount.

If the installer is running more than one hour late on their installations, they should call the customer and let them know they are running late. The customer should be given a new, approximate time of arrival. The installer should strive to keep at all costs the new promised arrival time.

Problems that Arise During Installation

If any problem should arise during installation that prevents the installer from completing the installation, the installer should call the decorator or designer to notify them of the problem. Installers should educate the designer/decorator about what was wrong, and why. The installer should clarify to you what **they** are going to do to correct the problem, and **what your role is in correction of the problem**. The objective is to get the job completed as quickly as possible.

The customer should be called immediately by the designer/decorator, confirming that the problem is being corrected in a prompt manner, with an apology for the delay.

The studio assistant, the decorator/designer, and the installer must follow through and stay on top of the situation. The customer must be handled with kid gloves to prevent them from canceling, or demanding an adjustment. If the customer is extremely angry and ready to cancel, offer them an adjustment. Offer as little as you think they will take — such as 15 — 20% of the gross amount. Realize that any subsequent visits by the installer and the extra fabrication costs to rework or remake the item are quickly eroding the profits. Always try to learn from every mistake and do not repeat them. The mistakes may be generated from flawed fabrics, wrong colors, defective products, errors in the workroom, shipment of wrong items, incorrect items taken to the customer's home for installation, missing parts, installation errors, misinterpretation of what is requested by the designer/decorator, or misinterpretation of what the customer thought he or she was getting. Many controllable and uncontrollable particulars will go wrong. Interior design is that type of business.

Memory Stitch

Memory-stitch tape keeps the drapery-pleat folds the same at the bottom as at the top of the folds. Some fabrics, when made up into drapery, will not hang uniformly and have to have the addition of this tape to complete the job. Memory stitching is added at the bottom of the drapery or sheers.

Methods to Remedy Crooked Drapery Side Hems

Drapery anchors are available to remedy the problem of drapery that will not hang straight at the sides.

Another remedy is the use of T-cup hooks attached to the wall at the hem line of the drapery, right behind the return of the drapery with plastic rings or drapery hooks at the base of the drapery (to hold the drapery taut) that slide into the T-cup hooks.

Drapery and Window Treatment Installation

This section has been included because you need to understand how basic drapery are installed. You may be able to take a set of drapery out to a home and install them on an existing rod for the customer. You may want to do some simple installations for yourself, sometime. Sometimes, customers take drapery out to a dry cleaner that does not specialize in drapery cleaning and have to reinstall the drapery themselves. They often get them hung up incorrectly, and call and say there is something wrong with the rod. You can glance at the way the drapery is hung, and will be able to tell they did not rehang them correctly.

Breaking the Crinoline

Before you proceed to install the drapery, you need to properly break the crinoline at the header of the drapery. **Breaking the crinoline is needed so the drapery will properly traverse back and forth on the rod, easily.** If you ignore the breaking of the crinoline in the header, when you attempt to traverse the drapery back and forth, the drapery will abruptly stop in the traversing process, midway, due to the pleats not folding properly. The pleats at the top will not fall nicely when drawn back together, either.

Depending on the hook set of the rod, or type of rod used, you either break the crinoline inward or outward.

On decorative rods, which have a ½" hook set, break the crinoline inward so the creases of the header will point out of the room when drawn back.

On regular traverse rods, break the crinoline outward, so the creases point outward into the room.

Breaking the crinoline is uniformly bunching all pleats together except the overlap pleat and the return pleats (first pleat and last pleat) **and creasing them in the middle area of the crinoline** inward or outward, to correspond with the type of rod to be used.

Hanging Drapery

When you have drapery fabricated in the workroom and request specific hook or pin sets for the corresponding rod and installation, the hooks come already attached to the drapery. Review the section on *Hook Sets* for more information on selecting the proper hook set.

The first thing you need to do after breaking the crinoline of the drapery, to correspond with the type of rod you are using, is to crimp the first two hooks of the leading edge or edges, for each side or sides of the drapery. Crimp the last hook on the other opposite end of the drapery. This is the hook that will end on the return by the wall. The reason for the crimping of the hooks is so the hooks will hug the master carrier and the return of the rod tightly, thus keeping the overlap standing-up uniformly while keeping the return hook against the wall.

If you have large panels to work with, it is preferable to do the job of hanging the drapery when you have someone else available, to hold up the other end of the drapery panel. Use a small ladder and step stool so you can get right up to the rod.

Pull the traverse open until you have the master and overlap carriers almost ½ the way to the center of the rod. On a one-way pull panel, start at the end with the master carrier. Insert the first crimped pin into the first hole in the master carrier. Place the second crimped pin into the second hole, about 3" away on the same strip of metal or plastic. Proceed to place pins in all holes for the hooks on the rod, until you get to the end hole of the rod. Place a pin at the end hole of the rod, swing drapery around, and place last crimped hook into the hole next to the wall on the return of the rod.

For decorative rods, place the last pleat hook of the drapery into the ring on the outer side of the bracket, at the end of the rod. The last hook on the drapery is placed in the hole in the bracket, next to the wall, on the return of the bracket.

Training the Drapery

Installers train the drapery so the pleats and folds will fall uniformly and evenly from the base of the pleats to the floor.

Pull the drapery open to the full-stack back position, where the drapery hangs in full folds. Smooth the folds of the drapery — the whole length of the drapery, from the base of the pleats or gathers down to the hem. Do this by combing the folds with your fingers. Smooth and recomb areas as you go up and down the folds.

When the sections are smooth, straight, and even-looking, tie the finished sections of drapery panels uniformly, folded up together, in place with light strips of fabric, yarn, or cord. Tie, slightly, tight enough to keep the strips from slipping off. If you need to pin the cord, yarn, or fabric in place to keep from slipping off, place the pins where the pin holes will not visibly mark the fabric.

Leave the bunches tied for 3 — 5 days, before removing the strips and traversing the drapery open and closed. Leaving the drapery tied-back forms a *"memory"* in the buckram so when they are untied, they will traverse smoothly, back and forth. Training the drapery will also allow the drapery to hang nicer with more uniform folds, when either opened or closed.

Customers Who Want to Install Their Own Window Treatments

Some customers will want to install their own window treatments due to installation costs, or personal satisfaction in doing the job themselves. If this is the case, you should **have them bring in their own measurements. You cannot be liable for mismeasurements if they are not having your installer install the window treatments.**

If they are purchasing a large quantity, you may want to send the installer to remeasure, or go out yourself to the home and remeasure for the customer. **Unless the customer is willing to pay a service charge to have the measurements checked, then do not go out and check the measurements.** Your company is a custom operation that does the installation, unless the customer comes to you and supplies their own measurements. *Out of courtesy for the customer, you will place the order.*

Below are some points to review with the customer about how to arrive at correct measurements:

For alternate window treatments with an I.B. mount:
- Reinforce to the customer that you will have **the factory or workroom take the allowances on I.B. mounts.**

- **The exact measurements are needed** — the smallest of the three measurements in width, and the smallest of the two measurements in length.

For drapery and top treatments on new rods and hardware:
- **Ask for the face width and tell the customer you will add the proper amount for the overlaps and returns.** For new rods, you should also plan the correct rods and hook set.

For drapery and top treatments mounted on existing rods, hardware, or boards:
- If the drapery or other treatment the customer is replacing had a good fit, ask the customer to bring in the old drapery or top treatments so you can measure them in the studio. Take note of the hook set, return size, and length. **Ask the customer if they shrank in length.** If they did shrink, would the customer like them an inch or so longer? **Ask the customer to measure the return size of any existing board for the top treatment.**

If the customer has already disposed of the drapery or is using the drapery for a drop cloth for painting, then the customer must measure the face width of the old rods, note if they are pairs or panels, the return size, and the placement of the rod so you can guess at the hook set. **If the drapery are off-set pairs, convince the customer to pay to have it installed so you can come out and double-check the measurements.**

Additionally:

- **Show the customer how to break the crinoline. Discuss the possibility that the hook set may have to be changed.** Demonstrate for the customer how to change the hook set. Also show the customer how to crimp the hooks at the overlaps and returns.

- **Make sure the customer realizes that if odd-split widths are used on a pair, that the split width should be used on the outside of the window — not in the more visible center area of the window (especially on prints).**

- Sell the customer cut-to-measure, custom hardware and have the rods cut to fit in the proper widths so they will go up easily. The problem is that cut-to-measure hardware is meant for installers, and does not come with directions. Have a printed sheet of directions available for your customer.

Ideally, you will always want to install everything you sell. Occasionally, good customers or customers that we want to retain for constant future sales, insist on doing the installations themselves. They believe they just need to simply hang the drapery on existing rods (it looks that easy to them).

Since repeat customers are important to you, you need to accommodate these requests. Let the customer order the goods if they are responsible for the measurements. Let them take the chance and the responsibility that the item may not fit. Always remind the customer when the items are professionally installed, your company is the one liable for mismeasurements. **When your company does not install the window treatments, your company is not responsible for any mismeasurements.**

Part 7

Alternate Window Treatments

Hard window treatments or alternate window treatments hang off of their own headrail and system. Unlike drapery and other fabric treatments that are fabricated in drapery workrooms, hard window treatments are fabricated at the workroom of the manufacturer offering the product. Various types of shades and verticals may be fabricated using decorative fabrics that may be used elsewhere in the interior.

For concise information and an overview of each of the alternate treatments covered in this section, refer to the end of this section to the *Alternate or Hard Window Information Chart.*

Hard window treatments may be inside or outside mounted. Follow the diagrams below for I.B. mounted treatments and O.B. mounted treatments. The arrows show the corresponding measurements to take for each.

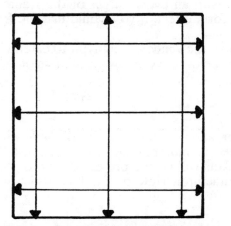

I.B. mount, measurements needed

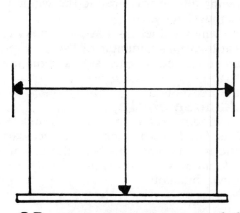

O.B. mount, measurements needed

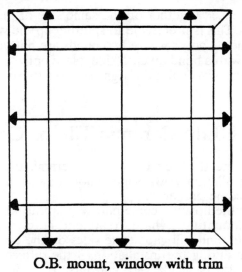

O.B. mount, window with trim

Measuring for an I.B. mount:

If the hard window treatment is to be inside mounted (or inside bracket measurement), measure the inside width across the top, middle, and bottom — to the nearest ⅛ of an inch. Write down the smallest of the three measurements. Next, measure top to bottom on the inside on each side, and in the middle area of the window, if the window is wide. Now, record the exact shortest measurement of the three measurements.

Note: If the I.B. mounted hard window treatment is to rest on the sill, when the length measurements are taken, take the *longest* of the three measurements. Remind the customer that bottom rails of mini blinds and other types of shades mark up the sill when they are pulled up and down, if they are allowed to rest on the sill.

When you order an I.B. mount on the workorder, and do not note that you have taken an allowance, the factory will take an allowance on the measurement, to ensure the item will fit into the window easily.

Measuring for an O.B. mount:

For an O.B. mount, measure on the outside the window from molding to molding areas, top and bottom, and label the workorder O.B. Or, label the workorder an O.B., and ask for an allowance on the measurement to be taken. When you take an allowance on an O.B. and are mounting the window covering to the outside frame and moldings of the window, you end up with an even margin of the frame of the window showing all the way around the window. It will be a uniform effect, if you would like the frame or molding to show slightly.

If the window does not have any molding or trim, then plan the window treatment to extend beyond the window at the top, a minimum of 1½" (2½" preferably); extend below the window a minimum of 1½" (2½" preferably); and extend on each side a minimum of 1" (1½" preferably).

Hold-down brackets:

Hard window treatments such as blinds, shades of all types, and woven woods are available with hold-down brackets. Hold-down brackets are necessary for door mounts and motor home and camper installations. Other situations will come up where the use of hold-down brackets will be the preferred way to go on the installation. Hold-down brackets are usually free from the manufacturer. Note on the P.O. which windows need hold-down brackets.

Operating Controls:

Operating controls may be placed together on the same side of the hard treatment, to keep clutter of cords and wands to one side only. This is preferable to splitting up the wand and cord with a cord on one side and a wand on the other. On sliding doors where two blinds are butted together, or are fabricated two-on-one headrail, or corner windows with a blind on each side, place both cords and wands for the left window on the left side. Place both cords and wands for the right side on the right side — freeing up the middle corner from dangling clutter.

Mounting Into Ceramic Tile or Concrete

Hard window treatments that need to be mounted into ceramic tile or concrete require a special drill bit for the drill to accomplish the installation. Always make note of a ceramic tile or concrete installation on the workorder, so the installer will come prepared.

Some windows have ceramic tile lips that come part way up the window and protrude in ½— 1¼ on the sides of the window. When mounting a hard treatment here, you can either take the smallest measurement at the bottom, and the blind will gap at the sides on the top portion of the window; or, have the installer trim the blind or shade during the installation, if the difference in the size is not an extreme (over 1"). The blind or shade may also be made with cut-outs. To order cut-out areas, you must be very precise on your measuring, and on the diagram or template supplied to the manufacturer. Charge the customer the necessary surcharges for this option.

Planning for Two-on-One Headrail Situations

Always check the price list of the manufacturer and the hard window product you are selling to see what the recommended break-off point is for two or more blinds or shades on-one-headrail. This will vary from one hard window product to the next, and from the quality of the product to the next.

It is an easier and more foolproof installation (if the spacing is off between the units, the hard treatment will not fit right) to plan the units as separate units, rather than placing the units on the more expensive (surcharges for two or more units on-one-headrail) multiple units on one headrail. The units can be spaced the correct distance apart by the installer, they are easier to handle, to clean, etc. The appearance is the same if a top treatment is planned or a valance strip of the hard treatment is ordered to cover all the units in one piece.

Blinds and Shades for Corner Windows

Blinds and shades may be overlapped to allow privacy for corner window situations. Mitered corners for blinds or shades are not available, so the blinds must be overlapped.

When planning a corner blind or shade situation, order the controls on the opposite, outer sides to the corner, for both blinds or shades. Below are the measuring guidelines for corner mini blind situations:

I.B. mounts:
- Measure across the width of the window, that is to go all the way to the corner. Do this by measuring from the inner corner of the window or edge of the glass itself, to the opposite, outer edge of the window frame, as you normally do for any blind.

- To measure for the blind or shade that is to *"butt-to"* the blind or shade that goes all the way to the corner; measure from inner corner of the window edge of glass or the corner of the window frame, to the opposite, outer window frame. Since the blind or shade must *butt only* and not go all the way to the corner, deduct 2" from this width measurement.

- When ordering from the manufacturer, note on the workorder that this is an I.B. mount, line #2; the butt-to blind or shade has already had 2" removed from its width, because it is a corner situation and *"butts-to"* the other blind or shade. The factory (depending on the width of the headrail and projection of the blinds or shade you are purchasing) may or may not take an additional ½" allowance off the width measurement for that particular window on line #2.

O.B. mounts:
- Review the above directions for an I.B. mount.

- Measure the width in the same way for both blinds or shades and add the wall-extension area or frame area desired for both width measurements. Take the same 2" deduction for the *"butt-to"* blind or shade.

- On the workorder, note the same information as an I.B. mount, except that this is an O.B. mount. The factory, when fabricating an O.B. mount, does not take *an additional deduction,* but will *check* the 2" deduction you took against the headrail and projection of the blind or shade.

Blinds and Shades for Bay Windows

When planning a job for blinds or shades that need to butt together on bay windows, the blinds or shades need to be placed as close together as possible, without overlapping, bypassing or mitering. Listed are the guidelines to follow when planning blinds or shades for a bay window when the windows are placed against each other or placed very close together:

- Place the controls for operating the side blinds or shades on the outer edges of the windows. The center window's controls may be placed on either side of the window.

- Measure each blind or shade separately.

- To be completely safe, have the window remeasured.

For an I.B. mount:

- Measure the width of the center window from corner to corner of the interior of the window's frame. If it is actually glass meeting glass on the bay window, hold the tape out about 1½" when you take the measurement for the width.

- The widths for the side blinds or shades are determined by measuring from the interior corner of the side window to the outer, interior corner of the window frame of the side window.

- Next, deduct 2" to allow the blinds or shades to butt-to the center window.

- Note on the workorder that there are side windows to a bay window on lines #3 and #4 and that you have deducted 2" for the blinds to *"butt-to"* the center window. The workroom will determine if they need to take an additional allowance for the width and check your 2" deduction against the size of the projection of the headrail.

For an O.B. mount:

- The widths for the side blinds or shades are determined by measuring from the corner of the window, out on to the opposite, outside frame about 1½" or more, depending on your customer's preference and wall space available.

- Follow the above guidelines for deducting 2" in width for both side windows, and for ordering the blinds or shades. On an O.B. mount the workroom does not take a deduction in width. They will note the 2" deduction you took, and compare it to your projection size of the blind or shade ordered.

Cut-Out Blinds or Shades

To order and plan for a blind or shade with cut-outs, follow the guidelines here:

- Draw a diagram and show all measurements for the width and length of the blind or shade.

- Next, draw and show the position of the cut-out area. Exact measurements for placement of the cut-out must be noted, in width and length. Note the exact measurement of the blind or shade above the cut-out area and in width that is left non-affected.

- All measurements noted must add up exactly. The balance area in the width and length added to the cut-out measurements must be exactly what you are measuring in width and length for the blind or shade.

- Do not take any deductions around the cut-out area. Leave this up to the factory. Measure exactly the obstruction and note to the factory that this is the exact measurement of the obstruction.

- For cut-outs over 5" in width that are needed in the center of the blind or shade, verify with the factory that it is possible to do.

Example: a pleated shade needs a cut-out of 3" in width on the left corner of the shade, and 2" in length from the bottom. The overall width of the pleated shade is 48" wide. The length is 36".

On the diagram you would draw in a square showing a width of 48", and a length of 36". Next, you would draw a square removed from the left corner.

Last, you will note on the diagram that the shade width to the right of the cut-out is 45", and the area of the shade left above the cut out is 34".

Striping for Mini Blinds and Mini Woods

If you are using striping for blinds to match graphic stripes on adjacent walls, advise your customer to be sure to wait until the blind is hung, before proceeding with the graphic striping on the wall. It is impossible to get the size and placement of the stripes of the window treatment accurately lined up if you have the graphics done before installing the mini blind or mini wood.

Mini blinds, mini woods and vertical blinds may all be striped. Pleated shades may be made in a double layer that gives a band of another color on the sides of the shade.

Wood Products

Any hard window treatment made out of a wood product is going to have the inherent qualities listed.

- Wood window products are imperfect natural products, each having its own individuality and character. You will not find two window products that will appear exactly the same.

- Paint or stain will appear different in different areas of the wood, causing the color to vary.

- The texture of the wood will vary with the grain in certain areas.

- Wood absorbs, releases moisture, and may warp. Very hot conditions, dry conditions, humid and moist conditions, or very cold conditions will contribute to the possibility that the wood product may warp. Generally, wood products will arrive slightly warped when the order is filled. The slats are thin — and they are naturally warped.

- Wood products for windows may be made only to a certain width before you need to place two-or-more-on-one headrail or butt separate units together. The weight is too great. Your customer will not easily be able to operate the item, and the wall will support only so much weight and pressure when the window treatment item is being operated. Additionally, the wider the wood window product is, the more apparent the warped strips or slats are.

- Wood window covering products are natural, insulating window coverings. The heavier the wood strip, slat or louver, the more insulating the window covering is. Wood window treatments virtually pay for themselves in money saved from heating and cooling costs.

- If you have an extremely particular customer, wood product inherent conditions should be thoroughly discussed and the customer switched to other products if the customer cannot easily accept the limitations.

Roller Window Shades

Roller window shades are a versatile product. They may be used in the full range of decorating styles. They may be obvious and noticeable, or may be concealed, and used for privacy, light control, and insulation behind an overtreatment. Shades may be used to eliminate all light with blackout shades, or to let subdued light through a colored, translucent shade. The color of the shade will be reflected into the room. Window shades range from light filtering to room darkening.

Shades are useful in protecting carpet, furniture, and drapery from fading and deteriorating. Depending on the selected fabric, they will still allow light to come in, or you to see out.

Window shades are more energy efficient than drapery or metal blinds — about 50% more effective. If the exterior temperature is cold, but the sun is out, it is preferable to raise the shades and let the sun's solar heat warm the room.

Shades placed under sheers and drapery are very energy efficient. In winter, shades can reduce heat loss up to 25% — 31% and reduce fuel consumption up to 8%. In the hotter months, shades can reduce heat coming in up to 50% — 54% and reduce air conditioning consumption up to 20% — 21%. The variance on the percentages depends on the fabric opacity used for the shades. Additionally, if the shade is mounted loosely in fit, the energy savings drops 10% — 15%.

Your customer may wish to use an interior fabric and have it laminated to a shade, and coordinate other fabric treatments in the room. Shades may be hand painted with scenes or graphic designs.

Window shades vary in quality and in price. The inexpensive ones will last a very short time, while the more expensive, higher quality ones have rollers that will last forever. Your customer can have the shade fabric replaced again and again, if desired.

Shade rollers are aluminum and consequently will not rust, sag, warp, or distort the fabric mounted on them. High-quality rollers roll straight and evenly. If you order a shade over 84" in width, the manufacturer will mount the shade on a heavy-duty roller. You can see the price jump up radically on the price list to allow for this more expensive roller.

Brackets for shades are usually of zinc. The proper brackets for installation will be provided, according to what type of mount you specify on the P.O. Shades are mounted with screws or molley bolts.

Fabrics for window shades are usually cottons, fiberglass-reinforced vinyls or polyesters, rayon or flax-blended fabrics. Fabrics are finished and stabilized for shade use by application of protective coatings. These coatings help in resisting dirt, preventing fading, wrinkling or curling. As with any fabric product, dyelots for shade fabrics will vary in color.

Printed or lace fabrics are usually fabricated by railroading the fabric. Railroading the fabric makes the length limited — double-check with your manufacturer to determine if the fabric you have selected needs to be railroaded.

Governmental and commercial installations will probably require that the fabric used is flame retardant. Some flame retardant fabrics may be ordered from the manufacturer for an optional charge. See the section under Flameproofing for other applications.

Installation is very inexpensive for basic window shades.

Note: The minimum width window shades can be fabricated in and still be operable is 18". The maximum width is 120".

Window Shade Upkeep

Upkeep for window shades is minimized if the shades are pulled up and down frequently. Pulling them up and down helps to keep dust off. Vacuuming them regularly with soft-brush vacuum attachments and occasionally sponging them off or spot cleaning with suds made from dish soap and warm water will keep them very clean. Advise you customer not to let the fabric soak when cleaning the window shades. When wet, they need to be blotted and towel dried. Allow shade to dry while down, before rolling them up.

Planning Trim or Scalloped Skirts

When planning trim or scalloped bottoms for shades on the skirt or bottom area of the shade, **note** if it is an I.B. mount, the scalloped area will not allow privacy and will not block out light on the bottom scalloped area. Scalloped skirts should be placed on an O.B. mount where you can pull the shade down far enough to cover the whole window.

For I.B. mounts, you may set the trim in a scalloped pattern up from the hem, to give the illusion of a scalloped bottom. **This is called a raised hem.**

An amicable combination that works well is to make the valance in a cut-out scalloped pattern, and copy the same design to the hem in the trim's design. Plan the hem to be straight bottomed with a raised, scalloped design out of the trim. If privacy and light filtering in are not problems, then make the hem's cut-out design match the valance's cut-out design.

Combination Valance and Shade

When planning and ordering a shade that has an attached valance, measure the valance width only. The manufacturer will take the allowance on the shade. They will deduct 1" on each side for a spring-roller type; they will deduct 1½" less on one side for a bead-chain operated system and deduct 1" on the other side.

The minimum width that a valance and shade combination may be ordered in is 20". This combination may be I.B. or O.B. mounted. If O.B. mounted, the return is standard at 2½" but may be ordered with a return up to 5½".

If I.B. mounted, you will need 2½" of recessed area in the window to mount the shade.

Separate Valance and Shade Combinations

The valance and shade may also be ordered separately for window shades. A separately ordered valance will come mounted on a board. Valances are usually 8" in length. If they are to be I.B. mounted, the separate valance will not have returns. If the valance is to be O.B. mounted, specify, return size from 2½" to 5½". The separate valance may be mounted separately or may be mounted with brackets in combination with the undershade.

A separate valance is a good combination when used with a shade mounted for an I.B. undertreatment. The valance is mounted O.B. for the overtreatment. You may want to add panels, tied back over the I.B. treatment, under the separate valance by using a 5½" return for the separate valance. The panels would have a return of 3½". If you attempt a multi-layer shade treatment like this, order and measure each layer separately with the measurements needed for each noted.

The minimum separate valance width is 12"; maximum width is 120". The minimum separate valance return is 2½"; the maximum return width is 5½".

Bead-Chain Operating Systems

Bead-chain operating systems are available to make operation easier for hard-to-reach areas, and for oversized shades 60" — 84" wide. Since the bead chain is handled, rather than the shade's fabric, the shade stays cleaner, much longer.

When measuring and planning for a bead-chain operated shade, allow a 1" allowance on one side of the shade for the bead-chain mechanism. You will also need to allow an additional ½" on the opposite side.

Brackets for bead-chain operations are mounted with the open-slot on the same side as the chain. The round-hole, closed slot goes to the opposite side.

Measuring and Mounting Window Shades

Measure as you would for any I.B. or O.B. window treatment. The manufacturer will take the allowances necessary, according to what you specify for the mount. Shades can be tricky for determining their size, if an I.B. or O.B. mount is not specified.

I.B. mounts:

For an I.B. mount, measure the exact distance between the window at the top, where the brackets will be installed. Note on the workorder that this is an inside-bracket mount, or I.B. The manufacturer will take an allowance of ⅛" off your exact measurements. The shade cloth will be 1" narrower, overall.

Measure the length to be covered and add 12" for the extra shade fabric needed to roll around the roll for the shade to function properly. This extra allowed fabric also prevents the shade from being torn off the roller.

Note: I.B. mounts require a recess area of at least 2" deep.

O.B. mounts:

To measure for an O.B. bracket, measure the exact width across the window where you want the shade fabric to start and end. Note on the workorder that this is an outside-bracket hang or O.B. mount For an O.B.

mount, measure over on to the wall or window trim 1½" — 2", for adequate coverage. **Measure the desired length and add 12" for the extra shade fabric needed to roll around the roll for the shade to function properly.** This extra allowed fabric also prevents the shade from being torn off the roller.

Brackets and rollers without fabric project 2⅝" from the wall. Fabrics vary in weight. The weight and the texture of the fabric selected will determine how much farther the shade will project out from the wall.

Mounting of I.B. and O.B. shades:

The brackets are mounted with the bracket with the open slot to be mounted on the left side. The bracket with the round hole goes on the right side.

To mount shades, always place the round pin in its hole first, and drop the flat pin into place on the opposite side.

Note: For reverse rolls, reverse the bracket positions.

Measuring for replacement window shades:

Measuring for replacement window shades is tricky, at best. The most foolproof way to measure is to remove the old shade from its rollers and measure the roller from tip to tip. Include the metal pins that fit into the brackets. Note on the P.O. that the measurement is tip to tip.

Ordering Information

Unless specified, you will receive a straight-bottom, plain-hem shade without a valance and trim. Decorative pulls are usually no additional charge, but must be selected and requested. The shade company you are ordering from should have examples of the trim styles, colors and decorative pulls available, in addition to a full range of fabric samples for shade fabrics.

Specify on the P.O. if the shade is to be a regular or a reverse roll. A regular roll is when the shade fabric pulls down from the back of the shade's roller. This is the most insulating type of mount for shades.

A reverse roll is when the shade fabric pulls from the front of the shade's roller. This is the best choice when using prints and blockout fabrics or when the fabric looks different on its reverse side. The reverse roll eliminates the back of the shade from showing into the room.

Note: Minimum shade width is 13". Maximum width is usually 121¼" — depending on the fabric selected. Many fabrics are only 96" in width.

Available Shade Options

Options available at no additional charge (usually):
Bead chain operation
Reverse roll
Decorative pulls

Options available for an extra charge:
Decorative trim on straight hem
Hem scallop on skirt, with trim
Decorative valance, with trim
Returns on valance, for O.B. mount
Separate valance, to be mounted O.B. over an I.B. mounted shade
Decorative pulls
Laminated-shade fabrics
Top-down shades
Heavy-duty rollers
Heavy-duty brackets
Flame-retardant fabrics

Laminated Shades

When planning to use laminated shades, furnish fabric at least 2" wider than the planned shade, and 12" longer. If the fabric is narrower than the planned width, the fabric can be pattern matched and widths put together.

Use an opaque room-darkening shade if it becomes necessary to seam the fabric for added width. The seams (and their several layers) will show up readily if the fabric is mounted to a translucent shade, and the light filters through the shade.

A stained-glass effect may be created with a printed fabric applied to a translucent fabric.

Operational Remedies

If the shade loses its tension due to the spring being too loose, check to see if the bracket is rubbing against the end of the roller. Pull the shade down all the way, remove the shade from the brackets and wind up the square, flat end of the barrel (of the roller end), restoring the tension. Now, roll up two turns of shade cloth on the roller and replace the shade in its brackets. Repeat this procedure again until the shade reaches its proper tension and easily rolls up.

If the spring is too tight, roll up the shade all the way. Remove the shade from its brackets and unroll two roller sections of shade fabric. Replace the shade to its brackets and roll back up, again. Repeat this procedure again until the spring regains its proper amount of tension.

Transparent Shades

Transparent shades help insulate from heat and cold, and help keep cooled or heated air inside. Transparent shades do this by forming an insulated, dead-air space, which helps keep the exterior climate from filtering through into the room.

Transparent shades are a versatile product that also helps reduce glare and fading. The daytime use of the shades will block out the sun's ultraviolet rays, which cause permanent fading and deterioration to many interior elements. At the same time, daytime use will give you privacy. Transparent shades are similar to having sunglasses for your windows. They may be pulled up or down, as needed.

Transparent shades roll up like regular window shades. In oversized widths, the shades will have to be seamed, and will require the use of gravity rollers. Transparent shades come in different tints and colors, and different gauges of material with different degrees of energy savings, visibility, fade and glare resistance.

Installation is very inexpensive for transparent shades.

Some of the key reasons to have transparent shades installed are outlined below:
- They help keep carpet from fading.
- To protect all furniture in the path of sun glaring through windows.
- They help preserve all window coverings.
- To help insulate in winter and summer, keeping the rooms more comfortable.
- They can be used under most window treatments.

Types of transparent shades:

- **Shades with one tint or color** are generally one sheet of shade material.

Clear, amber, or bronze Two-way visibility; will reduce heat and air conditioning loss 25% — 28%. Glare is reduced 7% on clear shades and 41% — 45% on the amber and bronze shades. All three shade colors have fade resistance effectiveness of 90% — 95%.

Smoke One-way visibility; will reduce heat and air conditioning loss 44%; glare 65%; and fading 97%.

●●   **Shades with two tints or colors** are generally two-ply and consist of two sheets of shade material adhered to each other.

Bronze/silver   These two types of tinted shades have one-way visibility; reduce heat and air
Silver/Polaroid   conditioning loss 85% — 89%; glare 90% — 94%; and fading 83% — 97%.
Smoke/silver

●●●   **Shades with three tints or colors** are generally three ply and are three sheets of shade material adhered to each other.

Gold/silver/smoke   These combination groups have one-way visibility; higher energy savings;
Smoke/silver/smoke   and higher fade resistance. Combination tints of shades take on different
Bronze/silver/bronze   colors and show the tones listed at various reflections. Heat loss is reduced 72%
                        — 73%; glare is reduced 90% — 96%; and fading is reduced 99%.

Comfort shades   Comfort shades are a very handsome shade that breathes. They actually let the
                        air through and help reduce heat and air-conditioned air loss. Comfort shades are
                        vinyl coated, fiberglass yarns woven into a striped, basketweave type of design.
                        They will soften and diffuse light. During the day, they allow daytime privacy,
                        while allowing outside viewing. At night, the reverse happens, so you need to
                        have a window treatment to draw over them for privacy.
                            Comfort shades will resist fading, tearing, stretching, shrinking, warping,
                        corrosion, rusting, raveling, and are fire resistant. Available colors are generally
                        ivory, fudge, cocoa, or charcoal. Comfort shades will help with energy savings, but
                        not to the degree that other transparent shades are able to.

Measuring for a Transparent Shade

O.B mounts:
To measure for an O.B. mounted transparent shade: The transparent shade should be measured to overlap the window frame or wall 1½" on each side of the window. Add 1½" above and below the window to total 3". Order an O.B. mount on the workorder.

I.B. mounts:
To measure for an I.B. mount: Measure the exact width across the top, middle, and bottom of the window opening and the exact height of the window opening (you have flexibility in the length, as the factory adds the extra amount needed to roll around the roller). Take the smallest measurement of the three width measurements and the length measurement. Order an I.B. mount on the workorder. The factory will take all allowances when you order an I.B. mount.

Tinted Windows

For windows that have extreme sunshine problems, tinted windows are a great solution. They perform like transparent shades, but have a film that is actually *applied* to the window. There are varying degrees of tinting and tones available, from light to dark, depending on the needs for the individual situation.

Tinted windows are not a window treatment, they act only to protect your interior's investments and help cut energy costs. Plan overtreatments to go along with tinted windows, unless your customer enjoys the effect of the plain tinting.

Some of the key reasons to have windows professionally tinted are outlined below. These are the same reasons for installing transparent shades as outlined above. Both selections are wise investments.

●   They help keep carpet from fading.

- To protect all furniture in path of the sun glaring through the window.
- They help preserve all window coverings.
- To insulate in winter and summer, keeping the rooms more comfortable.
- They can be used under all window treatments.

Silhouette®

Silhouette® window shadings are a very elegant, revolutionary type of shading system that combines the best features of curtains, blinds, and shades into one beautiful product. Silhouette® shades have the sheerness and softness of a curtain with the light control of a blind. The soft, woven vanes are suspended between two sheer knit facings. When the vanes are open, the view is a soft filtered image of the outdoors.

Silhouette® shades may be used alone or as an undertreatment with overdrapery, top treatments, or in the place of sheers or other undertreatments. Sheers may still be used as an overtreatment, if desired.

When pulled up or down, Silhouette® shades are extremely tight stacking, like pleated shades, taking only a few inches for a full-length shade. Silhouette® are more expensive than Duette® shades or pleated shades.

- Available in two-inch and three-inch vanes.
- Available in a full pallet of designer colors of anti-static 100% polyester fabric.
- Durable and easy to clean; exceptionally soil and dust resistant.
- One single continuous cord raises and lowers shading and tilts the vanes.
- A narrow headrail mounts inside or outside the window frame.
- The bottom rail is concealed inside headrail when completely raised.
- Hardware is color coordinated and snap-in bracketing allows easy installation on wall, header, or ceiling.
- Allow a minimum stack space of 2¼" when drawn open.
- 96" is the widest width that can be constructed in one piece on one headrail. Any width wider must be fabricated in multiple sections. Because the fabric must be made narrower, there will be a gap of at least ¾" between the shades.

Multi-panel shadings:

- Almost all shadings with ordered width measurements exceeding 73" will be split into two panels of equal width.
- All multi-panel shadings will operate with a single headrail, bottom rail and cord loop.
- Vane alignment may vary slightly.
- Specialty shades will be offered in the future.

Sheer fabrics should be viewed in the setting they are to be used in. The samples need to be held up to the window with the light filtering through them, to get a true perspective on the color. When shades are a tint of a color, the light filtering through the shade takes on the hue of the shade color.

The under fabric or the exterior fabric for Silhouette® shades is off-white for all colors.

Installation charges are very inexpensive, like any basic shade or blind. At this point, available options are limited to an extra long cord at no extra charge.

Dust with a feather duster, low-suction vacuum, or wash in mild detergent. Do not immerse headrail. For more thorough cleaning, professionally clean ultrasonically.

Note: Be very sure of your measurements, as Silhouette® shades cannot be cut down.

Note: If the shade is an I.B. mount, then no extra projection is needed for clearance for the overtreatment. If the shade is O.B. mounted, because of the depth of the headrail, the overtreatment should have a minimum clearance of 6".

Note: I.B. mounts are not recommended because the shade cannot rest on the sill (creating a light and privacy gap of ⅜" to ½"), a slight deduction in width of only 3/16" is taken, the headrail is deep — 2¾" in depth, and the fabric must be made 1" narrower than the headrail width. This creates a gap of ⅝" on the control side and a gap of ⅜" on the alternater side.

Note: Check for window cranks and other obstructions in opening. Ordered height must allow bottom weight to free-hang, for vanes to open and close properly.

Pleated Shades

Pleated shades were invented by a Dutch industrialist and have only been in the United States since the 1970s. As with most products, competitors are making similar products. Pleated shades are an excellent alternative for an undertreatment.

Pleated shades are made of pleated fabric with permanent pleats. Shade fabrics are fairly stiff and are pleated into pleats of ⅜" or ¾". Fabrics for pleated shades range in color from light whites to very dark colors. Fabrics are available in textured looks, sheer weights, opaques, prints and geometrics, lace looks, stripes, etc.

The fabrics available range from very private to very see-through. The see-through fabrics act like a sheer, letting you see out during the daylight hours, while preventing people outside from seeing more than interior shadows inside. At night when the light source is behind the shades, you will be able to see right into the interior from the outside, while from the inside you will not be able to see out, at all.

Pleated-shade fabrics range from light-filtering translucents to room-darkening opaques. The translucent fabrics allow viewing through; with the semi-opaque fabrics, shadows may be seen through the shade from outside; the opaque fabrics allow very good privacy and are light-blocking. The opaque fabrics do not provide complete block-out of light.

Sheer fabrics need to be viewed in the setting they are to be used in, at the window with the light filtering through them, to view the true color. When shades are mounted in a tint or a color, the light filtering in takes on the hue of the shade color.

The lace fabrics may be ordered with a liner of another shade color for a beautiful effect. Review the notes below under *Privacy Alternatives* on using a privacy liner and the negative points about liner fabrics.

Cord locks raise, lower, and lock the pleated shades in the desired position. Cord locks are located at the end of the headrail — taking up space on the headrail. When you have an inside mount, you lose about ⅛" to ¼" of the shade area. This allowance will create light leaks, and possibly not ensure privacy.

Installation charges are very inexpensive, like any basic shade or blind.

Privacy Alternatives

Since privacy is a problem at night for sheer or non-opaque fabrics, one manufacturer has come up with a type of a pleated shade that is actually two pleated shades mounted on the same headrail. Pull the right string, and you get the translucent shade; pull the other string and you get the opaque, private version of the same color. Unfortunately after a few years, the heaviness of having two shades on the same system, has the tendency to make the shades sag.

When determining which shade type your customer should purchase, help them decide on what it is they want — privacy or the ability to look out. If privacy is needed only occasionally, mount a pull-down shade behind the pleated shade.

Also available are the private shades which are able to pleat up with any selected fabric. This system is a permanent, unattached lining that lays against the pleated fabric, in a double layer. These do not work independently of each other, and are really for the customer who has found a fabric they must have — but the fabric only comes in a sheer weight, while they need a private fabric. The manufacturer adds the privacy layer during the fabrication process.

The only problem with the **privacy-layer shades are that they are not very tight stacking, and they have the tendency not to pleat up tightly with one another.** You may get complaints from very discriminating customers with the privacy-lined, pleated shades.

Points to consider when planning a job for pleated shades:

- The minimum width pleated shades can be fabricated in and still be operable is 6". The maximum width is 144".

- Pleated shades are one of the tightest-stacking window treatment products available. A floor-length shade takes only a few inches to stack. They are also light, airy, and cleanable.

- Aluminized shades are second only to Duette® shades (registered by Hunter Douglas) in insulation and energy savings.

- Pleated shades may be used alone, with a top treatment, or as an undertreatment.

- If the shade is an I.B. mount, then no extra projection is needed for clearance for the over-treatment.

- If the shade is O.B. mounted, the overtreatment should have a minimum clearance of 4½".

- Pleated shades for angled windows may be installed at angles of 30 degrees.

- On some fabrics, 24" is as wide as the width may be fabricated without adding overlapped seam areas to the shades, where the next width of shade fabric starts.

- If the length of the pleated shade exceeds 96", the pleats will appear very stretched out in the middle and top areas as opposed to the bottom of the shade.

- If the pleated shade arrives too short, **up to 5% may be added to the length of the shade by loosening the cord in the headrail.**

Insulation Abilities

Pleated shades can be wonderful for insulation, if you select a fabric with an aluminized backing. Unfortunately, these selections are limited within the collections, with the aluminized backing applied only to the most basic fabrics. Whites and pastel colors, unless extremely opaque and papery in feel, cannot be fabricated in an aluminized backing at this point. To do so would turn pastel colors and whites to grayed tones (on the front of the fabric). Deep, rich, medium-toned colors are good combinations with aluminized backings.

Pleated shades with aluminized backing have the backing vacuum bonded to the shade fabric.

Pleated Shade Upkeep and Cleaning

If the shades should get dusty, remove the dust by vacuuming with soft vacuum attachments or a hand-held, battery-operated vacuum. Shades may be easily spot cleaned with suds from dish soap, since the fabric is polyester.

Pleated shades with or without aluminized backings may usually be immersed in soapy water with mild detergent. Pleated shades are very lightweight and easily taken down and put back up.

Skylight Windows

Pleated shades are perfect for track mounting for skylight windows because they are capable of regulating heat and light. Skylights have the tendency to have heat buildup. If the fabric selected for the skylight has an aluminized backing and is translucent, the light is still able to come through but the heat rays are deflected. This allows the room to stay comfortable while still remaining light. Your customer will have to keep a stool handy to climb up and open and close the shade as desired.

When shades are mounted in a tint or a color on a skylight window, the light filtering in takes on a hue of the shade color.

Three-on-One Headrail

For a three-on-one headrail, order all the panels separately or order a two-on-one headrail for one unit, and the third panel separately. The installer will butt the third shade together at the same distance apart; cover the gap area with a bracket so it will appear to be a three-on-one headrail. It is preferable for better fit and cleaning ability to make all of the panels separately.

Duette® Shades

Duette® shades are shades that have two sides to them and form a honeycomb look with their pleats. Duette® shades are registered by Hunter Douglas. They are available in the ⅜" pleat and the ¾" larger pleat. The smaller pleat appears more traditional, the larger pleat more transitional or contemporary, depending on the setting they are used in.

Duette® shades are a very attractive, light-filtering window treatment. They are also the most insulating window treatment on the market. The air pocket formed by the pleats hold airs, similar to the way a double-paned window traps air between its layers. A layer of air is the most insulating way to insulate windows.

Additionally, the shades are sophisticated, soft, easily cleaned, airy, and able to be used alone or as an undertreatment with overdrapery, top treatments, or in the place of sheers or other undertreatments. Sheers may still be used as an overtreatment, if desired.

When pulled up or down, Duette® shades are extremely tight stacking, like pleated shades, taking only a few inches for a full-length shade. For an additional surcharge, Duette® shades are available made into a top-down shade, where the top stacks to-the-bottom, rather than stacking bottom-to-the-top.

Many fabrics styles and colors are available, with more styles and colors coming out all the time. Some of the available patterns and fabrics include prints, geometrics, patterns, sheers, stripes, textured sheers, plain solids, opaque solids. The earliest appearing fabrics for Duette® shades were felted fabrics rather than woven fabrics, and they came in solid colors. These fabrics are still available in the solids and are very basic, and easily combined with other fabrics. Privacy for Duette® shades varies with the fabric selected, from private, with shadows only showing through; to semi-private for sheerer fabrics.

Sheer fabrics need to be viewed in the setting they are to be used in. The samples need to be held up to the window with the light filtering through them, to get a true perspective on the color. When shades are a tint of a color, the light filtering through the shade takes on the hue of the shade color.

The under fabric or the exterior fabric for Duette® shades is off-white for all colors.

While the shade fabrics appear very fragile looking, you can actually wad up an area of shade fabric and it will recover its pleats and hang as if it has not been mishandled.

The fabrics usually carry a warranty for a few years, to cover against fraying, fading, or sagging.

I have seen only one fault so far with the shades: possibility of occasional tearing with **hard use** at stress points, in areas where the two fabrics are fused together.

I would not select this product for use in areas that it will be abused, given hard use, easily dirtied, or where children may handle and pull on the shades.

Duette® shades are spot cleanable — but one manufacturer's representative said that when spot cleaned you may leave a circle or large spot. It would be better to take the whole shade down and immerse the whole shade in soapy (mild soap you use to wash lingerie and fine washables) water and clean the whole shade. Air dry and hang back up, while still damp.

Duette® shades are more expensive than pleated shades. They do have the added advantages of having better insulation, more sophistication, come in a beautiful range of pastel colors, and a wide range of fabrics from very sheer to quite opaque.

Installation charges are very inexpensive, like any basic shade or blind.

See the options list, below, to see what options and specialty windows are available for fabrication of Duette® shades.

Note: If the shade is an I.B. mount, then no extra projection is needed for clearance for the overtreatment.
   If the shade is O.B. mounted, the overtreatment should have a minimum clearance of 4½".

Note: The minimum width Duette® shades can be fabricated in and still be operable is 6". The maximum width is 174".

Insulation Abilities

Both Duette® shades and Vertiglide systems are **significantly** more energy efficient than any other window covering. Their insulative ability is due to the air pocket formed by the pleats, which holds air. Trapped air is the most insulating way to insulate windows. This insulative process is similar to the way a double-paned window traps air between its layers. Over a period of several years, these products will virtually pay for themselves in energy savings.

Duette® Shades for Skylight Windows

Duette® shades mounted in a track for skylights can be operated either manually or by a motor. Duette® shades are a very effective insulation method to use against the natural heat build-up on skylight windows. They may not be as light emitting as pleated shades.

Available Duette® Options

Options available at no additional charge:
Hold-down brackets
Chains substituted for cords
Special cord lengths
Placement of cords together on one side

Options available at an additional charge:

Arched windows	—	maximum width of diameter	—	84"; template required
Quarter arch	—	maximum width of radius	—	42"; template required
Angled window	—	maximum width of headrail	—	84"; template required
Circle windows	—	maximum width of diameter	—	42"; template required
Octagon windows	—	maximum width of diameter	—	30"; template required
Skylight windows	—	maximum widths vary with style; template required	

Greenhouse windows
Top-down shade
Cutouts
2 or more on one headrail

Duette Vertiglides®

Duette Vertiglides® are another product registered by Hunter Douglas, similar to Duette® shades. They are made of the same fabric, but hang off a different system. They have a vertical comb appearance, rather than the horizontal-comb appearance of the Duette® shade.

Duette Vertiglides® are made by railroading (turning the fabric on its side) Duette® shade fabric, mounting track on the top and bottom, and making the unit into a pair, a one-way pull or a center-stacking panel.

Vertiglides®, like Duette® shades, are extremely insulating, soft looking, cleanable, and much more durable than they appear. These are great for sliding glass doors or any expanse of glass that needs insulation at different times of the year.

Vertiglides are very tight stacking when pulled back, taking only a few inches of area to stack. They can be easily stacked-back and hidden under a pulled-back overdrapery or stationary panels, using them as needed.

The Vertiglide® system is available in the narrow ⅜" pleat or the wider ¾" pleat. The pleated fabrics are the same as the Duette®-shade line and come in opaques, textures, prints, and sheer fabrics.

If you plan to use Duette® shades that are horizontal on some windows and use the Vertiglide® system on others, do not combine the two systems if the windows are near each other. They will need to be fairly far apart for this to work. This is because the Duette® shade has horizontal combs, and the Vertiglide® has vertical combs — they do not look good right next to each other.

Vertiglide® systems are a good selection for a window covering if you want a soft, lightweight feel. Top treatments and overdrapery can be easily used over this product.

They may *be easily* taken down, immersed in soapy water and easily cleaned.

The product is engineered for smooth, efficient operation. Magnetic locks hold the shade together when closed. A tension system holds the shade open, when in the open position. Rollers guide the fabric and the side rail/rails. A spring tension control system controls the movement. As with the fabric, the hardware is lightweight yet very durable. The fabric is suspended from the headrail.

The hardware is available in white, grey or bronze. In the future, the hardware will probably more closely match the fabrics in color.

The price of a Vertiglide® system will run about 50% more than a standard Duette® shade will. Included in this extra price is the expensive track for the top and bottom and all the additional hardware needed for this finely engineered window product.

Installation for Vertiglide® systems is more expensive. It will run approximately $40 per sliding door, since the installer is installing track, both top and bottom.

Mini Blinds

Mini blinds are a type of venetian blind that is made up of narrow horizontal slats, usually of aluminum (aluminum will not rust). Mini blinds have ladder supports and color-coordinated cords, headrails, and bottom rails. They may be I.B. mounted or O.B. mounted.

When mini blinds are closed, the surface looks solid, and is able to darken a room. Mini blinds are not completely black-out; some light will enter. When closed, they are excellent for providing privacy (depending on the coverage of the slats of the blinds you are selling).

When opened, the thin lines of the slats in their open position are barely noticed. They are able to diffuse light, glare, and control the amount of sunlight and its damaging rays.

Mini blinds are the most versatile hard window covering available today. Mini blinds may be used in formal, traditional settings as an undertreatment under sheers or drapery, or in a casual, contemporary room with a top treatment to finish them off.

They are also the least expensive hard window treatment and have become extremely common. Mini blinds can completely regulate light, air, or the view. They are an excellent, unobtrusive, almost unnoticed undertreatment if fabricated in a neutral color. The slats may be reverse tilted to let light in, while preventing people from seeing in from the outside. The blinds may be pulled up off the window and take a small amount of room to stack. They may be repaired, restrung — with only the damaged portion requiring replacement, instead of replacing the whole blind.

Mini blinds do have two negative points — they are dust catchers, and in comparison to other undertreatments available, not very insulating.

They are much more insulating when used in combination with another window treatment such as an overdrapery. Mount a pull-down shade behind an I.B. mounted mini blind to pull down during the winter to help insulate the windows, if you feel the need is necessary.

Mini blinds still have a bad reputation with some die-hard customers — they are the customers who had venetian blinds in their homes, suffered through the cleaning and the restringing when the tapes wore out. Mini blinds are much more refined today, less bulky, and have really caught on with most people.

Mini blinds came out in the 1960s, slowly caught on, and became widely accepted. Although mini blinds have become quite common, they are an exceptional undertreatment to open and close for privacy that will not detract from the overtreatment. What other undertreatment has the versatility that mini blinds have?

Mini blinds come in very narrow slats — micro minis; our industry standard, 1" slats; and wider 2" slats. The 2" slats emulate 2" wide, wood blinds, wide, shutter louvers, or our past venetian blinds.

Depending on the width of the slat, the gauge of metal may vary. If you are showing the micro mini blinds to your customer, be sure the customer really wants to spend more money for a micro mini blind than they would for a good-quality mini blind. They will end up getting thinner and less durable slats (with many more slats). There will be less distance between each slat, when the blind is opened.

Some manufacturers have come up with privacy blinds that interlock slats over each other, lock extra slats over the overlaping slats, or slats that overlap in the opposite direction to prevent anyone from seeing in. These types all use twice as many slats as a standard mini blind and are consequently about twice the price. Privacy blinds are very fine-quality mini blinds and use top-of-the-line materials for fabrication.

Mini blinds come in the full range of colors, textures, special effects, finishes, etc., that is imaginable. Ladders and cords are color matched and invisible. Nicer quality blinds feature polyester ladder cords. End caps are composed of non-marren plastic.

Unless your customer wants to use the blind alone with a top treatment over the top to finish off the blind, it is usually best to stick to the off-white colors. Any future owner of the home will *(easily)* be able to live with an off-white blind.

Duotone colors are available in a limited selection of colors. Duotone blinds have alabaster white, or another off-white shade on the exterior side, and the color of your choice (within their selection of duotone shades) on the interior side of the room. The colors available are limited. If the duotone blind is slightly tilted a bit too far, or if you are sitting down and looking up near the blind, you will see the white exterior color in the interior. Overall, duotone blinds are wonderful if you want an off-white color on the exterior and want a colored blind in the interior.

Most homeowners' associations today will not consider any color other than off-white to be visible on the exterior of the home. If the rule is violated, the offender is fined and made to replace the offending items with white or off-white items.

If the customer cannot afford to do anything else at the time you are in the home but buy mini blinds and really does not know what they want to do in the future; if you sell that customer blinds in an unusual color, that customer in the future will probably only add a top treatment over the odd-colored mini blinds. They will be unable to use sheers, because the blind's color will show through the sheers. If you sell a neutral shade, the customer will have many more options available as to what they may add over the top of the blinds in the future. They will be able to add at least an extra layer of sheers, and probably stationary panels or drapery if you stick with the neutral shades and work with the customer on future purchases.

Colors come and go, in and out of fashion. White and off-white blinds a customer cannot go wrong with — especially if the blinds are fabricated in lasting, quality materials.

Installation of mini blinds is very inexpensive.

Note: When mounted O.B., mini blinds require 2" clearance between the blind's headrail and the overtreatment.

Note: Blinds **under** 10½" in width will either be able to pull up or tilt, not both. If the blinds are 10½" — 18", controls must be on opposite sides. On 1" sized blinds, the maximum width is 140". On ½" sized blinds, the maximum width is 102".

Mini blinds aid in prevention of mildew growth:
Position mini blinds on windows where the window is closed most of the time, and where there is a tendency toward mildew growth. The addition of mini blinds will help hold moisture off window sills, and help prevent mildew from growing.

Mini Blind Quality

With mini blinds as with most anything else — you get what you pay for. Mini blinds vary widely in quality and slat coverage. Good quality mini blinds will hold up to much abuse. Their steel gauge is higher, which allows the blind slat when bent to bounce back to its original shape. Mini blinds vary in gauges of metals from thin to thick; the headrail components from plastic to metal; the bottom rail's heaviness and stability; and the overall construction.

Inexpensive brands of mini blinds use less slats — giving you less overlapment, cutting down privacy abilities. They use lesser quality, easily bent metal slats (that do not bounce back); plastic components in the headrail instead of metal; inferior parts and components overall. Even the quality of the cord holding the blinds together is inferior. Some lower quality mini blinds virtually fall apart on the window with minimum use. Instruct a customer who is price comparing your higher quality brand against lower quality blinds to thoroughly examine and *operate the blinds roughly* to see if they can really take abuse, before buying. Have the customer compare the guarantee and ask specific questions about the coverage of the warranty.

Unless the house is up for sale and the disadvantages of the inferior quality have been clearly pointed out — do not sell a low-quality mini blind to your customer. You will generate many complaint calls.

In their cheapest quality, least expensive form, mini blinds are made of vinyl. Wider vinyl blinds may not survive the installation. Their headrail's have the tendency to snap in two — due to their weight and width.

Mini Blind Cleaning

Mini blinds may be cleaned on the window with a damp cloth with suds made from dishsoap. They may also be dusted with glass cleaner or furniture polish. Additionally, a feather duster or a duster made for mini blinds may be used.

There are many companies that professionally clean blinds on site or elsewhere for a modest fee.

Mini blinds are easily removed from their brackets for easy cleaning in the bathtub or outside by the do-it-yourselfer. Instruct your customers to dangle the mini blind over a clothes line and hose them off. This cleaning technique will work if the dirt is not a greasy film, that needs to be soaked or scrubbed off. Advise your customer to remove the end-caps on the bottom rail, allowing the water to escape, rather than stay in the bottom rail and erode and rust the metal on the inside.

Available Options for Mini blinds

Options available at no additional charge:
Hold-down brackets
Extension brackets
Special wand or cord lengths
Tilt controls instead of wand controls
Controls grouped on either side

Options available at additional charges:
Specialty colors, or duotone colors
Valance strips — may not be an optional charge
Two or more on one headrail
Striping
Cutouts

All mini blind types listed below require a template;
Angled
Circle shaped
Octagon
skylights — slanted or horizontal
slant top
Inverted triangle

Decorator options for mini blinds:
Mini blinds may be painted, or have fabric or wallpaper applied to their surface. Splattered or wavy designs may be added to their surface or unique design effects created, such as marbling or faux finishes.

Mini Wood Blinds

Mini woods are a very functional and versatile undertreatment, like mini blinds. Mini woods allow you regulate the amount of light allowed to come in, control amount of privacy, and allow you to oversee the amount of view desired. Like mini blinds, mini woods may also have their slats tilted in reverse, to let light and air in, and preventing someone to view in from the outside. When closed, mini woods are room darkening, but not black out. Some light will enter. They are excellent for privacy control.

The slats and headrail are made of wood and vary in width from 1" to 2" in width. Mini woods are very handsome, and have a very warm effect. The woods are stained or painted in various shades from white to very dark. Colors such as red, greens, blues, and yellows are also available.

Basswood, birch wood, ramin wood, and other hard woods are the woods generally used. Slats are usually stained twice, buffed, stained, painted or acrylic lacquered (acrylic lacquer contains ultraviolet light inhibitors to resist fading and other elements) and sealed. Mini woods usually have wooden valances, bottom rails, wands or batons, and are stained or finished to match the wood slats. Plastic wands may be substituted for strength for blinds on windows wider than 48".

Mini woods are very easy to care for. They simply need to be dusted with a soft cloth and furniture polish or vacuumed with a soft brush. Do not use water or abrasive cleaners on wood products.

On widths that exceed 72" in width — some manufacturers list 52" in width—it is advisable to break the blinds up into sections for two or more on one headrail, due to the weight of the slats. If you break the blind into sections (on the same headrail), as opposed to butting the separate blinds together and covering with one valance strip over all the blinds, there will be an added surcharge to pass on to the customer. **It is usually preferable for a good fit and easy cleaning to break up the blinds into separate units.**

Some of the slats may waver in their straightness as they are made up in wood. This is a characteristic of wood. Review the *Wood Product* section. You will get complaints and have to replace some slats to please some customers.

Ladders and cords are color matched and invisible. Installation of mini wood blinds is very inexpensive.

To preserve wood blind finishes:

For added protection for regular blind finishes on southern and western exposures, be sure to advise your customer to wax the back of the blind with paste wax, periodically. Waxing the blind protects the finish from blistering heat that may shine on them regularly, and prevents the finish from peeling off after a few years.

Natural variations in grain and porosity of the wood will cause color and color-intensity variations within the slats, headrail, bottom rail, and batons.

Stack space:

To determine amount of stack space wood blinds will take up, use this formula: 1 foot of length takes 2" of stack space, plus the headrail and bottom rails.

Note: The minimum width wood blinds can be fabricated in and still be operable is 12". The maximum width is 102".

Insulation Abilities

Mini wood blinds, like shutters, are very insulating. They are exceptional, natural-insulating window coverings. The heavier the wood slats, the more insulating the mini wood is. Mini wood blinds essentially pay for themselves in energy savings. During summer and winter they work to prevent heat, cooling and energy loss through windows and sliding doors.

Available Options for Mini Wood Blinds

Available options, normally at no additional charge:
1" or 2" blinds are generally the same price

Hold-down brackets
Extension brackets
Special wand or cord lengths
Tilt control instead of wand control on either side
Grouped controls

Options available for an additional charge:
Two or more on one headrail
Cut-outs
Mitered returns
Cotton 1" tape for 2" blinds
Color matching
Striping
Angled blinds
A-frame blinds

Shutters

Shutters are permanent window coverings. They should last the life of the house, if professionally installed. They never really wear out. They also help raise the value of a home that they are installed in.

Light control with shutters varies with the type purchased. If a horizontal or slat is the style of the shutter, light can be readily controlled with opening and closing the slats. When the slats are closed, shutters provide excellent privacy.

Shutters are excellent for insulation against heat, cold, loss of heated air or air-conditioned air. See the section below on *Insulation Abilities* for a more in-depth view of how insulating they really are. Shutters virtually pay for themselves from heat and cooling bill savings.

Shutters are probably the easiest window treatment to maintain and clean that there is. Just wipe them off, occasionally. The wider the shutter slat, the easier to dust.

Shutters are the most expensive base treatment that a customer can buy. Shutter prices vary with the type of wood used, the finish selected, the size of the window, the style and options added, and the extra installation charges for remeasures, and any extra options.

Shutters may be fabricated in many different styles and effects. Generally, shutters are made up in the traditional 1¼" horizontal slat width, or the plantation 2½" or 3½" horizontal slat width. Shutters also may be made up into 4½" and 5½" slat widths for a *"Palm Springs" look.* The width of the slat selected depends on the look you are trying to achieve — traditional, transitional, or contemporary; and the amount of light you want to come through the slats when they are opened. See the section below under *Additional Styles and Available Options* for an overview of other options that are available for styling.

The woods available vary from the least expensive sugar pine, a soft wood and not as durable as other selections, to cedar, which is still a softwood, but a bit more durable and prestigious than pine; basswood, a harder softwood; alderwood, a hardwood; to oak, the most expensive and most obvious, grained wood available for shutters. Basically, the usual adage applies here: *"you get what you are willing to pay for."*

If your customer is set on having an open-grained wood for staining, but unwilling to pay the price of oak, cedar would be the next best choice to oak. Sandblasting and rough-wood finishes may also be applied to whatever selection of wood you are using.

Shutters are for the customer who wants maximum durability at affordable prices. While the initial cost of the shutters may be higher then other hard window treatments, their durability, lasting good looks, and insulative abilities will make up for the initial higher cost in the long run.

Shutters tend to have the longest delivery of any window treatment item. Remeasures take time, fabricating and finishing the shutter takes a lot of time, and getting the job scheduled for installation all take weeks and weeks. Depending on the manufacturer you use, you may have a start to finish time of six to eight weeks or twelve to sixteen weeks. When you have to tell the customer twelve weeks or more for delivery, you clearly turn them off from buying the item from you.

In the future, expect to see further innovative ideas for shutter designs. Expected innovations include textured finishes, laser-carved louvers and panels, embossing, hand-sawn louvers, tooled, grooved, laminated types, wood frames with molded plastic or die-cut louvers. These are just some of the future ideas for this popular window covering.

Windows With Odd Proportions

Shutters are an ideal alternative to use for odd-proportioned windows. If the same color shutter finish is used as the wall color, you are able to mask or camouflage the window's poor proportions and end up with a very elegant window treatment. Windows placed high up on a wall that are used with draped windows in the same room look excellent combined with shutters. This would be one of the rare times where keeping window treatments consistent within the same space may vary. Certainly, a shutter the same color as the wall, placed high up on the wall, would look superior to a very short drapery, oddly placed, higher and shorter in length than other drapery in the same room.

When planning a shutter job, keep in proportion panel-width sizes of the various windows within the space or room and their varying proportions. Find a close common denominator, proportionately, for all windows in the same space. Work it out by dividing various amounts of panels into the window width measurement on all varying windows to determine the closest match you can, for panel-width sizes.

When varying the panel sizes slightly from one window to the next, it is possible to make the outside panels of the shutter unit slightly wider, about ½", than the inside panels on the same unit. You will not notice the slight difference. With track installations, this is frequently done to allow the panels to stack properly.

Example: You are planning a shutter job for a 96" wide window and a 35" wide window in the same room. Take the 96" wide window and divide by 6 (panels). This equals 16" width for each panel. Divide the 35" window by 2 (panels) = 17½" wide each panel. These two measurements will be close enough — your eye is not going to notice that the 96" window has each panel 1½" narrower.

Shutters Need to be Remeasured

Shutters need to be remeasured, as mismeasurement of a shutter is a very expensive mistake to make. They are one of the most difficult window treatment to **exactly** measure and get to fit properly. Measurements must be exact. Perfectly square windows are rare and hard to find today. A good installer plans the shutter to compensate for unsquare windows, and has the ability and knowledge to camouflage the gaps that unsquare windows will have.

If the shutters are planned to be an I.B. mount, the window must be perfectly square or fit perfectly, or the shutters will not properly function.

Shutters cannot be reworked to make them slightly wider or slightly longer. They can only very carefully, be shortened or made narrower. Shortening a shutter or making a shutter narrower, changes the position of the divider rail, and the shutter may only be reworked if the shutter is the only one in the room. If there are other shutters in the same space that have the same panel proportions, you may not be able to rework it at all, as to do so will make that window stand out and appear different in proportion and placement of the divider rail.

General Shutter Pricing

The general price listed in the price list of shutters covers:

- Hanging strips, hardware, trim for top and bottom of the shutter, hinges, knobs, and the shutter panels fabricated in the wood that the manufacturer uses to fabricate shutters.

- Shutters are standard in semi-gloss paint or stains, selected from choice of color of the samples provided by the manufacturer.

- Joints are glued and doweled.

- Antique brass or bright brass hardware.

- Frame stock of 1⅛" or 1⅜".

- Louver sizes are 1¼", 2½", 3½", 4½", or 5½".

Note: The manufacturer will take allowances by taking ⅜" off in width and ¼" in height.

Louver Sizes:

Horizontal shutters now come in sizes from 1¼" wide up to 5½" wide. The narrower louvers are a traditional Early American style. The wide louvers are a very contemporary *"Palm Springs" look.* The 2½" or 3½" size louvers are a good, medium size. The narrower or wider the louver is, the wider or narrower the distance is between each louver to view out and to let light in.

Standard installations:

Standard installation charges cover a normal installation of the above listed items. **Remeasures of shutters are an additional charge** (and considered mandatory). Any optional item selected or needed, as listed at the end of this *Shutter* section, are also an optional installation charge.

Shutter installer:

You need an installer capable of doing an exceptional job of installing shutters. Otherwise, you will suffer with complaint calls from unhappy customers.

If the installer needs to bring a tall ladder, make a note on the workorder for both the installation and remeasure.

Shutter Terminology

Bottom rail	The bottom, plain portion of the shutter's frame. Varies from 2" to 6⅝" in width. May be wider for an extra charge.
Double-hung	Two separate units of shutters, placed one above the other on a window. The two units are independent of each other, and each unit may be open and closed separately, or the individual panels may be tilted individually.
Fixed	Non-movable slats on shutters. Normally found on cafe doors and closet doors.
Hanging strip	Band of wood applied to the window edge or trim that the shutter is hinged to and hangs off.
Louver	Slats that usually tilt on a shutter. They may also be fixed slats.
Stile	Frame width.
Tilt rod	Bar that enables the louvers to move back and forth, open and closed. The tilt rod is at right angles to the slats, fastened to one slat.
Top rail	The top, plain portion of the shutter's frame. Varies from 2" to 6⅝" in width. May be wider for an extra charge.
Trim	Mitered wood frame applied around the shutter (like a picture frame), mounted on the wall or molding; may be on all four sides, on the top and sides only, or may only be on the sides of the shutter — depending on the style of the window; or if you are striving to retain visibility of any wood trim surrounding the window.

Stop strip   A strip of wood that matches the shutter. The stop strip is usually about ½" by ½", and the same length as the shutter; screwed to the window sill; to keep the shutter from going back to far and hitting the window, when closed. The stop strip is visible from the exterior of the window, and only visible from the interior when the shutter is folded back.

Insulation Abilities

Wood shutters have insulation abilities equal to a brick 8⅓" wide or concrete 21" thick.

Climates and conditions that shutters will be installed in do vary, and the properties for shutters will deviate with them. In general, homes lose about 50% — 60% of their heat through uncovered windows in the average home, with average insulation.

The high initial cost of shutters will be *completely* recovered in insulation savings on heating and cooling bills, in two to three years.

Paint, Stain, and Wood Grain

When color matching or selecting the color for the shutters from the shutter sample, remember that there are not two pieces of wood that will take the stain the same way. Additionally, the wood grain will only be an approximate match to the sample.

Compare the wood grain of the shutter sample, if the shutters are going to be stained rather than painted and decide if it goes well with other wood elements within the same room. Hold the sample up to the wood paneling, wood furniture, wood floors, wood frames, etc. Consider if the shutters are to be stained a wood tone, if they are going to appear heavier than anything else within the room.

In climates that are sun intensive, recommend to your customers to give the shutters, both front and back (back especially), a good coating of paste wax on painted or stained shutters, to preserve the paint and finish from peeling off in a few years. Have the customer periodically reapply the paste wax to the back to ensure long-lasting, good looks.

Double-Hung Shutters

Shutters can be easily double-hung on older homes with double-hung windows. This is an ideal situation to use double-hung shutters, because of the horizontal strip of wood dividing the double-hung windows in half horizontally. In newer homes, without a horizontal strip of wood dividing the window, double-hung shutters may sag after a period of time. Since there is not a wood strip across the middle of the window, sunlight streams, in through the gap of the double-hung window. Light streaming in a gap is always accentuated and will appear about five times wider than it really is.

Double-hung shutters will sag in the middle, if the shutter's width from the center exceeds its height from the hinges more than two or three inches.

To remedy this situation (very common on rectangular windows where the window is wider than it is long, or on rectangular shaped windows with sliding windows at each end, with a fixed section in the center), divide the unit into two or three sections, conforming with the size and style of the window.

Have the shutters fabricated into separate shutter units, as you would if you were working with separate windows. Have the installer add wooden vertical posts to the interior of the window area at the various points you have decided, or at the window, mullion sections so the individual shutter units may be hinged to and hang off of these posts. Join adjacent windows with wider connecting strips to give the appearance of one large window. Windows can also be connected with corner posts to give a nicely finished appearance. Discuss and plan this situation with the installer.

An alternative remedy follows in the next section of *Appearance of a Double-Hung Shutter with a Full-Length Panel*.

Note: Price double-hung shutters as two separate units, not as one large window. Most price lists have a double-hung column for corresponding sizes.

Note: Orders must specify distance in inches, from the bottom of the shutter to the cut-line or division point of the two separate units.

Appearance of a Double-Hung Shutter with a Full-Length Panel

You may achieve the appearance of a double-hung shutter by the placement of a divider rail midway up the shutter panels. A divider rail is the plain, wood portion of a shutter, which may be placed anywhere on a shutter, from ¼ of the way up or down from the top or bottom, to 3¾ of the way up-or-down from the top-or-bottom.

The divider rail divides the moveable or fixed portions of the louvers from the top or bottom portions of the panels. Dividing a shutter with a divider rail allows only part of the shutter to be opened or closed for light, air, or viewing out. Depending on the look you are trying to achieve, some shutters may not have a divider rail at all. This is almost always true in the case of short windows.

Additional Notes on Full-Length Panels

Full-length, paneled shutters, made of narrow louvers under 42" in length, or wide-louver, paneled shutters, under 75" in length, will not require a divider rail on full-length panels. You may choose to use a divider rail if desired, but may be charged extra if you do.

For full-length panels with narrow louvers over 42" in length, or wide louver panels over 75" in length, a divider rail is recommended. List on purchase order distance from bottom of shutter to center area of divider rail.

Shutters for Sliding Doors

Shutters for wide-width areas such as sliding doors will need to have overhead track folding one way. You may need to box-out or project out the shutter frame for the sliding door, because of the sliding door's protruding handle.

Louvers project behind shutter frames when tilted open. If there is not enough clearance for louver movement, shutters must be installed on special hanging strips to provide proper clearance.

Additional Information

- Units of shutters folding to one side that are wider than they are longer usually require a track to support and guide the panels. Common uses are sliding doors and pass-through areas.

- All shutters with an even number of panels will open from the center, unless otherwise specified on the purchase order and workorder.

- For a 1¼" wide louver, 18" is the recommended width. 3¾" is the standard frame width and depth.

- For vertical louvered shutters, the maximum louver length is 25". This would be a 30" panel height without a divider rail.

- For bottom tracks, cutting into floor coverings is not required; the sliding guides attach to panels.

- For I.B. mounted shutters, the hanging strips may be mounted I.B. when this type of installation is requested. The shutter is usually hung off of aluminum hanging strips, or wood hanging strips. A flat surface of ⅞" is required to hang the hanging strips.

- Double-hung installations are not recommended for track installations.

Additional Styles and Available Options for Shutters

Different ways to treat shutters:

Fabric inserts; other types of inserts	May consist of gathered fabric inserts in the panels, etched, beveled or stain-glass panels, caning inserts, metal-mesh inserts, woven-wood inserts, plastic which has a glass appearance, or fret designs inserted before or after installation; vertical-louvered panels (which will not collect much dust).
Horizontal louvers	Slats come in sizes from very narrow to very wide.
Fixed louvers	
Non-movable louvers/slats	Usually found on cafe doors, closet doors
Solid panels	Usually beveled-wood inserts, raised on whole panels or in sections of panels.
Slope, curved, arch-tops	For the top of the shutter; template needed.
Contour types	Template needed.
Slant-tops	Template needed.
Sliding doors	
Cafe doors	
Folding doors	
Dividers	
Sunburst styles	

Other options for shutters and shutter installations: (Options include manufacturers surcharges.)

Special cut-outs
Custom paint, color matching, high gloss or flat finishes
Sandblasted finishes
Special mortise to relocate hinge in different area
Laminations to make rails larger for cut-outs
T-handles available to replace cranks on windows
Magnetic catches to hold shutters straight. Some included with each order — one for each two panels.
Special wood strips to be used as light stops behind shutters; or to hold shutter away from the bottom of the window, or other window obstruction.
Track installations — fittings, track, header, fascia, and necessary trim needed to complete the job.
Sliding-door hardware — track, rollers, and bottom glides for 1⅜" panels.
Box-out frames and "L" frames — needed when shutter needs to project from the exterior of the wall due to protrusions, cranks, louvered windows, etc.
Curved, hanging strips
Packaging for shipping

Installer, extra charges:

Working off of a ladder for high installations
Remeasures
Installer distance charges
Installation of special hardware
Box-out installations
Track installations
Installation of specialty window options
Template charges
Two or more installers needed for an installation **Example:** when the bottom of the window is 8' or more off the floor.

Measuring for Shutters

Window type:

Metal sash; no trim, or sill trim	Measure window, opening size — width and length. Finished shutter unit will consist of 3¾" x 1¼" hanging strips on all four sides. Overall width will increase 3⅜" in width and 3⅜" in length.

Metal sash; without trim but with sill	Measure window, opening size — width and length from top of sill to top of window edge. Finished shutter unit will consist of hanging strips on both sides and no trim at sill, trim of 1¾" at top. Overall width will increase 3⅜" in width and 1¾" in length.
Wood-sash window; with trim on three sides with sill	Measure from outside edge of trim to other outside edge of trim; top of trim to bottom of trim. Finished shutter unit will consist of standard hanging strips at sides only, which will be mounted on top of trim of window. Unit will be the same size as trim areas included in the window size.
Wood-sash window; with trim on four sides	Measure as listed in wood-sash window, above. For length measurement, measure top of trim edge to bottom of trim edge. Finished shutter unit will consist of hanging strips on sides of shutter only, which will be mounted on top of the trim of the window. Length will be the same as the length from top of the trim to bottom of the trim area.

Note: For all windows listed above, when measuring, make sure there is ⅜" clearance behind the width of louver you are planning to use, when opened.

Woven Woods

Woven woods are a versatile selection for a window covering or an undertreatment. If you or your customer like a woven wood full of colorful yarns with a very patterned texture or design, this is best used by itself as a total window covering without adding any additional treatment to the window. This type of woven wood provides excellent privacy and light control when closed. More openly woven types are going to provide less privacy and light control.

Woven woods that are more natural in color and design, with strings as the woven material, are more plain and easy to combine with other treatments on the same windows. The trend today is for an all-over, same color, plainer effect; or a combination weave of two-colored yarns or strings. These can be very elegant if woven in sophisticated colors.

Woven woods are a heavier window treatment (depending on the weight of the wood, and the amount of yarn used), and if you live in a harsh climate, may be the right choice for you.

There are a variety of styles available for woven woods: Roman styles, spring-roller styles, duo-fold styles, all types of drapery systems, cafe curtain styles, etc. See the options list below.

Woven woods may be hung as an I.B. mount or an O.B. mount.

Woven-wood shades are usually used by themselves on a window, unless fabricated in a plain, unvalanced style. Over an unvalanced style, you can give them a finished look by adding a decorative top treatment or valance, possibly in a solid color or in a complementary pattern; or by using the unvalanced, style woven wood in combination with a cantonniere.

Woven woods are raised and lowered by a pull cord on the right or left side of the shade. The position up or down desired is held by a cord lock with a die-cast locking roller that will not fray or damage the cord.

If you use an overtreatment over the woven wood and the woven wood is I.B. mounted, you do not need a projection of more than 3⅓" for the overtreatments. If you have an O.B. mounted woven wood, you will need a projection of 5½" to 6½" to clear the headrail for the regular, valanced Roman types; or 5½" to clear the unvalanced types of woven woods. If you are using a cornice over an I.B. mounted woven wood, you need to use a return on the cornice of 4½". Installation of woven woods is very inexpensive.

Note: Woven-wood shade styles and valances are made with their wood slats woven **horizontally**. All woven-wood drapery styles and cornices are woven with their wood slats, **vertically**. You will not want to combine these two different types of treatments in the same room, for good design.

Note: The minimum width woven woods can be fabricated in and still be operable depends on the vendor. The maximum width is 144".

Insulation Abilities

Air pockets formed with the yarns and woven strips of wood, along with wood being a great window insulator, work together to make woven woods a natural for effective insulation against heat and cold.

Depending on the closeness of the weave, the insulation ability will vary. The tightest weaves have an R-value of 1.71. If this same woven wood was used in combination with an energy liner — fabricated with the woven wood, at time of the order — the R-value would go up as high as 5.5.

Cleaning and Maintenance

Woven woods traditionally have been used in the kitchen. This is not the preferred application for them, as greasy dirt is their enemy. Woven woods collect and absorb greasy dirt and dust. Use them in areas that will not be exposed to grease, such as in the family room, recreational room, study, library, and possibly the bathroom (excess moisture is not good for them, either).

For regular maintenance, vacuum them monthly to prevent dust buildup.

If the woven woods are greasy, use foam on upholstery cleaner, or apply mild dish soap or laundry suds with a sponge and rinse with lukewarm water. Do not soak either the woods or the yarns. Never soak the trim. Towel dry. If they are in a greasy setting, this process will need to be applied to them regularly.

With regular upkeep and care, and average exposure to sunlight, woven woods will last about five years.

Quality Construction

Woven-wood shades are constructed of ramin-wood reeds, Lauan mahogany, or poplar slats. The wood is left natural, painted, or stained. Yarns for weaving are made of both natural and synthetic fibers. They are spun, twisted, and made in various weights to achieve specific results and looks. The yarns are dyed under pressure so they will hold their dye colors. Stable yarns, rather than stretchable yarns, are selected for use.

Quality points to look for in selection of woven woods:
- Kiln-dried wood that will retain its shape.
- Straight grain within slats, evenly cut.
- Finish coat, applied to the slats.
- Use of synthetic yarns resistant to fading, moisture, and soil.

Woven Wood Negative Points

Tendency to absorb grease and dirt:
Woven woods are a rather expensive product, and because of their ability to absorb dirt and grease, have fallen out of favor. While expensive, they are *not a very* durable product.

Fading:
The room side of the woven woods will retain its colors; while the exterior side exposed to western or southern exposures *(especially)* will fade, rapidly. Southern and western exposures also contribute to the

yarn's deteriorating and the strings coming loose from the hooks on the back, which raise and lower the shades. Yarns at the edges of the shades, if not glued in place, easily start to unravel after minimum use.

Woven woods are not tight stacking; in fact, they take a maximum amount of space to stack.

To allow light in on tightly woven, private, woven woods you must pull the shade up. If the woven wood is not tightly woven, light will come in at all times, and may not be private.

Ideal Situation for Use

Woven wood's ideal use is on windows not exposed to greasy, dusty dirt; windows with northern or eastern exposure (unless otherwise protected with patio covers or awnings); and on windows where the woven wood will not be handled frequently. Woven woods look exceptional when used under cantonnieres for a tailored effect.

Woven woods are expensive and fragile. You will want to protect your investment and get as much life and years out of them as possible. While they can be very rich and textured in effect, they are not very durable, and do not have the ability to last in a hard-use area.

Woven Wood Available Styles

Woven woods come in various styles. The listing below gives you the styles available:

- With decorative self-valances, attached or fabricated separately.

- In plain unvalanced styles, with a wood strip or trim to finish them off, with scalloped or straight skirts.

- With trim scalloped and cut out in a pattern on the valance or skirt.

- In straight-bottomed skirts; with the trim raised up and scalloped in a design on the skirt.

Plain, unvalanced styles with wood trim:
Plain, unvalanced styled woven woods are a simple look for a plain, tailored effect when used alone. They may also be used in combination with a top treatment and/or stationary panels. This style is finished off at the top with a strip of wood in a selection of stains.

This is the most reasonable style available for woven woods; a simple style that is usually the nicest looking and most workable.

Regular Roman styles:
On regular woven woods, the valance, which is a 6" flap of the same woven wood material, covers the headrail, cord mechanism and all hardware. End flaps are available for O.B. mounts.

When pulled up, the woven wood falls into folds, stacked against each other.

Cord and pulley shades:
This system rolls up from the bottom. Cord locks hold the shade in the desired position on the window. When this type of shade is rolled up, the reverse (possibly faded from being exposed to the exterior) side of the woven wood shows into the room. A 6" valance flap is standard, to cover the headrail and hardware. Cords from rolling up the shade are very visible on the face of the system.

Duo-fold systems:
This system may be used as either a top-down or a regular Roman-up shade. Included are separate cord locks for either operation. A 6" valance covers the headrail and hardware. This is an excellent solution for windows that you want to cover the bottom area rather than the top, for privacy and light problems.

Spring-roller shades:

This system of woven woods is like a spring-roller shade that pulls down or up. They are mounted on a spring roller. This style is not recommended for sizes that exceed 72" x 72" or for patterned woods with very wide slats. This style is preferably used in combination with a separately mounted woven-wood valance to match, or a decorative top treatment to use over the top of it. Allow plenty of room for the large, rolled-up woven wood in its up position, under the separately mounted valance or top treatment.

If you use the regular-roll system, the reverse of the woven wood will show into the room (it may be faded). Select the reverse roll for long-term good looks.

Separate valances or cornices:

Woven-wood separate valances or cornices are available for use in a variety of situations. Valances are made loose with lose returns at the sides (same as shades with valance and lose returns). The fabric is woven in the same direction as the shades are — horizontal. They may be scalloped and trimmed.

Cornices are made like a cornice with returns mounted (attached to the sides) on a board. They have a 5½" drop and may be scalloped and trimmed. If you are opting to order a cornice to be used with another woven-wood treatment underneath or nearby, check to see that the woven-wood pattern is going to be made in the *same direction* as the undertreatment. They are usually railroaded.

Vinyl Linings

Some companies have available vinyl linings which are sprayed on to the back, exterior surface of the woven wood to give a coating that will increase privacy on very open patterns. This sprayed-on coating provides privacy while allowing light to still filter through.

This is not recommended for railroaded or vertical goods. This lining may become brittle or discolored with age and should not be used where the woods are mounted in recessed areas against thermopane glass.

Energy Liners

A separate lining may be applied to the back of the shade during the fabrication process. This energy liner will triple the R-value of the shade insulation ability. The energy liner will protect the back of the shade from the sun's damaging ultraviolet rays and keep the back of the shade from fading. This is an option that will go a long way in protecting your customer's investment. Unfortunately, light is blocked completely and you will not be able to see out between the slats.

Woven-Wood Drapery

Woven woods are available in systems like drapery. The woven-wood fabric is railroaded so the slats hang vertically and hang off a track or rod. They hang in folds that traverse open and closed. They are available in sharp or soft folds.

Woven-wood drapery systems may hang off a track system especially made for this system; off of a decorative rod with pins; or a regular rod, with pins. If you opt for the decorative or regular rod with pins, the woven-wood drapery will lean toward the wall at the bottom, and also require more stacking space.

Woven-wood drapery are usually used as an overtreatment. If the drapery is to be hung over an I.B. mounted window treatment, no extra clearance is needed for the O.B. mounted drapery system. If you are going to use the woven-wood drapery over an undertreatment such as sheers or another woven-wood product, the woven-wood drapery will need a minimum projection of 8".

If you add a woven-wood cornice or other top treatment over the top of the woven-wood drapery, you would need a projection of 12" for the cornice or top treatment.

Stain-Repellant Finishes

This option is available for woods that are to be used in greasy, dirty environments. This finish is applied to both sides of the woods and seals yarn fibers against soil penetration. Cannot be used with woven woods with applied sprayed-on vinyl linings.

Available Options for Woven Woods

Options available at additional charges:

Valance
Skirt
Scalloped designs for valance or skirt
Trim added to valance or skirt
Additional rows of trim
Tassels
Side caps — returns, added for an O.B. projection of 1½" or more.
Cords — right or left or grouped (not an additional charge).
Spring-roller system
Canopy styles
Cord and pulley systems
Separate valance — not attached to a woven-wood body, loose returns at sides.
Cornices — 5½" drop, mounted on a cornice box, with returns attached, is available with vertical weaving to go with drapery styles. Can have fabricated with a scalloped bottom.
Duo-fold shades — shade will pull up or down. Has two sets of cords to achieve this.
Angled-top shade — will open only to lowest point, must include template.
Arch-top — top will remain stationary, must include template.
Two or more on one headrail
Mitered windows — for corner situations, bay windows.
Baseboard cut-outs — for shades or drapery systems. Need to provide a template.
Vinyl lining
Energy liner
Flameproofing — must be applied by a licensed company to meet codes. Flameproofing cannot be used with vinyl lined woods or stain repellant finishes.
Stain-repellant finishes

Additional options for woven-wood drapery systems:

Sharp or soft pleats
Room dividers — these are hung from the top of the door frame or ceiling. Floor track is not needed. These may be pairs or one way. Made like a drapery system with vertical, railroaded material.
Cafe curtains — Pleated at the factory — 50% fullness is added. Order returns if desired, at no additional charge. Included in the cafe package are oval clip-on rings.
Panel track — Comes with batons for use in drawing flat panels open and closed;
systems   hung off a track that stacks one panel behind the other. May be O.B. mounted or I.B. mounted or hung from the ceiling. Use with the woven-wood cornice to finish off this treatment.
Folding doors

Note: Any of the more complex systems such as skylights, slant-tops, or arch-tops should be remeasured and have templates made, where noted.

Vertical Blinds

Vertical blinds consist of a headrail and vertically hanging vanes which overlap each other slightly — about ¼". These vanes are uniformly spaced. The headrail is similar to a drapery rod, because you pull a cord to traverse them back and forth. They may open from the center, one-way right, or a one-way left. The vanes, slats, or louvers can be rotated all together, 180 degrees. Some verticals have 360 degree rotation to diffuse the sun and control indirect lighting. When the slats are open or closed, they may be traversed to the sides.

The slats, vanes, or louvers are controlled by a chain that pivots a gear or pinion rod, which is the rod which runs the length of the headrail. A group of gears in each vane carrier intertwines with the pinion rod. Pivoting of the rod causes all the vanes to pivot at once. Vanes are hooked into the carriers individually, through the hole in the top of each vane or slat.

Vertical blinds are very flexible and can provide as much light as may be desired within a room. They may be fully opened, letting in maximum light, or closed — shutting out almost all light. By positioning the vanes, sunlight may be diverted, yet still let in some light and still allow you to view out the window. Light-filtering fabrics when the vanes are closed, allow light to filter through. Depending on the fabric selected and the opaqueness or sheerness of the fabric or material, the amount of light filtering through the slats will vary.

Privacy will vary with the slat material selected. Privacy is excellent for aluminum, vinyls, and inserted slats. Medium to minimum privacy is to be expected with open weave and light-emitting fabric slats.

Vertical blinds come in a large variety of fabrics and materials: vinyls, aluminums, soft, free-hang fabrics, and inserts.

Vertical slats, vanes, and louvers are all synonymous with each other in their meaning. They are the vertical strips of material that make up the vertical blind. They rotate and slide back and forth across the window. Vinyl holders are like slats, vanes, or louvers, except that they have fabric or wallpaper inserted into their holder. Once inserted, they are considered a slat, vane, or louver.

Inserts are fabrics inserted into a rigid P.V.C. vinyl holder — usually with clear edges and a white or off-white exterior color, to keep them stable and long lasting. Wallpapers or interior fabrics may be used for inserts if your customer is not finding the exact fabric they would like in your collections. Fabrics or wallpaper may also be replaced later at the whim of the customer. Most materials are not stiff enough by themselves to be inserted and must be applied to a stiffening backing before insertion. Self-adhesive cardboard is a good choice. The peel-off cardboard comes in 3½" widths made for this purpose, and may be directly applied to the fabric or wallpaper.

Aluminum vanes may also have fabrics or paper applied to them. The material is cut slightly larger than the size of the vanes; the material and the vane is sprayed with contact-cement adhesive and applied together.

Free-hang vertical louvers have weighted hems and have an optional chain available, to hook into the bottom of the louvers to hold them together. The optional chain helps hold the slats together, instead of them being whipped across the room, knocking items off the table due to a strong breeze coming in through the window.

Free-hang verticals are about 25% — 30% less expensive than inserted louvers, and a more attractive vertical style (personal opinion). They have weights to hold them taut and keep them from curling. The hooks and weights are sealed into the hem and the headers of the vertical vanes.

Inserted louvers are more expensive and have a longer life span. The older inserted louvers, and probably some still on the market, tended to yellow with age and sun exposure.

Verticals are an excellent product to use with stationary panels (they accent and cover the exposed sides of the verticals) and top treatments of all types. Cantonnieres are also an interesting treatment to combine with vertical blinds. If verticals are to be layered, they usually end up on the bottom, as the undertreatment.

Notes: I.B. mounted verticals do not require their overtreatments to need additional clearance. Treatments mounted O.B. over verticals need a clearance of 4½" to 6" to clear the vanes, and allow the verticals to be rotated.

If using verticals with a cornice top treatment, the cornice should have a 6" to 9" return, depending on the return of the vertical underneath.

Verticals Are Not for Everybody

In many cases, vertical blinds will not be able to be planned to be private enough or light eliminating enough for certain customers with particular window situations. The slats barely overlap — in most cases as little as ¼" on each side. Windows with little metal interior trim, where your customer insists the verticals must be I.B. mounted, will gap at the sides, causing sunshine to leak in and their privacy to be questionable. I.B. mounts in many cases will appear to be to short, due to the style of the vanes and the sunlight accentuating the gap between the bottom of the vanes and the window sill.

Many customers, especially older people who have always had drapery and tend to have traditional furnishings, will not be able to get used to the differences verticals have from drapery, and will not ever really like them. Their son or daughter has them and loves them; their parents may *think* they want them. After they get the verticals installed, they will not be happy with them; and will put you in the uncomfortable position of having to explain and reinforce to them, *"I explained the vertical's limitations, you made the final decision to go ahead with selecting verticals. We are not able to replace a whole room full of verticals with drapery for you and be able to resell the verticals to someone else. The possibility of someone else wanting that exact color and fabric in those exact measurements is not realistically going to happen."* You, of course, do not want to lose the future business of this customer. These situations must be handled carefully and delicately.

Fully explain and discuss vertical blinds' limitations and positive points with every customer before they go ahead and decide to purchase vertical blinds. Make sure that this is the correct product for each customer and their individual situation. Rarely will an older customer who has had nice custom drapery before, end up liking vertical blinds as much as nicely hanging drapery. Drapery have returns, insulation, and many fabrics hang beautifully.

Verticals barely overlap on the slats, have light leaks, lack privacy in many cases, may be cold and commercial in feeling, may yellow and curl due to sunlight, and may be noisy if made of P.V.C. or metal.

On the other hand, **verticals are loved by many people young and old.** It really depends on the customer's personality, the look they are trying to achieve, and furnishings that they want to use with the verticals. **They are light, airy, take a minimum of space to stack, and are a "today" window product.** Inserts allow a wide selection of fabrics or wallpapers to be used. Many people like a contemporary feel, and verticals fit right in.

Additional Points to Consider About Vertical Blinds

Points to consider when planning a job with vertical blinds:
- The minimum width that a vertical **pair** can be, and still be able to traverse is 24".

- The minimum width that a vertical **panel** can be, and still traverse is 15".

- **An individual vertical unit may not be wider than 188⅛".**

- **Inserts or vinyl slats may not be longer than 144".**

- Butt two or more vertical units together and achieve the appearance of one vertical.

- Provide **exact measurements for the width and length.** The factory will take the allowances.

- The **measurement in width at the top is the only *width* measurement** for a vertical that needs to be taken — this is where the inflexible headrail sits. The slats are moveable and flexible and sit in from the sides of the headrail.

- When **reordering for the louvers or slats only, provide the exact length needed for the slats.** Note on the workorder *"exact length needed, do not take an allowance."*

- Verticals can be made into **one-way pull reverse or opposite-stack** to provide for the controls to be placed on the opposite side of the normal stack area. You must specify this in the workorder and check for the additional charge from the price list of the manufacturer. **When you do a reverse stack, the cord is visible at all times.**

- **Verticals are fairly tight stacking.** Depending on the manufacturer, some brands (due to the headrail quality) are tighter stacking than others. Stack space needed is generally 1⅜" stack space per foot in width of the vertical blind.

- A typical higher quality vertical blind system has over 150 moving parts.

- **Intense sunshine against hot glass will warp the inserts or any other vinyl P.V.C. slat, causing them to curl.** Slat manufacturers are working hard to correct this problem. Do not sell P.V.C. slats on unprotected windows in sunny climates with southern or western exposures.

- **Some of the clear vanes or louvers used for inserts will yellow from the sun and from time.** Other companies have found the answer to correct this problem — their product is said to hold up, remaining clear and unyellowed.

- **Plastic parts will also yellow with exposure to sunlight and age.**

- **Many fabrics and wallpapers may be inserted in louvers.** Use lighter weight fabrics. The inserts may be changed as the customer wants to change their interior.

- **I.B. mounted verticals**; more than any other window treatment when made to the correct specifications, **many times appear too short.** If vanes are made longer to alleviate this problem, some slats will drag in an unsquare window.

- **Vertical lengths may be lowered up to 1" for all types of vanes** — *if there is any type of a valance used with the vertical blind.* Specific hooks are designed to give *too short* slats an extra 1" in length and remain hidden, under a valance.

- When measuring widths for vertical blinds, **the first slat on each side of the headrail will be 1" narrower in width and coverage than the headrail on each side.** Therefore, if you order an extension of the window of 6" on each side, the area covered by the slats on each side of the window is 5".

- **Since vertical blinds do not have returns on the sides and project out from the wall, measure over 6" on each side for privacy needs and light leaks.**
  To ensure complete privacy and prevent light leaks almost completely, **the only way to plan the vertical blind is from wall to wall, floor to ceiling.**

- **Metal, vertical slats are known for their clankiness** whenever a slight breeze causes any movement to the slats. They are also famous for their **cold, commercial feel.**

- When planning a vertical blind for a sliding door with a southern or western exposure, if the room is carpeted, the carpet will fade all along the exposed strip of carpet (the strip between the verticals and the door) against the sliding door. If the verticals are left open during hot, sunny days, a much larger portion of the carpet will be faded — and probably other furnishings damaged, as well. *Strongly suggest,* if this area must be carpeted to have tinted film applied to the window for protection against the sunlight.

- Vertical blinds' life span are affected by: vertical blind quality; if the slats are free-hang or inserted (free-hang slats have a shorter life); amount of harsh sunlight.

- Many of the materials available, P.V.C., some fabrics, and aluminum, are fire retardant or flameproofed. **Check with your manufacturer on the materials available, in the line that you carry.**

- Order an extra slat for each window that you are selling vertical blinds for. Have the customer nail a nail in the back of a closet and slip the vertical slat over the nail and hang it up. This will keep the slat in a vertical, straight position, available if any slats should become damaged.

- Store sets of uninstalled vinyl louvers flat in their original box until they are installed, to prevent them from warping.

Insulation Abilities of Vertical Blinds

Insulation varies with the type of material or fabric selected for the vertical blind. If an inserted slat is selected, the inserted slat can eliminate 75% of the air-conditioned, air loss in the summer and up to 50% of the heated air loss in winter.

P.V.C. slats and some of the free-hang slats provide less insulation ability than unlined drapery.

Care of Vertical Blinds

Because vertical blinds hang vertically, they do not get very dusty or dirty. Most vertical blinds' material surfaces are easy to spot clean. The areas on the vanes where the verticals are handled, will get very dirty. Instruct your customer to **have all family members handle the chain and cord only.** Follow the guidelines below for regular maintenance and upkeep:

- Vacuum regularly with soft vacuum attachments or a hand-held vacuum.

- For fabric verticals that are made up of washable fibers, clean with a damp cloth and mild detergent suds. Do not soak the fabric. Towel dry the wet areas. Leave the slats in their vertical position to dry.

- Foam on upholstery cleaner is an alternate cleaning method for fabric vanes or fabric inserts.

- For wallpaper inserts, follow the direction on the wallpaper for cleaning. Most are scrubbable.

- For macrames, use a feather duster to clean. Be sure that macrame types of vanes are not handled and are mounted in areas where they will stay reasonably clean.

Available Vertical Options

Options available for an additional charge:

Chains with clips,	For use with free-hang fabrics
Chains w/keyhole punch	For use with aluminums, vinyls, inserts
Reverse stacking	
Single stack valance	One strip of the self-fabric.
Double-stack valance	The use of two strips of different colors of the same fabric.
Accent strips of fabric	Using a different color in some vertical vanes or in the valance strip.
Heavy-duty track	
Bottom track and hardware	
Cut down slats in length	
Cut down track	
Cut-outs	
Angle blinds	Must specify, angle blind on the workorder.
Angle cuts	Made by the workroom. The installer may be able to cut inserts and vinyls right on the job.
Bay window blinds	Check with your vendor. These are now able to be hinged in sections for bay windows.

Measuring and planning for an outside mounted vertical:

Use the following guidelines outlined below when planning a vertical for an O.B. mount.

- **The headrail should be placed a minimum of 4" above the window to conceal hardware from the outside of the home or building.**

- Headrail placement in width should be equal distance on both side of the window.

- Minimum wall extension should be 4" on each side. Preferably, **the extension should be 6" on each side to ensure privacy and eliminate light leaks.** Vertical blinds do not have returns on the sides and project out from the wall; this extension amount is needed to do the job properly.

    To ensure complete privacy and prevent light leaks as much as possible, the only way to plan the vertical blind is from wall to wall, floor to ceiling.

- Decide if the vertical is to be a pair or a one-way pull.

- **When floor-to-ceiling styles are planned, measure the length in several places in the overall width.** If the width is wide, measure 5 length areas at various intervals. Use the shortest measurement and deduct 1".

- For sill length measurements, plan the vertical to go below the sill a minimum of 3".

- **The valance width must be 1" wider than the headrail for an O.B. mount.** The workroom automatically makes this allowance for an O.B. mount.

Measuring and planning for an inside mounted vertical:

Inside mounted verticals are to be avoided as much as possible. Windows are rarely square, and when you need to take the smallest measurements in width and length, you end up with light leaks, questionable privacy, and vanes that appear too short. The vane style and light coming in accentuate the gap between the bottom of the slats and the window sill. If the slats are made longer, some of the slats will drag if the window is unsquare.

Explain to your customer the reasons it is best to O.B. mount the vertical blind. Discuss the reasons you hesitate to do an I.B. mount, and let the customer make the determination to go ahead, though they now realize the limitations of an I.B. mount.

Record on the sales slip that the customer has opted for an I.B. mount over an O.B. mount. In discussing the situation and letting the customer determine the correct course of action to take for them, you are vastly cutting down the complaints on I.B. mounted vertical blinds. Since you have already spelled out on the sales slip that it was their decision, that customer is going to hesitate to call you with a complaint, and probably decide to go ahead and live with their decision.

Note: If an I.B. vertical's vanes are fabricated short or appear too short, vertical vane lengths may be lowered and made longer at increments of ½", 3¾", and 1" for all types of vanes — if there is any type of a valance used with the vertical blind. Specific hooks are designed to give too-short slats this extra length and remain hidden — under a valance.

Use these additional guidelines outlined below, when planning a vertical for an I.B. mount:

- Be sure that the **window frame is deep enough to allow the vanes to pivot.** 3½" slat verticals have a projection of 3½" and require 4½" of space to pivot. 2" slats have a 2" projection and require 3" of space to pivot.

- **Measure the width across the top** (where the I.B. mounted headrail will sit) **exactly.** When you order an I.B. mount, the factory will take the allowance.

- **Measure the length in three places.** Write the shortest of the three length measurements on the workorder. Again the factory will take the allowance for the length.

- Decide if the vertical is to be **a pair or a one-way pull.**

Measuring and Planning for an Angled Blind

Angled windows look very professionally done in angled, vertical blinds. The degree of the angle will determine whether the blind will traverse and rotate normally; whether the blind will rotate only; or whether the blind will only sit there in a fixed position.

To eliminate problems, do not use free-hang fabrics. Select P.V.C, aluminum or inserted vanes, because they can be custom-cut for a good tight fit on the job site, by the installer.

A vertical valance, a sleeve valance, or other top treatments are very nice additions for finishing off angled windows.

Follow the guidelines below for measuring an angled blind:

- Measure across the window at exactly the top corner, opposite from the where the angle starts aiming up at the top of the window. Keep the tape level all the way across. You are giving the angled window an even-leveled, horizontal plane across the window from the shallowest top corner, across.

- Take a pencil and lightly mark the wall on the angled side of the window, where the tape horizontally ended up when you evenly held it up.

- Measure from the pencil mark up to the top corner of the angled window. **This measurement will determine whether the angled blind is going to completely work, only rotate, or stay in a fixed position.**

  - If the **measurement** up to the corner is **6" or under**, the vertical **will both traverse and rotate.**
  - If the **measurement is 6" to 9"**, the vertical blind is **will only rotate.** You will not be able to traverse it.

  - If the measurement is **9" or more**, the vertical may be mounted, but only in a **fixed, non-moveable state.** Your customer will be able to hand twist the slats to vary the light or privacy, occasionally.

- Determine the I.B. measurement, and both the short and long points for the length for the vertical manufacturer.

- Decide if the treatment is to be a pair or a panel, and which side/sides for the operating controls.

- Select the valance or other top treatment.

- **Record on the workorder that you are ordering an angled blind.**

Measuring and Planning for a Bay Window

To measure and plan a vertical blind for a bay window, you would follow the guidelines pointed out in the beginning of this section for *Measuring and Planning Blinds or Shades for a Bay Window* if the manufacturer that supplied you did not have the vertical headrails that are now available for hinged verticals for O.B. mounts. Hinged vertical blinds have the appearance of a split-draw, with control placement for either side available.

If you have to go the traditional method of planning a vertical blind in three separate pieces for a bay window, deduct the amount of projection that the vertical has for the vane width (the size vane you are working with) from the side window's width measurement, instead of the 2" deduction that you take for shades or blinds.

If your manufacturer has available the hinged headrails for vertical blinds, follow the guidelines outlined here for planning and measuring:

- Measure the bay window as it lays out on the wall area, exactly (place the tape directly against the wall, and measure each angle). Draw a diagram of exact measurements.

- Measure the back window width. Measure out from the wall 3½", corner to corner.

- Measure the side windows 3½" out from the wall from the corner of the center window's measurement, out to the desired wall extension measurement.

- Note the new set of measurements on the workorder for the factory. They will check your perceived measurements against the actual wall measurements and catch the errors before they make up the verticals. It is preferable to have a remeasure.

- Specify *"butting blinds,"* and how many are butting on the workorder.

Alternate or Hard Window Information Chart

Roller Window Shades

Minimum width	18"
Maximum width	120"
Headrail depth	1¾" — 2"
Minimum I.B. depth	1½"
Minimum O.B. amount above window	1½" above the window frame
Minimum extension on sides of window	1" on each side
I.B. length when measuring	Take the longest measurement, plus 1 foot.
Privacy	Ranges from semi-private with translucent fabrics, to completely darkening.
Light Control	Ranges from light filtering to room darkening, depending on the selected fabric. Some light will still enter.

Metal Blinds

Minimum width	10½" O.B.; 11" I.B.
Maximum width	140"
Slat size	½", 1", 2"
Headrail depth	1½"
Minimum I.B. depth	1½"
Minimum O.B. amount above window	1½" above the window frame
Minimum extension on sides of window	1" on each side
I.B. length when measuring	Take the longest measurement
Maximum blinds on headrail	4 blinds
Striped blinds	Yes
Bay windows	Yes
Skylight or incline windows	Yes
Arched windows	Yes
Available for cut-outs	Yes
Other options	Other shapes of windows available
Privacy	Very private
Light control	Flexible. When slats are tilted open, light is not restricted. Tilted, amount of light can be controlled and diverted. Closed, fairly room darkening. Some light will still enter.

Mini Woods

Minimum width	12" O.B. or I.B.
Maximum width	102"
Slat size	1" or 2"
Headrail depth	1½"
Minimum I.B. depth	1½"
Minimum O.B. amount above window	1½" above the window frame
Minimum extension on sides of window	1" on each side
I.B. length when measuring	Take the longest measurement
Maximum blinds on headrail	3 blinds
Striped blinds	Yes
Bay windows	Yes
Skylight or incline windows	N/A
Arched windows	N/A
Available for cut-outs	Yes
Privacy	Very private
Light control	Flexible. When slats are tilted open, light is not restricted. Tilted, amount of light can be controlled and diverted. Closed, fairly room darkening. Some light will still enter.

Duette® Shades

Minimum width	6"
Maximum width	174"
Pleat size	⅜", ¾"
Headrail depth	1¼"
Minimum I.B. depth	1¼"
Minimum O.B. amount above window	1½" above the window frame
Minimum extension on sides of window	1" on each side
I.B. length when measuring	Take the longest measurement
Maximum blinds on headrail	2 shades
Bay windows	Yes
Skylight or incline windows	Yes
Arched windows	Yes
Available for cut-outs	Yes
Privacy	Very private with solid fabrics; shadows will show. Semi-private with sheer fabrics.
Light control	Light filtering.

Silhouette®

Minimum width	12"
Maximum width, single fabric panel	73"
Maximum width, multiple fabric panels	96". There will be a gap between the two shades.
Minimum height	12"
Maximum height	96"
I.B. widths	Not recommended because the large headrail size and the small 3/16" deduction on the headrail. The fabric is 1" narrower than the headrail — ⅝" on the control side, ⅜" on the other side creates privacy and light gaps.
Vane size	2", 3"
Stack space	Minimum stack of 2¼" when opened
Headrail depth	2¾"
Minimum I.B. depth for flush mounts	2⅞"
Minimum rear fabric clearance	⅛"

Minimum O.B. surface above window	¾"
Recommended extension - sides of window	3" on each side
I.B. length when measuring	Take the shortest measurement. The bottom must not touch the sill. The vanes must hang free. There will be a gap of ⅜ to ½ at the bottom of the window.
Speciality windows	Not available at this time
Available for cut-outs	Not available
Options	Long cord loops available
Insulation	Good with lined or honeycomb constructed fabrics
Privacy	Some degree of privacy. Duette Eclipse® is recommended for room darkening.
Light control	Some degree of light control. Lined or honeycomb constructed fabrics give better light control.

Pleated Shades

Minimum width	6"
Maximum width	144"
Pleat size	½", 1"
Headrail depth	1¼"
Minimum I.B. depth	1¼"
Minimum O.B. amount above window	1½" above the window frame
Minimum extension on sides of window	1" on each side
I.B. length when measuring	Take the longest measurement
Maximum blinds on headrail	2 shades
Striped blinds	Yes, striped banding on sides only.
Bay windows	Yes
Skylight or incline windows	Yes
Arched windows	Yes
Available for cut-outs	Yes
Privacy	Translucent fabrics, see-through. Semi-opaque fabrics, shadows show through. Opaque fabrics, fairly good privacy. No fabrics will provide complete block-out of light.
Light control	Ranges from light-filtering to room darkening, depending on fabric selected.

Woven Woods

Minimum width	Depends on the manufacturer I.B.
Maximum width	144"
Slat size	¼", ½", 1"
Headrail depth	1" for valanced styles, ½" for wood trim styles.
Minimum I.B. depth	1¾" for valanced styles, 1" for wood trim styles.
Minimum O.B. amount above window	3" above the window frame
Minimum extension on sides of window	1" on each side
I.B. length when measuring	Take the shortest measurement
Maximum blinds on headrail	4 blinds
Bay windows	Yes
Arched windows	Yes
Available for cut-outs	Yes
Privacy	Very private depending on the tightness of the weave of the woven wood.
Light control	Ranges with the woven-wood fabric selected. Tilted, amount of light can be controlled and diverted.

Closed, fairly room darkening. Some light will still enter.

Shutters

Minimum width	Varies with the size of the slat and the manufacturer.
Maximum width	If made in separate units with posts, may be made as wide as needed.
Slat size	1¼", 2½", 3½", 4½", 5½"
Headrail depth	Varies with the size of the slat
Minimum I.B. depth	N/A; most shutters are not I.B. mounted
Minimum O.B. amount above window	Usually made to the I.B. length size of the window and any trim is mounted above the window.
Minimum extension on sides of window	Usually made to the I.B. width size of the window and any trim is mounted on the sides of the window.
I.B. length when measuring	Take the exact measurement
Bay windows	Yes
Skylight or incline windows	Yes
Arched windows	Yes
Available for cut-outs	Yes
Other options	Other shapes of windows available
Privacy	Very private with slats, insert privacy will vary
Light control	Flexible. When slats are tilted open, light is not restricted. Tilted, amount of light can be controlled and diverted. Closed, fairly room darkening.

Vertical Blinds

Minimum width	24" for a pair, 15" for a panel
Maximum width	188¼"
Slat size	2", 3½"
Headrail depth	3½"
Minimum I.B. depth	3" for the 2" slats; 4½" for the 3½" slats
Minimum O.B. amount above window	1" to 3" above the window frame
Minimum extension on sides of window	5" on each side; 6" is better
I.B. length when measuring	Take the shortest measurement
Striped blinds	Yes
Bay windows	Yes
Skylight or incline windows	Yes, for incline windows; must be a track on the bottom for skylight windows.
Arched windows	N/A
Available for cut-outs	Yes
Other options	Angled top windows are available
Privacy	Very private in vinyls, metals, or groover inserts. Minimal to medium privacy from other fabrics.
Light control	Flexible. When slats are tilted open, light is not restricted. Tilted, amount of light can be controlled and diverted. Closed, fairly room darkening or light filtering, depending on the fabric.

Part 8

Custom Bedspreads, Fabric Accessories, Slipcovers, and Reupholstery

Bedrooms

When decorating bedrooms, you will work with many different personalities and types of people. They may be young children, boys, girls, teenagers, middle aged or older people. As a designer or decorator, you need to express the personality of the occupants of the bedroom, while creating a comfortable environment to retreat to and relax in.

Your customers should allow their personality to flow freely in this room. The room should be comfortable, warm, casual, and very relaxing. A bedroom may also be a library, gathering place, or a place to escape to. When considering the best use of an interior space, consider the size, the shape, and the location of the bedroom.

The use of companion prints for bedspreads and drapery is a very comfortable and easy way to coordinate fabrics in a bedroom. For other ways to combine print fabrics, see the section on *Combining Print Fabrics*.

Here is a list of bedspread terminology, as applied to various types of bedspreads and bedroom accessories:

Terminology

Bedcap   Quilted or unquilted, fitted cover that covers mattress and box springs.

Bedsack   Quilted or unquilted, fitted cover that covers mattress only, similar to the bedcap.

Bedspread   Decorative bed covering that reaches almost to the floor.

Bell corners   Bottom-corner sections of a bedspread found at the foot of the bed that are cut and shaped on a radius.

Bonded polyester   Polyester filler placed between the self-fabric and the liner fabric of bedspreads and other quilted objects to add body, and to achieve a quilted effect.

Corded mattress edge   Cording applied in the seams, which sits at the top of the mattress edges between the drops and the top of the bedspread.

Coverlet   A bedspread with a short drop, finished a few inches below the mattress, used with a dust ruffle.

Drop   The measurement and section of the bedspread from the top of the mattress down to the desired length.

Dust ruffle   Fabric skirt made to fit over the box springs and made to drop almost to the floor on three sides. Covers the bed frame and prevents you from seeing under the bed.

Duvet cover	Unquilted slipcover to cover (usually) down comforters, to keep the comforter clean. Easily removed for cleaning or laundering.
Fill	The interior-bonded polyester (usually) placed between the self-fabric and the lining fabric on quilted items. Fill adds body and enables quilting of the item.
Fitted bedspread	A type of bedspread that fits snugly against three sides of the bed. Has straight, vertical, tailored sides and flat corners which conform to the bed shape. Corners may be split, or split with a gusset.
French sham	Same as a reverse sham, except the sham is attached only at the top edge, across the mattress end, not at the sides of the bottom edge.
Gusset	A section of fabric placed and sewn behind split corners of a bedspread to cover the split area and the corner of the bed.
Kick pleat	Tucked corner, used at corners of coverlets at the foot of the bed. Also called an inverted pleat.
Pillow shams	Covers that go over pillows, which are generally quilted. May be ruffled at the edges, pleated, or flanged in styling.
Quilting patterns	Various standard, custom and outline styles of designs available for quilting.
Reverse sham	A portion of fabric that generally is attached to the top of a bedspread. Reverse shams are placed in reverse of the body of the bedspread that it is attached to, and folds back over the pillow area of the bedspread. The loose end of the reverse sham ends up at the base of the pillow area. The sides are sewn to each other, and form a pocket to slip the pillow into.
Sham	The length of the bedspread that tucks under the front of the pillow, lays over the top of the pillow area, and tucks down behind the bed.
Split corners	Edges of a bedspread that are split and finished at vertical corners, at the foot of the bed. Corners may be split because a tailored effect is desired; the bed has a foot board, which requires the corners being split; or the customer is afraid of tripping over bell corners.
Throw style bedspread	A bedspread made into a single panel of flat fabric, lined, quilted, or plain; may have bell corners. Completely covers the mattress, box-springs and drops nearly to the floor.
Welting	Fabric-covered cord, sewn into the seams and edges of bedspreads and upholstery. Size may be ¼", ½", 1", and may be used single, doubled, or tripled.

Appropriate Fabrics

Most fabrics may be used to make bedspreads, but the durability and the fiber content of the selected fabric should be considered. Some satin fabrics will be ruined when one drop of water hits them.

Certain styles of bedspreads are better suited to certain types of fabrics than others. Flounced styles fabricate and look better in lightweight fabrics; the throw styles and fitted styles fabricate and look better in medium to heavier fabrics with some body. If your customer decides that they want a particular fabric that is lightweight for a throw type bedspread, then line the bedspread. Quilting is also an answer to this problem. If you line the bedspread with another self-fabric rather than lining fabric, the bedspread will become reversible. All custom bedspreads should be dry-cleaned only.

Steps to planning a bedspread:

- **Select the fabric desired** for the bedspread.

- **Choose the quilting style** (if any). Choose between standard styles or outline quilting patterns supplied by your bedspread fabricator.

- **Select the style** of the bedspread design.

- Choose **any coordinating fabrics** for dust ruffles, linings, ruffles, cordings.

Note: Satin fabrics are not recommended for use as trims and cording. When fabrics are selected to be combined together in a bedspread or other treatment, select fabrics that are similar in fiber content, for cleaning purposes and general overall effect.

Fill and Quilting

Bedspread fill usually comes 6-ounce; 8-ounce (many workrooms use 8-ounce as their standard weight, so specify if you want a lighter weight); and 12-ounce comforter-weight fill.

Bedspreads fabricated with 8-ounce fill and put on the bed generally seem too short. You will probably get a call from the customer on this issue. If you delay doing anything about it for 2 — 3 weeks, and insist that the customer go ahead and *use* the bedspread, **the loft of the quilting will flatten out and the bedspread will *grow* to the originally ordered size.** The loft of the quilting on 8-ounce fill or 12-ounce fill will really puff-up during the quilting process and will stay that way, until the bedspread is spread out and used for a few weeks.

Many bedspreads *get remade* with lighter-weight fill after the customer complains about the heaviness of their new bedspread.

Always discuss with your customer how heavy or lightweight they would like the bedspread to be. Many customers, especially older people, do not want to be lifting a heavy bedspread daily. Select a fill of 6-ounces to get a semi-lofty appearing, lightweight bedspread for *this* customer.

Heavier fill on throw bedspreads also causes the bell corners at the foot of the bed to flare out. Older people and children may trip over the bell corners flaring out, and may suffer serious injuries. It is safer and preferable for some customers to sell them fitted bedspreads with gussets to take care of these problems. Discuss these possibilities with your customers and suggest having the bedspread fabricated with split corners and tongues. This makes a well-fitting bedspread, and an easy bedspread for the customer to fold back at night and make up in the morning.

There are presently several methods of quilting a bedspread. Quilting is achieved by computerized machines, lockstitch quilting machines, and by feeding the fabrics and filling through a machine by hand.

Outline quilting methods:

Lockstitched   The fabric, fill, and lining fabric are pre-seamed together and the design is stitched with a *type* of sewing machine. The design is either stamped on the fabric, or the design of the top, self-fabric is outlined before being stitched freehanded. Lockstitching is used with this application. This is the most common outline stitching application.

Bonaz   Same type of application as above, with the lockstitch machine. A special Bonaz embroidery machine is used for the stitching process. This machine makes a decorative crochet or cable stitch with the thread, that becomes part of the design of the bedspread.

Machine quilting patterns and methods:

Computerized machines

Computer programmed machines are very expensive and very few workrooms have them. Computerized machines use preprogrammed designs. Quilted designs are not quilted free-hand as an outline-quilted design is. Outline-quilted designs also may be programmed in for individual fabrics, but the labor expenses in programming the design into the machine is prohibitive. The use of preprogrammed designs for quilting achieves a beautiful fabrication method for quilting, but labor charges are *expensive* due to the high cost of the machine.

Multi-needle machines

The fabric, filler, and lining are fed together into a multi-needle machine, *before* the fabric widths are seamed together. A machine operator rolls the layers of the widths of the bedspread and fill through the machine and also moves the fabric and fill from side to side. The side to side movement causes the rows of stitching to form the desired patterns and designs.

Note: With multi-needle machines used on solid-color fabrics, the *quilting* is matched at the seams. On prints, the *pattern of the fabric* will match at the seams, *unless the quilted pattern is more predominant.* Therefore, **either the pattern will match up, on printed fabrics at the seams, or the quilted pattern will match at the seams.** Because of the nature of the multi-needle application, **it is *not possible* to match both the pattern and the quilted pattern.**

Note: The quilting process lofts up the fabric; therefore, add slightly more fabric for anything that is quilted.

Measuring for Any Type of Bedspread

Before proceeding to measure the bed, ask your customer if the amount of bedding on the bed is the same amount of bedding that is *normally* on the bed. **Inquire if the bedspread you are fabricating should be made to fit the bedding on the bed.** *If not*, the bed must be remade up with the appropriate bedding *before* you proceed to measure.

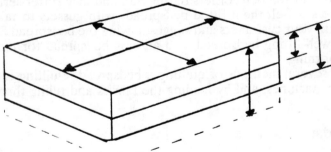

Measuring for bedspreads:

A.   Measure the length of the bed from the tip of the mattress at the head board, to the tip of the mattress at the foot board.

B.   Measure the width across the bed from the tip of the top of the mattress at one side, across the bed to the other side.

C.   Measure the drop, the distance from the tip of the top of the mattress to the desired drop. Check this drop at various points around the bed. If the drop is to go to the floor or nearly to the floor, **ask your customer what *their* preference is** - does the bedspread need to touch the floor, or should the bedspread be made ½" or 1" shorter, to make vacuuming easier?

•   **Measure and note on the workorder where any slits are to be fabricated** at the foot of the bed, and where they are to fall.

- **Add the length measurement + the pillow allowance** (standard is 16", you may add more or less). Next, **add the drop desired to determine the finished length of the bedspread.**

  Example: the length is 72" + 16" (pillow allowance) + 21" (one drop) = 109". Write this length measurement in the finished length box, on the workorder.

- **Add the width measurement + the two drop measurements, to determine the finished width of the bedspread.**

  Example: the width is 60" wide from tip to tip across the width, 60" + 21 + 21 (two drops) = 102". Write this width measurement in the finished width box on the workorder.

Note: It is good practice to note the mattress length, mattress width, and the drop length on the workorder. Record these measurements, regardless if these measurements are requested or not. This shows the workroom how you arrived at the measurements for fabrication. If you write these measurements in, the workroom will *normally* double-check your measurements for you.

Bedspreads

Many different styles of bedspreads and types of applied design are available for fabrication in individually selected fabrics, to express your customer's wants and needs. **There are two basic types of bedspreads: the throw style and the coverlet style.** *All other types of bedspreads are a variation of these two.* The basic styles are listed below:

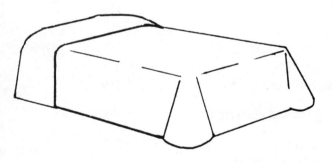

Throw Style Bedspread

Coverlet Style Bedspread

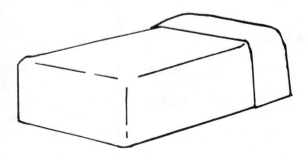

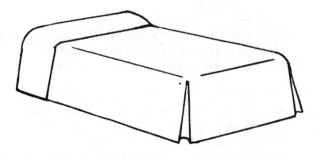

Fitted Bedspread

Split and Gusseted Style

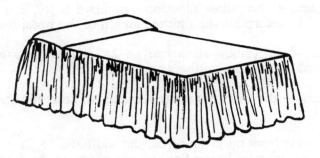

Shirred Drop Style

	Extra fabric needed
Basic throw style bedspreads:	
• Basic throw bedspread, with bell corners.	0 yards
• Basic throw style, with regular tuck in sham.	0
• Basic throw style, with welting at the top edge of the mattress.	1½
• Fitted bedspread, sewn together at the bottom corners at the foot of the bed. Welted all around the top of the mattress edge. **Outline quilting is not suitable for a fitted bedspread.**	½
• Waterfall style, fitted. **Outline quilting is suitable.**	0
• Split or split and gusseted corners at foot of the bed. *If the body of the bedspread is ordered quilted, the gussets will come quilted also.*	½
• Quilted top, shirred drop.	0
• Quilted top, shirred drop, with welting.	1½

Basic throw coverlet style bedspreads:	
• Basic throw coverlet, with bell corners.	0
• Basic throw coverlet, welted at top edge of mattress, with unquilted kick-pleat corners at the foot of the bed.	1½
• Basic throw coverlet, without welting, and split and gusseted corners at the foot of the bed.	½
• Bedcap — fitted cover that covers mattress and box springs.	0
• Bedsack — fitted cover that covers mattress only, similar to the bedcap.	0

Bedspread options:		
• One or two split corners with tongue/tongues.		½
• One or two split corners with tongue/tongues; corners finished off with welting.		1½
• Two split corners, throw style.		0
• Split corners with corner tabs (to hold split together) and tongues.		1½
• One or two corners, with closed cap.		0
• Corded bottom edges of bedspreads.	½" cording	1
	1" cording	2
	2" cording	3
• Scalloped bottom edges of bedspreads/coverlets.		2
• Single welting — ¼" at top of mattress.		1½
• Quilted tops and shirred drops.		3
• Quilted top and shirred drops, double ruffled.		6

- Plain reverse or separate shams.

twin	2½ yards
full	3
queen/king	3½

- Reverse sham with cording on leading edge only. Regular or
  1" size — *add* to reverse sham yardage.   1½

- Reverse sham with cording on three sides, or separate sham
  with cording on three sides. Regular or jumbo sized cording.   5¼

- Reverse sham with scalloped edge only on leading edge — *add*   2
  to reverse sham yardage.

- Reverse sham with scalloped edge on three sides — *add* to reverse   2
  sham yardage.

- Reverse sham with a short drop.

twin	2½
full	3
queen/king	3½

- Comforter with jumbo welting.

1" cording	1
2" cording	2

- Comforter with ruffle/ruffles.   3
- Double layer of fill.   ½
- Lining for an unquilted bedspread — extra charge price includes
  lining; if you use a coordinating fabric, then *double* the amount
  of yardage in the bedspread chart.
- Round bedspreads, with or without welting at the mattress edge.
  Figure the size to the closest corresponding larger, regular
  bedspread in the style of your selection.
- Four-sided bedspreads.   4¼
- Attached shirred underskirt, one tier — *add* amount, corresponding
  to the size needed, from the dust ruffle chart.
- Attached shirred underskirt, two tiers — *double and add* amount,
  corresponding to the size needed, from the dust ruffle chart.
- Attached shirred underskirt, three tiers — *triple and add* amount,
  corresponding to the size needed, from the dust ruffle chart.
- Attached box pleated underskirt — *add* the correct amount, corres-
  ponding to the size needed for the dust ruffle size from the dust
  ruffle chart.
- Monograms on bedspreads.
- Special yarn colors.
- Double fill, or heavier fill.
- Underliner for sheer or lace fabrics — *double* the amount for the
  yardage needed.
- Fringe or trim applied on top of a bedspread — *determine* the number of lineal
  feet needing coverage. *Divide* the lineal feet by 36" to arrive at the
  yardage amount needed for ordering and charging the customer.
- Ruffles — 3" is standard size, 6" is maximum size.   3 yards
- Double ruffles — 3" is standard size, 6" is maximum size.   6
- Fringe or trim applied to the bottom hem of the bedspread, coverlet —
  determine the number of lineal feet needing coverage. *Divide* the lineal
  feet by 36" to arrive at the yardage amount needed for ordering and
  charging the customer.
- Banding 2", 4", 6".
- Extra quilted yardage for other interior items. Specify standard,
  quilted pattern, or outline quilting.

Note: Unquilted bedspreads come unlined. *Bedspreads may be lined for an additional charge.*

Basic Bedspread Sizes and Yardage Requirements

8-ounce fill is the standard fill that most workrooms use for bedspread fill. 4-ounce fill is available on request.

	Mattress size	Finished size	48" Yardage	54" Yardage
Twin	39" x 75"	81" x 112"	2 widths 7½ yards	2 widths 7½ yards
	39 x 80	81 x 118	8	8
Full	54 x 75	96 x 112	3 widths 11½ yards	2 widths 8 yards
	54 x 80	96 x 118	12	8½
Queen	60 x 80	102 x 118	3 widths 11½ yards	3 widths 12 yards
King (Cal)	72 x 84	114 x 122	12	12
Dual	78 x 75	120 x 113	11½	11½
King (Dual)	78 x 89	120 x 118	12	12

Note: Add a full repeat for every width of fabric needed for fabrics with repeats. *Amount of fabric widths needed are listed above the yardage amount.*

Note: These sizes include a standard pillow allowance of approximately 16", and a standard 21" drop for bedspreads. *Specify* **the correct drop length.**

Reverse Sham Bedspread Size and Yardage Requirements

	Mattress size	Finished size	48" Yardage	54" Yardage
Twin	39" x 75"	81" x 124"	2 widths 8½ yards	2 widths 8½ yards
	39 x 80	81 x 130	9	9
Full	54 x 75	96 x 124	3 widths 12½ yards	3 widths 12½ yards
	54 x 80	96 x 130	13	13
Queen	60 x 80	102 x 130	13	13
King (Cal)	72 x 84	114 x 134	13½	13½
Dual	78 x 75	120 x 125	12½	12½
King (Dual)	78 x 80	120 x 130	13	13

Note: Add a full repeat for every width of fabric needed for fabrics with repeats. *Amount of fabric widths needed are listed above the yardage amount.*

Coverlets

Coverlets are short bedspreads that end approximately 3" below the mattress, and are usually combined with a dust ruffle. Coverlets may be flounced, pleated, or plain at the sides. See the option list above for bedspreads' available additions.

Coverlets have 8-ounce fill as their standard fill; 4-ounce is available upon request.

Coverlet Sizes and Yardage Requirements

	Mattress size	Finished size	48" Yardage	54" Yardage
			2 widths	**2 widths**
Twin	39" x 75"	65" x 104"	7 yards	7 yards
	39 x 80	65 x 109	7½	7½
Full	54 x 75	80 x 104	11	7½
	54 x 80	80 x 109	11	7½
			3 widths	**2 widths**
Queen	60 x 80	86 x 109	11	7½
			3 widths	**3 widths**
King (Cal)	72 x 84	98 x 113	11½ yards	11½ yards
Dual	78 x 75	104 x 104	12½	12½
King (Dual)	78 x 80	104 x 109	13	13

Note: Add a full repeat for every width listed, *in addition to* the yardage amounts listed, for fabrics with a repeat.

Note: These sizes include a standard pillow allowance of about 16". **Specify the drop needed for coverlets.**

Comforters

Comforters may be made reversible by using a contrast fabric on the reverse side. 8-ounce fill is usually an industry standard; for more loft, request 12-ounce fill.

Because of a comforter's loft, pillow tuck-ins are *not available* for comforters.

Comforter Sizes and Yardage Requirements

If you do choose a coordinating fabric for the reverse side, use the yardage chart below for *each* side. *Outline quilting is not available for comforters.*

	Mattress size	Finished size	48" Yardage	54" Yardage
			2 widths	**2 widths**
Twin	39" x 75"	65" x 88"	5½ yards	5½ yards
	39 x 80	65 x 93	6	6
Full	54 x 75	80 x 88	5½	5½
	54 x 80	80 x 93	6	6
			3 widths	**2 widths**
Queen	60 x 80	86 x 93	9	9
			3 widths	**3 widths**
King (Cal)	72 x 84	98 x 97	9	9
Dual	78 x 75	104 x 88	8½	8½
King (Dual)	78 x 80	104 x 93	9	9

Note: Add a full repeat for every width listed, in addition to the yardage listed, for fabrics with a repeat.

Duvet Covers

Duvet covers are slipcovers made to cover down comforters. These are made unquilted and easily slip off, since they have Velcro closures for ease in cleaning or laundering. The fabric amounts shown are for the use of the same fabric for both sides of the duvet cover. If you want to use a contrast fabric for the reverse side, simply divide the yardage in two, ½ for the self fabric, ½ for the contrast fabric.

Size	48" Yardage	54" Yardage	Up to 12"	Repeats 12 — 24"	Over 24"
Twin	12 yards	12 yards	12 yards	13 yards	14 yards
Full	18	18	18	19	20
Queen	18	18	18	19	20
King	18	18	18	19	20

Measuring for duvet covers:

- Measure the size of the existing comforter in width and in length. Add 3" to each of these measurements.

Dust Ruffles

Dust ruffles are gathered, pleated, or have pleats only at the corners. Dust ruffles have the function of hiding the box springs. Dust ruffles combine well with coverlets and comforters. Lighter weight and sheer fabrics are the best fabric selections for gathered dust ruffles. If the fabric is medium or heavy in weight, use the fabric in a tailored-styled dust ruffle.

The dust ruffle's gathered sides, or the tailored-pleated sides, attach to a rectangle of fabric that is cut to the measurements of the top of the mattress plus the seam allowances. The rectangle may be a fitted sheet that covers the box springs and the dust ruffle attaches to the sheet. The dust ruffle may also be attached by Velcro to the sides of the box springs.

Gathered Dust Ruffle   **Tailored, Pleated Dust Ruffle**

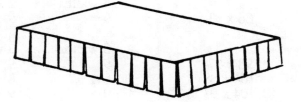

Box Pleated Dust Ruffle

Dust ruffle basic styles:

- Gathered.
- Cluster gathered at foot corners, *and* cluster gathered in the middle of the sides.
- 4" box pleated (standard); pleats may be fabricated wider or narrower.
- Tailored, pleated at the corners only.
- Tailored-pleated style, pleated once in the middle on each of the three sides.

Dust ruffle extra charges:

- Dust ruffles with split corners.
- Four-sided dust ruffles. For the additional side, add ⅓ of the amount of fabric listed below under *Yardage Needed for Dust Ruffle Fabrication.*
- Quilted dust ruffles.
- Multiple-layered dust ruffles. Double the amount of yardage listed for two layers.
- Attach Velcro for affixing to the sides of the box springs.

Yardage Needed for Dust Ruffle Fabrication

	36" goods		48" goods or wider	
Size	Tailored	Shirred or box pleated	Tailored	Shirred or box pleated
Twin	3¾ yards	8½ yards	3¾ yards	6½ yards
Full	3¾	8½	3¾	7
Queen	4½	10	4	7½
King	4½	10	4	7½
Dual king	4½	10	4	7½

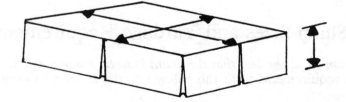

Measuring for dust ruffles:

A. **Measure the length** from the edge of the corner of the box springs (take measurement from the side of the mattress) at the head of the bed, to the edge of the corner of the box springs at the foot of the bed.

B. **Measure the width** from the edge of the corner at the foot of the bed, across to the opposite corner's edge.

C. **Measure the drop of the ruffle** from the top edge of the box springs, to the desired length placement near the floor. Ask your customer what their preference is in the length. Does the dust ruffle need to touch the floor, or does the customer prefer for the dust ruffle to be ½" or 1" shorter to make vacuuming easier?

- **Add the length to *one* drop length, to determine finished length.** If the bed is covered on *all four sides* with a dust ruffle, add an additional drop length to the measurement, and note on the workorder that this is a four-sided dust ruffle.

- **Add the width, plus two drop lengths to determine finished width.**

Note: It is good practice to note the mattress length, mattress width, and the drop length on the workorder. Record these measurements, regardless if these measurements are requested or not. This shows the workroom how you arrived at the measurements for fabrication. If you write these measurements in, the workroom will *normally* double-check your measurements for you.

Pillow Shams

Pillow shams are covers that go over pillows. They are quilted or unquilted, ruffled at the edges, pleated, or flanged in style.

Pillow shams are usually fabricated to go with coverlets, comforters, or flounced bedspreads. Most throw style bedspreads and coverlets will not need pillow shams, if you are trying to achieve a more tailored or simple appearance. **Remember not to add in the extra length needed for a bedspread *that is not* using pillow shams, since the tuck-in excess is no longer needed.** The extra length is for the tuck-in area around the pillow and down the back of the bedspread, 14" — 16".

- Standard prices includes flanged, ruffled, or welted shams.

- Indicate a zipper or overlap closure.

- Interior of shams are packed with fill.

Options available:	Extra yardage needed
Inset welt, ¼"	½ yard
Jumbo cord, ½", 1"	1½ yard
Additional ruffles	1½ yard, each additional ruffle

Pillow Sham Sizes and Yardage Requirements

Fabricate the pillow sham to fit the bed that the sham is to be made for. These sizes listed are *only* guidelines. **Adjust the yardage requirements** to fit the pillow that the sham is fabricated for.

Pillow sham sizes		48" — 54" yardage Unquilted	48" — 54" yardage Quilted
Size			
Standard	21" x 26"	2½ yards	3 yards
Queen	21 x 30	2½	3
King	21 x 36	2½	3

Bolster Sizes and Yardage Requirements

Bolsters come in two shapes for studio beds: wedge shaped and round. Below are the standard dimensions and yardage requirements to fabricate a bolster. Bolsters come standard with welted, tight fitting covers on all sides. Zipper closures are standard.

Size	Dimensions	Yardage
Wedge shape	12" wedge, up to 36" — 48"	1½ yards each
	12" wedge, from 48" — 80"	3
Round shape	8" round, up to 36" — 48"	1½
	8" round, from 48" to 80 "	3 yards each

| Oblong | 12" oblong, up to 36 — 48" | 1½ |
| | 12" oblong, from 48" to 80" | 3½ |

Pillows

Depending on the personality your customer is projecting in his or her interior, there are many pillow styles to go with an individual's character and nature.

Pillows are actually available in three categories of styles. These styles are tailored types, transitional, and ruffled-gathered types. All other types are variations of these three types. When selecting pillow styles for a room, stay consistent with the styling you have already started in the rest of the room.

For a tailored room, select a pillow type from the tailored group. If the room is romantic, ruffly, feminine, select a pillow type from the ruffled, gathered group. If you want to soften up a fairly tailored room, use a transitional style. Self-fabrics may be quilted or left plain, depending on the type of pillow style.

Tailored styles:
- Round or square, plain styles, with welting.
- Round or square, plain styles, with a covered button in the middle, or multiple buttons placed in a pattern, and welting.
- Square or round, with welting banding, or other design inset on face.
- Round or square, with flange (flat, border area stitched around the pillow, without stuffing in the border area).
- Round or square, with flange, with covered button in the center.
- Square-boxed or round, with welting.
- Square-boxed or round, with welting, banding, or other design inset on face.
- Square-shape, with mini-horizontal pleats on the face, with welting.

Tailored-roll types of pillows:
- Round, fitted at sides with a flat inset of fabric, with a button.
- Round, fitted at sides with a flat inset of fabric, with welting.

Transitional styles:
- Square or round, with gathered welting sewn into the side seam.
- Heart shaped, with welting.
- Heart-boxed shaped, with gathered sides.
- Boxed square or round, with welting, with gathered face, with button in the middle.
- Square or round-boxed style, with gathered sides, and welted seams.
- Square or round, plain or boxed style, with gathered ruching set in on face, echoing the pillow's shape.

Transitional-roll styles:
- Round, fitted inset gathered piece at sides, with a button, and welting.
- Round, gathered at sides, with a button.

Gathered, ruffled styles of pillows:
- Round or square style, with loose ruffles at sides, welted or not welted.
- Round or square style, with loose ruffles at sides, with a button in the center, welted or not welted.
- Heart shaped, with gathered, loose ruffles.
- Multiple layers of fabric and lace ruffles, for ruffled styles.
- Round or square box pillow; with ruffles on both sides of boxed edges, welted or not welted.

Gathered, ruffled-roll styles:

- Round, with loose ruffles at each end.
- Round, with multiple ruffles attached at each end around face of pillow.

Pillow Sizes and Yardage Requirements

Make the pillow size *fit* the situation. These sizes are only guidelines. Adjust the yardage requirements to fit the size of the fabricated pillow.

Corded or ruffled pillows:

- Standard sizes for pillows are 14", 17", 22" square or round. Each of these sizes requires1½ yards of plain, unquilted fabric. For quilted fabrics add ¼ yard more fabric; for fabrics with a repeat, add one whole repeat.

Flanged square or round:

- Standard sizes for pillows are 14", 17", 22". Each of these sizes requires2 yards of fabric. For quilted fabrics add ¼ yard more fabric; for fabrics with a repeat add one whole repeat.

Table Covers

Table covers are made in one or two tiers; trimmed, banded, ruffled, or left plain. A contrast or coordinating lining may also be used for reversible table cloths and covers.

Size	Yardage needed; 48" or 54" wide
For a small bedside table	4½ yards for the long tier, 1 yard for the top short tier, + additional trim, banding, ruffle yardage.

How to measure for a table cover:
The directions for measuring apply to both round, square, or rectangular shaped tables.

A. **Measure the diameter** of the table (at the top of the table).

B. Measure from the tip of the top of the table to the floor, or desired length of the drop.

C. Determine yardage: *You will need the same measurement for the width as the length.* Add the diameter, plus two drop lengths (each side). Allow 4" of fabric for the hem to determine the cut size. Next you determine the widths of fabric needed. Take the cut size, and divide by the width of fabric you are using. If the resulting number is not an even, whole number, round up to the next width of fabric.

Example: Your customer has selected 48" wide, plain fabric. The top of the bedside table has a diameter of 18". The drop to the floor is 28". 18" (diameter) + 28" + 28" (two drops) = 74". Add in hem allowance of 4". 74" + 4"= 78". 78" divided by 48" fabric = 1.63 widths. Round up this number to 2 widths of fabric. The length needed is 78". 78" by 36" (yards) = 2.17 yards. Figure in any repeat here, and determine the length with the repeat added (we are using plain fabric for this example. Multiply this number by the widths needed, in this case 2. 2 x 2.17 = 4.34. Round up this number slightly, to 4.5 yards. Order a minimum of 4½ yards for this example.

Note: Figure the horizontal repeat by dividing the cut length by the repeat size. Round up the resulting number, if it comes out uneven.

Note: If lining the table cover in a coordinating or contrast fabric, **double** the fabric amounts above.

Table Placemats

Custom placemats are usually lined, and may be fabricated quilted or unquilted. Quilted placemats are quilted on one side only. Contrast or coordinating lining may also be used for reversible placemats.

<u>Size</u>	<u>Yardage needed: 48" or 54" wide</u>
12" x 18"	½ yard for one side only.

Note: If lining the placemats in a coordinating or contrast fabric, *double* the fabric amounts above.

Table Runners

Table runners are fabricated usually 12" wide times the length needed for the situation. Table runners have lining. If table runners are quilted, they are quilted on one side only. Corners are mitered and hemmed. Any quilt design may be selected; designs such as applique, or monogramming may be applied. A contrast or coordinating lining may also be used for reversible table runners.

<u>Size</u>	<u>Yardage needed: 48" or 54" wide</u>
12" width x 60" finished length	2 yards needed. Add 1 yard additional per 30" of length needed.

Note: If lining the table runner in a coordinating or contrast fabric, double the fabric amounts above.

Headboards

Nicely shaped and proportioned headboards covered in fabric are a welcome addition to a bedroom. This is especially true when the customer does not want a traditional wood headboard, but may still want a traditional shape, or is opting for a new look. They may want to echo a design-shape found elsewhere in the room.

Note: Headboards are fabricated quilted and non-quilted.

Headboard Yardage Requirements

Basic headboard styles:	Size	Yardage	Repeats up to 12"	12"— 24"	over 24"
	twin	2 yards	2½ yards	3 yards	3½ yards
	full	2½	3	3½	4
	queen	3½	4	4½	5
	king	3½	4	4½	5

Sunburst styles:

twin	3 yards	4 yards	4½ yards	4½ yards
full	5	5	5	5½
queen	5½	5½	5½	6
king	6	6½	6½	7

Designs options available: Extra yardage needed

- Plain roll   2½ yards
- Quilted panel   1
- Shirred roll edge with welting   2½
- Diamond or biscuit tufting — *double* the yardage requirement
- Gathered panel areas — *triple* the yardage requirement
- Sunburst styles — yardage requirement below
- Scalloped or curved exterior shapes   0
- Quilting   1
- Mounting to mount to the wall
- Cleats for mounting to bed

Canopies

Canopies are usually fabricated with tailored, tailored-pleated, cluster-pleated, shirred or box-pleated ruffles and valances. The standard length of ruffles or valances is 8" in length. Below are the yardage requirements for ordering a canopy.

Unless specified, canopies will come unlined. Canopies may be lined with self-fabric or regular lining fabrics. If self-fabric is selected, double the amount of yardages listed here. If lining fabric is selected, order the same amount of lining fabric as the self-fabric listed.

Canopy style:	Yardage requirements: 48" or 54"		
	Twin	**Full**	**Queen/King**
Tailored, pleats only in corners	7 yards	7 yards	7 yards
Tailored pleated, with one pleat in the middle of each section and in the corners.	9½	9½	9½
Cluster shirred, at corners and in the middle of each section	10½	10½	10½
Shirred or box pleated	8	11½	12½

Note: Specify buttonholes size and placement on the workorder for bedposts that pass through the canopy. Check price list for the fabrication charge for buttonholes.

Measuring for canopies:

- **Measure the length of the canopy frame.** Allow for any curve in length. Walk the tape along the frame of the canopy from tip to tip in length.

- To determine the width of the canopy, **measure across the width, tip to tip.**

- **Decide how deep to make the drop.** 8" is a standard drop for canopy ruffles and valances.

- **Add the length, plus one or two drops, to arrive at finished length.** Add two drops, if there is to be a drop behind the head of the bed.

- Next, **add the width plus two drops, to arrive at the finished width.**

- **Note and draw in on the workorder the accurate locations and measurements of any bedposts.** Also **note the size of any buttonholes** needed for slipping the bedposts through the canopy.

Note: Always have canopies remeasured. Have a template made to fit the canopy, since canopies are an item that requires an exact fit.

Other Fabric Decorating Items

Many other decorating items and furnishings are also fabricated with fabric. Some of these include:

- **Upholstered benches** Plain or quilted top; diamond or biscuit tufted; with or without banding. Plain or shirred sides. Legs may be covered with fabric.
- **Boudoir chairs**
- **Chaise lounges**
- **Folding screens** Straight top; arch tops; or rounded tops
- **Custom beds**
- **Table napkins**
- **Kitchen accessories**

Slipcovers and Reupholstery

Slipcovers

Slipcovers can unify, harmonize, balance, and give rhythm to a room if the right fabrics are selected for the design situation.

Color and texture are the most important design elements to consider for slipcovers. Durable fabric is the next consideration for long-lasting slipcovers.

Here on the West Coast, slipcover fabricators are hard to find. If and when you do find a slipcover fabricator, *they charge about the same* as having the piece reupholstered. In the eastern states, slipcovers are extremely popular. Eastern people who relocate to the West *constantly* request slipcovers from western upholsterers who are unfamiliar with them. Slipcovers are an exceptional idea that needs to be adopted everywhere.

Slipcover skirts for furniture items are left unskirted, shirred, or box- or kick-pleated at the bottom. Slipcovers are tied or tacked to the underside of the seat. Seams are finished off with single or double welting, or short fringe is applied in the seams.

Note: The finished slipcover should not have any wrinkles, as wrinkles will cause the slipcover to fade and wear at the wrinkles. Wrinkles also *look* very unprofessional.

When should you recommend slipcovers?

- When **the furniture is still in good condition**, but may be the wrong color, design, texture, or the furniture's original fabric covering has faded.

- When the **color** of the existing furniture is preventing the customer from doing what he or she wants to do with color in the room.

- When the existing furniture is a variety of **unrelated patterns, textures, styles, and colors.** Slipcovering a few pieces can really help tie the furniture together with other fabrics in the room.

- When the customer **wants the furniture's fabric to match the drapery.**

- When the customer would like **a summer look, and the ability to change easily to a winter look** as the seasons change.

- When the customer **wants to protect the original upholstery** from the grandchildren or pets with an easily cleaned, nicely fitting cover.

- When the customer **would like easy upkeep and cleaning** with easily removed covers. Slipcovers may be handwashed and put back on, while still damp, if made of cotton, or taken to the cleaners. This is much less expensive than having the upholstery cleaner come in and clean each upholstered piece.

Sell winter scheme upholstery jobs *and* summer scheme slipcovers for maximum enjoyment of the furniture by your customers. It is a preferable to change a furniture's covering when the seasons change to a heavier or lighterweight fabric. Consequently, both fabrics last a long time, due to being used only half the time.

When reupholstery would be a better idea:

- When you can see that the fabric is badly worn, and the springs need retying. Always check the furniture piece the customer is considering for a reupholstery job for loose joints, worn springs, sagging cushions, and too much stress on the webbing.

- When the customer really wants a heavy upholstery fabric rather than a lighterweight fabric.

- When the customer indicates to you that they are not going to be removing the slipcover to enjoy the upholstery underneath. They may not *do* their own upkeep or *want* to remove the slipcovers for the change of seasons. Most elderly customers will not want to remove the slipcovers.

- When the customer really wants only one color selection for the furniture, to use year around.

- When you can see that this is a living room *that does not get used much*, and the upholstery will not receive much wear and abuse.

Fabric Selection for Slipcovers

The selection of quality fabrics for slipcovers is the key to them having a long life. Vat dyed, preshrunk, soil-repellant finishes and washable fabrics are the preferable fabrics to use. The fabric should be of a tight and strong weave. If the fabric is not firm and tightly woven, any applied stress, as when someone sits on the furniture, will tear the fabric at the seams.

Recommended fabrics are 100% cottons, linens, and medium-weight fabrics that have the ability to mold to the furniture. If you select a heavier fabric, the curved areas of the fabric will not lay flat and smooth, as a medium-weight fabric will.

Always check with the fabricator you are planning to use for their recommendations on fabric requirements. They will supply you with a chart or guidelines to meet *their* fabric requirement needs. If not, use the guidelines in this section and ask the fabricator to cut the fabric the most economical way.

Slipcover fabrication requires more fabric than regular reupholstery. You should calculate 2 — 3 yards *more* per item. Most fabricators will need 9 yards for an overstuffed chair and 16 yards for a sofa with three cushions, for slipcovers.

If you are adding contrast welting, then you will need to add 1⅓ yard more fabric in the contrast fabric. If you add this contrast fabric, reduce the self-fabric amount by 1 yard. The chair now becomes 8 yards, plus 1½ additional yards of contrast fabric. The sofa becomes 15 yards, plus 1½ yards of contrast fabric.

Fabrics to avoid using for slipcovers:

For slipcovers, avoid using sheer fabrics, foam-backed fabrics or heavy rubberized fabrics, frieze fabrics, loosely woven fabrics, fabrics with less durable satin weaves, corduroy which will rub off (unless it's nylon), and velvets which will crush.

Measuring for slipcovers:

The example shown is a chair. A sofa, or any other item is measured in the same way. Draw yourself a diagram of the item front and back, and take these essential measurements for determining how much yardage to use. You are taking the furniture item and measuring it in sections: width and length. Take all measurements from the widest point, taking length measurements to the floor. Decide which way the lengthwise grain of the fabric should run. Usually the lengthwise grain runs up and down the piece, not across the piece.

- <u>Measuring the basic structure of the chair:</u>
  Remove all loose cushions from the piece before proceeding.

- **Measure the back length,** from the floor to the top of the item. If the item is a chair or a sofa without a skirt, take the measurement from the bottom of the item and add 4".

- **Measure the front length.** Measure from the top front of the item, down to the front of the cushion, plus 3" allowance for a fabric tuck-in.

- **Measure the top horizontal width** of the item.

- **Measure the back width.**

- **Measure the seat width;** add 3" to each side, for a total of 6" for tuck-ins.

- **Measure the front width. Include the sides of the item.**

- **Measure the side of the arm to the floor.**

- **Measure the side, front to back.**

- **Measure the inside width of the arm area;** add 3" for tuck-in.

- Measure the inside of the arm in length; measure front to back. Add 3" for tuck-in.

- <u>Measuring the loose cushions:</u>
  Measure the cushion length.

- Measure the cushion width.

- Measure the depth of the cushion.

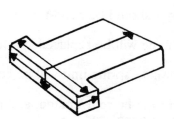

Reupholstery

Reupholstery allows you and your customer to select the perfect fabric to change their existing fabric-covered furniture, which will help tie the room together.

Note: Do not reupholster a piece of furniture that was inexpensive and of poor quality to begin with.

Reupholster the finer-quality pieces of furniture that were expensive at the time of purchase. These are generally heavy and well made — well worth reupholstering. Reupholstery is an expensive proposition and if the piece is not that high quality, the customer may just want to start over with a new piece of furniture, which may be even a less expensive alternative.

If the furniture is of good quality, the result after reupholstering will be a fine, irreplaceable piece by today's standards. You will not be able to easily find the resulting quality, even from the finer manufacturers.

When you have reupholstery done, the *same* person works on the piece of furniture from start to finish. The same upholsterer goes through the whole structure of the piece; reties the springs, retightens the screws, replaces the cushions or revitalizes the existing ones, and adds new foam for padding. Much more attention and detail is virtually given to the piece than a piece of furniture which is rolling off the assembly line, where a multitude of people have worked on each piece.

- Most upholsterers require 5 yards of 54" wide fabric for a chair with one seat cushion, without a skirt.

- Add 2 yards more for a chair with a skirt.

- Wing chairs require an additional yard of fabric.

- Occasional chairs require 4 yards.

- Most sofas will require 10 yards of 54" wide fabric for a two — three-cushion sofa.

- Add two yards more for a sofa skirt.

- If the seat is to be self-decked, reversible, or covered on both sides with the same self-fabric, add 1 yard of fabric for the chair, and an additional 2 yards for a two-cushion sofa, 3 yards for a three-cushion sofa.

- Measure the furniture to decide accurately how much yardage to order and charge the customer.

- Add the repeats to each cut, if the fabric is patterned.

A quality reupholstery job will consist of the following:

- Furniture is stripped to the frame.

- The frame is redoweled, reglued where needed, and all joints checked and reinforced.

- Worn or broken springs will be replaced.

- All springs should be hand-tied with eight-way ties.

- Old webbing will be replaced.

- The complete spring-unit will be covered in burlap.

- All filling will be rejuvenated, and more filling added, where needed. Filling should be reused when possible, not replaced.

- All exposed wood will be touched up, cleaned, and polished. On antique pieces the finish should not be refinished.

- Fresh, sterilized cotton padding will be added to the arms, back, and seat of the piece for firmness and added plumpness.

- Seat cushions will be replaced. Available replacement cushions are normally polyurethane types, or down types, available for an optional charge.

- The covering of the fabric is tacked on, and any skirt to be used added.

Fabric Selection for Reupholstery

Fabrics for reupholstery should be firm, tightly woven, made of durable fibers, coated with soil-repellant finishes, and be medium heavy to heavy in weight. These guidelines are for furniture pieces that will receive hard wear. If the piece is only for show and only occasionally sat in, then you may feel comfortable in going with a lighter weight fabric with a less durable weave.

- Dark-colored fabrics and large-patterned fabrics in contrasting colors will make the room appear smaller.

- Light-colored fabrics and fabrics with small patterns tend to give a room a feeling of lightness and will expand the space.

- Busy patterns in the room should be used with solid fabrics in the reupholstered pieces, to help calm down the other fabrics.

- A room with predominantly solid-colored fabrics needs patterned reupholstery to liven it up.

- Use one dominant color, add several shades of the dominant color, and then add in accent colors for contrast.

- In a bright, sunny room, tone it down by using cool colors such as blues, greens, lavenders and purple tones.

- To warm up a cold room, use sunny colors, such as reds, yellows, oranges, and browns.

Quality Upholstered Furniture

The better upholstered furniture frames are made of hardwoods, preferably ash wood. Hardwoods make solid, sturdy, dependable pieces of furniture. Hardwoods are harder to work with and are more expensive than softer woods.

Woods used in frames should be kiln dried. Kiln drying avoids future warping, shrinking, and possible future, uneven joints. Frames are glued and doweled together to give the piece a long life.

Unexposed frame areas are usually made of birch and other hardwoods. The exposed areas of the frame are usually fruitwoods, mahogany, or walnut.

Quality pieces also include eight-way, hand-tied springs with strong webbing attached. Also included are: 14-ounce burlap, Italian twine, hair filling, fine cotton, a cover of the cushioning made of muslin, and then the piece is finished off with the selected upholstery fabric. Furniture of this quality does not *really* wear out, only the fabric-upholstery covering does. The springs may need to be retied, the joints may need to be checked and tightened, and the filling may need to be revitalized or replaced.

Poor-Quality Upholstered Furniture

Poor-quality upholstered furniture pieces are referred to as *"borax."* These frames are made of oak or pine and rarely kiln dried. The frames are reglued and nailed. This quality would not be worth reupholstering.

Start by examining the furniture piece considered for reupholstery: check for loose joints, worn springs, sagging cushions, frames, and webbing that is falling apart due to excess weight and stress on various points.

Care and Maintenance of Upholstery Fabrics

To keep your upholstery looking as good as possible, instruct your customers to:

- Vacuum and turn the loose cushions of your upholstered pieces once a week.

- Twice a year, a general cleaning of upholstered pieces is needed. Read the attached labels on the upholstered pieces; have the customer pull the sales slip to review the fabric's fiber content (always list on the sales slip at the time of sale); or check the original sample of the fabric for the fiber content.

- **Test a hidden area or scrap of the upholstery fabric to see how the fabric is going to react to shampooing.** If the fabric is considered washable, and the fabric does not bleed or shrink, then proceed by cleaning with spray-on upholstery cleaner. Never use soap — once applied, you will not be able to ever, completely remove it. The soap residue becomes like a magnet for attracting soil and dirt.

  Make your own home remedy cleaner easily whipped up much less expensively, without requiring a trip to the store: Make suds (as mentioned throughout this book) with dish soap and water, whipped up until sudsy. Apply the suds to a small area or section at a time by using a sponge or soft brush. Scrub lightly in a circular motion. Remove remaining suds and rinse the area with warm water. Towel dry as much as possible. Turn a fan on the piece of furniture, to aid in rapid drying.

- **Fabrics that are non-washable will need to be cleaned professionally, or with a dry-cleaning solution available at the drug store.** Use a small amount of the solution in a hidden area to see how the fabric will react before proceeding. Use a thin application of the solution over the upholstered piece, you are working on. It is better to use a thin application and do the piece more often than to over-saturate the fabric all at once.

Yardage Requirement Chart for Reupholstery and Slipcovers

Below is a listing of a range in yardages for both reupholstered and slipcovered sofas and chairs. The chair and sofa range in yardage shown reflects using 48" or 54" goods, and the difference in a size range from a 75" - 78" *"small"* sofa to a large 108" sofa. Adjust your yardage requirements according to the size sofa you are working with and the width of fabric you are working with: small, medium or large. If the sofa is medium size and you are using a 54" wide fabric, use the amount between the small and large. For a large sofa with a 48" fabric, use the maximum amount of fabric listed. **For sofa skirts add an additional 3 yards; yardage for chair skirts is already reflected in the maximum amount of yardage shown.**

Reupholstery 10 — 14 yds.
Slipcover 15 — 17

Reupholstery 10 — 14 yds.
Slipcover 18 — 20

Reupholstery 10 — 14 yds.
Slipcover 15 — 17

Reupholstery 10 — 14 yds.
Slipcover 15 — 17

Reupholstery 10 — 14 yds.
Slipcover 14 — 16

Reupholstery 10 — 14 yds.
Slipcover 15 — 17

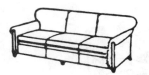

Reupholstery 10 — 15 yds.
Slipcover 15 — 18

Reupholstery 10 — 14 yds.
Slipcover 15 — 17

Reupholstery 6 — 7 yds.
Slipcover 8 — 11

Reupholstery 8 — 12 yds
Slipcover 12 — 15

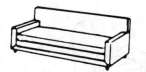

Reupholstery 9 — 13 yds.
Slipcover 14 — 17

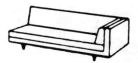

Reupholstery 10 — 12 yds.
Slipcover 13

Reupholstery 10 — 15 yds.
Slipcover 15 — 18

Reupholstery 3½ — 5 yds.
Slipcover 5 — 7

Reupholstery 4½ — 6½ yds.
Slipcover 7 — 8

Reupholstery 4 — 5 yds.
Slipcover 5 — 7

Reupholstery 5 — 7 yds.
Slipcover 8

Reupholstery 7 — 8 yds.
Slipcover 13

Reupholstery 5 — 7 yds.
Slipcover 8

Reupholstery 6 — 7 yds.
Slipcover 9

Reupholstery 5 — 7 yds.
Slipcover   8

Reupholstery 5 — 7 yds.
Slipcover 8

Reupholstery 5 — 7 yds.
Slipcover 8

Reupholstery 3 — 4 yds.
Slipcover   6

Reupholstery 6 — 7 yds.
Slipcover 8

Reupholstery 5 — 7 yds.
Slipcover 9

Reupholstery 5 — 6 yds.
Slipcover 8

Reupholstery 5 — 6 yds.
Slipcovers 8

Reupholstery 6 — 7 yds.
Slipcovers 9

Reupholstery 6 — 7 yds.
Slipcovers 9

Reupholstery 5 — 6
Slipcovers 8

Reupholstery 5 — 6 yds.
Slipcovers 8

Reupholstery 7 — 9 yds.
Slipcovers 10

Glossary

Accent fabric Cloth selected to trim or provide interest to top treatments, drapery, tiebacks, accessories, bedspreads, etc. May be used in the form of banding, banding with welting, inset areas, braided fabric areas, etc. Any fabric used in the treatment other than the self-fabric.

Acetate Manmade fiber made from cellulose acetate; weaker than most fibers, has a silky appearance, is lustrous, resistant to moths and mildew. Some colors may fade. Acetate's main enemy is sunlight, which will weaken the fiber.

Acrylic A manmade fiber. A generic term which is made into filament and staple forms of yarn.

Allowance Deductions taken from exact measurements by the workroom, to allow the item to be fabricated to fit correctly.

Antique satin Fabric that is made to resemble silk satin. Usually of uneven texture. May be made of acetate and rayon, cotton blends, may be 100% cotton. Very common, broad fabric category used for many interior applications.

Angora Hair from the Angora goat. Also know as mohair.

Apron The wood facing below the sill on double-hung windows.

Arch-top Curved top or opening of windows; or the curved top of shutters and woven woods that are used with cathedral-top or arch-top windows.

Art Nouveau Decorative style popular around the turn of the 19th century. The Art Nouveau style broke away from previous styles and was a beginning of new original forms. Known for its free form, flame, wave-like patterns, and curved designs. A very original, curved style of design.

Austrian shade Fabric shade controlled by tapes. Austrian shades have vertical gathers of lightweight fabric, gathered on shirring tape every 12 — 15 inches.

Austrian valance Fabric top treatment similar in looks to the shade above, but shorter in length and immovable. Used as an accent above a window, over an undertreatment or overdrapery.

Balloon shade Fabric shade controlled by tapes. May be gathered or tailored in styling. Balloon shades pouff or balloon out. May be raised or lowered.

Balloon valance Fabric top treatment similar to the balloon shade above, but shorter in length and immovable. Used as an accent above a window, over an undertreatment or overdrapery.

Banding Strips of contrast fabric applied to any interior fabric treatment or accessory for an accent.

Bartack Group of stitches that hold the drapery pleat together.

Basket weave A type of weave. A plain weave that incorporates two or more warp and filling threads woven together, to give a basket weave look. A flat, loose, and moderately open weave. May be heavy, lightweight, and made up in any fiber. Popular fabrics where this weave is common; burlap, polished cotton, linen, and homespun appearing fabrics.

Batik Traditional fabric application for resist dyeing. Wax is applied in areas to resist the dye. Dye will penetrate cracks in the wax. Many fabrics today are printed to emulate batik fabric. This is done by roller or screen printing.

Batiste   Sheer fabric of manmade fibers. Fine quality construction. Known for its lengthwise streaked effect. Usually used for sheers or lining.

Baton   Wand, made of plastic, wood, or metal, attached to the leading edge of drapery; or used to operate by tilting mini blinds or mini woods.

Bay window   Three or more windows which are set at near angles to each other, which project out of a normally square or rectangularly shaped room.

Bleeding   Color which changes, moves from its original area, or disappears during the washing or dry-cleaning process. Familiar fabrics where bleeding is favored are the madras cloths from India.

Blend   To combine two or more fibers in weaving of fabrics to achieve better performance and new fabric types, different textures, dyeing capabilities, and finishing effects.

Block printing   Application of design to fabrics, achieved by hand stamping with dyes and carved wooden or linoleum-faced blocks.

Bolt   The entire length of fabric made on the loom at one time.

Border print   Fabric which has a distinctively different design from its other design areas, printed along one selvage in the full ength of the fabric's bolt. The design may be narrow or may be half the width of the fabric's width. The border may also be placed on both edges of the selvages. Border-printed fabrics require special planning to make use of the print, such as railroading the fabric for border-print placement.

Bottom hem   The double-fold of fabric at the bottom of the drapery, forming the finished edge.

Boucle   Fabric with a knotted or looped surface, whether knitted or woven. Boucle also refers to yarn with this type of effect.

Bow window   Curved bay window. See bay window.

Box pleated   Folds of fabric stitched to make even folds that are then flattened and pressed to make pleats that are of the same size and evenly spaced.

Bracket to bracket   Length in inches of the rod width needed to cover the wall area.

Brocade   Fabric of jacquard design with designs of raised figures or flowers. The background areas may be satin, twill, or combinations of other weaves. Brocade has an embossed appearance, and may incorporate gold and silver threads in the design.

Brocatelle   Heavy drapery and upholstery fabric with cross-ribbed, jacquard designs raised in high relief.

Buckram   Stiffly finished woven fabric used in drapery headers and tiebacks.

Calendaring   Finishing process where the fabric is passed through heated, pressurized rollers to create textures and effects on the fabric.

Canopy   A lightweight awning type of covering for exteriors and interiors. May be mounted with a curved rod, may be supported by poles, or mounted to a handrail on the ceiling or wall. Usually fabricated out of canvas, decorative fabrics, woven woods, or mosquito netting.

Cantonniere   A three-sided window treatment similar to a cornice. Sides may go all the way to the floor or finish below the window. Made on boards with padding, covered in fabric, and welted.

Carrier   Moves the rod and holds the hook which is fastened to the drapery. There is only one carrier to each drapery hook. Carriers are usually made of plastic, but may be found made of metal.

Cartridge pleat   Rounded folds of fabric sewn in place and stuffed with paper, to maintain roundness, to give fullness to drapery and top treatments.

Cascades   Shaped, pleated decorative ends for top treatments. Cascades usually hang in zig-zag folds down to a point, on the sides of the window or undertreatment of the top treatment.

Casement fabric	Loosely woven fabric used for drapery, unlined or lined.
Casement window	A window that has hinges at the sides, to swing in or out of the room.
Cashmere	The finest wool fabric available on the market. A warm and lightweight fiber made from fleece. The finest fleece is derived from the cashmere goats of Tibet, Mongolia, and China. The fibers from India, Iran, and Iraq are coarser.
Center draw	Pair of drapery that opens from the center of the window, or the center of a set of drapery.
Center support	Brace used with a drapery rod to help support the weight of the drapery and rod. A center support will not interfere with the traversing of the drapery, but does prevent the rod from sagging in the middle.
Ceiling mount	Installation of window treatments where the brackets are mounted into the ceiling, rather than into the wall.
Chain weights	Bead-chain weights covered with fabric and put in the bottom hems of drapery, for uniform hanging ability. Sheer fabrics will show a bumpy appearance at their hems.
Check	Woven or printed fabric, patterned of squares.
Chevron	Fabric printed or woven in zig-zag stripes. May be knitted or woven in a herringbone weave.
Chintz	Printed fabric of glazed cotton. Many finishes may be applied to achieve the highly polished sheen of chintz fabric. Wax glaze and starched glaze will wash out. The most durable finish is resin.
Classic	Term used for traditional design, pattern, and style.
Complementary	Opposite colors on the color wheel are used to achieve complementary color schemes.
Clerestory windows	Group of small windows placed near the ceiling, usually found in homes with cathedral-type ceilings.
Cluster pleats	Group of pleats placed together at regular intervals, to add fullness to a treatment or drapery, that also give a decorative design by the way the pleats are placed.
Colorfast	Fabrics that do not fade noticeably during their normal life span. Fabrics used in decorating have colorfast ratings in hours.
Combed cotton	Yarn that is cleaned by wire brushes after carding, to remove short fibers and impurities.
Contemporary	Modern styling of decorative furnishings. Updated, current, new styling.
Continuous filament	Continuous strand of a manmade fiber or raw silk.
Contrast fabric	Same as accent fabric.
Convertor	Distributor of fabrics who purchases greige goods, puts his own designs on them, finishes them, and resells them to buyers, cutters, and stores. Many mills will also do their own converting.
Corduroy	Cut-pile fabric, woven in wales, wide or narrow, or a combination of both. This is done with an extra fill yarn. The backing may be a plain weave or a twill weave. The fabric with the twill weave backing is the higher quality product.
Cornice	Padded, upholstered board top treatment covered in fabric; or a wood top treatment made of boards or wide moldings.
Cotton	Natural vegetable fiber with a soft hand from the seed pod of a cotton plant. The longer the fiber, the better the quality. The average length is 1 inch, but the length may vary from ½ inch to 2 inches. Usually cotton is creamy white, but may be brownish or reddish white.

Count of cloth Number of yarns per square inch of the fabric.

Crease resistance Fabrics which have been treated to have wrinkle resistance. Usually this is done by adding a certain amount of permanent synthetic resin to the fabric.

Crepe Fabric with pebbly, crinkled, or puckered surface obtained by finishing techniques. Crepe fabrics come in weights from light to heavy.

Cretonne Fabric scenes printed on unglazed cotton.

Crinoline Similar to buckram. Crinoline comes in a variety of colors and is used with sheer, lightweight, open-weave fabrics to prevent buckram from showing through the fabric.

Custom made An item individually made for a consumer in his or her selection of style, size, and material.

Cut length The length of fabric needed, with the amount added in for hems and headers, for fabrication of the treatment.

Cut to measure Drapery rods, cut to specific measurements, needed to do the job.

Cut yardage Quantity in yards. Amount of fabric which is less than a full bolt of fabric.

Damask Jacquard-woven fabric that is flatter than brocade. Has a firm hand and a glossy surface.

Decorative rod Drapery rod which may traverse, or a pole rod which is stationary. Usually made of metal, wood, or plastic, and may be simulated to look like wood, brass, pewter, chrome, bronze, etc. Traverse rods have rings to hold pleats, or carriers to hold the hooks; fabric rod pockets slip over pole rods. Some decorative rods have decorative finals at the ends, some have smooth elbows that return to the wall.

Delustering The dulling or elimination of yarns by using titanium pigment in the fiber solution, or other chemicals in the finishing process.

Denier A unit of weight which indicates the size of a fiber filament. The higher the denier number, the heavier the yarn. This term is used with silk, rayon, acetate, and other manmade fibers.

Depth The length of a decorative item or treatment.

Dormier window Small window in an alcove area.

Dip dying Fabrics are dyed by dipping into the dye bath after they are woven. Also known as piece dying.

Double hem A hem which has been folded twice to give drapery weight, eliminate shadows, and place all raw edges to the inside.

Double-hung shutters Two units of shutters placed one above the other, with a slight gap between the separate units.

Double-hung windows Windows that have upper and lower sashes, hung separately. Each may be raised and lowered separately.

Drape Refers to the way a fabric falls when pleated, draped, or hung up.

Drapery Widths of fabric pleated or gathered up and mounted on a rod to cover windows for privacy, light control, insulation or decorativeness.

Drift Amount that the crosswise design of a pattern, woven or printed on fabric, will vary in position on the opposite side. 1½ inch is considered acceptable by the industry. Check the fabric before cutting; send back for a replacement piece, or reselection if not acceptable.

Dropped-pattern Repeats of patterns that *do not* match up on points directly above or below each other, but *will* match up across from each other. The pattern has been moved over in the horizontal position, so the sides match at different points from each other. Check with the workroom to see if the selected fabric pattern is appropriate for your design selection, if in doubt.

Dust caps   Top boards of top treatments, which use covered boards. Dust caps cover the top of the window treatment to prevent dust from getting on the top treatment and undertreatments. Dust caps give a finished look, and hold the top treatment in front of the traverse rod, so the traversing drapery will not drag against the top treatment.

Dyelot   Color variation in color, from one dyed batch of fabrics to the next. Always purchase all quantity of fabric needed out of the same dyelot, at the same time.

Dyes   There are natural and chemical synthetic dyes. Dyes vary in their resistance to washing, cleaning, effects from gas, perspiration, sunlight and alkali. Dyes also vary in the way they *take* to different fibers. Some dyes are more soluble than others, and have to be applied differently.

Eclecticism   Mixing and blending of various styles in decorating and furnishings, harmoniously.

Ecru   The natural color of fabric in its non-dyed or bleached grey goods state.

End bracket   Support that hold up a drapery rod or hard treatment headrail. Fastens to the wall or ceiling. End brackets control the amount of projection and are usually adjustable.

Fabrics   Manufactured textiles. Fabrics may be woven, felted, knitted, plaited, braided, or may be other non-woven materials made of fibers or yarns.

Faille   Fabric known for its horizontal ribs, soft hand, and good draping qualities.

Felt   Fabric made of densely matted fibers of wool, fur, or mohair mixed with cotton or rayon. The materials are mixed, carded, hardened with moisture, heat, and pressure, and flattened into sheets.

Fiber   Natural or manmade synthetic substance made of thread-like strands, capable of being spun, knitted, or woven.

Fiberglass   Fine filament fiber, made of glass.

Filament   Single, continuous strand of manmade fiber or silk. Filaments are wound together to make yarn.

Fill   Same as weft yarns. Also called picks.

Finial   Decorative end piece used on decorative rods.

Finish   Treatment applied to a fabric, to give *certain* surface effects or performance.

Finished length The length of drapery needed after the hems and headers have been finished. The original length needed for the finished treatment.

Finished width The width of drapery or other treatment with the overlaps and returns included in, after the drapery or window treatment is already pleated or gathered up. The actual width of the drapery or treatment needed to do the job.

Finishes   Applied processes to create finished fabrics. Some of these are bleaching, mercerizing, steaming, singeing and dyeing.

Flame repellant Applied treatment, usually chemical, that retards burning.

Flax   Plant of the genus Linum, whose fiber from the stem is used to make linen.

Float   In weaving, section of a warp or fill yarn that sits over the top of two or more adjacent warp or filling yarns. A weaker weave for surface effect.

Foam-backed fabric A thin layer of synthetic foam, attached to the back of the fabric and bonded by heat, pressure, and adhesives.

Frieze   Hard-handed fabric, usually used for upholstery. Frieze has a rough, raised surface texture.

Fullness   Extra fabric added in width to make pleats or gathers.

Gauge   Number of needles per inch in knitted goods. The larger the number, the finer the knit.

Gimp	Flat, decorative, tape-type trim used on drapery, upholstery, and other interior items.
Greige (gray)	Fabric; after being woven in its natural state, before finishes and *sometimes* dyes have been applied.
Hammered satin	Satin fabric treated and finished to have a hammered-metal effect.
Hand	The way the fabric feels, hangs, the amount of body and weight of the fabric. Hand also refers to how much flexibility and resilience the fabric has.
Heading	The top portion of drapery or top treatment that is to be pleated or gathered up. Headings are usually folded up, and if pleated, contain buckram or crinoline.
Heavy-duty hardware	Rods and hardware designed to hold medium- to heavy-weight drapery.
Holdback	Hardware that attaches at the sides of drapery; holds the drapery back for style and viewing out. May be a holder that allows drapery to be released as needed; may be ornate and made of brass.
I.B.	Denotes inside mounting of a window treatment. Mounted on the inside of the window frame or window area.
Interlining	A middle layer of flannel, chamois, or quilted material that is applied between the self-fabric and lining fabric, for added body and warmth.
Jacquard	An intricately patterned and woven weave. Brocades, damasks, and tapestry types of fabric are jacquard woven.
Lamination	Joining two or more layers of material by using adhesives, binding agents, or heat.
Leno weave	A weave where warp yarns are arranged in pairs, to twist one around the other, forming figure-eights between each fill yarn. Marquisette fabric is woven using this weave.
Lift cord	Cord attached to shade and blinds; lifts or lowers the shade or blind as the cord is used.
Lineal feet	Measurement in feet along the selvage of the fabric, or around the perimeter of the area to be covered. Encompasses all yardage *across* the area.
Lineal yards	Measurement in yards along the selvage of the fabric, carpet, or around the perimeter of the area to be covered. Encompasses all yardage *across* the area.
Linen	Crisp, firm-handed fabric made of flax. Has poor resistance to wrinkling. May have finishes applied to help resist wrinkles.
Linen finish	A type of finish applied to non-linen fabrics, to give the appearance of linen.
Louver	Wooden slats placed horizontally in a shutter, may be movable up and down to control light, view and air. Vertical slats for vertical blinds are also called louvers.
Marquisette	Thin, transparent fabric with a leno weave. Marquisette is usually made of polyester, glass fibers, nylon, or cotton. Usual use is for sheers.
Master carrier	On traverse drapery rods, the two carrier arms that overlap each other, usually in the middle of the rod, when the drapery is drawn closed.
Matelasse	Woven fabric with a puffy, raised texture. This texture is created by weaving coarse yarns into the fabric face. Matelasse fabrics are normally used for upholstery.
Matte finish	Non-glossy and non-reflective finish.
Mesh	Open-texture fabric. May be fine or coarse; may be woven or knitted mesh.
Mildew resistant	Applied finish to fabrics to retard mildew and mold.

Mohair   A fiber from the wool family. Derived from hair from the Angora goat. Has a coarse hand, is lightweight, and appears silky. Mohair fabric is puffy in appearance.

Moire   Finish applied to fabrics to give a watered, wavy, or wood grain appearance to fabrics. This is achieved by pressing the fabric through engraved rollers.

Monk's cloth   Heavy, basket-weave type of fabric. Usually used for upholstery.

Monofilament   A single filament fiber used for sheer fabrics or used as thread.

Motif   The main or dominant figure or design in woven or printed fabrics.

Mullion   The vertical or horizontal divider in windows, usually made of wood. Mullions divide the glass and the window.

Multi-filament More than one filament. Used to make yarn.

Multiple draw The capability of being able to open and close more than one drapery on the same rod, at the same time. This is not the same as an even pair that simultaneously opens *both sides* of the pair at the same time. This is a drapery rod that has been *engineered by the installer* to draw open more than one drapery at the same time.

Mutin   Wood or metal strips that divide individual panes of glass in windows.

Mural   A pattern scene in drapery or wall coverings that does not repeat itself *anywhere*. Different paneled areas may be eliminated, according to the size of the area the panels are to be used in.

Muslin   A cotton fabric. Muslin comes in many weights; usually off-white in color.

Nap   The surface of fabric that is produced by wire brushing or napping. All cuts of napped fabric must go in the same direction, as a change in direction will produce a different color.

Natural fibers Strands of fibers derived from natural sources such as animals, silkworms, and vegetables.

Ninon   Sheer fabric with a crisp hand, in a plain weave, used for sheers.

Non-woven   A felted fabric.

Novelty weave A weave in fabrics that combines the three basic weaves: plain weave, satin weave, and twill weave.

Novelty yarns Nubby fibers twisted to make yarns in varying degrees of thick to thin yarn, boucle, metallic, and any other decorative yarns that may be *added in*, during the weaving process, to achieve a distinctive look.

Nubby   A texture achieved by using a nub yarn.

Nub; Nub yarn A yarn, that has varying degrees of thin to thick areas within the yarn. When the yarn is woven into fabric, a lumpy, nubby surface is created. Nub yarns are also known as slub yarns.

Nylon   Manmade fiber that is long wearing, durable, with a harder hand than most fibers.

O.B.   Outside mounted window treatment. Treatments are mounted on the wall or exterior window frame of the window.

Off-center window   A window that does not fall to the center of the wall.

Offset pairs   Drapery pairs that have been engineered by the designer to fall in the center of the window by making one panel smaller, and the other panel larger.

Olefin   Manmade fiber usually used for upholstery fabrics. A fiber that will take a lot of wear.

Open-weaves   Loosely woven fabrics, also known as casement fabrics. Has loosely woven designs and woven areas.

Overlap	The areas on the leading edges of drapery that fasten to the master carrier by hooks and overlap on top of each other; usually overlapping in the center of the drapery, when the drapery is drawn shut to give a uniformly hanging drapery and to help ensure privacy and prevent light leaks.
Panel	One section or width of a pair of drapery. May also mean one individual width of fabric within a drapery section.
Pattern	Design or motif.
Permanent finishes	Coatings applied to fabrics to improve their shine, glaze, hand, body, and performance. Permanent finishes are durable and long lasting. They will not wash out or come out during a normal life span of the fabric.
Piece dyeing	Technique for dyeing woven fabrics. Achieved by running the bolt of fabric through a dye bath.
Pile	The yarns that stand up on the surface of the face of the fabric, due to mechanical finishing equipment. This pile may be cut or uncut. Fabrics with pile finishes are velvets, velveteens, velours, corduroys, plushes, friezes, carpeting, and rugs. All fabric cuts must go in the same direction or there will be a difference in shade or color.
Pinch pleat	Means the same as French pleat. Pleating up fabric at definite intervals, into exact folds. Pleats are then stitched in place to hold them together.
Pilling	Fuzzy balls that form on the face of fabrics due to abrasion.
Piping	A decorative finish or trim added usually in seams and edges. May be in the form of binding or cording.
Pique	Fabric with rib weaves and textures; formed by raised ribs or wales, varying in width and thickness. Pique is used usually in bedspreads and drapery.
Plaid	A pattern of stripes that cross at right angles, in a basket-weave fashion, under and over each other, to create distinctive patterns and color formations.
"Pleat-to"	Finished width needed to have the fabric panels pleated-to, for proper fullness.
Pleating	Folded and sewn sections of the header, to add fullness to drapery or valances.
Plisse	A crinkled, puckered effect given to fabric with caustic soda, which shrinks areas of the fabric and creates a puckered effect. Usually used in window treatments, bedspreads, and accessories. Usually made of cotton, some manmade fibers.
Plush	Cut-pile surface; longer than velvet, but not as densely woven.
Ply yarn	Two or more yarns twisted together.
Polyester	Manmade fiber of a chemical solution, ethylene glycol and terephthalic acid.
Print	Term for fabric that has had designs applied to its surface by roller printing with engraved rollers, wood blocks, or screen printing.
Projection	Extension of drapery rod, window treatment, or drapery that extends out from the wall. The part of the drapery, window treatment, or rod that *returns* to the wall, from the face of the rod or treatment.
Quilting	Two layers of fabric with an inside layer of batting, joined by a stitched design. Outline quilting is in the outline of the self-fabric's pattern.
Ramie	Similar to flax, comes from the ramie plant. Hard-handed, brittle fiber, usually used for table linens.
Raw silk	Silk fiber, taken from the silkworm cocoons before the natural gum has been removed.
Rayon	A manmade fiber, derived from cellulose.
Rep	Plain-woven fabric with rib effect, used in drapery and bedspreads.

Repeat   The distance from any part or point of a design; the interval from where it appears again and again, regularly. Whenever possible, repeats need to be lined up when widths are sewn together in uniform, pleated areas.

Repossessed wool   Wool yarns that have previously been woven, felted, or knitted into fabrics that were never used. They have been returned to their original, fibrous state; rewoven or refelted back into fabric.

Reselection   The process of having to choose another selection of fabric, design, or style due to unavailability, poor quality, or unworkableness of the original selection or design.

Resilience   Ability to bounce back or recover from crushing or crimping. Ability to go back to an original state after cleaning, washing, or use.

Resist dyeing   Dyeing method; fabric or fiber is treated in a certain way, so certain areas will resist being dyed when the fabric or fiber goes through the dyeing process.

Resist printing Resist method of printing; where certain areas of a design are treated in a certain way, so the design areas will resist printing when the fabric goes through the printing process.

Return   The section of drapery or window treatment on the side of the drapery or treatment that folds back and returns to the wall, covering all hardware and undertreatments.

Rib   Raised cord, formed by a weaving pattern.

Rolled heading During the drapery fabrication process, when the drapery fabric is folded over crinoline twice to conceal raw edges, to cover crinoline, and to get it ready for pleating.

Roller printing Printing process, where engraved rollers are used to apply a design to fabric.

Roman shades   Fabric shades with soft or sharp horizontal pleats. A type of shade that controls light, has a tailored appearance, and is a fabric window treatment that uses a minimum of fabric.

Sash   Window frame that holds the window's glass.

Sash window   Same as a double-hung window.

Sateen weave   Fabric with floating fill yarns. Usually found in drapery linings, or satins.

Satin   Lustrous fabric created by floating yarns. Satin fabric comes in many varieties, from soft to stiff.

Satin backed   Fabrics with their backing in a satin weave. Face of the fabric may be the same as the back of the fabric, or very different.

Screen printing Printing process where silk screens or other types of screens are used to apply a design to fabric.

Self-fabric   The main body fabric of the treatment. The fabric to be used in the majority of the treatment or item.

Serged seam   Seaming formed by an overcast-sewing machine, with a special joining seam that completely encompasses raw edges within its stitching. Any excess selvage or seam allowance is automatically cut off, during the process.

Selvage   Finished edge along both lengthwise edges of any fabric.

Sheer fabric   A thin, transparent fabric used to make sheers such as batiste, ninon, polyester, marquisette, etc. Comes in varying opaqueness, from very sheer fabric, such as ninons and voiles — to batiste (which will vary from light and sheer to more opaque). Many of the sheer fabrics are available in 118" wide, goods, rather than just 48" wide.

Shirr   Means the same as to gather up fabric. Special shirring tapes are usually used to shirr fabrics.

Shirring   Gathering up fabric with the shirring tape, to create several rows of shirring on the face of a treatment. Also means to gather up fabric on a rod. The rod does the job of gathering the fabric, or shirring up the fabric.

Shrinkage   The loss in width and length that occurs in fabrics due to washing, cleaning, or exposure to humidity.

Side hem   Doubled, 1½" folded area to finish off the side edges of a drapery panel.

Side panels   Stationary panels of drapery that are hung for decorative effect, sometimes tied back, non-traversing.

Silk   Natural fiber from silkworms.

Slipper satin   Heavy-weight satin fabric; with a cotton back and a lustrous floating yarn face. Slipper satin is usually used for drapery and upholstery.

Sizing   Finish added to fabrics to give fabrics body, smooth appearance. Glue sizing gives a permanent sizing, while a starch sizing gives a temporary finish, which washes out when laundered.

Skip-dent   Semi-sheer fabric with an open-spaced design due to the weaving pattern, skipping stitches. Lightweight shirting fabric with open design in weaving.

Slub; slub yarn Terms having the same meaning as a nub, nub yarn.

Smocked pleats   Created by special smocking tape similar to shirring tape, but when it is drawn up, looks like smocking.

Soil repellant   Chemical finishes applied to fabrics; helps most stains and soils wipe off or wash out easily.

Solution dyed   Dye process where manmade fibers are dyed in the spinning solution before being hardened into fibers. The most permanent dyeing process.

Spacing   Refers to the space or area between pleats or other design elements in the planning or fabrication of interior window treatments.

Stabilizing   Applied treatment; helps prevent fabrics from stretching and shrinking.

Stacking   Amount of wall or window area needed, for a drapery or other window treatment to *take up* when the treatment is drawn open.

Stack-off   Amount of wall area needed for a drapery or other window treatment to *clear* the window, when drawn back.

Stain and spot resistant finishes   Many companies make variations of finishes which, when applied to fabrics, help the fabric repel water, stains, soil, and spotting.

Staple yarns   Short lengths of fiber make up staple yarns, rather than long filament fibers. All natural fibers are staple yarns, except for silk. Manmade fibers may be made to emulate staple yarns by being cut or formulated into shorter fibers.

Stenciling   Printing method using precut stencil or patterns where paint, ink, or dye is pressed through the cut-out design areas.

Stock dyeing   Fiber is dyed in its raw state before the fiber is spun into yarns and woven into fabric.

Stripe   Fabric pattern usually woven in bands of various color. The bands of color may be in weaves different than other areas of the fabric, may be in a different yarn texture, or may be the same color as the other areas of the fabric, but woven in different yarns or weaves.

Sunfast   Dyed fabrics that will not fade appreciably when exposed to normal repeated sunlight.

Support   Hardware to hold up rods; needs to be installed every 4' for good support.

Swags   Draped top treatment pleated horizontally, mounted on a board in a scalloped effect, usually with other swags overlapping each other.

Swatch   A small sample of fabric used to represent a larger piece of the fabric.

Synthetic fibers Also known as manmade fibers. Manmade from chemicals, rather than derived from a natural source.

Tabling A workroom process with drapery. Tabling *is when* widths of fabric are sewn together and laid flat on a table. Even length and even heading are then achieved for the drapery or other item.

Taffeta A plain, woven fabric with a surface sheen. Taffeta is normally smooth on both sides. May be printed, plain, striped, plaid, checked, or woven with slub types of yarns. Taffeta comes in varying weights of heaviness. Known for its rustly sound and firm body.

Tapestry An ornamental textile. Originally a hand-woven fabric of wool, cotton, or linen. Scenic type of designs. Today, usually made on a jacquard loom.

Tartan Plaid, woven designs of wool derived from Scotland. Each Scottish clan had their own distinctive plaid designs.

Tassel Highly decorative ornament. Tassels are made of yarns fabricated in clumps in various designs. Tassels may be used alone or in combination with fringe on interior treatments and accessories.

Tensile strength Amount of pressure needed to make a yarn or fiber reach its breaking point.

Tension pulley Used with traverse rods. Device mounted at side of drapery; keeps tension on traverse cord, keeps drapery traversing smoothly, and keeps cords in order if more than one cord is used for a multiple draw.

Tergal French-imported sheer; wide-width, 118" fabric.

Texture The evenness or unevenness of yarns or fabrics.

Textured yarn Filament yarn that has been reprocessed to change its form from its original, smooth surface to an uneven, textural surface. Some of the textural effects achieved are boucle, crepe, pebble looks; or yarns may be textured to add stretch to fabrics, to bulk up a light yarn, to add resilience, opaqueness, and to change the normal hand and body of the fabric.

Tieback A strip of fabric, usually with a buckram interior, used to hold drapery back off of a window. Tiebacks are used for effect, light and air control, or for viewing out of a window.

Tier Short drapery or curtain used by itself, or with other short drapery or curtains (tiers). Each tier is usually one above the other, overlapping 4" on top of each other. The top tier needs a wider projection from the wall than the lower tiers, so it may hang free. Each tier beneath the top tier needs a progressively shallower return.

Toile de Jouy Classic pastoral, 18th-century French scenes printed on fabrics. The designs were in one color against a neutral, white background color. Fabric was usually toile or a fine-count cotton.

Top treatment Decorative top to a window treatment to add style, elegance, and to finish off a window treatment.

Transitional A style that is made up of two consecutive styles in its design.

Traverse rod Drapery rod with a pulley mechanism to draw drapery open and closed by using a traverse cord, mounted at the side of the drapery.

Tweed A fabric that has a soft hand, but a masculine appearance with a rough texture. Tweed usually has flecks of other colors in it. May appear within plaids or striped fabrics.

Twill weave A weave that has a diagonal appearance. There are many variations to these. Some of the different types are serges, surahs, and gabardines.

Twist How many turns per inch a yarn has.

Underdrapery The drapery under an overdrapery. May be a sheer, liner, or other drapery fabric. Underdraperies are used to control light, privacy, or to be decorative.

Valance Simpler styles of top treatments. Usually refers to pleated, box pleated, or gathered on the rod, styled top treatments.

Vat dyed   Dye process where insoluble dye is reduced to a soluble form in its application process, and then oxidized to the original insoluble form. One of the most resistant dyes available to sunlight and washing.

Velcro tape   Double nylon tape which has loops on one of the two pieces of tape, and pile on the other. When the two tapes are stuck together, the tape holds fast. Multiple uses. In the decorating business, used mainly to attach top treatments and valances to boards.

Velour   Upholstery fabric with a soft pile and hand. Velour fabric is usually woven in a satin or plain weave, with a finished thick, short, pile. Velour is the same as plush.

Velvet   Short, piled fabric. Velvet has a smooth, rich appearance. The fabric is made by weaving two face fabrics together and then shearing them apart. Velvet pile may be chemically dissolved in areas to create designs. Velvet may be left with its loops uncut, or certain patterns may be created with a combination of cut and uncut loops. The pile may be crushed or pressed flat to make panne velvet. This is a napped fabric that needs to have all cuts go in the same direction.

Virgin wool   Wool that has never been used or reused; any spun, woven, knitted, felted, manufactured or used wool product. Any grade of wool may be called virgin wool.

Voile   Fabric that is lightweight, sheer, and of a plain weave, with a crisp hand. The crisp hand is achieved by using yarns with a large degree of twist. Used predominantly for sheers and curtains.

Warp   Threads that run lengthwise in weaving. Warp threads or yarns are stronger than weft threads or yarns. The filling or weft threads interweave or lace with the warp yarns.

Waterproofing   Treatment for fabrics with coatings of rubber, resin, or plastic to resist water.

Water repellant   Treatment applied to fabrics by chemicals, resin, silicone, or fluoride to make fabrics more resistant to water, spots, or stains.

Weaving   The process of making fabric by interlacing warp and weft threads or yarns at right angles.

Weft   Filling threads or yarns. The threads or yarns that run crosswise in fabric. Filling threads are weaker than warp yarns or threads. Warp yarns interlace or weave over and under warp yarns. Also called picks or woof yarns.

Weights   Leads encased in plastic or cloth, placed at bottom hem seams and leading edges of drapery to help with the hanging.

Welting   Trim that has cord running through it, to be used as a decorative finish at seams; for top treatments, bedspreads, upholstery, slipcovers, or other accessories.

Width   The crosswise expanse of all fabrics.

Widths   How many widths of fabric are needed or sewn together to achieve a specific width of drapery or other decorative treatment.

Wool   Made from fleece of sheep; can be spun in many sizes or denier, and variations of thread count.

Woven wood   Window treatment available in various styles that combine wood slats with yarns and cords.

Yarn   Manmade or natural fibers twisted together to form a continuous strand to be used in weaving or knitting.

Yarn-dyed   Yarn is dyed before being made into fabric.
fabrics

Index

Secrets of Success for Today's Interior Designers and Decorators
Easily Sell the Job, Plan It Correctly, and Keep Your Clients Coming Back

This book provides a <u>wealth</u> of knowledge, experience, and benefits for *all* interior designers and decorators. Your guide to accurate planning, measuring and selling the job, whether you are new to the ID field or are very practiced, *everyone* gains knowledge and experience from this book. Improve your sales ability, design planning/measuring skills, and fabric selection expertise. Determine what will and won't work for the specific situation and gain an overall increased knowledge in the ID field. The realm of alternate and fabric window treatments is thoroughly covered. Follow the advice, use the information, and become a window treatment expert.

Complete explanations and extensive professional advice are included. Learn methods for getting better leads, proven marketing and advertising techniques, how to eliminate your competition, and how to be financially successful *today* in this career. Buy this book <u>now</u> if you want to *increase* your sales and profits and eliminate problems. **You get a reference packed with information to ensure your success. 336 pgs. (8 ½" x 11").** **SATISFACTION GUARANTEED!** Written by Linda M. Ramsay.

Start Your Own Interior Design Business and Keep It Growing!
Your Guide to Business Success

You'll find a complete and lucrative business plan covering *everything* you need to know from A to Z to start and grow a successful interior design business. There are many more Touch of Design® prospecting, marketing, and advertising secrets. Don't start an ID business without *this* book. This is *your* guide to business success. This book is *filled* with successful, useful, practical, helpful, and profitable ideas for anyone starting or attempting to grow an interior-design business. A <u>must</u> for interior-design businesses just starting up — *but* should be read by *all* interior design business owners who want to prosper and flourish and earn more money in today's business climate. *All* will benefit from this new book. <u>**Extremely comprehensive and complete.**</u> **384 pgs. (8½" x 11").** Written by Linda M. Ramsay.

Successful Window Dressing and Interior Design
Your Guide to Achieving Excellent Results!

Consumers guide to creating successful interiors. Included are the extensive window planning and measuring sections, and fabric details from *Secrets of Success for Today's Interior Designers and Decorators* and directories from *Start Your Own Interior Design Business and Keep It Growing!* How to make correct selections, avoid mistakes and problems, find and work with superior designers if you don't want to do it yourself, get the most for your money, find your style, achieve custom results, select what is right for your home, situation, personality, and budget, cut the price down, get the best possible pricing, work with existing furnishings, measure, plan, and determine yardage for all types of window and fabric accessories, make effective fabric selections, determine what will and won't work are all included. Written by Linda M. Ramsay.

Interior-Design-Furnishings Directory of Discounted 800-Number and Hard-to-Find Companies
Insider's Home Decorating Guide to Lower-Priced and Little-Known Companies that Offer You <u>Substantial Savings</u> and <u>Higher Values</u>

If you are interested in buying goods less expensively, whether you are a designer, decorator, or a consumer attempting to stretch your decorating dollars further, this is the interior-goods resource book for you. Includes hard-to-find sources that offer quality goods with lower prices. Designers will be surprised to find how to get better prices through these companies than through their regular sources. You get many sources for mini and wood blinds, vertical blinds, Duette® shades, pleated and roller shades; drapery rods and hardware; drapery, curtains, valances, bedspreads, quilts, linens, and fabric accessories; fabrics; art; carpeting and rugs, wood flooring, marble, resilient floorcoverings; wallcoverings; furniture; lighting and lamps; lamp shades; accessories, clocks, and collectibles; outdoor furnishings and garden accessories; historic hardware and fixtures; office furniture and accessories; stencilling; table pads; architectural details; appliance reproductions, and wood stoves. Written by Linda M. Ramsay.

Ordering Information

These books are <u>filled</u> with details to ensure your success and are <u>real values</u>.

Yes, I am interested in investing in my future. Please send me:

- *Secrets of Success for Today's Interior Designers and Decorators* $39.99 _____

- *Start Your Own Interior Design Business and Keep It Growing!*   39.99 _____

- *Successful Window Dressing and Interior Design*   24.99 _____

- *Interior Design-Furnishings Directory of Discounted 800-Number.......*   19.99 _____

California residents add sales tax — 7¾% _____

USA Shipping/handling: one book $3.45, $1.50 for each additional book

_____

International orders: Insured Surface Delivery; one book - $6.30, two books - $13.00, three books - $18.00. For each additional book add - $5.00. If type of delivery is not specified, we will ship by surface delivery. International Insured Airmail: $20.00 for 1st book, each additional book - add $10.00 _____

Total _____

- **Need more information or volume rates?**
  Contact our sales department by phone, mail, FAX, or e-mail.

Only prepaid orders will be accepted. Order by check, money order, Visa, or Mastercard.

Name/Firm_____ Address_____

City_____ State_____ Zip_____

Signature_____ Card Number_____

Credit Card Expiration Date _____

Phone Number_____ E-Mail Address_____

Type of credit card: ☐ Visa   ☐ Mastercard

Order by mail, phone, FAX, or e-mail:

Touch of Design ®

475 College Blvd., Ste. 6290, Oceanside, CA 92057
FAX: (619) 945-4283
voice: (619) 945-7909
e-mail: todesign@electriciti.com or todesign@cyber.net

Visit our web site at http://www.electriciti.com/todesign for free interior design reports and information.

Are you on our mailing list? If you did not purchase this book directly from Touch of Design®, send us your name and address for future available books by Touch of Design®.

Please tell your friends and associates in the interior-design field about these books.

Ordering Information

These books are <u>filled</u> with details to ensure your success and are <u>real values</u>.

Yes, I am interested in investing in my future. Please send me:

- *Secrets of Success for Today's Interior Designers and Decorators* $39.99 _____

- *Start Your Own Interior Design Business and Keep It Growing!*   39.99 _____

- *Successful Window Dressing and Interior Design*   24.99 _____

- *Interior Design-Furnishings Directory of Discounted 800-Number*.......   19.99 _____

California residents add sales tax — 7¾% _____

USA Shipping/handling: one book $3.45, $1.50 for each additional book _____

International orders: Insured Surface Delivery; one book - $6.30, two books - $13.00, three books - $18.00. For each additional book add - $5.00. If type of delivery is not specified, we will ship by surface delivery. International Insured Airmail: $20.00 for 1st book, each additional book - add $10.00 _____

Total _____

- **Need more information or volume rates?**
  Contact our sales department by phone, mail, FAX, or e-mail.

Only prepaid orders will be accepted. Order by check, money order, Visa, or Mastercard.

Name/Firm_____Address_____

City_____State_____Zip_____

Signature_____Card Number_____

Credit Card Expiration Date _____

Phone Number_____E-Mail Address_____

Type of credit card: ☐ Visa   ☐ Mastercard

Order by mail, phone, FAX, or e-mail:

Touch of Design ®

475 College Blvd., Ste. 6290, Oceanside, CA 92057
FAX: (619) 945-4283
voice: (619) 945-7909
e-mail: todesign@electriciti.com or todesign@cyber.net

Visit our web site at http://www.electriciti.com/todesign for free interior design reports and information.

Are you on our mailing list? If you did not purchase this book directly from Touch of Design®, send us your name and address for future available books by Touch of Design®.

Please tell your friends and associates in the interior-design field about these books.

Touch of Design ®

Linda M. Ramsay
Owner/Publisher